Handbook of Life Design

Handbook of Life Design

From Practice to Theory and From Theory to Practice

Laura Nota and Jérôme Rossier (Eds.)

Library of Congress Cataloging in Publication
information for the print version of this book
is available via the Library of Congress Marc Database under the
Library of Congress Control Number 2014952548

National Library of Canada Cataloguing in Publication Data
   Handbook of life design : from practice to theory and
from theory to practice / Laura Nota and Jérôme Rossier (Eds.)

Includes bibliographical references.
Issued in print and electronic formats.
ISBN 978-0-88937-447-8 (bound).--ISBN 978-1-61676-447-0
(pdf).--ISBN 978-1-61334-447-7 (html)

   1. Counseling psychology--Handbooks, manuals, etc.
I. Nota, Laura, 1966-, author, editor II. Rossier, Jérôme, 1969-, author,
editor

BF636.6.H35 2015   158.3   C2014-908039-5
                                               C2014-908040-9

© 2015 by Hogrefe Publishing
http://www.hogrefe.com

PUBLISHING OFFICES
USA: Hogrefe Publishing Corporation, 38 Chauncy Street, Suite 1002, Boston, MA 02111
              Phone (866) 823-4726, Fax (617) 354-6875; E-mail customerservice@hogrefe.com
EUROPE: Hogrefe Publishing GmbH, Merkelstr. 3, 37085 Göttingen, Germany
              Phone +49 551 99950-0, Fax +49 551 99950-111; E-mail publishing@hogrefe.com

SALES & DISTRIBUTION
USA: Hogrefe Publishing, Customer Services Department,
              30 Amberwood Parkway, Ashland, OH 44805
              Phone (800) 228-3749, Fax (419) 281-6883; E-mail customerservice@hogrefe.com
UK: Hogrefe Publishing, c/o Marston Book Services Ltd., 160 Eastern Ave.,
              Milton Park, Abingdon, OX14 4SB, UK
              Phone +44 1235 465577, Fax +44 1235 465556; E-mail direct.orders@marston.co.uk
EUROPE: Hogrefe Publishing, Merkelstr. 3, 37085 Göttingen, Germany
              Phone +49 551 99950-0, Fax +49 551 99950-111; E-mail publishing@hogrefe.com

OTHER OFFICES
CANADA: Hogrefe Publishing, 660 Eglinton Ave. East, Suite 119-514, Toronto, Ontario, M4G 2K2
SWITZERLAND: Hogrefe Publishing, Länggass-Strasse 76, CH-3000 Bern 9

Hogrefe Publishing
Incorporated and registered in the Commonwealth of Massachusetts, USA, and in Göttingen, Lower
Saxony, Germany

Cover design: Daniel Kleimenhagen, Designer AGD

International Life Design Group logo © Guy Soyez and the International Life Design Group

Printed and bound in Germany

ISBN 978-0-88937-447-8 (print) • ISBN 978-1-61676-447-0 (PDF) • ISBN 978-1-61334-447-7 (EPUB)
http://doi.org/10.1027/00447-000

Table of Contents

Part I
Introduction

Chapter 1
Introduction

Laura Nota[1] and Jérôme Rossier[2]

[1]Department of Philosophy, Sociology, Education, and Applied Psychology, University of Padova, Italy
[2]Institute of Psychology, University of Lausanne, Switzerland

The contemporary world and our recent history are characterized by a very rapid evolution of social and economical structures. This is very clear both to the authors of this volume and to readers. Rapid technological changes, the globalization phenomenon, economic and social insecurity, new migrations, prolonged economic crises, and much more are before the eyes of everyone. These changes have important implications for each individual and each citizen, but also for career counselors and professionals in the field of vocational and career psychology. These new challenges underlie the development of the new life design paradigm, first presented in a scientific article in 2009, and now further developed in this handbook.

There has been a downturn in people's quality of life due to lower pay, loss of health insurance, fewer pension benefits, poorer labor conditions, and greater income inequality and instability. All this is increasingly affecting large groups of the population, among whom young people, older workers, short-term contract workers, migrants, and families having to manage long periods of school–work transitions experienced by their children, could be listed. It is evident that the change that characterizes the history of human beings is occurring so fast that it is resulting in significant hardships and difficulties. This present is also changing the idea of the future. Current conditions tend to stimulate a negative vision of it. Fairly frequently, it is perceived as involving considerable discomfort and feelings of despair and bewilderment. The tendency to think about the future as characterized by multiple perspectives, progress, improvement of living conditions, and new opportunities is lower than in the past. These unpleasant feelings and emotions are also associated with the spread of pessimism and the belief that it will be very difficult to get out of the crisis that is affecting different parts of the world and to contain its deleterious effects. Even counselors and career counselors themselves are not immune to all of this, as they often experience the same conditions of insecurity and underemployment as their clients.

Bearing in mind the conditions we are all living through, the increased number of at-risk individuals, the barriers and needs of career counselors themselves, the Life Design International Research Group was created in 2006, included scholars from diverse countries – Belgium, France, Italy, Portugal, Switzerland, The Netherlands, and the United States, who strongly believed that it is important to find answers which are different from those given in the past. The group is composed of Jean-Pierre Dauwalder (University of Lausanne, Switzerland), Maria Eduarda Duarte (Universidade de Lisboa, Portugal), Jean Guichard (Institut National d'Etude du Travail et d'Orientation Professionnelle – Conservatoire National des Arts et Métiers, France), Laura Nota (University of Padova, Italy), Jérôme Rossier

(University of Lausanne, Switzerland), Mark Savickas (Northeastern Ohio University College of Medicine, USA), Salvatore Soresi (University of Padova, Italy), Raoul Van Esbroeck (Vrije Universiteit Brussel, Belgium), and Annelies E. M. van Vianen (University of Amsterdam, The Netherlands). The Vrije Universiteit in Bruxelles hosted this group for 3 consecutive years, from 2006 to 2009. During that period, the group wrote a position paper that appeared in one of the most prestigious scientific journals of our field, the *Journal of Vocational Behavior*, to also stimulate a discussion and an international debate on some critical issues of vocational guidance and career counseling (Savickas et al., 2009). This position paper has since been translated into several languages – Brazilian Portuguese (Duarte et al., 2010), French (Savickas et al., 2010c), German (Savickas et al., 2011a), Greek (Savickas et al., 2010b), Italian (Savickas et al., 2011b), and Portuguese (Savickas et al., 2010a) – and it was one of the most cited articles from the *Journal of Vocational Behavior* in 2012.

With the aim of continuing the work of deepening and further developing ideas for research, training, and intervention actions, the group has met every year in different locations: at the University of Lausanne, at the University of Lisbon, at the INETOP of Paris, and at the University of Padova. We have organized several symposia in international conferences, to present our ideas and proposals, and discuss them with all of the colleagues of our field. In 2011, at the University of Padova, the idea of this book was born, to discuss how to use life design models, methods, and materials to assist people with coping strategies for important changes in our world.

This handbook is organized into five parts. Part II includes five chapters that address theory and conceptual reflections. Part III includes four chapters that apply life design to four different age groups. Part IV includes eight chapters that present ideas and suggestions for working with more at-risk people, in different contexts, and to facilitate the training of life design counselors.

In Part II, called "The Life Design Paradigm," the conceptual structure of the life design approach is examined, and reflections derived from the position paper are provided. Also, a specific in-depth analysis, conceptual elaborations that enrich the early formulations, new developments, and relationships with other approaches, which are considered useful for further enrichment, are proposed.

The first chapter by Jean Guichard gives an introduction to the economic and cultural globalization that has taken place over recent decades, which in turn, has produced a reformulation of the major vocational and life design issues that people face. His chapter traces the conceptual developments that led to the birth of the career and life design paradigm. After a description of salient points, the author proposes three types of interventions – information, guidance, and dialogue – to focus on life design dialogues, which are useful to develop the reflexivity that clients need to design their lives.

Andreas Hirschi and Jean Pierre Dauwalder are the authors of the second chapter. After emphasizing the complexity of constructing careers today, the authors focus on the new life design paradigm, as a perspective that highlights the relevance of the complex dynamics and the unforeseeable results of multiple nonlinear interactions. They state that life design provides the basis for career interventions from a contextual and dynamic perspective. Moreover, the authors highlight the suggestion that career counselors should focus on the interaction between client and environment to obtain possible favorable career outcomes.

The third chapter was written by Maria Eduarda Duarte and Paulo Cardoso. After exploring the question of the gap between career counseling theories and reality that contributed to the emergence of the life design paradigm, they underscore the fact that life design involves not only the context of the self but also the construction of the self. They then provide considerations on some topics which are currently debated in light of the life design paradigm for counseling, such as working alliances, co-construction of meaning, etc. Lastly, the chapter illustrates the practical contribution of the life design framework to counseling.

Jacques Pouyaud wrote the fourth chapter. He tries to make a synthesis of different, but quite close, approaches that could be included in the life design paradigm, under the auspices of the concepts of Ricoeur, the Savickas approach to career construction, the contextual action model of Young and colleagues, the active socialization conception of Malrieu and colleagues, and the making oneself self approach by Guichard. The personal reworking, synthesis, and conceptual anchor efforts allow him to emphasize the importance of the connection between meaning and action in the counseling process, pushing him to formulate a metaphor of identity constructing and directing as being like riding a bicycle.

The fifth chapter, by Mark Watson and Mary McMahon, addresses how several theoretical perspectives that have emerged in career psychology nowadays are embedded in postmodern, constructivist, and social constructionist approaches. It emphasizes a collaborative approach between the counselor and the client in which the focus is on making personal meaning and moving the client toward an action-oriented approach. Further, the authors delineate in particular the potential convergence and divergence between the life design and the systems theory framework, as an effort to ensure a new identity for the field and also to increase the opportunity to provide more personalized responses to clients.

Part III includes four chapters that apply life design to four different age groups. It is entitled "Life Design Across the Life Span," and provides an overview of the issues relating to reflections that the life design approach has stimulated so far about what people are facing at different ages of their lives, as well as information on the processes that are important and should be strengthened to promote professional design and working lives.

The first chapter of this part, written by Paul Hartung, concerns children and childhood. He emphasizes how life design, which represents a third paradigm for career studies and career intervention, applies to childhood. After a review of the established results in relation to what happens in the developmental age, he points out that life design aims to fosters self-making through work and relationships toward achieving life design's core goals of activity, adaptability, narratability, and intentionality. In the conclusion, comments and future directions for advancing life design in childhood are presented.

In the next chapter, Gudbjorg Vilhjálmsdóttir gives an account of life design for the adolescent age group. After pointing out how previous theoretical paradigms that have centered on the person–environment fit are not adequate in an ever-changing work environment and new set of competencies are needed, she directs our attention to the key competences in adolescence in the light of life design approach, such as creating a life story, exploring how work fits into that story, and adapting to inevitable career changes. The author gives an example of an intervention with a teenager to highlight how we can proceed in line with what she has proposed.

The third chapter, written by Jonas Masdonati and Geneviève Fournier, examines young adults and the school-to-work transition, conceived as a subjective process. Referring to the life design approach, they propose four key processes to consider in facilitating transitions: contextual factors, relational environments, being a worker with an occupational identity, and the relationship to school and work, including work values and its importance. In the second half of their contribution, the authors focus on the implications of the life design paradigm for career counseling.

Finally, the last chapter in Part III, written by Mark Savickas, considers adulthood, during which people make new choices repeatedly. Particular attention is paid to the greater complexity and diversity of life paths that we observe nowadays, which involve a shift from standardized, institutionalized life course patterns to individualized biographies. He suggests that career counselors and researchers have moved to the life design paradigm, which provides a model and methods for career intervention. He concludes the chapter describing biographical bricolage, through which clients engage in a dialogue with the sources of their own self.

In Part IV, special attention is paid to the potential contribution of the life design paradigm in proposing interventions to promote adaptability and new ideas to help people through career coaching and life design prevention. Thoughts and stimuli for working with those who experience more difficulties or are vulnerable – for example, the unemployed, people with disabilities, people with low economic resources – are provided. Particular attention is given to prevention activities, to interventions in different cultural contexts, and to the skills advocated for practitioners. This section is titled "Life Design Interventions and Activities."

Developing the life design paradigm, Jérôme Rossier in the first chapter underscores the need for career interventions to be available throughout life, to be holistic, taking into account different roles and identities, and to be attentive to contextual factors. These interventions should increase adaptability, narratability, activity, and intentionality. The author emphasizes that interventions aimed at increasing career adaptability contribute to the development of the life design competencies. After describing the evolution of the concept of adaptability and the role of this construct in the current research, he then focuses on interventions that enhance it.

In the second chapter, Raoul Van Esbroeck and Marie-Thérèse Augustijnen underscore the fact that translating the life design paradigm into adequate career intervention models and methods requires major changes in the intervention approach. In view of the increased attention to coaching in the managerial context, they state that coaching should be considered as a fourth type of career intervention. They specify therefore that in the life design approach, coaching is to be considered as a separate type of intervention that fits between education and counseling, and describe a case study as an example of a life design coaching intervention.

In the third chapter, Laura Nota, Maria Cristina Ginevra, and Sara Santilli underline why the bond between life design and prevention is an optimal one, in particular when regarding goals to pursue, characteristics of interventions, and individuals to be helped. Both environment-centered and person-centered prevention efforts are considered, providing examples of what can be done in the family, with parents, and with those who are constructing their future – the children. Conclusions include a series of competences that life design counselors interested in prevention should have.

Annelies E. M. van Vianen, Jessie Koen, and Ute-Christine Klehe initiate the fourth chapter of Part IV by reminding us that uncertainty and identity threats are components of the distress that people encounter during unemployment. Building upon the life design approach and conservation of resources theory, they propose that several key resources are necessary to cope with unemployment and new-economy careers. These resources involve people's preparation by means of building mental models of careers and self. In the final part of this chapter, they discuss possible ways in which counselors can help clients to develop these key resources.

In the first part of the fifth chapter, Lea Ferrari, Teresa Maria Sgaramella, and Salvatore Soresi present innovative trends underlying the current cultural-scientific debate on disability. In particular, their relevance to realization and work inclusion of individuals with impairments are addressed. Subsequently, the role played by some important and positive constructs, such as identity, time perspective, hope, and optimism, which are essential to life design, are discussed. Finally, competences and attitudes that should characterize life design counselors, especially those who work with people with disabilities, are examined.

In the sixth chapter, Jacobus G. Maree shows how the theory of life design can be applied in real-life contexts to help disadvantaged people from an impoverished rural village design successful lives. After discussing the impact of poverty in a developing country, he explains why it is useful to interpret impoverished contexts from a life design perspective. This is followed by some thoughts on possible ways of interpreting and applying the principle of active mastery of what has been passively suffered. He then reports a case study that demonstrates how life design can be applied, concluding with specific recommendations.

In the seventh chapter, Hsiu-Lan Shelley Tien considers the life design approach from a multicultural perspective. Western versus Eastern, traditional versus modern/postmodern, and masculine versus feminine are the primary dimensions discussed. She also presents cultural differences and similarities in the global world. Attention is given to the relationship between career and life competences and other important variables such as personality, self-efficacy, and life satisfaction in Eastern cultures. Based on her work, she also proposes some suggestions for career and life design competence counselor training in Eastern cultures.

Lastly, Peter McIlveen analyzes the competences required to perform life design counseling and what constitutes the core processes of construction, deconstruction, reconstruction, and co-construction of clients' stories toward action. Extending beyond the fundamental competences of career development practice, the enhanced competences of life design counseling are overviewed – namely, the ethic of critical reflexivity and dialogical interpretation. In summary, this chapter articulates conceptual and radical research dimensions of the agenda set by the Life Design International Research Group.

The book highlights how the life design approach has stimulated conceptual arguments and research studies in line with the times we currently live in, thus involving a growing community of researchers in making it more meaningful and putting into practice what was proposed in 2009.

At the same time, it has captured the need to provide answers to the discomforts experienced today by many individuals and to abandon the wait-and-see approach that has typically characterized our research context. This, besides a revision of procedures adopted in career counseling activities, has consequently stimulated new ideas for intervention activities.

Consider as examples coaching or career education proposals – which we might refer to as life design career education to better differentiate it from traditional views – or prevention, or even the relevance given to the willingness of helping the largest number of individuals. It clearly and powerfully emerges that scholars who refer to life design are emphasizing the need for thinking, studying, and considering the issues of those who are experiencing the greatest needs, those who suffer most of all from the negative outcomes of the times we are currently passing through.

In addition, it clearly turns out that this perspective strongly emphasizes the need for adopting new modalities when facing difficult situations and current challenges. Diverse, high-quality, multidisciplinary and interdisciplinary interventions are needed, in which not only people's work life but also other, contiguous domains are taken into account. These interventions should therefore care for both individuals and their living contexts.

In reading the chapters, it will be found that the life design approach, besides fostering the development of new ideas, takes itself inspiration from the concepts it suggests. The approach can be seen as *a corpus of thoughts*, characterized by constantly taking shape, dynamic, careful of context and regarding what happens within it, waiting for researchers and life design counselors to give value to it all.

References

Duarte, M. E., Lassance, M. C., Savickas, M. L., Nota, L., Rossier, J., Dauwalder, J.-P., … van Vianen, A. E. M. (2010). A construção da vida: Um novo paradigma para entender a carreira no século XXI [Life designing: A paradigm for career construction in the 21st century]. *Revista Interamericana de Psicologia, 44,* 203–217.

Savickas, M. L., Nota, L., Rossier, J., Dauwalder, J.-P., Duarte, M. E., Guichard, J., … van Vianen, A. E. M. (2009). Life designing: A paradigm for career construction in the 21st century. *Journal of Vocational Behavior, 75,* 239–250. http://doi.org/10.1016/j.jvb.2009.04.004

Savickas, M. L., Nota, L., Rossier, J., Dauwalder, J.-P, Duarte, M. E., Guichard, J., … van Vianen, A. E. M. (2010a). A construção da vida: Un novo paradigma para compreender a carreira no século XXI [Life designing: A paradigm for career construction in the 21st century]. *Revista Portuguesa de Psicologia, 42,* 13–47.

Savickas, M. L., Nota, L., Rossier, J., Dauwalder, J.-P., Duarte, M. E., Guichard, J., … van Vianen, A. E. M. (2010b). Σχεδιασμός ζωής: Πρότυπο για τη διαμόρφωση επαγγελματικής σταδιοδρομίας τον 21ο αιώνα [Life designing: A paradigm for career construction in the 21st century]. *Επιθεώρηση Συμβουλευτικής και Προσανατολισμού, 90/91,* 99–126.

Savickas, M. L., Nota, L., Rossier, J., Dauwalder, J.-P., Duarte, M. E., Guichard, J., … Bigeon, C. (2010c). Construire sa vie (Life designing): Un paradigme pour l'orientation au 21e siècle [Life designing: A paradigm for career construction in the 21st century]. *L'Orientation Scolaire et Professionnelle, 39,* 5–39.

Savickas, M. L., Nota, L., Rossier, J., Dauwalder, J.-P., Duarte, M. E., Guichard, J., … van Vianen, A. E. M. (2011a). Life designing: Ein Paradigma für die berufliche Laufbahngestaltung im 21. Jahrhundert [Life designing: A paradigm for career construction in the 21st century]. *dvb-forum, 1,* 33–47.

Savickas, M. L., Nota, L., Rossier, J., Dauwalder, J.-P., Duarte, M. E., Guichard, J., … van Vianen, A. E. M. (2011b). Life design: Un nuovo paradigma per la costruzione della vita professionale nel XXI secolo [Life designing: A paradigm for career construction in the 21st century]. *Giornale Italiano di Psicologia dell'Orientamento, 11,* 3–18.

Part II
The Life Design Paradigm

Chapter 2

From Vocational Guidance and Career Counseling to Life Design Dialogues

Jean Guichard

Institut National d'Etude du Travail et d'Orientation Professionnelle (INETOP),
Conservatoire National des Arts et Métiers (CNAM), Paris, France
UNESCO Chair of Lifelong Guidance and Counselling, University of Wroclaw, Poland

Introduction

As a result of economic and cultural globalizations, Western societies have undergone some major transformations during the last 3 decades. Terms such as *postmodern*, *late-modern*, or *liquid* were coined to describe these changes. Within these societies, the dominant form of work organization also changed: Work and employment became very flexible. Subsequently, the career development issues that people needed to face were modified to such an extent that it could be said that a new paradigm emerged in this domain. The concepts that had formed, for almost a century, the core of vocational guidance and career counseling (centering on the relationships between individuals and work activities) were replaced by a model that concentrated on the individuals themselves, considered as governors of their own work pathways and, more generally, of their lives.

This chapter first recalls the three kinds of factors that played a role in the construction and evolution of the first paradigm – namely (1) a certain organization of work within societies having some specific characteristics, (2) ideological debates about the ultimate end or purpose of the interventions that could be offered to help individuals make their vocational choices, and (3) a domination of some scientific models that led to a consideration of human behavior in a certain way. The following section describes the major characteristics of the paradigm that had begun to emerge in the 1970s, and tries to understand the reasons for its being constituted as it was. The third section intends to answer the following question: Which kinds of interventions are suggested by this paradigm so as to help individuals living in "liquid modernity" face their life and career design issues? As will be shown, two major types of help may be distinguished. But will they suffice to contribute to the resolution of some acute crises with which our world is confronted (as e.g., a deficit of decent work, global warming, etc.)? Shouldn't we try to give an answer to a quite pressing issue? How to help people combine the care of themselves – and the governance of their lives and career – with the care for distant others and for the "permanence of a genuine human life" (Jonas, 1984, p. 11)?

Construction and Evolution of the Matching Paradigm

Vocational guidance came into existence in Western societies at the end of the 19th century as a consequence of new problems that people had to face: How to find an occupation they could succeed in? This issue appeared at that time and place because of changes in technology (Industrial Revolution) and social transformations (rural depopulation, immigration, etc.), and because these societies were focused on the individual (Elias, 1991), where work was seen as a major occasion to achieve something in life (Schlanger, 2010). In such a context, the "choosing an occupation" issue was seen as a task that should be completed by the individuals themselves, but at the same time as a quite complex one for which they might be helped (Parsons, 1909).

This gave birth to the first paradigm in the domain of career counseling, which may be referred to, in a general way, as the matching of individuals and work. Three different kinds of factors played a major role in the construction of this paradigm. The first one was the Industrial Revolution and the kind of work organization that prevailed then. Alain Touraine (1955) and Claude Dubar (1998) named this the "professional system of work." In such an organization, workers had stable occupational or professional identities made up of specific knowledge, know-how, skills, etc. These identities were also made of shared values and beliefs and of collective representations, and so on – corresponding to their particular trades. Therefore the first paradigm was initially conceived as a matching of individuals and occupations or professions.

The second category of factors that played a role in this paradigm's elaboration was an economic, societal, and political dispute about the purpose (or the *end*, to use a more philosophical term) of vocational guidance's interventions (Gysbers, 2010; Huteau, 2002, 2009). Was the ultimate goal of these interventions to reproduce the society as it was (children having an equivalent position in the social structure to that of their parents, and men continuing to do "masculine activities" and women, "feminine ones")? Or was it to develop an overhauled society which would be both wealthier (because all would have a job corresponding to their capabilities) and fairer (because jobs wouldn't be distributed any longer in relation to the individual's ethnic or social origins and gender)? This second conception – endorsed notably by Alfred Binet (1907), Edouard Toulouse (1913), and Edouard Claparède (1922) – was close to the views of the American Progressive Movement formed around 1900 by scholars such as John Dewey, Felix Adler, Edward L. Thorndike, and G. Stanley Hall. As Willis Rudy (1965, p. 11) wrote: These people's hope was "that American education could be made more socially responsive, more helpful in the meaningful reconstruction of the modern social order, more recognizant of the needs of the individual child, more solidly based on an objectively established science of learning" (quoted by Gysbers, 2010, p. 6).

This ideological dispute about the purposes of vocational guidance was entangled with another about the possible role of scientific knowledge in that guidance. The conservative advocates (e.g., in France, Fernand Mauvezin, 1922; see Huteau, 2009) asserted that counselors should only rely on common sense observations (such as "you need physical strength to have this occupation," "you don't see women doing this kind of job," etc.). In contrast, the defenders of the reformist view were scientists (e.g., Binet, 1907; Toulouse, Piéron, & Vaschide, 1904) who wanted to show that some interventions actually reached their goals and that they reached it for precise reasons their scientific approach could explain.

This gave rise to a scientific reconstruction of the career issues. This reformulation formed the third kind of factors that played an important role in the elaboration of the first paradigm. Indeed vocational or career issues are always about actions and decisions to be made. They deal with questions such as "What occupation or profession should I choose?" In contrast, scientific questions are only about factors and processes – for example, which factors and processes explain that people succeed in some occupations and fail in others? A point needs to be stressed here: These two kinds of approaches (either about action or knowledge) belong to two different categories. Indeed, observations made in the knowledge domain do not provide any imperative as regards actions or decisions to be made. At most, they permit a hypothetical reasoning when a purpose (an end) is previously defined. As in the following example: If you consider it important that a person learns quickly and performs in a given occupation well, you have to consider that research has shown that learning and performing depend on a person's mastering particular aptitudes.

Scientists studied the scientific questions they constructed from the career issues people had to face, referring to the models which were dominant in the social and human sciences of their time. These models insisted on the stability of the human subject's psyche. To describe these stable characteristics which were thought to give an "objective" view on the human mind, they relied on concepts such as *aptitudes*, *personality traits*, *mental age*, etc. In addition, most of these models insisted on either the genetic origins of these characteristics or on the lasting role of early or childhood experiences in their construction.

In such a context (where work was organized this way and where the dominant scientific models insisted on stable and objective personality characteristics), the relationship between individuals and work was described as a matching between individuals and occupations or professions, in terms of aptitudes, work values, interests, etc. The theory of work adjustment (TWA) model by René V. Dawis and Lloyd L. Lofquist (1984) was probably the most comprehensive approach to the first formulation of this first paradigm: A formulation, which gave birth to quite directive career interventions (as counselors were supposed to be able to know "objectively" the kind of occupations or professions that matched individuals' stable characteristics).

This first paradigm evolved during the 20th century as a result of the changes in work organization and in the scientific models within which the research questions were formulated. For example, as a result of the Taylorist–Fordist work organization, many workers lost their occupational identities (in the sense described above). They became undifferentiated "operators" (Dubar, 1998). This led to the emerging of a new broad hypothesis as regards the scientific approach to the relationship between individuals and work: People who share some common interests (in various domains: leisure, sports, work, or home activities, etc.) should be more able than others to form an efficient work collective. This gave birth to the Vocational Interest Blank by Edward Strong (1927) and, more recently, to John Holland's theory of types of personalities and environments (1966).

Donald Super's work represents this first paradigm's final evolution and a transition to the second one. When Super (1957) approached the relationships between individuals and work, a new form of work organization was progressively appearing as a consequence of production's automation (and later, it's computerization). As described by Touraine (1955) and Dubar (1998), this "technical work system" consisted in long-standing work teams forming a functional network. The functions of each of the team's members were much less precisely defined than the jobs in the Taylorist or occupational work systems. These functions indeed depended on the capabilities of other people forming a team, on the technical features of the machines and their rapid evolution, on the currently manufactured objects, etc. Nevertheless, these "technical work systems" were implemented in a context where companies were still supposed to offer their loyal employees a career and where societies still provided individuals with grand models for successful lives (Havighurst, 1952; Levinson, Darrow, Klein, Levinson, & McKee, 1978; Levinson & Levinson, 1996).

In the meantime, new scientific approaches to human subjects had developed. Thus, Carl Rogers's work (1951) had shown the importance in behaviors of the subjective perceptions of a situation, Kurt Lewin (1936) had insisted on the role of the "psychological field," and Robert Havighurst (1952) had described the "development tasks" individuals must accomplish according to their ages, etc.

Taking stock of these advancements, Super introduced three major changes in the matching model. First, he stressed that the subjective views of the persons themselves (their vocational self-concepts) were as important – and perhaps more so – in this matching, as their personality's "objective" descriptions (in terms of personality traits, aptitudes, values, etc.). Second, he considered that in such renovated and evolving work settings, the work pole of the relationship between individuals and work should be approached in terms of "careers" and not any longer in terms of occupations, professions, or jobs. Third, Super underlined the fact that understanding the subjective relationships between individuals and work – and their development throughout the life span – also required a consideration of the individuals' subjective relationships with their other life settings.

All of these changes resulted in the concept of "life span, life space career development" (Super, 1980) and in the view of the human person as a developing system of self-concepts. Vocational guidance became "career counseling," and "career education" developed: These interventions' core goal being to help people cope by themselves with all decisions they might make in order to direct their career from school to retirement.

The Career and Life Design Paradigm

During the last 3 decades, the development of information and communication technologies and of inexpensive ways to carry goods has had a major impact on the definition of the career issues that people face. Hence, a second paradigm has emerged progressively in the field of life and career counseling as a consequence of changes (1) in modern societies, (2) in the organization of work and the distribution of jobs, and (3) in scientific approaches to studying human behaviors.

Liquid Modernity and the Self-Identity Issue

"Globalization" has greatly transformed most societies and, more particularly Western ones. To use a concept coined by Zygmunt Bauman (2000), they have become *liquid*. This means that, within these societies, social forms (structures that limit individual choices, institutions that guard repetitions of routines, patterns of acceptable behaviour) can no longer (and are not expected) to keep their shape for long, because they decompose and melt faster than the time it takes to cast them, and once they are cast for them to set. (Bauman, 2007, p. 1)

As these social forms are not to be given enough time to solidify, they cannot serve as frames of reference for human actions and long-term life strategies. Indeed these forms' life expectations are "shorter than the time it takes to develop a cohesive and consistent strategy, and still shorter than the fulfilment of an individual life project requires" (Bauman, 2007, p. 1).

Liquid societies no longer furnish individuals with the strong social, organizational, and ideological frames that solid ones offered to their parents (a certain lifestyle considered as a "normal" one, specific roles for men and women, shared conceptions about what gives one's life meaning, etc.). The function of support, or "holding" (Winnicott, 1986), provided by major social institutions (religions, ideologies, parties, guilds, syndicates, etc.) has faded. As a result, individuals increasingly

> emerge as the possessors of many voices. Each self contains a multiplicity of others, singing different melodies, different verses, and with different rhythms. Nor do these many voices necessarily harmonize. At times they join together, at times they fail to listen one to another, and at times they create a jarring discord. (Gergen, 1991, p. 83)

In such a context, as authors such as Charles Taylor (1989) and David Parker (2007) have discussed, individuals don't have any other alternative than to determine by themselves what life means to them. They must identify for themselves their fundamental values or "key goods" that serve this holding function and allow them to construct their lives and careers. People now have to get their life bearings, and to get them not only once and for all, but repeatedly: They have to engage in an ongoing process of designing their lives. In liquid modernity, as stressed by Giddens:

> self-identity becomes a reflexively organised endeavour. The reflexive project of the self, which consists in the sustaining of coherent, yet continuously revised, biographical narratives, take place in the context of multiple choice as filtered through abstract systems.... Reflexively organised life-planning ... becomes a central feature of the structuring of self-identity. (Giddens, 1991, p. 5)

Flexible Work and Employment: From Predictable Career to Insecure Work Pathways

The technologies of information have permitted an extraordinary growth of a financial capitalism in search of short-term investments yielding quick profits (Marazzi, 2010). This phenomenon in conjunction with the development of transportation has had some major consequences as regards work and employment. On the one hand, many companies relocate their production facilities to countries where labor is cheap, and labor law is in its embryonic stages (which allows for extremely flexible work and employment conditions). On the other hand, to be able to yield such rapid profits, many firms have developed their marketing of innovative products. Its purpose is to continuously supply consumers with new products which they should consider so innovative that they would buy them to replace similar – but older – ones. To attain such a goal, many companies have deeply transformed their work organization (Ashkenas, Ulrich, Jick, & Kerr, 2002). Four kinds of changes may be described. First, it is often considered that work should be organized as networks of workers gathered only for the duration of an assignment (Amossé & Coutrot, 2010). Such collectives must achieve a certain goal in a given amount of time, and they have to organize themselves accordingly: The notion of clear-cut occupations, jobs, or professions fades away. This very flexible work organization requires, second, a differentiation between "core workers" (who form the "memory" of the company's know-how) and peripheral ones (who are hired when the economic conjuncture is good, and laid off when it deteriorates). Different studies have shown that many employees remain peripheral ones for a very long period of time and, in some cases, never accede to the first segment of the labor market (that of long-term employment) (Edwards, Reich, & Gordon, 1975). The third change is the replacement of some employment contracts by commercial ones (with, e.g., self-employed people) (Parker, 2004). The fourth transformation is the consideration that a company no longer has any obligation as regards the careers of their employees, who are seen as entirely responsible for the governance of their work pathways (Arthur & Rousseau, 1996; Rousseau, 1995).

All of these changes combine to render more and more undeterminable the work pole of the relationship between individuals and work, which formed the first paradigm's core of career counseling. As a consequence, the second paradigm concentrates on the individuals themselves. These are seen as governors of their work pathways. To describe this new view, authors have coined the terms *protean careers* (Hall, 1976, 2002) or *boundaryless careers* (Arthur, 1994; DeFillippi & Arthur, 1996). These "careers" (which should be more precisely named "work pathways") are quite different from what careers were previously, when people were supposed to be able to draw future plans as regards their future at work. Individuals now have to develop a strategic mindset – that is, an ability to spot potential work activities (opportunities) that might become theirs in the environment. This is an important change, as these two perspectives differ regarding their anchoring points and their time spans. The starting point of a planning attitude was the definition of a future goal: A more or less far away ideal to be attained. The means and resources were then defined in relation to this goal. In contrast, the starting point of a "strategic" attitude is current reality. In a given context, a certain individual anticipates such and such an opportunity at the same time as he/she identifies the resources they might rely on to make this possibility become real.

Such a strategic mind-set requires that individuals know what matters to them. Indeed, they are able to discover what might become an opportunity only if they have already thought about (or immediately begin to think about) what is important to them. Recognizing a potential opportunity implies that the possibility is meaningful to the person. Using the terminology of Gibson (1979), it can be said that an opportunity is an *affordance*: something that is perceived – and perceived in this particular way – by a person because he/she immediately anticipates from this phenomenon a particular possibility, one that matters to him/her.

A New Look Into the Human Subject

In the meantime, the perspectives from which human and social scientists consider the human subject has changed. First, human subjects are now seen as less unified than previously. They are now described as "plural" (Lahire, 2010), as speaking with different voices (Gergen,

1991), as combining different "I" positions (Hermans & Kempen, 1993), as composed of different "subjective identity forms" (Guichard, 2005, 2009), as made of a collection of various self-efficacy beliefs (Bandura, 1977), etc. Second, their behaviors are seen as less immediately determined by their early or past experiences than was the case before. In contrast to previous perspectives, these new views of the human subjects insist on the importance of the meaning-making process (Malrieu, 2003), the symbolic power, which can introduce a "margin of freedom" between objective chances and explicit aspirations (Bourdieu, 2000, p. 235), the substantial role of (re)interpretations, symbolizations (Wiley, 1994), dialogues (Jacques, 1991), reflexivity, modes of relating to oneself and one's experiences (Foucault, 2010), etc., in the determining of human self-conceptions and behaviors. As a consequence, human actors are now conceived of as endowed with a greater (at least potential) agency than before (Bandura, 2006). Thus, Pierre Bourdieu, who in the first part of his work underlined the role of past conditioning (via, notably, the concept of "habitus"; see Bourdieu & Passeron, 1990) stressed, at the end of his career, that

> symbolic power can loosen the adjustment of expectations to objective chances and open a space for liberty by a more or less purposeful positing of more or less improbable possible goals, utopia, projects, programs or plans, that a pure calculation of probability would have led [one] to rule out. (Bourdieu, 1997, p. 277; English translation: 2000)

Third, these new approaches to "plural" human subjects describe them as searching to give their lives unity, coherence, and meaning, notably through certain life themes (Csikszentmihalyi & Beattie, 1979) and the construction of life stories which imply notably a *biographying* (Delory-Momberger, 2009) or a *narrative emplotment* (Ricoeur, 1992), etc.

These renewed views of the human subject combined with the obligations made to individuals living in liquid modernity and working in flexible work organizations, to design by themselves their lives and their occupational careers led researchers working in the field of life and career counseling to concentrate on individuals. Their grand research question may be outlined this way: What are the factors and processes involved in individuals' governance of their work pathways and of their lives? As regards the direction of their work pathways, one model dominates: Individuals are now generally described as holders of a certain capital of competencies they must judiciously invest in the work opportunities they are able to elicit. These competencies are described either in terms of career capital (Arthur, 1994; Arthur & Rousseau, 1996; DeFillippi & Arthur, 1996) or of identity capital (Côté, 1996, 1997). Concepts such as *serendipity* (Merton & Barber, 2003) or *planned happenstance* (Mitchell, Levin, & Krumboltz, 1999) were either retrieved or constructed to describe the capability to spot certain opportunities and seize them. Decision-making processes have also been scrutinized (Gati, 1986; Peterson, Sampson, Lenz, & Reardon, 2002) as well as the ability to adapt to these continuously changing conditions (Savickas, 1997; Savickas & Porfeli, 2012), etc. As regards the life design processes, researchers have investigated from different theoretical perspectives, the ways people build their midterm projects, their future goals, or their life plans (Lent, Brown, & Hackett, 1994; Young, Valach, & Collin, 2002). A few general models were also conceived to describe the reflexive processes via which individuals give their lives and work pathways a meaning, and direct them accordingly (Collin & Guichard, 2011; Guichard, 2004, 2005; Guichard & Dumora, 2008; Savickas, 2005, 2011).

Three Major Kinds of Intervention: Information, Guidance, and Dialogue

Within the framework of this second paradigm, two major categories of supports offered to individuals may be distinguished according to the major goal of those supports: the design either of the individual's work pathways or of their life. As regards the first goal, two subcategories may be distinguished: Some (education or counseling) interventions aim to help individuals learn how to find exact and relevant information about today's work and employment, while others attempt to help individuals build a vocational self-concept appropriate to the current world of work.

The main purpose of the interventions forming the first subcategory is to help individuals give an answer to questions such as, What major activities does one do in this job? How is work organized? What are the employment prospects in this career domain? What are the requirements to do such a job? Are there some specific curricula or training programs that prepare for such a job? What are the usual recruiting procedures (résumé, letter of application, other)?

The objective of the interventions making up the second subcategory is to help clients construct a vocational self-concept that matches the current social norms of employability. This means an adaptable vocational self-concept made up of the diverse types of career competencies (DeFillippi & Arthur, 1996) distinguished by researchers and forming a part of an encompassing identity capital (Côté, 1996). This requires that clients engage in a certain type of reflection on themselves and their diverse experiences: They have to create or develop specific ways to relate to these experiences and themselves. These interventions' core object is about the competencies that are required to do such or such work functions, the way that people doing them have developed these competencies, the competencies that clients involved in such interventions have already constructed, the way they have developed these competencies (at school, in training, leisure, sport, job, family, other experiences), the competencies that clients may now construct and how. Such interventions are intended thus to develop a reflexivity guided by the current norms of work and employment. Therefore they can be called career guidance or advising interventions. The *bilan de compétences* (competency elicitation guidance) (Lemoine, 2002) or competency portfolios (e.g., Aubret, 2001) and some career education workshops are prototypical examples of this kind of intervention.

Life design dialogues – which form the second large category of interventions – are intended to assist people in developing the reflexivity they need to design their lives (Savickas et al., 2009). Indeed, as described above, in current liquid societies, individuals must think about their lives to define (and redefine at each period of their lives) the major expectations that give their lives a meaning (expectations and meaning that permit them, in addition, to adopt the strategic mind-set they need to manage their job pathways). In contrast to career guidance, life design dialogues don't aim to aid clients in thinking about their lives from the perspective of the current social norms of employability. Their purpose is more fundamental: It is to help them define their own norms; norms from which they can give a meaning to their lives and design them. This means assisting clients in finding the life bearings that will play the support role in their lives that stable institutions and established ideologies offered in solid modernity. Reflecting on the perspectives that make their lives meaningful implies that people embark on dialogues with themselves and others. Therefore, interventions that aim to assist clients in developing such reflexivity take the shape of counseling dialogues. They are deliberation processes (Lhotellier, 2001) which help clients to look at their various experiences from various potential future perspectives and give them a (never fully established) meaning.

Conclusion

As shown, three major kinds of factors determine the interventions that career counselors implement with their clients in modern Western societies. The first one is the organization of work. Career issues that people have to face depend first on the way work is organized. During the 20th century, the prevailing modes of employment successively took the forms of occupations and professions in professional systems of work, of jobs in Taylorist organizations, of functions embedded in stable networks of work within the technical system of works, and of uncertain jobs and functions in networks based on short-term assignments within flexible work systems. Second, these interventions have depended on the ongoing ideological disputes about the ultimate purpose of such interventions. These debates are mainly about the kind of society that these interventions should contribute toward developing. For example, all through the 20th century, in many countries (including Western ones) and on various occasions, a (more or less overt or covert) controversy has opposed those who believed that women should first ("because of their nature") be at home and nurture their children, with those who thought that men and women should have similar roles and equal positions as regards both paid and home work. Third, these career interventions have also depended on the transformation of the career issues faced by people, into research questions. Such research questions are always about factors and processes, whereas career issues are about decisions to be made or behaviors to be implemented. Therefore scientific observations can only provide counselors with data showing that where a certain final (career or life) goal is set (its selection being beyond the scope of science), such and such factors need to be taken into account. Thus, such scientific reconstructions of career issues contribute to the implementation of less hazardous interventions. Nevertheless, these reconstructions necessarily occur in relation to the scientific models which are dominant at a given time within the scientific field.

All of these factors contributed to the emergence at the end of the 20th century of a new paradigm in career counseling. Where the first one focused on the relationship between individuals and work, the second paradigm concentrates on individual subjects considered as (1) holders of a certain capital of competencies they must know how to invest in occupational opportunities they elicit from the settings where they interact and as (2) designers and governors of their lives. Three kinds of support seem to be appropriate for helping these individuals cope with such tasks: teaching them to find relevant information, guiding them in the construction of the adaptable vocational self-concept they need to direct their flexible work pathways, and entering into dialogues with them to help them design and govern their lives.

Although this paradigm of individuals considered as managers of their lives and work pathways matches well with the demands made on individuals in current Western societies, it raises two kinds of problems. The first are about the great differences between people as regards their capabilities of governing their work pathways. The second refers to a broader interrogation: Can such a paradigm make individuals contribute to the solving of the major crises that the world is now facing?

As noted, this paradigm posits that individuals rely on a group of competencies to manage their careers and lives. This observation raises the issue of how those competencies are constructed. Numerous studies (e.g., Bronfenbrenner, 1979; Côté, 1997; Guichard, 1993; Law, 1981; Vondracek, Lerner, & Schulenberg, 1986; Young, Valach, & Collin, 2002) have suggested that the activities, interactions, and interlocutions which individuals carry out in their different life settings (family, occupational, academic, sports, community, etc.) play a determining role in this construction. Indeed, as a consequence of their activities, interactions, and dialogues in each of these settings, individuals construct certain competencies, certain ways of acting and behaving, certain mind-sets, certain self-concepts, certain social roles, certain assumptions about the world, a certain ideology, certain anticipations as regards their future, certain self-determination beliefs, etc. But individuals' involvement in such settings depends closely, on the one hand, on the volume of the different types of capital (economic, cultural, and social; see Bourdieu & Wacquant, 1992) that they inherit, and, on the other hand, on their gender (Oakley, 1972). In addition, the experiences that individuals can have in some settings lead them to construct certain competencies that have a higher social utility or value – that is, in the construction of their protean career – than the experiences they can have in other settings. Furthermore, individuals can interact and engage in dialogue in a greater or smaller number of settings (in general, the better a person is endowed with the different types of capital, the greater is the number of settings he or she will participate in). These different settings may also be more or less dissonant or consonant. The more dissonant they are, the more the individuals have to get involved in what Urie Bronfenbrenner (1979) called mesosystemic transitions – that is to say, in repeated switching back and forth from one setting to the other that leads them to develop a great flexibility in who they are, and how they act, interact, and relate to themselves (Cohen-Scali, 2010).

These various factors combine to produce the same result: The capital of competencies a person may rely on to govern his/her protean career may differ considerably – in terms of nature and volume – from that of another person. Individual agencies in this matter differ considerably and appear to be closely bound to the individuals' positions within the different social fields forming the society where they live (Bourdieu & Wacquant, 1992). Therefore, one is forced to subscribe to the analysis of Michèle Grosjean and Philippe Sarnin:

> The almost exclusive transfer of career management to the individual (...) could appear as an improvement to those who have greater decision-making powers over their system of activities, or as a social regression to workers with no job security, which is worsened by psychological hardship because they are placed in the paradoxical situation of having to consider that they are responsible for their careers even though it is a process to which they are subjected. ... It is the same for blue-collar workers, because the assertion that individuals should manage their own careers hits hard in the absence of future career possibilities. (Grosjean & Sarnin, 2002, p. 16)

Admittedly, some relevant counseling interventions (be they information, guidance, or dialogue) can partially compensate for such inequalities. But it is likely they are not enough. Indeed, this new paradigm presupposes that everyone – at least from childhood to emerging adulthood – should be considered as a creative being to whom possibilities should be given to develop his/her idiosyncratic potentials via activities, interactions, and dialogues in a variety of settings having a developmental component. Such a view profoundly differs from the way education is considered today in most Western societies (where school is often organized as a more or less covert competition between young people, and where what is at stake is access to the best possible societal positions) (Bourdieu & Passeron, 1990; Gottfredson, 1981). Therefore a new look at education is badly needed. In addition, some international regulations as regards work and employment need also to be implemented. In their absence, one may fear that this new paradigm – which provides individuals with the possibility of greater agency and liberty – produces in many people something totally different: Social despair, which might result, in some states, in a situation close to the one that occurred in Germany in 1933.

More fundamentally, one may also wonder whether this conception of individuals governing their work pathways and designing their lives can bring about an answer to the major challenges that humanity is confronted with today. These are of different kinds: (1) economic challenges – with a financial crisis in many countries, high unemployment rates, considerable disparities between countries in the Northern and Southern hemispheres (Thompson & Reuveny, 2009); (2) ecological challenges – with climate change, an oncoming water crisis, extinction of living species, etc. (Fotopoulos, 2007); and (3) human challenges – with what the International Labour Office has called a "deficit of decent work" (International Labour Office, 2001, 2006), a world demographic explosion, and mass migrations of populations who can't survive in their native environment (Ehrlich & Ehrlich, 2009).

Yet, our current paradigm implies that individuals concentrate on the governance of their protean career. They have to care about their work pathways. Certainly, when they get involved in such a reflection process, they are generally led to care about others around them. This is the case, for example, when they wonder about the possible repercussions of their career decisions on close relatives. It is not excluded they take into account the consequences their choices might have on distant others or on mankind in general (Devine & Maassarani, 2011). Nevertheless, most people don't enter into such considerations when they have to make a decision as regards their work pathways. Sometimes it even happens that certain people get involved in duties that they know will have consequences that can only be harmful to others. The subprime mortgage crisis is an example of such involvements, as one of its causes was the supply of loans to people who bank credit officers and their supervisors knew should not receive them.

At the same time, when people design their lives, they usually enter into broader considerations (questions such as, What will be my legacy to my children? And more generally, what kind of world are we going to leave for the next generations?). When they do so, they embark necessarily on an ethical reflexion about what really makes a life worth living. Indeed, as stressed by Charles Taylor, the self is something which "can exist only in a space of moral issues" (1989, p. 49). To make sense of their lives, people must follow a guiding question: What is it good to be? What gives human dignity to my life? Therefore it may be said that designing one's life always occurs against a background of more or less explicit and developed ethical considerations (Eakin, 2004). In some cases, profound dissonances exist between these ethical considerations and the decisions a person has made or needs to make about his/her work pathways. Taking stock of such dissonances is a major element of the plot that structures the life narratives of people at work who wants to redirect their career toward jobs belonging to the social and solidarity economy (De Calan & Guichard, 2013).

One may wonder whether life design dialogues should not be used to help clients develop such ethical considerations. As we have noted, such reflections are necessarily involved in the processes of designing one's life. But, wouldn't it be appropriate, in the current alarming world juncture, if counselors introduced the issue of caring about distant others and just institutions (in particular, the topic of decent work) – an issue which, according to Paul Ricoeur (1992) is at the very heart of any ethical intention – when it is not tackled by a client? Such considerations might also be related to the "imperative of responsibility" maxim proposed by Hans Jonas: "Act so that the effects of your action are compatible with the permanence of genuine human life on earth" (Jonas, 1984, p. 37). Such a reflection on their lives would probably have some consequences as regards the way people see their work pathways and their current or expected job. Of course, such individual considerations will probably be without any immediate effects on the world of work as it is now organized – that is, in view of a maximization of financial profits. One may nevertheless imagine that a further development of these thoughts might lead to the outlining of both a world organization of work and a world distribution of jobs, in relation to the maximization of the human development they might foster. Couldn't we dream of a World Work Organization implementing international regulations that would enforce the standard of decent work for a sustainable and equitable development?

References

Amossé, T., & Coutrot, T. (2010). *A dynamic overview of socio-productive models in France (1992–2004)*. Paris, France: Centre d'Etudes de l'Emploi.

Arthur, M. B. (1994). The boundaryless career: A competency-based perspective. *Journal of Organizational Behavior, 15*, 307–324. http://doi.org/10.1002/job.4030150403

Arthur, M. B., & Rousseau, D. M. (Eds.). (1996). *The boundaryless careers: A new employment principle for a new organizational era*. Oxford, UK: Oxford University Press.

Ashkenas, R. N., Ulrich, D., Jick, T., & Kerr, S. (2002). *The boundaryless organization: Breaking the chains of organizational structure* (2nd ed., revised and updated). San Francisco, CA: Jossey-Bass.

Aubret, J. (2001). *Le portefeuille de compétences. Le portefeuille de compétence des acquis de formation et d'expériences* [Competency portfolio: A portfolio of experiential, education and training knowledge]. Paris, France: Editions Qui Plus Est.

Bandura, A. (1977). Self-efficacy: Toward unifying theory of behavioral change. *Psychological Review, 84*, 191–215. http://doi.org/10.1037/0033-295X.84.2.191

Bandura, A. (2006). Toward a psychology of human agency. *Perspectives on Psychological Science, 1*, 164–180. http://doi.org/10.1111/j.1745-6916.2006.00011.x

Bauman, Z. (2000). *Liquid modernity*. Cambridge, UK: Polity Press.

Bauman, Z. (2007). *Liquid times: Living in an Age of Uncertainty*. Cambridge, UK: Polity Press.

Binet, A. (1907). Préface. *L'Année Psychologique,14,* pp. v–vi.

Bourdieu, P. (1997). *Méditations pascaliennes*. Paris, France: Editions du Seuil.

Bourdieu, P. (2000). *Pascalian meditations*. Stanford, CA: Stanford University Press.

Bourdieu, P., & Passeron, J. C. (1990). *Reproduction in education, society and culture*. London, UK: Sage.

Bourdieu, P., & Wacquant, L. (1992). *An invitation to reflexive sociology*. Chicago, IL: University of Chicago Press.

Bronfenbrenner, U. (1979). *The ecology of human development*. Cambridge, MA: Harvard University Press.

Claparède, E. (1922). *L'orientation professionnelle, ses problèmes et ses méthodes* [Problems and methods of vocational guidance]. Geneva, Switzerland: Bureau International du Travail (Etudes et Documents).

Cohen-Scali, V., (2010). *Travailler et étudier* [Working and studying]. Paris, France: PUF.

Collin, A., & Guichard, J. (2011). Constructing self in career theory and counseling interventions. In P. J. Hartung & L. M. Subich (Eds.), *Constructing self in work and career: Concepts, cases and contexts* (pp. 89–106). Washington, DC: American Psychological Association.

Côté, J. (1996). Sociological perspectives on identity formation: The culture-identity link and identity capital. *Journal of Adolescence, 19,* 417–428. http://doi.org/10.1006/jado.1996.0040

Côté, J. (1997). An empirical test of the identity capital model. *Journal of Adolescence, 20,* 577–597. http://doi.org/10.1006/jado.1997.0111

Csikszentmihalyi, M., & Beattie, O. V. (1979). Life themes: A theoretical and empirical exploration of their origins and effects. *Journal of Humanistic Psychology, 19,* 45–63. http://doi.org/10.1177/002216787901900105

Dawis, R. V., & Lofquist, L. H. (1984). *A psychological theory of work adjustment: An individualdifferences model and its applications*. Minneapolis, MN: University of Minnesota Press.

De Calan, C., & Guichard, J. (2013). Oasis ou mirage: qu'attendent de l'ESS les personnes qui souhaitent s'y reconvertir ? [Oasis or mirage: What do people intending to redirect their career toward the social and solidarity economy expect from it?]. In P. Braconnier & G. Caire (Eds.), *L'économie sociale et solidaire et le travail*. Paris, France: L'Harmattan.

DeFillippi, R. J., & Arthur, M. B. (1996). Boundaryless contexts and careers: A competency-based perspective. In M. B. Arthur & D. M. Rousseau (Eds.), *The boundaryless career* (pp. 116–131). Oxford, UK: Oxford University Press.

Delory-Momberger, C. (2009). *La condition biographique. Essais sur le récit de soi dans la modernité avancée* [The biographical condition: Essays on self-narratives in late modernity]. Paris, France: Tétraèdre.

Devine, T., & Maassarani, T. F. (2011). *The corporate whistleblower's survival guide: A handbook for committing the truth*. San Francisco, CA: Berrett-Koehler.

Dubar, C. (1998). *La socialisation: Construction des identités sociales et professionnelles* [Socialisation: Construction of social and occupational identities] (2nd rev. ed.). Paris, France: Armand Colin.

Eakin, P. J. (2004). *The ethics of life writing*. Ithaca, NY: Cornell University Press.

Edwards, R. C., Reich, M., & Gordon, D. M. (1975). *Labor market segmentation*. Lexington, MA: D. C. Heath.

Ehrlich, P. R., & Ehrlich, A. H. (2009). The population bomb revisited. *Electronic Journal of Sustainable Development, 1*, 5–13. Retrieved from http://epsem.erin.utoronto.ca/desrochers/The_Population_Bomb.pdf

Elias, N. (1991). *The society of individuals*. Oxford, UK: Blackwell.

Fotopoulos, T. (2007). The ecological crisis as part of the present multi-dimensional crisis and inclusive democracy. *International Journal of Inclusive Democracy, 3*. Retrieved from http://www.inclusivedemocracy.org/journal/

Foucault, M. (2010). *The government of self and others: Lectures at the College de France, 1982–1983*. New York, NY: Palgrave Macmillan. http://doi.org/10.1057/9780230274730

Gati, I. (1986). Making career decisions: A sequential elimination approach. *Journal of Counseling Psychology, 33*, 408–417. http://doi.org/10.1037/0022-0167.33.4.408

Gergen, K. (1991). *The saturated self: Dilemmas of identity in contemporary life*. New York, NY: HarperCollins / Basic Books.

Gibson, J. J. (1979). *The ecological approach to visual perception*. Boston, MA: Houghton-Mifflin.

Giddens, A. (1991). *Modernity and self-identity: Self and society in the late modern age*. Stanford, CA: Stanford University Press.

Gottfredson, L. S. (1981). Circumscription and compromise: A developmental theory of occupational aspirations. *Journal of Counseling Psychology Monograph, 28*, 545–579. http://doi.org/10.1037/0022-0167.28.6.545

Grosjean, M., & Sarnin., P. (2002). Les parcours professionnels [Job pathways]. *Education Permanente, 150*, 9–22.

Guichard, J. (1993). *L'école et les représentations d'avenir des adolescents* [School experience and future representations in adolescents]. Paris, France: PUF.

Guichard, J. (2004). Se faire soi [Making one's own self]. *L'Orientation Scolaire et Professionnelle, 33*, 499–534.

Guichard, J. (2005). Life-long self-construction. *International Journal for Educational and Vocational Guidance, 5*, 111–124. http://doi.org/10.1007/s10775-005-8789-y

Guichard, J. (2009). Self-constructing. *Journal of Vocational Behavior, 75*, 251–258. http://doi.org/10.1016/j.jvb.2009.03.004

Guichard, J., & Dumora, B. (2008). A constructivist approach to ethically grounded vocational development interventions for young people. In J. A. Athanasou & R. Van Esbroeck (Eds.), *International handbook of career guidance* (pp. 187–208). New York, NY: Springer.

Gysbers, N. C. (2010). *Remembering the past, shaping the future: A history of school counseling*. Alexandria, VA: American School Counselor Association.

Hall, D. T. (1976). *Careers in organizations*. Glenview, IL: Scott, Foresman.

Hall, D. T. (2002). *Careers in and out organizations*. London, UK: Sage.

Havighurst, R. (1952). *Developmental tasks and education* (2nd ed.). New York, NY: David McKay.

Hermans, H. J. M., & Kempen, H. J. G. (1993). *The dialogical self: Meaning as movement*. San Diego, CA: Academic Press.

Holland, J. L. (1966). *The psychology of vocational choice: A theory of personality types and model environments*. Walthman, MA: Blaisdel.

Huteau, M. (2002). *Psychologie, psychiatrie et politique sous la troisième république; la biocratie d'Edouard Toulouse (1865–1947)* [Psychology, psychiatry and politics during the third Republic: Edouard Toulouse's biocraty]. Paris, France: L'Harmattan.

Huteau, M. (2009). *Un pionnier de l'orientation professionnelle: Fernand Mauvezin* [Fernand Mauvezin: A pioneer in vocational guidance]. Paris, France: Documents de l'INETOP.

International Labour Office. (2001). *Reducing the decent work deficit. International conference 89th session 2001* (Report to the Director General). Geneva, Switzerland: Author.

International Labour Office. (2006). The decent work deficit: A new ILO report outlines the latest global employment trends. *World of Work, 56*, 12–15.

Jacques, F. (1991). *Difference and subjectivity: Dialogue and personal identity*. New Haven, CT: Yale University Press.

Jonas, H. (1984). *The Imperative of responsibility: In search of an ethics for the technological age*. Chicago, IL: University of Chicago Press.

Lahire, B. (2010). *The plural actor*. Cambridge, UK: Polity Press.

Law, B. (1981). Community interaction: A "mid-range" focus for theories of career development in young adults. *British Journal of Guidance and Counselling, 9*, 142–158. http://doi.org/10.1080/03069888108258210

Lemoine, C. (2002). *Se former au bilan de compétences: Comprendre et pratiquer cette démarche* [To be trained in competency elicitation guidance: Understanding and implementing such interventions]. Paris, France: Dunod.

Lent, R. W., Brown, S. D., & Hackett, G. (1994). Toward a unifying social cognitive theory of career and academic interest, choice. and performance. *Journal of Vocational Behavior, 45*, 79122. http://doi.org/10.1006/jvbe.1994.1027

Levinson, D. J., Darrow, C. N., Klein, E. B., Levinson, M. H., & McKee, B. (1978). *The seasons of a man's life*. New York, NY: Knopf.

Levinson, D. J., & Levinson, J. D. (1996). *The seasons of a woman's life*. New York, NY: Knopf.

Lewin, K. (1936). *Principles of topological psychology*. New York, NY: McGraw-Hill. http://doi.org/10.1037/10019-000

Lhotellier, A. (2001). *Tenir conseil; délibérer pour agir* [Counselling: A deliberation for action]. Paris, France: Seli Arslan.

Malrieu, P. (2003). *La construction du sens dans les dires autobiographiques* [The construction of meaning in autobiographical narratives]. Toulouse, France: Erès. http://doi.org/10.3917/eres.malri.2003.01

Marazzi, C. (2010). *The violence of financial capitalism* (2nd ed.). Cambridge, MA: MIT Press.

Mauvezin, F. (1922). *Rose des métiers. Traité d'orientation professionnelle, qualités et aptitudes nécessaires à l'exercice de 250 métiers différents et défauts rédhibitoires* [Occupational compass. Treatise on vocational guidance: Qualities and aptitudes required for 250 different occupations and redhibitory defects]. Paris, France: Editions littéraires et politiques.

Merton, R. K., & Barber, E. G. (2003). *The travels and adventures of serendipity: A study in sociological semantics and the sociology of science*. Princeton, NJ: Princeton University Press.

Mitchell, K. E., Levin, A. S., & Krumboltz, J. D. (1999). Planned happenstance: Constructing unexpected career opportunities. *Journal of Counseling and Development, 77*, 115–124. http://doi.org/10.1002/j.1556-6676.1999.tb02431.x

Oakley, A. (1972). *Sex, gender and society*. London, UK: Temple Smith.

Parker, D. (2007). *The self in moral space: Life narrative and the good*. Ithaca, NY: Cornell University Press.

Parker, S. C. (2004). *The economics of self-employment and entrepreneurship*. Cambridge, UK: Cambridge University Press. http://doi.org/10.1017/CBO9780511493430

Parsons, F. (1909). *Choosing a vocation*. Boston, MA: Houghton Mifflin.

Peterson, G. W., Sampson, J. P., Jr., Lenz, J. G., & Reardon, R. C. (2002). A cognitive information processing approach to career problem solving and decision making. In D. Brown (Ed.), *Career choice and development* (4th ed., pp. 312–369). San Francisco, CA: Jossey-Bass.

Ricoeur, P. (1992). *Oneself as another*. Chicago, IL: University of Chicago Press.

Rogers, C. R. (1951). *Client-centered therapy*. Boston, MA: Houghton Mifflin.

Rousseau, D. (1995). *Psychological contracts in organizations: Understanding written and unwritten agreements*. Thousand Oaks, CA: Sage.

Rudy, W. S. (1965). *Schools in an age of mass culture: An exploration of selected themes in the history of twentieth-century American education*. Englewoods Cliffs, NJ: Prentice-Hall.

Savickas, M. L. (1997). Career adaptability: An integrative construct for life-span, life-space theory. *Career Development Quarterly, 45*, 247–259. http://doi.org/10.1002/j.2161-0045.1997.tb00469.x

Savickas, M. L. (2005). The theory and practice of career construction. In S. D. Brown & R. W. Lent (Eds.), *Career development and counseling: Putting theory and research to work* (pp. 42–70). Hoboken, NJ: Wiley.

Savickas, M. L. (2011). *Career counseling*. Washington, DC: American Psychological Association.

Savickas, M. L., & Porfeli, E. J. (2012). Career Adapt-Abilities Scale: Construction, reliability, and measurement equivalence across 13 countries. *Journal of Vocational Behavior, 80,* 661–673. http://doi.org/10.1016/j.jvb.2012.01.011

Savickas, M. L., Nota, L., Rossier, J., Dauwalder, J.-P., Duarte, M. E., Guichard, J., . . . van Vianen, A. E. M. (2009). Life designing: A paradigm for career construction in the 21st century. *Journal of Vocational Behavior, 75,* 239–250. http://doi.org/10.1016/j.jvb.2009.04.004

Schlanger, J. (2010). *La vocation* [Vocation] (2nd ed. rev.). Paris, France: Hermann.

Strong, E. K. (1927). *Vocational Interest Blank*. Stanford, CA: Stanford University Press.

Super, D. E. (1957). *The psychology of careers: An introduction to vocational development*. New York, NY: Harper & Row.

Super, D. E. (1980). A life-span, life-space approach to career development. *Journal of Vocational Behavior, 13,* 282–298. http://doi.org/10.1016/0001-8791(80)90056-1

Taylor, C. (1989). *Sources of the self: The making of the modern identity*. Cambridge, MA: Harvard University Press.

Thompson, W. R., & Reuveny, R. (2009). *Limits to globalization: North-South divergence (rethinking globalizations)*. London, UK: Routledge.

Toulouse, E. (1913). *La vie nouvelle* [The new life]. Paris, France: Fayard.

Toulouse, E., Piéron, H., & Vaschide, N. (1904). *Technique de psychologie expérimentale* [Techniques of experimental psychology]. Paris, France: Douin.

Touraine, A. (1955). La qualification du travail: histoire d'une notion [Work qualification: History of an idea]. *Journal de Psychologie Normale et Pathologique, 13,* 27–76.

Vondracek, F. W., Lerner, R. M., & Schulenberg, J. E. (1986). *Career development: A life span developmental approach*. Hillsdale, NJ: Erlbaum.

Wiley, N. (1994). *The semiotic self*. Cambridge, UK: Polity Press.

Winnicott, D. W. (1986). *Holding and interpretation*. London, UK: Hogarth Press.

Young, R. A., Valach, L., & Collin, A. (2002). A contextualist explanation of career. In D. Brown (Ed.), *Career choice and development* (4th ed., pp. 206–252). San Francisco, CA: Jossey-Bass.

Chapter 3
Dynamics in Career Development: Personal and Organizational Perspectives

Andreas Hirschi and Jean-Pierre Dauwalder
Institute of Psychology, University of Lausanne, Switzerland

Introduction: The Dynamic Nature of Careers

Due to advances in technology, increased workforce diversity, and changes in organizational structures, the nature of careers has changed remarkably over the past 3 decades (Sullivan, 1999). One important consequence of today's career environment is the increased importance of each employee's performance and the increasing inability of organizations to plan long-term career development or to manage careers for employees (Stickland, 1996). As one consequence of this change, psychological contracts between employers and employees have also changed. Current psychological contracts are no longer based on the promise of job security and automatic advancement as provided by the employer, in exchange for loyalty and good performance as provided by the employee. Instead, the support of the employee's personal career development and learning in exchange for temporally limited contributions to the organization's success increasingly form today's tacit agreement between parties in organizations (Rousseau, 2001). As a result of these changes in how careers are developed in today's world of work, employees face an increased need for career self-management because companies are increasingly pursuing a human resource policy that shifts accountability for career management from the employer to the employee (Kossek, Roberts, Fisher, & Demarr, 1998). These changes have profound effects on how careers develop, resulting in more nonlinear and less predictable career patterns. Accordingly, increased self-directedness, flexibility, and adaptability are required on the part of employees if they are to successfully cope with the changes in the realm of work (Sullivan, Carden, & Martin, 1998).

As outlined by Guichard (2015; see Chapter 2), the dominant theories and practices of career counseling have always been a reflection of contemporary societal, political, and economic conditions. Faced with the above mentioned new career context, the field is hence in need of new theoretical and practical conceptualizations that are aligned with the current realities in organizations and the labor market. Although they still have merit, linear models of career development such as that proposed by Super (1990) or models of stable individual differences that need to be matched with aligned work environments such as implied in the model proposed by Holland (1985) seem inapt to fully reflect this new reality.

As a consequence, the field of career studies – particularly, its management-oriented branch – has proposed a vast array of career concepts over recent years that aim at addressing the new career reality. Prominent among these are the notions of employability (Forrier & Sels, 2003; Fugate, Kinicki, & Ashforth, 2004), career motivation (London, 1983; London & Noe, 1997), career self-management (King, 2004; Kossek et al., 1998; Stickland, 1996), career competencies (Akkermans, Brenninkmeijer, Huibers, & Blonk, 2012; Kuijpers & Scheerens, 2006), or a protean (Hall, 1996) and boundaryless (Arthur, Khapova, & Wilderom, 2005) career orientation. From the domain of vocational psychology, the happenstance learning theory (Krumboltz, 2009) and the chaos theory of career (Bright & Pryor, 2005) have equally addressed the dynamic nature of careers.

Common to all of the modern approaches to career development is the notion that career development cannot be restricted to career decision making that focuses on finding a suitable profession corresponding to personal skills, values, and interests. As a consequence, classical notions of career guidance which aimed at assisting clients in finding a good match between their personal characteristics and work environments or professions are deemed insufficient. Moreover, many of the current career concepts are limited by the fact that they propose solely different sets of attitudes, competencies, or behaviors that are deemed important for successful career development in the new context. However, they mostly fail to adequately address the *processes* by which career development can be conceived.

The life design paradigm has the potential to address these issues and shortcomings. It is based on the epistemology of social constructivism (Young & Collin, 2004) and acknowledges that professional development is highly contextualized and individualized. Similar to the general developmental-contextual theory of human development (Lerner, 2006), the life design paradigm proposes that career development must be understood as a dynamic interaction of person and environment. As a consequence, focusing solely on personal attitudes or competencies as a basis for successful career development is insufficient. A truly comprehensive notion of career development must address which personal characteristics in combination with what kind of environmental conditions produce what kind of career outcomes. While it is beyond the scope of the present chapter to develop such a theory (see Vondracek, Lerner, & Schulenberg, 1986; Vondracek & Porfeli, 2008, for elaborations), we will outline some of the implications for career counseling based on a life design approach.

According to developmental contextualism, people are active agents of their own development. Their development is the result of a dynamic interaction between personal characteristics and actions and environmental affordances and constraints. As a consequence of this process, human development shows great plasticity and contains the potential for systemic change and adaptation. The resulting individual trajectories of development may vary across time and place and are dependent on individual differences as well as constraints and opportunities in the environment (Lerner, 2006). In contrast to the notions of chaos or happenstance, such trajectories are in principle predictable and lawful, albeit very complex and dynamic.

From Dynamic Reasoning ...

Understanding – and taking advantage of – complex dynamics therefore becomes more and more important for career counselors. Classical scientific reasoning is linear and deductive.

It proved to be useful and efficient to apply a general law (e.g., all human beings die) to the single case (e.g., X is a human being) and deduce a foreseeable consequence (e.g., X will die). By analogy and for decades now, traditional career counseling has desperately looked for such linear relationships between single "causes" (e.g., abilities, interests) and their foreseeable "consequences" (e.g., professional choice, career development).

Unfortunately, neither the "law" that interests or abilities are sufficient to obtain any "job" or "training" opportunities, nor even the premise that these prerequisites remain stable or at least predictable, are valid anymore. During actual processes of resolving professional problems, not only the premises but also the definitions of the problems themselves continuously change in an interactive manner. *Chains of causality* become multiple, complex, and permanently changing, sometimes complicated by the influence of reciprocally dependent elements. Nonlinear relationships are the rule; simple and linear causalities remain the exception.

This challenge, however, also opens unexpected opportunities to position life design as a science of understanding and managing such complex interactive problem-solving processes at the interface of many other traditional disciplines (Haynes, 1992). Rather than continue to apply classical reasoning, which has not proven to be false but rather weak in our fields, we should develop more adequate forms of reasoning, taking advantage of a better understanding of *interaction*, *complexity*, and *dynamics*. In other words, we have to replace the prevalent linear (or "medical") sequence – for example, (1) differential diagnosis, (2) indication, and (3) prescription of choice or treatment – with iterative or even circular interventions – for example, identifying invariants and variable elements in a client's interaction with his or her environment, formulating dynamic hypotheses, exploring the space of potential changes, testing different solutions. A single contact will thus rarely be sufficient for life design; dynamic reasoning needs time. Furthermore, introducing and developing dynamic reasoning in the field of counseling – for the time being – mainly relies on ideas and concepts developed in other disciplines such as mathematics, physics, thermodynamics, biology, or meteorology (Gleick, 1988).

One principle is to understand each person as just one element within an ongoing process of mutual shaping between himself/herself and his/her environment. There is no singular or unidirectional causality, but at best a *coevolution* which can be observed. For life design, this means that there exists no "independent" or "neutral" point of reference. Looking at a client's perception of her environment includes looking at the counselor's role as just one element among others within this environment, sometimes helpful, sometimes not. This might explain why in psychotherapy research the working alliance (Horvath & Greenberg, 1994) or therapeutic relationship (Grawe, Donati, & Bernauer, 1994) proved to be so fundamental, just as it seems determinant for counseling outcomes (Masdonati, Massoudi, & Rossier, 2009). But understanding and accepting each single person as acting within the constraints of her (perceived) specific environment or ecosystem also means being particularly attentive to the dynamic patterns resulting from these interactions, including the client's plans to influence the counselor (Caspar, 2007).

A second principle is to understand complex systems as not being directed or controlled by any agent or subsystem – whether that be the client herself or even the counselor – inside or outside the system itself. The multitude of interactions generates, however, some form of global order, emerging spontaneously. Such *self-organization* is wholly decentralized over all components, typically robust and able to survive and self-repair even with substantial perturbations. Understanding and accepting the power of self-organization is crucial for any life design intervention (see also Schiersmann & Thiel, 2012). For example, labor markets continually change at a local level (e.g., innovative products from smaller companies or start-ups create new jobs), but they are at the same time constrained by macroeconomic conditions (e.g., taxes or consumer behavior). There is no need for an "invisible hand" to explain the emergence of a state of equilibrium among the locally changing attractors (due to local control parameters) and the more stable potential landscape (Haken, 2006), growing together into a comprehensive general picture (due to emerging order parameters).

Another example is to be found in clients looking for vocational guidance, where perceptions and expectations about possible professional pathways form many coexisting attractors linked through quite random dynamics and large "basins" of attraction. Any choice then selectively reinforces one attractor among all others and thereby also reshapes the whole potential landscape. Counseling outcomes usually result in reduction of uncertainty and undecidedness, mainly by working out a comprehensive dynamic understanding (metaperspective) and reshaping of such complex configurations (Dauwalder, Rossier, Massoudi, & Masdonati, 2011).

A third principle calls for an understanding of the emergence of order and disorder as being both necessary and complementary for *sustainable evolution* in living systems. A completely "ordered" system would be immune to change or evolution (e.g., entropy in a thermodynamic system). Local disorders allow for emergence of new dynamic patterns, which enter into competition with existing patterns and generate new attractors, sometimes able to trigger a bifurcation. This corresponds to a sudden qualitative or topological change in the behavior of an entire dynamic system (Gleick, 1988). Described as *équilibration majorante* in cognitive development during childhood, by Piaget (1985), or *dissipative structures* with a role in dynamic systems far from equilibrium (Prigogine & Stengers, 1997), these fundamental reorganizations often mark irreversible *steps of evolution* within dynamic systems, usually accompanied by substantial increase in efficiency. This means that life design might be particularly helpful in critical situations (far from equilibrium), when bifurcations toward a new order parameter (Haken & Schiepek, 2010) become possible. In such "bi-stable" configurations, a (irreversible) decision often depends on small or insignificant details. This might explain why even university students retrospectively often declare having decided the choice of their studies "at random" (Bäumler, Scheller, & von Maurice, 1994). On the other hand, the emergence of a macroscopic order parameter such as somebody's professional identity is usually maintained through a multitude of interactions and constraints in their daily environment and acts back according to the *slaving principle* (Haken, 1991) on what is possible or not in one's life (e.g., a butcher will not practice as a surgeon and vice versa). Effective life design has to be aware of these dynamic constraints too.

A fourth principle opens, by understanding the dynamics of a complex system, the whole perspective of *anticipation*. The emergence of macroscopic order parameters facilitates the understanding of possible or potential evolutions of a whole dynamic system for any observer. It drastically reduces the information (e.g., into a set of mathematical equations) necessary to describe its dynamics. Not only in the present but also for the future.

A discipline which has achieved mastery in *modeling* complex dynamic systems is meteorological science (Lynch, 2006). Today's weather forecasts are usually fairly reliable and adapted to local conditions for up to 10 days in advance. However, according to the particular configuration of the control parameters, sometimes practically no prediction is possible, or sometimes very reliable predictions are possible for long periods. By analogy, for some clients or some professional identities, given the dynamics of their interactions and/or constraints within their local environments, no forecast is possible, whereas for others it seems easy. In life design, the first attempts to systematically anticipate possible professional identities through specific interview techniques have recently be proposed by Jean Guichard (2008). He puts into perspective the multiple *subjective identity forms* of one person in their evolution from the past through the present toward the future.

Thus, the emergence of order and the control of local dynamics appear to be indivisible and mutually linked phenomena. The classical distinction between cause and effect or between independent and dependent variables no longer makes sense. The life design paradigm goes far beyond such traditional reasoning, as the understanding, analysis, and shaping of naturally occurring processes of change leads to the need for new kinds of interventions.

... to Life Design Interventions

Usually, *change* continuously happens within the limits of self-organization. Noise, disorder, or perturbations regularly appear within the dynamic equilibrium of a given system. They are generated through environmental influences or the nonforeseeable results of multiple nonlinear interactions within the system itself. Persisting perturbations give raise to fluctuations and instability within system dynamics, potentially leading to states far from equilibrium. Finally, bifurcations toward new order parameters may restabilize dynamic patterns at a new integrative level (équilibration majorante).

At this point, we should ask what this (different) understanding of change from a dynamic perspective implies for life design interventions and counselors' approaches. Efficient counselors usually do not apply theories strictly, but refer to their intuition. In fact, their intuition reflects a holistic understanding of complex dynamics, which are different for each client within his or her ecosystem. Intuitively most counselors know when a client is really ready to actively engage in a process of counseling, problem solving, or vocational guidance. In a particular case, a 15-year-old boy may well understand and integrate the preoccupation of his parents about his need for professional choices without asking for vocational guidance (assimilation), without any substantial perturbation. In another case, such a message may be understood (assimilation), but also generate increasing questioning regarding the client's personal and professional identity (fluctuations) and result in a need for intensive counseling (crisis) or life design interventions, and, if successful, lead to a mature choice and increased assertiveness (accommodation). Beyond their intuition and this fundamental distinction between assimilation and accommodation processes, however, counselors need theoretical constructs to help clients negotiate continuous change without losing a sense of self and social identity (Guichard, 2005).

From our life design perspective, *motivation to change* is elicited from the client and not imposed by outside forces. Readiness to change is not a trait of the client, but a fluctuating result of dynamic interactions and environmental influences. At best, counselor and clients thus can achieve a co-construction, sufficiently efficient to modify the client's readiness to change. Miller and Rollnick (2002) have developed specific motivational interviewing techniques based on five effective principles: (1) express empathy, (2) develop discrepancy, (3) avoid argumentation, (4) roll with resistance, and (5) support self-efficacy. These client-centered but also directive techniques aim particularly at the examination and resolution of any ambivalence in the client before engaging in more specific problem solving or career counseling.

From our life design perspective, the concepts of *constructivist and narrative career interventions* fit particularly well with the actual needs for effective interventions, which are adapted to our global understanding of dynamic change (Savickas, 2012). Savickas, building on a common epistemological position about contextual boundedness, dynamic processes, nonlinear causalities, multiple subjective realities, and needs for modelization (Savickas et al., 2009), and his former work on career construction by narrative techniques (Savickas, 2005), proposes substantial evolutions of heuristics for life design interventions. His model involves construction, deconstruction, reconstruction, and co-construction, which lead to action in the real world. First, the counselor asks clients to tell stories, illustrating how they have constructed their self, identity, and career. Storytelling means active construction of multiple subjective realities through words, but also building new local attractors or control parameters in dynamic reasoning. Second, the counselor assumes a critical role by confronting the client with self-limiting ideas or biases in his or her stories. This deconstruction is only efficient when clients become aware of their own contradictions (assimilation) and then include alternative ideas in their own future reasoning (accommodation). For dynamic reasoning, this contributes to enhancing fluctuations or instability, leading finally to "states far from equilibrium" and is therefore essential for systemic changes.

Third, from all of the microstories told by the client, the counselor has to identify clients' macrostories (or identity), which explain their past, orients them in their present, and guide them into the future. This reconstruction gives a holistic sense to the stories, but also defines at least one order parameter in dynamic reasoning. In our view, offering different explanations or order parameters to the client at this moment might increase the probabilities for bifurcations or restabilizations (équilibration majorante) at new integrative levels.

Fourth, the counselor has to constantly revise the life portrait developed so far, together with his or her client. This co-construction opens perspectives of new language, fresh perspectives, or extended vistas not only to clients but also to counselors. In life design interventions, one might perhaps stress somewhat more the "anticipation" perspective, exploring the potentials and the limits of the modelization designed together, for the client's future options for life. Finally, the counselor should help clients turn their intentions into action. Albert Bandura (2001) defines perceived self-efficacy as the necessary foundation of human agency: People are self-organizing, proactive, self-reflecting, and self-regulating because of their interaction with their environment. For dynamic reasoning, this monitoring and coaching of the client's actions provides the necessary test of the integration of change into the whole dynamic system: decentralized, robust, and able to self-repair. In other words, the counselor is no longer necessary.

Some might criticize the life design interventions presented so far as being too normative. Haken and Schiepek (2010) tried to define some very general generic principles as being less normative, because they should be present during the whole process of any systemic intervention: (1) Create stable conditions for change processes; (2) Identify the system and its patterns; (3) Develop visions and goals; (4) Energize and identify control parameters; (5) Destabilize and reinforce fluctuations; (6) Foster symmetry breaking; (7) Secure restabilization; and (8) Facilitate synchronization. In their excellent book, Schiersmann and Thiel (2012) analyzed, however, in detail theses eight generic principles and criticized their relative proximity to more classical problem-solving techniques.

What we definitely need are new global assessment tools and research methodologies to better describe and monitor life design interventions and their efficacy (Dauwalder, 2007). The emerging concepts, however, seem sufficiently promising to position life design as a science of understanding and managing complex interactive problem solving at the interface of many other disciplines.

Beyond such interventions in personal situations, which already include an ecosystemic perspective, there exist a variety of organizational contexts. To further advance the life design paradigm, it is important to connect it with the literature on personal and organizational career management (Savickas et al., 2009). In the following paragraphs, we will specifically focus on how self-directed career management can be seen as a part of life design.

Career Management: Proactive Regulation of Person–Context Interactions

Focusing on the dynamic nature of careers, lifelong career management within, between, and outside of organizations becomes pivotal. The notion of career management implies that career counselors should focus on the interaction between client and environment and how this interaction can be optimized to result in favorable career outcomes. To achieve this, career counseling and career development in organizations should focus on (a) the promotion of proactive career behaviors and (b) the development and unitization of personal and environmental resources of the client.

First, career counseling practice based on the life design paradigm should focus on promoting proactive career behaviors. Modern concepts of career emphasize self-directed career management as vital for positive career development (Hall, 2002; King, 2004; London & Noe, 1997). For example, Savickas (2011) asserted that the modern career and work context requires career management – not career planning – and action – not verbal expression of decidedness. As a consequence, different researchers have noted that the current career context increases the need to be engaged in proactive career behaviors (e.g., career planning, networking, exploration) to achieve objective and subjective career success (Fuller & Marler, 2009; Thomas, Whitman, & Viswesvaran, 2010). One of the major functions of different proactive behaviors is to achieve a good person–environment fit (Parker & Collins, 2010).

We propose three fundamental ways for how people can interact with their environments through different proactive career behaviors aimed at (1) the selection of environments, (2) the adaptation of oneself to current environments, and (3) the active shaping of the current environment to oneself. According to this conception, the person–environment fit is a temporal state that results from the alignment of personal needs and preferences to environmental demands and resources. This state of fit can be achieved through a process of person–environment interaction that consists of three previously named processes.

First, people can select environments that correspond to their personal needs, skills, and preferences, which allow an alignment between personal needs and environmental resources. This notion is related to various classical models of career development and career decision making (Hirschi & Läge, 2007; Holland, 1997; Savickas, 2005; Savickas et al., 2009; Super, 1990), where a clear self-awareness is seen as the foundation for being able to make sound career choices and implementing one's self-concept in the work role. Empirical research has shown, for example, that a clearer career identity relates positively to career choices congruent with one's interests (Hirschi et al., 2011; Srsic & Walsh, 2001) or that unemployed adults reporting more career planning were more successful in finding employment with a good person–job fit (Saks & Ashforth, 2002). These components therefore refer to the classical approach in career guidance which aims at helping clients make self-congruent career choices and implementing their choice (Sampson, Lenz, Reardon, & Peterson, 1999).

Second, people can adapt themselves to better correspond to existing and future work environments. This aspect is related to the notion of personal flexibility, which is often mentioned as a requirement to succeed in the modern work context (Hall, 1996). For example, Pulakos et al. (2002) showed in an empirical study that more facility in adjusting to new work situations predicts better job performance. This flexibility is often referred to as career adaptability, which has been defined as the ability to adapt to changing career circumstances and proposed as an indicator of openness to change and the ability to handle the stresses of a new career context (Kossek et al., 1998), or as a component of employability, which refers to wage and occupational flexibility or a propensity to learn combined with a sense of control and efficacy (Fugate et al., 2004; McQuaid & Lindsay, 2005). Likewise, adaptability in the workplace is described as the individual characteristic that allows people to increase their level of fit with the work environment through adaptive performance measures, such as dealing with uncertain and unpredictable work situations (Pulakos, Arad, Donovan, & Plamondon, 2000).

Third, people can shape their environments according to their personal needs, skills, and preferences. This notion is similar to the concept of job crafting proposed by Wrzesniewski and Dutton (2001), which envisions employees as active crafters of their jobs, who change actual task boundaries, cognitive task boundaries, and social task boundaries. According to Wrzesniewski and Dutton, the degree to which such job crafting occurs depends on the individual work and motivation orientations of the employee and on the job characteristics in terms of task interdependence and the level of freedom and autonomy at one's job. Emerging empirical work supports the assumption that people in different professions and at different levels within organizations are active in job crafting, and that work orientation and self-image are predictors of crafting behaviors (e.g., Berg, Wrzesniewski, & Dutton, 2010).

In sum, all three proposed approaches to career management can enhance person–environment fit. In contrast to static models of person–environment fit, however, they depict that fit as dynamic and an ongoing process of constant person–environment interactions. Such interactions stem from the application of different proactive career behaviors. As such, this dynamic notion of fit, based on career management, reflects the theoretical approach in the life design paradigm that career development is a contextualized and individualized process of self-construction (Savickas et al., 2009).

Promoting Resources and Readiness Among Clients

To promote different types of proactive career behaviors among career counseling clients, career counseling based on a life design approach should focus on promoting the necessary resources, abilities, and readiness that allow clients to actively take charge of their working lives.

Several recent theoretical accounts have promoted such an approach. First, Savickas and Porfeli (2012) have proposed career adapt-abilities as essential for career development, extending Savickas's (1997) earlier conceptualizations of career adaptability. *Career adaptability* is described as a psychosocial construct that denotes an individual's resources for coping with current and anticipated tasks, transitions, and traumas in their occupational roles that, to some degree large or small, alter their social integration (Savickas, 1997). According to Savickas and Porfelli, *career adapt-ability* is seen as a set of resources that a person can draw on to master challenges in the domain of work. They emerge from the intersection of person–environment relations, represent a form of human capital, and are closely related to the recent notion of psychological capital (Luthans, Avolio, Avey, & Norman, 2007). Specifically, four manifestations of career adapt-abilities are proposed: concern, control, curiosity, and confidence.

Second, Lent (2013) has addressed the need to revise long-standing notions of career decision making and planning, and suggested that, while still valid, they should be complemented by career counseling aiming at enhancing clients' *life preparedness*. He describes this as a "healthy state of vigilance regarding threats to one's career well-being as well as alertness to resources and opportunities on which one can capitalize" (p. 7). One important function of this preparedness is that clients can use proactive behaviors to manage barriers, build support, and master the challenges in their working lives. Within the context of the social cognitive career theory (Lent, Brown, & Hackett, 1994), career and life preparedness can be enhanced by developing vocational interests, enhancing self-efficacy beliefs, correcting unrealistic or negative outcome expectations, setting attainable career goals, and managing environmental barriers and supports.

A final example of a recently proposed model is Hirschi's (2012) career resources model. Based on a qualitative review and integration of different theoretical models and empirical studies regarding the competencies, behaviors, and attitudes that are important for successful career development, Hirschi proposed that four basic and interrelated career resources situated in the person and the environment can be intensified, which are important for career counselors to assess and develop to promote positive career development among their clients: human capital resources, social resources, psychological resources, and identity resources. *Human capital resources* include factors such as education, experience and training, and cognitive ability within the broader category of work-relevant knowledge, skills, abilities, and other characteristics (KSAOs). *Social resources* (often referred to as social capital) refer to "the goodwill available to individuals or groups" (Adler & Kwon, 2002, p. 23) in terms of the information, influence, and solidarity it makes available to the person. The availability and characteristics of a mentor is one form of social capital, but it can be more broadly conceived of as one's developmental network, which can be characterized according to its structure and diversity (e.g., range and density) and quality or strength (Higgins & Kram, 2001). *Psychological resources* refer to the positive psychological traits and states, such as the cognitions, motivations, and affect of the person, which are generalized and expressed in different contexts and more specifically in relation to the work role. Finally, *career identity resources* indicate one's conscious awareness of oneself as a worker; of one's occupational interests, abilities, goals, and values; of the importance of one's work; and of the structure of meanings in which such self-perceptions are linked with career roles (Ibarra & Barbulescu, 2010; Meijers, 1998). At the core of career identity is the question, who am I and how is my work meaningful to me? Hence, career identity resources can be distinguished from more general psychological resources in the sense that they specifically refer to how one consciously views oneself in relation to one's work.

In sum, all of these three briefly reviewed concepts share the view with the life design paradigm that classic models of decision making and planning which dominated career counseling in the last century should be expanded by a career counseling approach that helps clients build readiness and use their resources in order to enable them to actively manage their working lives. As such, they actively help clients in a process of self-construction, taking their individual life stories and contexts into full account.

Conclusions

In this chapter we elaborated on some basic notions in the life design paradigm and specifically focused on the dynamic nature of modern career development and its implications for theoretical and practical perspectives on career counseling and career development interventions on the personal and organizational level. Based on the life design approach, we have shown that models which see careers as predictable, linear, and based upon deductive reasoning should be complemented by perspectives that take the dynamic interaction between person and context into account. Career counseling and career development approaches based on the life design paradigm should apply dynamic reasoning and interactive counseling approaches. Linking life design with career management at the individual and organizational level, we showed that career counseling should stimulate positive person–environment interactions, promote proactive career behaviors, and focus on developing and applying different resources for positive career development. We believe that enhancing career theory and intervention practice with these perspectives inspired by the life design paradigm will adequately reflect the realities of modern career development and promises to significantly enhance the quality, effectiveness, and relevance of career counseling and intervention for our clients.

References

Adler, P., & Kwon, S. (2002). Social capital: Prospects for a new concepts. *Academy of Management Review, 27*, 17–40. http://doi.org/10.2307/4134367

Akkermans, J., Brenninkmeijer, V., Huibers, M., & Blonk, R. W. B. (2012). Competencies for the contemporary career: Development and preliminary validation of the career competencies questionnaire. *Journal of Career Development, 40*, 245–267. http://doi.org/10.1177/0894845312467501

Arthur, M. B., Khapova, S. N., & Wilderom, C. P. M. (2005). Career success in a boundaryless career world. *Journal of Organizational Behavior, 26*, 177–202. http://doi.org/10.1002/job.290

Bandura, A. (2001). Social cognitive theory: An agentic perspective. *Annual Review of Psychology, 52*, 1–26. http://doi.org/10.1146/annurev.psych.52.1.1

Bäumler, T. Scheller, R., & von Maurice, J. (1994). Der Einfluss von Zufallserfahrungen auf die Studienfachwahl [The influence of chance experiences on what to study]. *Swiss Journal of Psychology, 53*, 166–177.

Berg, J. M., Wrzesniewski, A., & Dutton, J. E. (2010). Perceiving and responding to challenges in job crafting at different ranks: When proactivity requires adaptivity. *Journal of Organizational Behavior, 31*, 158–186. http://doi.org/10.1002/job.645

Bright, J. E. H., & Pryor, R. G. L. (2005). The chaos theory of careers: A user's guide. *Career Development Quarterly, 53*, 291–305. http://doi.org/10.1002/j.2161-0045.2005.tb00660.x

Caspar, F. (2007). Plan analysis. In T. Eells (Ed.), *Handbook of psychotherapeutic case formulations* (pp. 251–289). New York, NY: Guilford Press.

Dauwalder, J. P. (2007). Beratung: Herausforderungen für eine nachhaltige Entwicklung [Counseling: Challenges for sustainable development. *Report, 30*, 9–19.

Dauwalder, J. P., Rossier, J., Massoudi, K., & Masdonati, J. (2011). Effectiveness of guidance and controlling: The complex impact of guidance. In S. Kraatz & B. J. Ertelt (Eds.), *Professionalisation of career guidance in Europe: Training, guidance research, service organization and mobility* (pp. 221–232). Tübingen, Germany: Dgvt-Verlag.

Forrier, A., & Sels, L. (2003). The concept employability: A complex mosaic. *International Journal of Human Resources Development and Management, 3*, 102–124. http://doi.org/10.1504/IJHRDM.2003.002414

Fugate, M., Kinicki, A. J., & Ashforth, B. E. (2004). Employability: A psycho-social construct, its dimensions, and applications. *Journal of Vocational Behavior, 65*, 14–38. http://doi.org/10.1016/j.jvb.2003.10.005

Fuller, B., Jr., & Marler, L. E. (2009). Change driven by nature: A meta-analytic review of the proactive personality literature. *Journal of Vocational Behavior, 75*, 329–345. http://doi.org/10.1016/j.jvb.2009.05.008

Gleick, J. (1988). *Chaos: Die Ordnung des Universums* [Chaos: Order in the universe]. Munich, Germany: Droemer Knaur.

Grawe, K., Donati, R., & Bernauer, F. (1994). *Psychotherapie im Wandel: Von der Konfession zur Profession* [Psychotherapy in transition: From confession to profession]. Göttingen, Germany: Hogrefe.

Guichard, J. (2005). Life-long self-construction. *International Journal for Educational and Vocational Guidance, 5*, 111–124. http://doi.org/10.1007/s10775-005-8789-y

Guichard, J. (2008). Proposition d'un schéma d'entretien constructiviste de conseil en orientation pour des adolescents ou de jeunes adultes [Outline of a life designing counselling interview for adolescents and young adults]. *L'Orientation Scolaire et Professionnelle, 37*, 413–440.

Guichard, J. (2015). From vocational guidance and career counseling to life design dialogues. In L. Nota & J. Rossier (Eds.), *Handbook of life design: From practice to theory and from theory to practice*. Boston, MA: Hogrefe Publishing.

Hall, D. T. (1996). Protean careers of the 21st century. *The Academy of Management Executive, 10*, 8–16.

Hall, D. T. (2002). *Careers in and out of organizations*. Thousand Oaks, CA: Sage.

Haken, H. (1991). *Erfolgsgeheimnisse der Natur* [Nature's secrets of success]. Frankfurt/Main, Germany: Ullstein.

Haken, H. (2006). *Information and self-organization: A macroscopic approach to complex systems*. Berlin, Germay: Springer.

Haken, H., & Schiepek, G. (2010). *Synergetik in der Psychologie: Selbstorganisation verstehen und gestalten* [Synergetics in psychology: Understanding and shaping self-organization]. Göttingen, Germany: Hogrefe.

Haynes, S. (1992). *Models of causality in psychopathology*. New York, NY: Wiley.

Higgins, M. C., & Kram, K. E. (2001). Reconceptualizing mentoring at work: A developmental network perspective. *The Academy of Management Review, 26*, 264–288. http://doi.org/10.2307/259122

Hirschi, A. (2012). The career resources model: An integrative framework for career counsellors. *British Journal of Guidance & Counselling, 40*, 369–383. http://doi.org/10.1080/03069885.2012.700506

Hirschi, A., & Läge, D. (2007). The relation of secondary students' career-choice readiness to a six-phase model of career decision making. *Journal of Career Development, 34*, 164–191. http://doi.org/10.1177/0894845307307473

Hirschi, A., Niles, S. G., & Akos, P. (2011). Engagement in adolescent career preparation: Social support, personality and the development of choice decidedness and congruence. *Journal of Adolescence, 34*, 173–182. http://doi.org/10.1016/j.adolescence.2009.12.009

Holland, J. L. (1985). *Making vocational choices*. Englewood Cliffs, NJ: Prentice Hall.

Holland, J. L. (1997). *Making vocational choices: A theory of vocational personalities and work environments* (3rd ed.). Englewood Cliffs, NJ: Prentice Hall.

Horvath, A. O., & Greenberg, L. S. (1994). *The working alliance: Theory, research and practice*. New York, NY: Wiley.

Ibarra, H., & Barbulescu, R. (2010). Identity as narrative: Prevalence, effectiveness, and consequences of narrative identity work in macro work role transitions. *Academy of Management Review, 35*, 135–154. http://doi.org/10.5465/AMR.2010.45577925

King, Z. (2004). Career self-management: Its nature, causes and consequences. *Journal of Vocational Behavior, 65*, 112–133. http://doi.org/10.1016/S0001-8791(03)00052-6

Kossek, E. E., Roberts, K., Fisher, S., & Demarr, B. (1998). Career self-management: A quasi-experimental assessment of the effects of a training intervention. *Personnel Psychology, 51*, 935–960. http://doi.org/10.1111/j.1744-6570.1998.tb00746.x

Krumboltz, J. D. (2009). The happenstance learning theory. *Journal of Career Assessment, 17*, 135–154. http://doi.org/10.1177/1069072708328861

Kuijpers, M. A. C. T., & Scheerens, J. (2006). Career competencies for the modern career. *Journal of Career Development, 32*, 309–319.

Lent, R. W. (2013). Career-life preparedness: Revisiting career planning and adjustment in the new workplace. *The Career Development Quarterly, 61*, 2–14. http://doi.org/10.1002/j.2161-0045.2013.00031.x

Lent, R. W., Brown, S. D., & Hackett, G. (1994). Toward a unifying social cognitive theory of career and academic interest, choice, and performance. *Journal of Vocational Behavior, 45*, 79–122. http://doi.org/10.1006/jvbe.1994.1027

Lerner, R. M. (2006). Developmental science, developmental systems, and contemporary theories of human development. In R. M. Lerner & W. Damon (Eds.), *Handbook of child psychology: Vol. 1. Theoretical models of human development* (6th ed., pp. 1–17). Hoboken, NJ: Wiley.

London, M. (1983). Toward a theory of career motivation. *The Academy of Management Review, 8*, 620–630. http://doi.org/10.5465/AMR.1983.4284664

London, M., & Noe, R. A. (1997). London's career motivation theory: An update on measurement and research. *Journal of Career Assessment, 5*, 61–80. http://doi.org/10.1177/106907279700500105

Luthans, F., Avolio, B. J., Avey, J. B., & Norman, S. M. (2007). Positive psychological capital: Measurement and relationship with performance and satisfaction. *Personnel Psychology, 60*, 541–572. http://doi.org/10.1111/j.1744-6570.2007.00083.x

Lynch, P. (2006). *The emergence of numerical weather prediction.* Cambridge, UK: Cambridge University Press.

Masdonati, J., Massoudi, K., & Rossier, J. (2009). Effectiveness of face-to-face career counseling and the working alliance. *Journal of Career Development, 36*, 183–203. http://doi.org/10.1177/0894845309340798

McQuaid, R. W., & Lindsay, C. (2005). The concept of employability. *Urban Studies, 42*, 197–219. http://doi.org/10.1080/0042098042000316100

Meijers, F. (1998). The development of a career identity. *International Journal for the Advancement of Counselling, 20*, 191–207. http://doi.org/10.1023/A:1005399417256

Miller, W. R., & Rollnick, S. (2002). *Motivational interviewing: Preparing people to change.* New York, NY: Guilford Press.

Parker, S. K., & Collins, C. G. (2010). Taking stock: Integrating and differentiating multiple proactive behaviors. *Journal of Management, 36*, 633–662. http://doi.org/10.1177/0149206308321554

Piaget, J. (1985). *Equilibration of cognitive structures.* Chicago, IL: University of Chicago Press.

Prigogine, I., & Stengers, I. (1997). *The end of certainty: Time, chaos and the laws of nature.* New York, NY: Free Press.

Pulakos, E. D., Arad, S., Donovan, M. A., & Plamondon, K. E. (2000). Adaptability in the workplace: Development of a taxonomy of adaptive performance. *Journal of Applied Psychology, 85*, 612–624. http://doi.org/10.1037/0021-9010.85.4.612

Pulakos, E. D., Schmitt, N., Doresy, D. W., Arad, S., Borman, W. C., & Hedge, J.W. (2002). Predicting adaptive performance: Further tests of a model of adaptability. *Human Performance, 15*, 299–323.

Rousseau, D. (2001). Schema, promise and mutuality: The building blocks of the psychological contract. *Journal of Occupational and Organizational Psychology, 74*, 511–541. http://doi.org/10.1348/096317901167505

Saks, A. M., & Ashforth, B. E. (2002). Is job search related to employment quality? It all depends on the fit. *Journal of Applied Psychology, 87*, 646–654. http://doi.org/10.1037/0021-9010.87.4.646

Sampson, J. P., Lenz, J. G., Reardon, R. C., & Peterson, G. W. (1999). A cognitive information processing approach to employment problem solving and decision making. *Career Development Quarterly, 48*, 3–18. http://doi.org/10.1002/j.2161-0045.1999.tb00271.x

Savickas, M. L. (1997). Career adaptability: An integrative construct for life-span, life-space theory. *Career Development Quarterly, 45*, 247–259. http://doi.org/10.1002/j.2161-0045.1997.tb00469.x

Savickas, M. L. (2005). The theory and practice of career construction. In S. D. Brown & R. W. Lent, (Eds.), *Career development and counseling : Putting theory and research to work* (pp. 42–70). Hoboken, NJ: Wiley.

Savickas, M. L. (2011). New questions for vocational psychology: Premises, paradigms, and practices. *Journal of Career Assessment, 19*, 251–258. http://doi.org/10.1177/1069072710395532

Savickas, M. L. (2012). Life design: A paradigm for career intervention in the 21st century. *Journal of Counseling and Development, 90*, 13–19.

Savickas, M. L., Nota, L., Rossier, J., Dauwalder, J.-P., Duarte, M. E., Guichard, J., . . . van Vianen, A. E. M. (2009). Life designing: A paradigm for career construction in the 21st century. *Journal of Vocational Behavior, 75*, 239–250. http://doi.org/10.1016/j.jvb.2009.04.004

Savickas, M. L., & Porfeli, E. J. (2012). Career adapt-abilities scale: Construction, reliability, and measurement equivalence across 13 countries. *Journal of Vocational Behavior, 80*, 661–673. http://doi.org/10.1016/j.jvb.2012.01.011

Schiersmann, C., & Thiel, H. U. (Eds.). (2012). *Beratung als Förderung von Selbstorganisationsprozessen* [Counseling as support to self-organization processes]. Göttingen, Germany: Vandenhoeck & Ruprecht.

Srsic, C. S., & Walsh, W. B. (2001). Person-environment congruence and career self-efficacy. *Journal of Career Assessment, 9*, 203–213. http://doi.org/10.1177/106907270100900207

Stickland, R. (1996). Career self-management: Can we live without it? *European Journal of Work and Organizational Psychology, 5*, 583–596. http://doi.org/10.1080/13594329608414881

Sullivan, S. E. (1999). The changing nature of careers: A review and research agenda. *Journal of Management, 25*, 457–485. http://doi.org/10.1177/014920639902500308

Sullivan, S. E., Carden, W. A., & Martin, D. F. (1998). Careers in the next millennium: Directions for future research. *Human Resource Management Review, 8*, 165–185. http://doi.org/10.1016/S1053-4822(98)80003-X

Super, D. E. (1990). A life-span, life-space approach to career development. In D. Brown & L. Brooks (Eds.), *Career choice and development: Applying contemporary theories to practice* (2nd ed., pp. 197–262). San Francisco, CA: Jossey-Bass.

Thomas, J. P., Whitman, D. S., & Viswesvaran, C. (2010). Employee proactivity in organizations: A comparative meta-analysis of emergent proactive constructs. *Journal of Occupational and Organizational Psychology, 83*, 275–300. http://doi.org/10.1348/096317910X502359

Vondracek, F. W., Lerner, R. M., & Schulenberg, J. E. (1986). *Career development: A life-span developmental approach*. Hillsdale, NJ: Erlbaum.

Vondracek, F. W., & Porfeli, E. J. (2008). Social contexts for career guidance throughout the world: Developmental-contextual perspectives on career across the lifespan. In J. A. Athanasou & R. van Esbroeck (Eds.), *International handbook of career guidance* (pp. 209–225). Heidelberg, Germany: Springer.

Wrzesniewski, A., & Dutton, J. E. (2001). Crafting a job: Revisioning employees as active crafters of their work. *The Academy of Management Review, 26*, 179–201. http://doi.org/10.5465/AMR.2001.4378011

Young, R. A., & Collin, A. (2004). Introduction: Constructivism and social constructivism in the career field. *Journal of Vocational Behavior, 64*, 373–388.

Chapter 4
The Life Design Paradigm: From Practice to Theory

Maria Eduarda Duarte[1] and Paulo Cardoso[2]
[1]Faculty of Psychology, University of Lisbon, Portugal
[2]Department of Psychology, University of Évora, Portugal

Introduction

There are two fundamental processes applied in the building of knowledge: one theoretical and the other practical. The first, usually designated as top-down, is the process through which scientists make use of theory to give order to reality, to formulate hypotheses, and to offer guidance in chaos and the multiplicity of that reality. The second, designated as bottom-up, is the starting point and reality which, in acting as the source of new experiences, updates or innovates scientific theories, thereby allowing for a continuous development and adaptation to that reality.

The life design framework for counseling aims to frame counseling (practice intervention) as an intersubjective process, focused primarily on work or career issues, and is structured to be a life-long, holistic, contextual, and preventive practice (Savickas et al., 2009). The origin of the framework can be viewed as being the result of a complementary approach to top-down and bottom-up, the two processes through which knowledge is built.

The epistemology of social constructionism (Gergen, 2001), particularly as related to research methodology (research methods in favor of qualitative approaches) and also in the emphasis that it places on "social and cultural milieu as the lens or medium through which individuals construct their experience, [and it] positions culture as a primary force in human development" (Richardson, Constantine, & Washburn, 2005, p. 57) and the theory of life span/life space of Donald Super (1957, 1980), supports a conceptual structure capable of guiding the actions of researchers and the practices applied in analysis and intervention in the field of career guidance. The complexity of the current context of the globalized economy also presents challenges, both in terms of research and of practice, which are fundamental for the continuous development of theory.

The importance of the theory for the evolution of the life design paradigm is recognized in the research agenda that considers a range of studies based around theories, and other studies that are based around the analysis of practices (Savickas et al., 2009). From the theoretical arises the use of intervention methods and techniques, such as the development of self-knowledge and ecological variables, in that they can be facilitating or inhibiting, in decision-making processes. The stories and activities developed by individuals are the focal point of method-ological aspects, rather than the utilization of test scores or profile interpretations. The existing techniques and tools are reconfigured for use in a social constructionist approach. From the practical arises contact with the complexity of reality and an invitation to reflect on the ideas that guide actions, which is fundamental to the innovation of that which had previously been believed.

In this chapter, after some brief observations of a theoretical nature, the focus is directed toward an analysis of practices that contribute to the improvement and evolution of the life design framework for counseling. The chapter has four main sections, followed by a conclusion. It begins by highlighting how the gap between career counseling theories and reality has contributed to the emergence of the life design paradigm. In the second section, consideration is given to some topics which are currently debated in light of the new life design paradigm, and its relationship with counseling activity. An approach to the process of counseling according to life design perspectives and the importance of the analysis of practices for the continuous updating and innovation of this framework for counseling follows. Finally, research into the practice of career counseling and a case study that illustrates the practical contribution to the life design framework for counseling is discussed.

The Existence of a Gap between Career Counseling Theories and Reality

The following presents an attempt to demonstrate the existence of a gap between career counseling theories and reality. The realities of change, including significant changes in the nature of work and employment, lead to a conclusion that traditional career counseling theories failed due to the fact that the fundamental elements that such approaches were built upon were being ignored. These changes signal many important transitions in the territory in which career counselors work or will work.

Career counseling has traditionally been linked with a positivist epistemology. The traditional concept of counseling may indeed be misleading, as it is based on the separation between the counselor, seen as the "owner of knowledge," and the counselee, seen as the "object of knowledge." This approach can be seen as one that is stricken by a relative lack of attention to the issues of conceptual clarity in favor of correspondence between theoretical propositions and evidence given by empirical observations. Such an approach is no longer applicable to the way of working in a contemporary world which requires attention to human variety, searching for uniqueness at an ever increasing rate, to stand up to the artificiality of technology, which imposes standard procedures.

The lack of equilibrium between career counseling theories and reality still exists, in part due to the utilization of preconstructed models, and in part the fact that reality is invariably more complex than theory, which represents only a small part of reality and of the context in which individuals act and live. Career counseling when seen as an objective process, in which assessments are made through the scientific method of collecting facts and "interpreting numbers and figures," is no more in tune with these new realities than the above-mentioned approach. It is an accepted fact that knowledge is fundamental to the development of both societies and individuals; it is also a known fact that technology has brought about the dissemination of such knowledge. However, it is through the importance of intellectual capital, giving rise to the creation of value and in which the structural changes to the economy, knowledge, and communication systems are rooted, that great differences emerge: A career counseling approach based on constructivism proposes addressing counseling activities as a process of individual meaning making rather than as a restricted analytical perspective of logical positivism (Duarte, 2010).

Following the thinking of Immanuel Kant (1781/1996) in his criticism of empiricism and rationalism, *criticism* is characterized by a critical analysis of the possibility, origin, value, laws, and limits of rational knowledge. It is a philosophical position in principle and not dependent on a person or, more specifically, on a sensitive experience and the limits imposed on knowledge. On the other hand, *critique* – originating from the Latin *Critica*, based on the Greek expression *kritikê tékne* (critical art), which refers to the ability to separate, judge, decide – is a voluntary act belonging to the sphere of the individual and is an activity of reasoning which sets out to distinguish true from false. In short, it is an act of the mind stemming from a doubt about a given situation (Duarte, 2012). Another way to examine the problem is related to the importance of "the critical art" as an attempt to minimize the gap. Applying such a critique to the construction of reflexivity, that means the self-awareness that emerges from the construction of social realities (Savickas, 2011b, 2012) can essentially lead to and drive an approximation between theory and practice.

To this end and in addressing what is fundamentally of interest here: Career counseling has been influenced by the tradition of empiricism, which is one of the reasons behind the current distance between theory and the reality of practice. The theories and practices that emerged to serve contingencies up to the end of the 20th century are no longer appropriate for the new, albeit transitory, reality. This is not an attempt to set a paradigmatic standard, rather it is more of a critical look at past theories, based on a consideration of the criteria of the new realities of the 21st century (Duarte, 2012).

Considering the framework of actions which are supported by theories and prediction techniques based on employment and environmental stability – for example, developmental theories and their subsequent model of intervention, along with those which set out to place the individual in a continuous process within certain contexts, in harmony with the critical perspective (Duarte, 2009a) – we can see which actions have the potential to create more value in a contemporary society characterized by uncertainty in the labor market.

As Herr and Cramer (1996) noted, developmental models tend to center on the longitudinal expressions of behavior, thereby highlighting the importance of self-awareness and driving conceptions for the understanding of development and career behavioral changes over time. Such models can be applied to both youths and adults as part of a variety of practical guidance settings and a diverse array of contexts. When dealing with youths who are part of the education system, the emphasis is generally on the decision-making process, as there is a basic assumption of a need to make vocational decisions (Savickas, 1992). In the case of adults, the focus is more toward the possibility of knowledge and comprehension of the life cycle, the discovery of values applicable to certain situations, the roles which are developed in adult life, and even the influencing of the careers of individuals. However, this is also a model which has already been overtaken by newer organizational structures present in both the professional environment and society: The results of career counseling done on the basis of an understanding of what each instrument measures do not take into account all of the needs of the individual – namely, those that cannot be satisfied via the application of tests (Duarte, 2009b).

In light of this, we are not only looking to understand the ways in which an individual can develop and progress in his or her career, but also a reflection of what is a key question in the making of a change: How do individuals construct their lives, and what are the factors and processes that form part of that construction? The construction of working lives is no longer independent of the construction of other areas of life, meaning that an understanding is needed of how individuals construct their other areas of life via their working life. It is on this basis that the life design paradigm has been developed (Savickas et al., 2009).

In terms of action, the consideration of not only the context of the self but also the construction of the self is fundamental. Thus, in more than simply aiding to clarify self-perception, it is important to aid in the co-construction of an understanding of the coherence and continuity of the construction process itself (Guichard, 2009). In other words, the focus is not placed solely on individuals – and they are not only viewed as actors but also as the authors of their own destiny.

As indicated by Guichard (2015; see Chapter 2), life design dialogues do not aim to aid clients in thinking about their lives from the perspective of the current social norms of employability. Their purpose is a more fundamental one: It is to help clients define their own norms; norms through which they can give a meaning to their lives and therefore design them.

In short, in taking a glance at the existence of a gap between career counseling theories and reality, it is possible to consider whether intervention models based on the life design approach are indeed capable of surpassing that gap. To reduce that gap, the promotion of an analysis of practices is needed, thereby permitting a particular understanding and contextualization which is needed to learn about nonlinear dynamics and to predict stable configurations for the multiple psychological variables that are part of the career guidance process. In that light, it would be possible to identify empirical evidence that indicates the efficiency of such activities, as is recommended by one of the five presuppositions of life designing counseling (Dauwalder, 2003; Savickas et al., 2009).

Theoretical Considerations Currently Debated in Relation to the New Life Design Paradigm and Their Relationship With Counseling

This section introduces some of the theoretical considerations which are currently being debated in relation to the new life design paradigm and its relationship with counseling activities. Life design – the paradigm for career construction – requires reflection on the self and the environment, as well as receptivity to feedback and the imagining of new opportunities for narrative self-construction (Savickas et al., 2009). The nature of certain changes that are taking place, which demand that people be flexible, necessarily results in dynamic and flexible practices (Niles & Karalic, 2009). The demands of action (counseling process) imply a new relationship that supports the process of self-exploration, thereby helping individuals to construct a narrative capable of expressing the central problem in their life and synthesizing their needs and resolutions by formulating goals and approaches to reaching those goals.

Some case studies carried out by the authors of this chapter (Cardoso, 2012; Duarte, 2012) and various other colleagues during interventions have given support to the possibility of using this model – noting that (a) it is an approach that is more explicative than explorative or descriptive, (b) it makes it possible to explore intraindividual variability, and (c) it gives space to the importance of contextual variables.

As proposed by the research agenda for life design activities – namely, bottom-up research – it is through the conducting of a wide variety of case studies that the conditions in which life design can lead to the redefining of one's vocational identity in terms of social processes in a given culture that the topic may be better understood. From one point of view, this is essentially the putting to one side of simple and linear causal explanations. The observation of these types of cases may assist in the understanding of a particular client's reference framework, through those that are described by counselors. The more relevant and widely utilized life design methodologies may also be discourse analysis, narrative, or ethnographic analysis. Such types of analysis can certainly help with the understanding of the influence that cultural context has on the process of career construction. With the combining of cross-cultural studies and ethnographic approaches, a great step forward can be taken in the field of career studies in a way that attempts to describe the influence of cultural aspects on career guidance issues (Duarte, 2011).

Research that identifies the underlying processes to be dealt with by life design, especially in relation to work roles, should be conducted. However, the direct assessment of these processes is not an easy task, as such processes are effective only temporarily or are unknown or inaccessible. It is in this context that studies could combine various methods to formulate a research strategy that draws information from a variety of fronts, thus increasing the external validity of findings, as similar results would come from several sources, while at the same time giving more information to aid in a more complete comprehension of the problem.

The promotion of a diverse range of perspectives, techniques, and methods contributes to the improvement and widening of an understanding of the construction of life projects, and better co-construction within one's dependent context and dynamic. This point of view is clear: A co-construction perspective is integrated into the life design paradigm and consequently counseling is conducted around a self-construction process. The nature of the changes that are taking place and the demands of action (counseling process) imply a new relationship process based on individual narratives and stories, along with the establishment of a dialogue that permits the expression of emotion and that seeks to reveal one's own life and allows the identification of the salient elements of the self.

What is at stake is that it is fundamentally important to transform the idea, or the model, into reality or, rather, to transform the concept into a real object guided by the individual as the construction instrument. This transformation would of course be motivating, as the construction of anything is based on motivation, and motivation can then lead to action. In short, the model does not consider implementation strategies, but rather the decision of implementation, of choice, and of involvement. Whenever one looks to implementation as a competency, the nonrational and nonformable aspects of the human condition are most certainly being ignored. All formulae and descriptions are essentially concepts, words, ideas, and theories. To this end, we can ask the question, what is it that makes counseling activities real? The answer is involvement, adherence, and commitment; it is a personal choice and not a decision of a strategic nature. The theories and concepts that each individual wishes to make real, and the "I" that exists in each of us, belong to two different worlds. What can be described, and, therefore, what exists? In a work relationship between a counselor and a client, what matters are life stories and not the concepts applied. Put another way, the human being is not an idea, but rather he/she is human because he/she is alive, and what is alive can essentially die when transformed into a disembodied idea. Therefore, the key to success may also be found in making something happen – namely, constructing or, better, co-constructing, and constructing is essentially having a vision (Duarte, 2011).

In conclusion, in taking a glance at the theoretical considerations and their relationship with counseling interventions, the focus should be on the "liaison" between the theoretical and the activity, in a way that involves a consideration of the characteristics and skills of each individual, so that each individual can sustain themselves without losing their condition as an active and supportive element within the historical chain from which he or she has emerged. Having obtained knowledge, the inclusion of his or her own experiences and the associated interpretations of those experiences can give continuity to this very chain and go on to project it into the future.

The Process of Counseling From Life Design Perspectives

This section is focused on the process of counseling from life design perspectives: The process of constructing and conducting a counseling process is a dynamic one that acts and reacts according to each individual element that is introduced. Whereas the success of this kind of relationship has traditionally relied upon a specific counselor's training, the most important difference found here in going against the grain of traditional approaches is that individuals are considered people who construct themselves from how they perceive others reacting to them, with those others not simply being considered as elements which are separate and located elsewhere (Markus & Kitayama, 1991). In this way, individuals use the notion of themselves to organize their understanding of life, inclusive of working life (Guichard, 2009). Based on the perspective of self-dynamics, the career counselor takes the role of a meaningful co-constructor, thereby trying not to come across as an expert of the client's experience, but instead acting as a facilitator of the deepening of such experience. The counselor's position is essentially to take up the problem and the experience of the client in a way that facilitates the client's own transformation process (another way to consider what a bottom-up process is). Much like an experienced jazz musician, there is no need to play a huge variety of notes, but simply those necessary to open the rest of the band up to new creative possibilities.

According to life design perspectives, when a counselor meets an individual, that person is not separate from him or her and that individual may condition the counselor's own behavior in much the same way as the counselor does the individual's. An interdependent relationship is thereby created in which nothing that is perceptible remains indifferent to either one of the parties involved. It is precisely here that the importance of identity as a process of social construction emerging from a molded continuum is recognized, thereby following new directions as other constructions are being edified. It is of course possible to question to what extent it is reasonable to think that collective well-being depends on one having to renounce one's own personality and become enclosed against one's own will and nature itself, within a rigid space which is, on the one hand, functional, but on the other, conditioning and restricting of one's creativity. Through this prism, the whole basis of the counseling process can be seen as unmolding the actual "I": It can be seen as the rewriting of one's own narrative in a way that allows for an understanding of how people interpret and represent reality. It is the understanding of how people look to perform the tasks that a particular context presents, what meaning they give to those tasks, and how such interpretations interact in a person's own personal history (Duarte, 2012).

The presentation and discussion of one particular case study and research based on career counseling practices helps to illustrate this new way of facing career counseling. In summary, the aim is to emphasize the role of the analysis of practices in the life design framework for counseling.

Examples of Practice-Based Contributions to Improve the Life Design Framework for Counseling

The following is a discussion of the results obtained from a qualitative investigation into the dilemmas faced by psychologists in the practice of career counseling, along with a case study in which the life design paradigm for career counseling was applied (Savickas, 2011b). The following analysis is structured along the lines of the recommendations presented by Stiles (2003), which highlight the need for case studies to not simply be an illustration of theoretical models, but rather an opportunity to verify and/or to innovate theoretical approaches.

Psychologists' Dilemmas in Career Counseling

Psychologists' dilemmas in career counseling were analyzed in a study by Cardoso, Taveira, Biscaia, and Santos (2012). The aim of that analysis was to further the understanding of the career counseling process in its complexity. The study of dilemmas fits this purpose because the experience of dilemma, such as when the counselor has doubts or suffers conflicts about what to say or do when all of the possible alternatives are equally unsatisfactory (Scaturo, 2005), reveals the interplay of the technical and the ethical dimensions of the intervention with the relational dimension and the context in which it takes place.

Participants included in the study comprised 24 Caucasian Portuguese psychologists who were or are working as career counselors (22 women and 2 men), ranging in age from 30 to 53 years ($M = 41.54$, $SD = 5.89$). Their experience in career counseling ranged from 7 to 30 years ($M = 15.56$, $SD = 6.69$). The activity of these psychologists was analyzed based on an interview constructed around the principle question, "Would you like to talk about the dilemmas you experience most when performing career counseling?" and a variety of secondary questions designed to clarify the experiencing of a dilemma. Responses were analyzed using the consensual qualitative research approach (Hill, 2011).

The multiplicity of the participants' dilemmas (neutrality, assessment, dual loyalty, role boundaries, and confidentiality) shows the intersubjective nature of the career counseling process. The results obtained are discussed from a perspective that touches upon the dimensions of the counseling process such as (a) a working alliance, (b) the co-construction of meaning, (c) the ethical challenges faced, and (d) the interface between career and personal issues. In this sense, this discussion seeks to deepen reflection about the career counseling process as an intersubjective experience, while contributing to the development of the life design framework for counseling.

The challenges posed to the quality of a working alliance are generally present as part of the dilemmas experienced by participants, which effectively demonstrates the management of dilemmas as one of the expressions of management of a working alliance. Indeed, most dilemmas reveal the psychologists' attention to possible ruptures in the working alliance resulting from the frustration of the client's hopes/dreams (e.g., to support vs. to confront career plans), expectations (e.g., asking oneself, "Should I satisfy demands for psychological tests?"), and needs (e.g., whether or not to intervene in the client's emotional problems and whether or not to give more time to this client).

For example, the *doubt about whether or not to confront the client's career plans*, which is a typical dilemma tackled by psychologists practicing career counseling, reveals that the balance between how much to confront and how much to support clients is especially challenging when psychologists confront clients' career plans. As stated by Savickas (2006), the challenge is to support clients to manage the dynamic balance between aspirations and realism, between personal goals and the conditions of the labor market, as well as to maintain the balance between keeping close to the client, which facilitates the exploration of new possibilities, and maintaining a position of greater distance, representing the society against which career plans are confronted.

If identity is indeed socially produced (Savickas, 2011b), then the double role of the counselor is therefore fundamental within the space of counseling, for the activation of a dialogue that replicates the client's daily life, thereby defining the client's identity in relation to the context in which he or she lives. From this perspective, the dilemma of the counselor is an extension of the challenge that clients have to cope with – namely, to design realistic career plans based on the balance between dreams and reality. This dilemma can be managed by the counselor with consideration for the co-construction matrix in which the career counseling process occurs. In this sense, counselors can negotiate the counseling alliance with clients by clarifying their double role. To this end, such developments can facilitate the client's acceptance of confrontation stemming from career plans and help to deconstruct the misconceptions surrounding the role of a counselor – in particular when it comes to indicating the most adequate path for a client to take. This suggestion complements the results of the research that highlight the importance of the working alliance for the effectiveness of career counseling (Masdonati, Massoudi, & Rossier, 2009) and the need to negotiate objectives, tasks, and the other dimensions of the relationship in a way that thereby strengthens that relationship (Masdonati, Perdrix, Massoudi, & Rossier, 2014).

The results of the study into the dilemmas faced by psychologists in career counseling also permit a better understanding of the process involved in the co-construction of meaning, which does, of course, have implications for the framework of life design for counseling. Generally speaking, the co-construction of meaning is understood as a collaborative process between the client and the counselor in a way that promotes changes within the client via, for example, empathic reflection, inference, and hypotheses about the client's behavior and motives (Hook, 2001). From a narrative perspective, it is a dialogical space which permits a mutual reflection rather than a cascade of ideas given by the counselor as solutions to the client's problems (Hermans, 2003). The study of dilemmas suggests that counselors also change as part of the process, in a way that facilitates the change of the client. To effectively deal with the client's dilemmas, the counselor must deal with his or her own dilemmas. For example, to solve the dilemma "to confront or to support career plans?" the counselor is opened to the client's experience and asks himself or herself what the meaning of client's career plans are. However, that is not sufficient to act (to support or to confront career plans) with sensitivity to the client's needs. It is also important to understand the reasons for the counselor considering the client's career plans to be irrational, and to review his or her position if necessary. The continuous exercise of this practice of self-reflection contributes toward the counselor becoming more flexible – that is, accepting both the experience of the client and the relativity of his or her positions. This opening up to both the client's experiences and to revising one's position is not only transformative for the client, but is also an effective model for the opening up of the client to change and preparing the client to better deal with his or her career challenges. In this sense, the co-construction process is also a cotransformation process, which is in accord with the life design framework for counseling herein presented.

The wider understanding of the co-construction process also touches upon the ethical dimension of career counseling, as the reflection by the counselor relative to the relationship with the client is also a reflection about the clash between two ethical positions. The epistemological perspective of social constructivism, within which the life design framework for counseling can be found, gives an important contribution to the understanding of this meeting of principles (e.g., ideas about solidarity, social justice, personal fulfillment, or liberty), which can guide the action of each of the participants in the career counseling process. In the life design paradigm for counseling, the emphasis given to intersubjectivity and the context of meaning construction results in a perspective in which ethical principles are not viewed as absolute truths, separated from the life of individuals, which therefore lead to rational and linear ethical decision making. On the contrary, ethical decision making is an interpretative act, as the definition of what is good and correct involves ethical principles as well as individual idiosyncrasies and contextual particularities which are characteristic of the counseling process (Betan, 1997). The confrontation between the ethical view point of the counselor and that of the client, along with the interpretative nature of ethical decision making, is particularly evident in dilemmas in which the counselor and the client shape their action around the same ethical principle. It is a typical dilemma faced by psychologists in career counseling – namely, *to confront or to support career plans*. As is suggested in the results of the study, the *good action* of psychologists is in fact guided by various ethical principles, of which concern for the client's well-being of course stands out – that is, the ethical principle of serving the client's benefit by acting as a reference guide for the assessment of what type of action to take in a given context (Cardoso et al., 2012). On their part, clients, in defining certain career plans, are also guided by ethical principles, which also include their own well-being. The dilemma results when the parties involved make different interpretations of the consequences resulting from the client's career plans. If, for the client, those plans are essentially the solution to problems which are being experienced, then such plans can aggravate this problem for the counselor. The following passage illustrates well the role of subjectivity in the evaluation performed by the counselor:

> The dilemma is between what one thinks is good for her and what I think are the person's abilities and cognitive limitations. This raises the dilemma whether to indicate what we think is good for the person or what the person really wants and intends. (Cardoso et al., 2012, p. 233)

In showing that the ethics of the counselor and the ethics of the client closely relate to each other in a way that aids in deepening the understanding of the relationship between the parties, this study highlights the importance of a reflection on dilemmas. This reflection is facilitated by research and practice and is a fundamental part of getting to know more about the principal ethics that direct the lives of people and for a deeper understanding of the processes involved in the construction of a life.

Finally, the analysis of dilemmatic experiences also reveals that career counseling is personal counseling. It shares with other forms of counseling (or psychotherapy) that it is a holistic practice, which opens up the possibility of intervention in emotional issues originating from career issues (Amundson, 2006; Hackett, 1993; Savickas, 2011b). In this sense, seven counselors (29.2%) in the study by Cardoso et al. (2012) referred to the dilemma of *whether or not to intervene in the client's emotional problems*. Among the study's participants, this challenge occurred when there was a risk of exceeding the limits of their competence and/or established boundaries for a career counseling relationship. The results also suggested an influence of the setting in the frequency of dilemmas. The dilemmas of *whether or not to intervene in the client's emotional problems* and whether or not *to give more time to this client* were almost exclusive to a work/employment setting. This result was explained by (1) characteristics of the target population in this setting, mainly consisting of unemployed and low-skilled people, in whom it is more likely that career problems coincide with personal problems; (2) limitations in training of the participants for intervening in emotional problems; and (3) pressure for cost containment, leading to pressure for briefer interventions. Of these factors, note is also given to the influence of productivity rates in the experiencing of dilemmas, as such rates are one of the main challenges for psychological intervention in general and for career counseling in particular, resulting from the economic logic of the best productivity for the lowest cost. The practices constituting the life design paradigm for counseling are advantageous in helping to deal with this challenge due to their flexible and dynamic nature and because they integrate career construction in the process of self-construction. In this sense, these practices reduce false dichotomies that may exist between career counseling and personal counseling and may easily be integrated into other practices. Thus we suggest that in future these practices should be integrated in new opportunities services (NOSs) and public employment services (PESs), where the dilemma *to give or not to give more time to this client* is more frequent. In the NOSs, employees manage the assessment and recognition of prior experiential learning. People of all ages and backgrounds receive recognition and formal credit for learning acquired in the past through nonformal and informal learning, as well as through work and other experiences. The methodology used is based on the analysis of life stories so that counselors who are familiar with narrative approaches can easily integrate life design practices into the accreditation of competencies, without reducing attendance levels. In turn, the integration of the life design framework for counseling in PES allows the possibility of continuing to benefit from the use of tests for assessing groups and thus achieve high rates of attendance. However, assessment results will serve the process of meaning construction rather than adjusting clients to courses and/or occupations.

The possibilities presented by the life design paradigm of offering brief interventions and integration into other psychological practices should not promote the status quo or the processing of people rather than the application of counseling. In this sense, the dilemmas of *whether or not to intervene in the client's emotional problems* and *to give or not to give more time to this client* should also function as markers for rethinking the organization's criteria of efficiency and productivity, to maintain professional standards in relation to personalized services (Sultana & Watts, 2006).

Case Study

Other possibilities for the analysis of practices for the innovation of theory can be found in case studies (Stiles, 2003, 2007). Such studies permit the analysis of the peculiarities of action and nonlinear processes, which are difficult to grasp through the application of nomothetic approaches (Savickas et al. 2009). The Maria case outlined in the following is illustrative of this, as the resolution of the case goes beyond what was anticipated by theory. However, the life design paradigm for counseling was fundamental in the exploration of new possibilities. In this sense, the novelty lies in the fact that change requires intervening in the repetition of maladaptive relationship patterns underlying career decision-making difficulties. The client was incapable of making a decision, because her life narrative was saturated by one single theme, thereby impeding a multifaceted representation of herself and reality, as she was continuously making a redundant construction of her experience. As such, she was incapable of choosing a new path in life that could break the cycle of maladaptive repetition (Cardoso, 2012).

Maria (pseudonym) is a 38-year-old woman who sought help in coping with her feelings of ambivalence regarding whether she should continue to pursue her career as a civil servant or become a full-time psychotherapist. Like many others, she faced a dilemma between pursuing her dream (the occupation she had always hoped to have) and facing reality (the economic security provided by her job and the avoidance of any risks involved in making a change). The Career Construction Interview (CCI; Savickas, 2011b) was used. This is a semistructured interview covering five topics that form life themes and inform decision making about the current transition. The topics are (1) role models for self-construction; (2) magazines, television shows, or websites for manifest interests, (3) favorite story from a book or movie, for the script for the next episode; (4) sayings or mottos of advice to self; and (5) early recollections, for the perspective on the present problem or transition. From the answers obtained, it was possible through a process of self-exploration to help Maria construct a narrative that expressed the central problem of her life – namely, the search for knowledge and caring for others. It also helped Maria to understand that working as a psychotherapist could accommodate the main roles of the characters in her narrative. On the one hand, it would allow her to act as a helper by being in contact with the real lives of people, and it would allow her to share experiences with them and aid them in overcoming the challenges that they face. On the other hand, it would also allow her to act as a thinker by reflecting on the human condition and allow her to delve into the mystery of the complexity of human behavior. This, in turn, would help quench her thirst for knowledge. However, the meanings that had been constructed failed to offer the level of coherence that was necessary to resolve her ambivalence. Her own words revealed the extent of that ambivalence: "I know what I want, but I cannot make the decision." The impasse was due to a cycle of maladaptive repetition which was interrupted when the counselor affirmed: "It is time to take care of yourself." The exploration of this affirmation allowed her to understand how the theme of helping others was permeating other dimensions of her life, and how it led to the suppression of the full expression of other needs. This dialogue gave a new meaning to her career decision and goals: Becoming a full-time psychotherapist meant choosing herself and breaking an interpersonal relationship pattern that had become saturated with the theme of helping others.

The discussion of this case begins with a focus on the contributions of the life design framework to counseling, and the solutions that it provides. A reflection on the contributions of this practice for the conceptualization of the life design framework for counseling will follow. This reflection considers a follow-up session which took place 10 months after the intervention. Finally, the four dimensions of career counseling (working alliance, the co-construction of meaning, the ethical challenges faced, and the interface between career and personal issues), highlighted in the study of the dilemmas (Cardoso et al., 2012) are discussed from the perspective of practice contributions for the life design framework to counseling. The first contribution of the life design paradigm for counseling for the resolution of the case is related to the repetition of life themes in explaining the process of career construction. The *dynamics of life themes* was the structure applied by the counselor to facilitate the client's own structuring. This dynamic is essentially the continuous search for a solution to the central problems of life that, in the vocational domain, reveal the close relationship between needs, interests, and objectives (Savickas, 1995, 2005). In this sense, it is a reflection of how the structure of an individual's early needs (past) leads to the construction of aspirations (future) that might meet those past needs. In addition, an individual's interests (present) are instruments used to meet goals and thereby satisfy his or her needs (Cardoso, 2012). Guided by the relationship between needs, interests, and objectives, it was possible to help the client in understanding the themes which structured her narrative. Attention was then given to the markers of narrative saturation, which involves an examination of whether a single personality/position dominates the different positions of a person's life, or if there are different personalities/positions present in the multiple areas of a person's life. This holistic dimension of the intervention facilitates a response to the challenges posed by the emotional issues of career problems and allows the intervention to consider other roles beyond those applicable to the work role. In this case, focus was given to the role of the family, as the indecision shown by Maria was identified as being related to the consequences of choices stemming from the economic stability of the family. This holistic character does, of course, have consequences in the holistic dimension of the results. Maria integrated her career problems within a global functioning dynamic, and the associated changes were extended to the other areas of her life. In this sense, her words about the experience of change are enlightening: "It is not only occupational.... it is an all-important aspect of knowing the direction that things should go" (Cardoso, 2012, p. 367). What is fundamentally being examined is a change that justifies career construction counseling as counseling for life design (Savickas, 2011a).

The second contribution was in the conceptualization of the process of career counseling as relative to the co-construction of meaning. The adoption of this approach is the practice of an epistemological position in the counseling process, in that the counselor rejects the role of omnipotence and of being the holder of the truth. On the contrary, the counselor reflects on himself or herself, on the client, and on the process of counseling itself. This closeness and attention to self-experience within relationships with others permits the identification of markers that guide decisions relating to what to say and do in the moment-by-moment unfolding of the counseling process. In the case of Maria, this allowed her to give attention to the feeling of being held prisoner by a repetitive cycle and ask herself about the reasons behind the impasse. The response was the identification of maladaptive repetition markers (Cardoso, 2012).

The third contribution was the proposal of resolution by contrast (Savickas, 2011b). This counseling task seeks to validate neglected but nevertheless vital aspects of lived experience (Gonçalves, Matos, & Santos, 2009; White & Epston, 1990). The use of contrast as a solution for the gaps being experienced in life permits the application of this solution to the needs of the person. In Maria's case, the identification of a problematic narrative that was saturated with the theme of caregiving suggested that a theme of helping herself could be used to resolve her dilemma. Thus diversity and complexity were added to the narrative, and consequently they facilitated the reorganization of self-experience in a way that attributed a new meaning to career decisions: The choice to become a psychotherapist was no longer made to help others, but to help herself.

We now focus on the innovation that the analysis of this case can bring to the life design framework for counseling, such as the integration of the concept of maladaptive repetition into the dynamics of life themes. The analysis of this case suggests that maladaptive repetition should be understood as a dysfunctional evolution of the concept of repetition leading to mastery, as proposed by Savickas (2011b). In this sense, it is considered that maladaptive repetition begins when early life experiences introduce and/or intensify certain themes, thereby leading to a subsequent tendency to exclude, distort, or avoid experiences that are inconsistent with the themes that have given order to the individual's previous experience. Individuals who have limited contact with experiences that threaten their precarious narrative organization may become prisoners of a redundant construction of their experiences, and as a result, such an individual may then become incapable of building a narrative that allows them to support a multifaceted view of themselves. This proposal is inspired by constructivist (Greenberg, Rice, & Elliot, 1993; Mahoney, 1991) and social constructionist (Fernandes, 2007; Hermans & Dimaggio, 2004; Ribeiro & Gonçalves, 2011) frameworks of human functioning, and by research showing the importance of the role of attachment (Blustein, Prezioso, & Schultheiss, 1995; van Ecke, 2007), early dispositions of personality (Savickas, 2003), and dysfunctional narratives (Cochran, 1997) in career construction difficulties.

The case also allows for a reflection on the process of a client's change in career construction counseling. The analysis of the client's perspective on her transformation revealed both what had changed and how it had changed. In the follow-up session, held 10 months afterwards, Maria described her experience of change as being one of peace and harmony and of now having meaning in her life. She had become aware that she had not been able to distance herself from her core self in order to follow a genuine path. This was essentially the reorganization of the narrative identity as something that was lived in a way that was fundamental for the establishment of the stability needed to deal with the challenges of her career construction. However, the case also reveals that the change was not a linear process but a cycle of advances and retreats that expressed the continuous management of tension between the new and the old order. In the follow-up session, Maria noted that she sometimes forgets to look after herself and that she needs to make an effort to not distance herself from what she needs. This gradual and nonlinear evolution reveals how the self-organization dynamics avoid discontinuities that threaten personal integrity (Mahoney, 2003; Ribeiro & Gonçalves, 2011). The gradual evolution of change was first revealed with Maria's understanding about the presence of the theme of helping others across the different dimensions of her life, then with the implementation of career changes and the subsequent search to break the maladaptive repetition cycle present in her relationship with family members. She purposefully affirmed that she was satisfied with the career choice that she had made but that she was worried about her nurturing tendencies in other aspects of her life, especially in relation to her dependent sister.

To clarify the dynamics of change in the epistemology of social constructionism, the integration of the construct of dialogical self in the life design paradigm for counseling is proposed, as has also been suggested by McIlveen and Patton (2007). The dialogical self means that the self is a dynamic multiplicity of relatively autonomous characters or voices. Each voice has the ability to move from one position or perspective to another, in accordance with changes in situation and time. This multiplicity entails divergence, conflict, and negotiation, all of which ensure the articulation of different perspectives (Hermans, 2006). From a dialogical perspective, the tension and ambivalence shown by Maria reveal the conflict between the dominant themes of helping others and the theme of helping herself. This conflict is one, on the one hand, of the opposition between the position of the caregiver and, on the other, the silenced position of helping oneself. As has previously been noted, the counselor's advice – "It is time to take care of yourself" – gave voice to the silenced character and permitted a rupture of the maladaptive repetition cycle. From a dialogical perspective, this change occurred because the "position moves from the background of the system to the foreground, ... when deeper layered positions are brought to the surface" (Hermans, 2003, p. 110), thereby introducing more complexity and differentiation into the narrative and subsequently permitting the establishment of a new order that requires constant dialogue between the various characters/perspectives for continuity.

Finally, Maria's case also adds to the reflection on the dimensions of career counseling (working alliance, the co-construction of meaning, and the interface between career and personal issues) approached in the study of psychologists' dilemmas (Cardoso et al., 2012). In that sense, the case shows how in the life design framework to counseling, the working alliance can be used both to obtain markers on what to say or what to do in the moment-by-moment advancement of career counseling and to favor meaning construction. For example, in the case of Maria, it was the counselor's awareness of his experience in the relation with the client that allowed him to recognize the therapeutic impasse and make the confrontation – "It's time to take care of yourself" – enabling innovation in the client's self-narrative.

The importance attributed to a working alliance favors holistic approaches placing career problems in the matrix of personal issues. Again, Maria's case is illustrative of both the holistic character of life design counseling and its possibilities for managing the dilemma of whether or not to intervene in the client's emotional problems. In this case, the counselor assessed the client's problem by taking into account the interface between family and work roles and then placing Maria's problem in the context of her psychosocial (dis)functioning. Finally, Maria's understanding of how her narrative was saturated in the theme of caring for others, which influenced other dimensions of her life, allowed her both to attribute new meaning to career decision making and to generalize the change to other career roles beyond the work role.

Conclusions

This chapter has discussed the contribution of the analysis of practices from the life design paradigm for career counseling, with the intention of contributing to the improvement and evolution of this model, thereby following one of the parts of the research agenda, while looking to complement theory and practice.

By analyzing the positivist approach, a search is made to demonstrate the intersubjective nature of the practices that are founded in the epistemology of social constructionism. Seeking a counterpower within human diversity, against the artificiality of technology, and finding solutions that do not shape the individual as if he or she were contained within a mold, may constitute a new, different way of approaching the work of career counselors.

In theory as well as in practice, one never knows all of the aspects of a system's definition. In this light, it is important not only to act but also to reflect on what is being done in order to reduce the gap between theory and practice. The life design paradigm opens up possibilities capable of responding to this challenge. On the one hand, the design of the counseling process as an intersubjective experience suggests that the counselor should listen and create conditions so that clients may affirm themselves relative to their specificity, thereby creating a situation that enables them to feel at ease as an active agent. Beginning with the client's experience demands that the counselor have a reflective posture that is capable of moving his or her own experience closer to that of the client. On the other hand, the appreciation of individual and localized understanding within this paradigm leads to the consideration of analysis of practices for the reduction of the gap between theory and practice. In this chapter, the practices analyzed reveal the complexity of the career counseling process and the possibilities that this type of study can offer for aiding in a better understanding of this complexity – namely, as relative to the working alliance dynamic, the ethical challenges faced throughout the process, and what it is that actually characterizes change. To provide this type of understanding is to project career counseling into new possibilities capable of responding to the challenges faced in the real lives of the people who seek its aid. As a Portuguese philosopher put it: "A theory that focuses on the same questions, that kneads and grinds without ever transforming them, that reproduces them without producing something else, without ever truly working on those questions, that is a dead theory" (Prado Coelho, 1967, pp. lvii-lviii).

Both theory and practice should be kept within the psychological domain, because the constant search to find the uniqueness of each is essentially the best thing that a psychologist can do. For that to happen, perhaps the best way to turn an idea into a reality is to feed theory with a touch of the real.

References

Amundson, N. (2006). Challenges for career interventions in changing contexts. *International Journal for Educational and Vocational Guidance, 6*, 3–14. http://doi.org/10.1007/s10775-006-0002-4

Betan, E. J. (1997). Toward a hermeneutical model of ethical decision making in clinical practice. *Ethics and Behavior, 7*, 347–365. http://doi.org/10.1207/s15327019eb0704_6

Blustein, D., Prezioso, M. S., & Schultheiss, D. P. (1995). Attachment theory and career development: Current status and future directions. *The Counseling Psychologist, 23*, 416–432. http://doi.org/10.1177/0011000095233002

Cardoso, P. (2012). Maladaptive repetition and career construction. *Journal of Vocational Behavior, 81*, 364–369. http://doi.org/10.1016/j.jvb.2012.09.003

Cardoso, P., Taveira, M., Biscaia, C., & Santos, G. (2012). Psychologists' dilemmas in career counselling practice. *International Journal for Educational and Vocational Guidance, 12*, 225–241. http://doi.org/10.1007/s10775-012-9232-9

Cochran, L. (1997). *Career counseling: A narrative approach*. Thousand Oaks, CA: Sage.

Dauwalder, J. P. (2003). Quality in educational and vocational guidance at the beginning of the 21st century: Some introductory statements. In J. P. Dauwalder, R. Kunz, & J. Renz (Eds.), *Quality development in vocational counselling and training* (pp. 22–25). Zurich, Switzerland: SVB.

Duarte, M. E. (2009a). The psychology of life construction. *Journal of Vocational Behavior, 75*, 259–266. http://doi.org/10.1016/j.jvb.2009.06.009

Duarte, M. E. (2009b). Um século depois de Parsons: escolher uma profissão ou apostar na psicologia da construção da vida? [One century after Parsons: Choose an occupation or a bet on the psychology of life construction?]. *Revista Brasileira de Orientação Profissional, 10*, 5–14.

Duarte, M. E. (2010). La questione dell' assessment: concetto, criteri e problem specifici [The question of assessment: Concept, criteria, and specific problems]. In S. Soresi & L. Nota (Eds.), *Sfide e nuovi orizontti per' orientamento* (pp. 91–99). Florence, Italy: Giunti Organizzazioni Speciali.

Duarte, M. E. (2011). Desaprender para ensinar os princípios (ou um outro modo de enfrentar a orientação) [De-learning to teach the principles or a new way to face guidance]. *Revista Brasileira de Orientação, 12*, 143–151.

Duarte, M. E. (2012). Reflections on the training of career counselors. *Cypriot Journal of Educational Sciences, 7*, 265–275.

Fernandes, E. M. (2007). When what I wish makes me worse…. to make coherence flexible. *Psychology and Psychotherapy: Theory, Research and Practice, 80*, 165–180. http://doi.org/10.1348/147608306X109294

Gergen, K. J. (2001). Psychological science in a postmodern context. *American Psychologist, 56*, 803–813. http://doi.org/10.1037/0003-066X.56.10.803

Gonçalves, M. M., Matos, M., & Santos, A. (2009). Narrative therapy and the nature of "Innovative moments" in the construction of change. *Journal of Constructivist Psychology, 22*, 1–23. http://doi.org/10.1080/10720530802500748

Greenberg, L. S., Rice, L. N., & Elliot, R. (1993). *Facilitating emotional change: The moment-by-moment process*. New York, NY: Guilford Press.

Guichard, J. (2009). Self-constructing. *Journal of Vocational Behavior, 75*, 251–258. http://doi.org/10.1016/j.jvb.2009.03.004

Guichard, J. (2015). From vocational guidance and career counseling to life design dialogues. In L. Nota & J. Rossier (Eds.), *Handbook of life design: From practice to theory and from theory to practice* (pp. 11–26). Boston, MA: Hogrefe Publishing.

Hackett, G. (1993). Career counselling and psychotherapy: False dichotomies and recommended remedies. *Journal of Career Assessment, 2*, 105–117. http://doi.org/10.1177/106907279300100201

Hermans, H. J. M. (2003). The construction and reconstruction of a dialogical self. *Journal of Constructivist Psychology, 16*, 89–130. http://doi.org/10.1080/10720530390117902

Hermans, H. J. M. (2006). The self as theatre of voices: Disorganization and reorganization of a position repertoire. *Journal of Constructivist Psychology, 19*, 147–169. http://doi.org/10.1080/10720530500508779

Hermans, H. J. M., & Dimaggio, G. (2004). *The dialogical self in psychotherapy*. New York, NY: Brunner-Routledge. http://doi.org/10.4324/9780203314616

Herr, E., & Cramer, S. (1996). *Career guidance and counseling through the life span* (5th ed.). New York, NY: HarperCollins.

Hill, C. E. (2011). *Consensual qualitative research: A practical resource for investigating social science phenomena*. Washington, DC: American Psychological Association.

Hook, D. (2001). Therapeutic discourse, co-construction, interpellation, role-induction: Psychotherapy as iatrogenic treatment modality? *International Journal of Psychotherapy, 6*, 47–66. http://doi.org/10.1080/13569080120042207

Kant, I. (1996). *The critique of pure reason* (W. S. Pluhar, Trans.). Indianapolis, IN: Hackett (Original work published 1781).

Mahoney, M. (1991). *Human change processes*. New York, NY: Basic Books.

Mahoney, M. (2003). *Constructive psychotherapy*. New York, NY: Guilford Press.

Masdonati, J., Massoudi, K., & Rossier, J. (2009). Effectiveness of career counseling and the impact of the working alliance. *Journal of Career Development, 36*, 183–202. http://doi.org/10.1177/0894845309340798

Masdonati, J., Perdrix, S., Massoudi, K., & Rossier, J. (2014). Working alliance as a moderator and a mediator of career counseling effectiveness. *Journal of Career Assessment, 22*, 3–17. http://doi.org/10.1177/1069072713487489

Markus, H., & Kitayama, S. (1991). Culture and the self: implications for cognition, emotion, and motivation. *Psychological Review, 98*, 224–253. http://doi.org/10.1037/0033-295X.98.2.224

McIlveen, P., & Patton, W. (2007). Dialogical self: Author and narrator of career life themes. *International Journal for Educational and Vocational Guidance, 7*, 67–80. http://doi.org/10.1007/s10775-007-9116-6

Niles, S. G., & Karalic, A. (2009). Training career practitioners in the 21st century. In J. A. Athanasou & R. Van Esbroeck (Eds.), *International handbook of career guidance* (pp. 355–372). New York, NY: Springer Science.

Ribeiro, A. P., & Gonçalves, M. M. (2011). Maintenance and transformation of problematic self-narratives: A semiotic-dialogical approach. *Integrative Psychological & Behavioral Science, 45*, 281–303. http://doi.org/10.1007/s12124-010-9149-0

Richardson, M. S., Constantine, K., & Washburn, M. (2005). New directions for theory development in vocational psychology. In W. B. Walsh & M. L. Savickas (Eds.), *Handbook of vocational psychology* (3rd ed., pp. 51–83). Mahwah, NJ: Erlbaum.

Prado Coelho, E. (1967). *O estruturalismo – antologia de textos teóricos* [Structuralism: Anthology of theoretical texts]. Lisbon, Portugal: Portugália Editora.

Savickas, M. (1992). New directions in career assessment. In D. H. Montross & C. J. Shinkman (Eds.), *Career development: Theory and practice* (pp. 336–255). Springfield, IL: Charles C. Thomas.

Savickas, M. (1995). Examining the personal meaning of inventoried interests during career counseling. *Journal of Career Assessment, 3*, 188–201. http://doi.org/10.1177/106907279500300206

Savickas, M. L. (2003, September). *Life portraits from Donald's Super Career Pattern Study*. Paper presented at the Congress of the International Association for Education and Vocational Guidance, Bern, Switzerland.

Savickas, M. (2005). The theory and practice of career construction. In S. Brown & R. Lent (Eds.), *Career development and counseling: Putting theory and research to work* (pp. 42–70). Hoboken, NJ: Wiley.

Savickas, M. L. (2006). *Career counseling*. (Specific treatments for specific populations, video series). Washington, DC: American Psychological Association.

Savickas, M. L. (2011a). The self in vocational psychology: Object, subject and project. In P. J. Hartung & L. M. Subich (Eds.), *Developing self in work and career: Concepts, cases, and contexts* (pp. 17–33). Washington, DC: American Psychological Association.

Savickas, M. (2011b). *Career counseling*. Washington, DC: American Psychological Association.

Savickas, M. (2012). Life design: A paradigm for career intervention in the 21st century. *Journal of Counseling & Development, 90*, 13–19. http://doi.org/10.1111/j.1556-6676.2012.00002.x

Savickas, M. L., Nota, L., Rossier, J., Dauwalder, J.-P., Duarte, M. E., Guichard, J., . . . van Vianen, A. E. M. (2009). Life designing: A paradigm for career construction in the 21st century. *Journal of Vocational Behavior, 75*, 239–250. http://doi.org/10.1016/j.jvb.2009.04.004

Scaturo, D. J. (2005). *Clinical dilemmas in psychotherapy: A transtheoretical approach to psychotherapy integration*. Washington, DC: American Psychological Association. http://doi.org/10.1037/11110-000

Stiles, W. B. (2003). When is a case study scientific research? *Psychotherapy Bulletin, 38*, 6–11.

Stiles, W. B. (2007). Theory-building case studies of counseling and psychotherapy. *Counseling and Psychotherapy Research, 7*, 122–127. http://doi.org/10.1080/14733140701356742

Sultana, R. G., & Watts, A. G. (2006). Career guidance in public employment services across Europe. *International Journal for Educational and Vocational Guidance, 6*, 29–46. http://doi.org/10.1007/s10775-006-0001-5

Super, D. E. (1957). *The psychology of careers*. New York, NY: Harper & Brothers.

Super, D. E. (1980). A life-span, life-space approach to career development. *Journal of Vocational Behavior, 16*, 282–298. http://doi.org/10.1016/0001-8791(80)90056-1

van Ecke, Y. (2007). Attachment style and dysfunctional career thoughts: How attachment style can affect the career counseling process. *The Career Development Quarterly, 55*, 339–350. http://doi.org/10.1002/j.2161-0045.2007.tb00088.x

White, M., & Epston, D. (1990). *Narrative means to therapeutic ends*. New York, NY: W.W. Norton.

Chapter 5
Vocational Trajectories and People's Multiple Identities: A Life Design

Jacques Pouyaud
Department of Psychology, Bordeaux University, France

Introduction

The life design paradigm stresses that individuals must now cope in a globalized society with new career and personal issues (Savickas et al., 2009). Life courses appear to be more uncertain, featuring many more breaks than previously, and career development is now seen as a construction of meanings that allow individuals to deal with multiple vocational life paths. As Savickas explains: "Building a subjective career resembles the task of building a self" (Savickas, 2011, p. 15). Vocational trajectories are thus integrated into a life design, a self-construction paradigm that emphasizes the question of multiple identities as potential resources for human development. The life design perspective stresses this idea that career counseling should be built on self-construction processes through narratives. One condition of this idea, noted by Savickas and colleagues, is that "the issue of interaction between personal agency and social structure must be transformed into scientific questions" (Savickas et al., 2009, p. 241). The aim of this chapter is to explore such processes and conditions within the four main contemporary approaches, and to propose an integrated model of self-construction based on Ricoeur's approach of narrative identity. Four theoretical and practical propositions are chosen for their complementarity and their description of such life design construction processes; the construction of career through narratives (the career construction theory; Savickas, 2011), the processes of personalization as a system of conflict resolution (active socialization; Malrieu, 2003; Malrieu, Malrieu, & Widlocher, 1973), the narrative process of construction of joint action (the contextual action theory; Young & Valach, 2008; Young et al., 2011), and the reflexivity processes that lead to the construction of a dynamic system of identity forms (the making oneself self model; Guichard, 2005, 2009). All of these models appear to be similar in their focus on identity as a fundamental dynamic concept to understand self-construction. All of these models underline the capacity of the individuals to take a reflexive stance on their experiences that endows them with self-determination ability. The first part of this chapter, then, presents the theoretical approach of narrative identity developed by Ricoeur (1992). This theory appears to be a very heuristic framework for the life design perspective because it helps understand the individual "biographicity" (Alheit & Dausien, 2000), the capacity of using biographical agency to bridge transitions. I then present the four approaches and explain how they enrich each other within Ricoeur's general framework in order to propose an integrative model of self-construction. This model is presented as a metaphorical tool for practitioners who would like to use the life design paradigm. Finally, I conclude with a consideration of the consequences of this proposition for career counseling practices from the life design perspective.

Identity in Life Design Approaches

The life design approach presents identity as a fundamental resource that supports career development. Although Ricoeur's theoretical work is not often cited in the life design literature, I think it constitutes a common foundation for most of these perspectives.

Narrative Identity as a General Framework

Paul Ricoeur always tried to combine multiple disciplines such as philosophy, history, and literature. His method was to organize a multidisciplinary dialogical discourse between disciplines to open up perspectives and create new points of view. He studied themes such as time, memory, history, evil, and identity by analyzing how human beings interpret, imagine, and represent reality, especially through narrative, in order to recreate reality.

Two main publications can be seen as the core references of his conception of narrative identity. In the three volumes of *Time and Narrative* (Ricoeur, 1984, 1985, 1988) and in *Oneself as Another* (Ricoeur, 1992), Ricoeur presents a hermeneutic of the self that can help the life design approach to take into account more precisely the relations among language, action, and social context in a more holistic perspective. His interpretation of the self is indeed described as a dialogue between three registers of human expressiveness: language (the subject who speaks), action (the subject who acts), and ethics (moral subject). The three levels refer first to a semantic and pragmatic vision of the self, a description built from action (who I am through my actions and language), and second to a prescriptive vision (who I want or would like to be). Between these two visions (descriptive – who I am; and prescriptive – who I would like to be), the subject built his or her identity. The notions of memory and narrative are used to explain how the two levels are embedded in the time perspective, from past to present, and from the short to long term. For Ricoeur, the subject is constructed between two identity poles: the *idem-identity* is the fact that we can feel ourselves to be identical and recognizable throughout time. The modality of idem-identity is the *character*. The second pole is *ipse-identity*, which corresponds to maintaining the self (self-constancy), the modality of which is the promise. The promise is the subject's commitment to become who she or he says she or he is, and who she or he wants to be.

Narrative Identity as a Space "Between"

The major concept for life design perspective is narrative identity. For Ricoeur, narrative identity is like the glue that holds the two poles of idem and ipse together within the different times of the self. The narrative identity is not stable or predefined. On the contrary, it is built through the interpretations of life events, and may always be redesigned by the plurality of new narratives and interpretations. Most of all, narrative identity is the responsibility of he or she who tells himself or herself. Ricoeur emphasizes here that "it is language that is the primary condition of all human experience" (1983, p. 191), and that language and narratives are the main processes of construction of the self, between immediate action and life pathways.

As pointed out by Mongin (1998), "if the event, which cannot be separated from action, should be told, then the identity needs to be split between idem-identity and ipse-identity" (p. 31, author's translation). This means that narrative is what allows action to be transformed into experience, leading the history of the construction of identity. This duality is the product of the specificity of language and its mediation by signs. Identity, language, and signs are at the heart of the interpretation processes involved in the development of the self. "There is no self-understanding that is not *mediated* by signs, symbols, and texts; in the final analysis, self-understanding coincides with the interpretation given to these mediating terms" (Ricoeur, 1983, p. 191).

Narratives are what make life possible, and language is a tool for building ipseity. "A life is the history of this life, in search of narration. Understanding oneself means being able to tell both understandable and acceptable stories about oneself, especially acceptable ones" (Ricoeur, 1995, as cited in Mongin, 1998, p. 126, author's translation). It's not a story that tells the truth of the fact, but a story rebuilt in relation with the fact, an analogy that makes sense of the event. "The pastness of an observation in the past is not itself observable but it is memorable" (Ricoeur, 1988, p. 157). Memory is a duty that links us to the past. Through our narrative memory, we again set up the world in which we live.

Ricoeur describes the interlacing of two forms of narratives. On the one hand, there is the historical narrative, which is a reconstruction of "real" traces. The function of this reconstruction is what Ricoeur terms its "representation" (*representance*) which is "the expectation attached to the historical knowledge of constructions constituting the reconstructions of the past course of events" (Ricoeur, 1988, p. 359). On the other, the fictional narrative is built on the unreal. This form of narrative allows exploration of different possibilities and reconstructs time in multiple ways. The main function of fiction is what Ricoeur calls its significance (*signifiance*). The first narrative is an attempt to combine the immediacy and the truth of the action, while the second is about the interpretation and the shaping of an identity trajectory. Between these two narratives live the characters and the plot that gives consistency to narrative identity. The plot and the characters allow events to be transformed into lived experience in the time of history. The development of the self is therefore associated with the capability to construct a fictional narrative. For Arrien (2007), "this is the movement of emplotment to the character that allows Ricoeur to enrich the concept of person, therefore designed as an intricate character in its own experiences and narratively fighting against the fragmentation of the self" (p. 447).

The Importance of Alterity

The plot is never isolated but is constructed through relationships with others. The person alters, changes, and crosses time within the relation to the other. Bringing others into the narrative plot is necessary to maintain the dialogical relationship between the pole of idem and ipse. Ricoeur describes here how humans can be "capable." He describes the capable man who is able to act, to tell, to judge into alterity through time.

Although fundamental, the dialogical relation between idem and ipse is not sufficient to describe the concept of identity. To go further, I need to explain how this dialectic is made dynamic by a second one: the dialogical relation to otherness. The difference enriches the narrative identity between idem and ipse by saying something new about ourselves.

As long as one remains within the circle of sameness-identity, the otherness of the other than self offers nothing original:

> "Other" appears in the list of antonyms of "same" alongside "contrary," "distinct," "diverse," and so on. It is quite different when one pairs together otherness and selfhood.... *Oneself as Another* suggests from the outset that the selfhood of oneself implies otherness to such an intimate degree that one cannot be thought of without the other, that instead one passes into the other.... To "as" I should like to attach a strong meaning, not only that of a comparison (oneself similar to another) but indeed that of an implication (oneself inasmuch as being other). (Ricoeur, 1992, p. 3)

The otherness of the other leads individuals to change and to learn something new about themselves. "The other one leads the individual towards a phenomenon of alterity. Otherness is a process from which a subject changes and becomes another, according to influences exercised by another one, without losing his identity" (Briançon, 2008, p. 2, author's translation). Viewing oneself as another also refers to the ethical dimension of identity: The self is constructed through the care given to others.

The Construction of the Self Through the Three Experiences of Alterity

For Ricoeur, three ways of experiencing alterity contribute to the construction of the self: alterity of the flesh (the experience of one's own body), alterity of the foreign (the experience implied by the relation of the self to other than self), and alterity of our own consciousness (the experience of relation of the self to itself, the conscience). The first alterity is related to power and leads humans to perceive themselves as a body among other bodies. The second modality of experience is the relation to others as a foreigner. Nevertheless, "the other is not condemned to remain a stranger but can become *my counterpart,* i.e. someone who, *like* me, says *I*" (Ricoeur, 1992, p. 335). The condition for this is a relationship of mutual friendship with others. This friendship is a way to support both our own identity and the promise of the identity of others. The third experience is the recognition of our own conscience. This is the "heart of hearts" (the innermost being – le "for intérieur," as it is called in French), a voice that seems strange but which resonates in us. To hear this voice is to live otherness of oneself by oneself (oneself as another), which is what Ricoeur calls being enjoined. "Being enjoined thus constitutes the moment of otherness proper to the phenomenon of conscience, in accordance with the metaphor of the voice. Listening to the voice of conscience signifies being enjoined by the Other" (Ricoeur, 1992, p. 351). Self-consciousness characterizes the ethical dimension of identity. The voice of conscience calls and invites individuals to a *good life.*

> The passivity of being enjoined consists in the situation of listening, in which the ethical subject is placed in relation to the voice addressed to it in the second person. To find oneself called upon in the second person ... is to recognize oneself as being enjoined to live well with and for others in just institutions and to esteem oneself as the bearer of this wish. (Ricoeur, 1992, p. 352)

Finally, *capable person* is he or she who crosses the tragic events of life by facing up to evil in a desire for accomplishment. Achievement of this desire to live well with and for others in just institutions is expressed in the relationship of friendship and love with others. For life design researchers and practitioners, Ricoeur's philosophy tells us something about the processes and conditions of the "biographicity." The next four theoretical approaches enrich this proposition in the field of career counseling.

First Theoretical Relation: The Career Construction Theory

Career construction theory (Savickas, 2011) is a well-known theoretical and practical approach of career counseling. Based on Super's contribution on career development (Savickas, 2001; Super, 1990), this perspective incorporates new challenges and issues of postmodern societies in a constructivist proposition that lies at the heart of the life design paradigm.

Like Ricoeur, individuals construct themselves through language and interpersonal experiences according to the career construction theory, which distinguishes self and identity. Self is larger and is "not actually self-constructed ... [but] co-constructed through active, collaborative processes" (Savickas, 2011, p. 17). This is close to Vygotsky's perspective (1978) that self is "an emergent awareness that is culturally shaped, socially constituted, and linguistically narrated" (Savickas, 2013, p. 148). As an adaptive dimension of humans, identity is unstable.

> It schematizes the self by locating it in a social context.... The schema called identity is a pattern imposed by the individual to mediate and guide his or her response to social realities.... Being a psychosocial construct, identity resides at the interface of self, context and culture. (Savickas, 2011, pp. 17–18)

Identity is therefore a developmental resource that updates in context. The implementation of the self in context lies at the source of self-knowledge. Again, the capable man derives from the confrontation with action, and from the creation of a temporally organized meaning.

> In committing to the facticity of their lives, individuals make some emotional compromises with reality and project them forward for some considerable amount of time. In so doing, they take hold of themselves by gripping viscerally certain convictions, and then they cling unflinchingly to these beliefs as they experience confusing and conflicting ideas.... An individual must repeatedly revise identity to adaptively integrate significant new experiences into the ongoing life story. (Savickas, 2011, p. 19)

There is a connection between the daily adaptation of individuals to contexts and the construction of the self through narratives. In career construction theory, this connection is explained by the construction of meaning between micronarratives and macronarratives, which is close to Ricoeur's distinction between historical and fictional narratives and their intertwining.

> Narrative processing of identity gathers *small stories* or *micro-narratives* about important incidents and episodes.... In working with the micro-narratives, the person actively gathers the story threads and weaves them together into one tapestry to craft a unified sense of individuality. The integration of small stories about the self in social situations constructs a *large story* or *macro-narrative*. (Savickas, 2011, p. 22)

The concept of *narrative identity* is again used to explain how the life story can make sense of ourselves to ourselves, stressing that "through narratives, individuals interpret the self as if they were another person" (Savickas, 2011, p. 21). The plot is expressed through the notions of *life themes* and *character arc*.

> A theme in a macronarrative traces how a person is identical with self despite diversity across micronarratives.... Recognizing the theme in a narrative identity enables individuals to see self as an integrated and inevitable whole, offering an important way of viewing self and explaining oneself to others. (Savickas, 2011, pp. 26–27)

While the life theme refers to the melody that constructs the narrative identity, the character arc is what allows this melodic line to be embodied through characters. It is an individual motive which drives the plot. It is constructed through needs that prompt individuals to act, and

> the progress from need to goal transforms individuals as they grow, develop, and learn.... This transformation represents the core of the character, that is, the character arc that defines the person and explains the driving force of the plot. (Savickas, 2011, p. 30)

Finally, as in Ricoeur's proposition, the construction of identity is mediated by the relation to others, and an ethical dimension also exists, mainly expressed in individual values: "Values name the constitutive concerns that make the identity narrative an ethical and aesthetic project because they connect the individual to a broader reality or greater story" (Savickas, 2011, p. 28). Even if these propositions, especially those of life theme and character arc, are very useful for the holistic purpose of life design paradigm, they omit to take into account daily activities as possible resources for self-construction.

Second Theoretical Relation: The Contextual Action Theory

While the previous approach may be seen as a focus on the long-term narrative dimension of identity described by Ricoeur, the contextual action theory (Young et al., 2011) offers a perspective more centered on the pragmatic and semantic level. Action is indeed the main concept that makes it possible to describe the role of interactions in the construction of the self. Even if the starting point is the concrete and immediate level of action, this perspective explains how this pragmatic level is redesigned in a more general long-term trajectory through joined actions. In that sense, contextual action theory can make links between the two first perspectives and complete the holistic life design view. In my opinion, the "redesign" of action described here is a process of "making sense" based on perceived alterity between idem and ipse. Young and colleagues describe identity construction in a temporal dimension that refers to different embedded levels spreading from internally directed behaviors to more socially constructed levels as projects and careers. "Short term actions can lead to mid-term projects, which, in turn, can lead to long-term careers (in the non-occupational as well as occupational sense)" (Young et al., 2011, pp. 89–90). Actions are directed to each level by goals constructed through internal feelings and emotions at the immediate level of action, and through meanings and thoughts, socially constructed in interactions with others. The duality of *idem* and *ipsé* identity may therefore be understood in relation with these embedded temporal dimensions of action (action–project–career).

Action theory identifies processes that steer and regulate actions and projects. Attention to these processes highlights the agency of individuals and their social partners in the construction of identity. The processes include internal (thought and feelings) and social processes.... Identity is socially constructed through joint actions with others. (Young et al., 2011, p. 90)

The authors make a distinction between goals involved in the level of action and those involved in the level of career. Each goal's category refers to more or less stabilized dimensions of the self. The whole process begins with the act of communicating.

Behind each communicative action is an identity goal which guides individuals toward trying to achieve compatible experiences and confirmation.... The specific goals of action are related to supra goals, such as identity, which extend over a much longer period of time. (Young et al., 2011, p. 90)

This "hierarchy" of goals is close to the proposition of Carver and Scheier (1998) who differentiate identity goals ("be goals"), which aim at self-achievement as a person from action, from action goals ("do goals") that aim simply to achieve a certain type of action. The "be" and "do" goals are integrated and form a hierarchical system of goals where "do goals" are involved in the implementation of "be goals." This description appears very useful to emphasize the interrelations of time levels and action levels in understanding the construction of identity. The next two perspectives complete the picture with a focus on the two main processes involved in the construction of the self: The role of conflict, for the former, and reflexivity processes, for the latter. The role of conflict as resource is indeed very important for the life design approach, which proposes to focus "upon strategies for survival and the dynamics of coping" (Savickas et al., 2009, p. 242). The reflexivity processes are also considered as principal tools to cope with situations.

Third Theoretical Relation: Active Socialization

The active socialization approach comes from the work of Malrieu and colleagues (1973) on the development of personality during childhood and adolescence. The fundamental dialogical relation between *idem* and *ipse* is now questioned through the socialization processes. Identity is constructed within the relation of individuals to social contexts in a conflict mode. Socialization fields, social contexts, and institutions have the power to alienate individuals. According to Malrieu (2003), socialization is "active" in the sense that this attempt to alienate, which corresponds to the "acculturation" processes, is counterbalanced by the activities of individuals trying to fight against acculturation conflicts. In trying to overtake the conflicts they face with institutions in which they live, individuals develop both themselves and the context. These activities are called personalization processes. Identity is therefore seen as a "system of conflict resolution" that aims to adjust reciprocally the person and the environment in a creative way. In other words, this approach deals like Ricoeur with the question of the capable man. Ricoeur presents the relation with others as a "productive conflictuality" and the individual as an "operator in mediations" (Ricoeur, 1960, as cited in Abel & Porée, 2009, p. 37, author's translation). The notion of personalization refers to the psychological processes used by individuals to transform conflict into development (of themselves and institutions). For Malrieu, personalization occurs as a result of two main articulated and integrated acts: acts of person and acts of personalization. Acts of person refer to the organization of behaviors in relation to goals and motives developed by the individual, while acts of personalization are activities undertaken by the individual to give meaning to life in a more long-term perspective. Through these latter activities, mainly narratives, individuals develop the ability to surpass themselves, that is to say, being more than what is expected of them by the environment in which they live. Identity is a quest implied by conflict experienced as alienating.

Identity is therefore a set of strategic processes. It tends to "defend and promote the self … through the quest for power (control of the self and the environment), the quest for meaning and significance, the quest for autonomy … and the quest for self-realization" (Esparbes-Pistre & Tap, 2001, p. 138, author's translation). Four strategies can be described: First, *identity strategies*, the function of which is to "maintain or increase the degree of self-worth, to assume the 'internal logic' through which the subject gives legitimacy to, invests in and controls himself" (Esparbes-Pistre & Tap, 2001, p. 189). All of these mechanisms can be active or defensive, conscious or unconscious. As Lipianski (1990) points out: "Some of these strategies are positive: assimilation, differentiation, affirmation, withdrawal, categorization, identification. Others are negative: collusion, rejection, exclusion, devaluation, and leading to a feeling of alienation and to difficulty in perceiving one's own identity" (as cited in Tap, Esparbes-Pistre, & Sordes-Ader, 1998, p. 190, author's translation). Second, *social positioning strategies* represent the efforts of individuals to find solutions to conflict by committing themselves to new social roles. Third, *coping strategies*, in reference to Lazarus and Folkman (1984), are responses made by the subject to adjust and cope immediately with conflictual situations. Finally, *project strategies* are solutions found by the subject as he or she projects himself or herself into the future. Projects are ways to escape and leave the situation. They help in "managing conflicts through anticipation" (Esparbes-Pistre & Tap, 2001, p. 138, author's translation). The same idea arises here of identity as movement in a "polarized space" between the dialogical experiences of alterity. Identity is therefore the "temporary and often revisited result … of the reciprocal structuration of the ontological and the pragmatic, of the individual and the collective" (Esparbes-Pistre & Tap, 2001, p. 141, author's translation). Within the structuration of the ontological and the pragmatic, the identity (existential) is a search for truths about oneself. These truths are expressed and constructed through values that allow identity to be what gives meaning to acts, but at the same time, acts are also what give meaning to oneself. The structuring of the individual and the collective summarizes the idea of oneself as another. Again the dialogical perspective is fundamental:

> Between meaning and action, the individual and the collective, and is directly related to personal time. [It consists of] managing the here and now, the present to resolve conflict, a personal story to defend and the future to invest in the construction of a life project (Esparbes-Pistre & Tap, 2001, p. 142, author's translation).

The personalization processes described above suggest how individuals navigate in the identity space composed of tensions between multiple experiences of alterity (relation to others) involving commitments and actions. Identity is an instrument of navigation through the time and space of existence. Synchronically, it allows us to act thanks to the "critical deliberation between the values attached to various domains of life and activities" (Dupuy & Leblanc, 2001, p. 69, author's translation). Diachronically, it links synchronical deliberations together into a subjective story. It is an "internal system, a cognitive and affective organization which helps individuals to rebuild the past, to regulate the present, and to guide the future" (Massonat, 1985, as cited in Tap et al., 1998, p. 187, author's translation).

Fourth Theoretical Relation: The Making Oneself Self Model

The making oneself self model (*se faire soi*) proposed by Guichard (Collin & Guichard, 2011; Guichard, 2005, 2009; Guichard, Pouyaud, & Dumora, 2011) synthesizes numerous elements of the previous theoretical approaches. Guichard describes the construction of the self from a cognitive point of view, but also with a dynamic perspective that explains the evolution of individuals' subjectivity over time. Again the core nature of identity is narration, even though actions and the body also play a role in the dynamic process. To grasp the plural and evolving nature of self-identity, this approach describes self-identity as a dynamic system of subjective identity forms (SSIF).

In the cognitive perspective, the construct of "subjective identity form" (SIF) describes each self that an individual constructs and implements (or has constructed and implemented, as well as expects to construct and implement in the future) in a particular setting. An SIF may be defined as a set of ways of being, acting, and interacting in accordance with a particular way of representing oneself – of conceiving oneself – within a given setting. In general, an SIF corresponds to a particular social role, but it also includes the way one thinks of oneself in this role, the way one sees oneself in that setting, what one says about oneself in that role.

The SIF can be seen as a behavioral, emotional, and cognitive identity compromise at a given instant. The SIF is thus bound to the moment and environment in which it is constructed. Indeed, according to the contexts in which individuals interact and communicate, they construct for themselves distinctive SIFs. Through their different SIFs, individuals can act, interact, and relate to themselves in a given way in one context, and differently in another context. Some SIFs refer to settings in which the individual interacts and communicates at the moment, other SIFs refer to expectations or ways of imagining oneself in the future, while other SIFs refer to past experiences that have had a lasting impression on the person.

All of these distinctions mean that at a given period of an individual's life, some SIFs are more central and play a major role in the current organization of that individual's system of SIF (SSIF). Nevertheless, although it is possible to "map" the SSIF at a given moment in a specific identity configuration, it is characterized mainly by its dynamism. Described from a psychological perspective, this dynamism involves a tension between two kinds of reflexivity.

In my opinion, the notion of reflexivity is close to what Ricoeur describes in the dialogical relation between me – myself and others. The value of this model is that it distinguishes different psychological modalities of reflexivity in the "oneself as another." In this model, the different kinds of reflexivity are articulated with each other during development, with a balance between stabilization and questioning of the self.

The first reflexivity, also called dual reflexivity, is a stabilizing factor. It may be described as a process of identification that leads a person to *want to become like this person* or *to be and act in accordance with the ideals of a specific belief system*. This process often involves some counteridentification processes – that is, a rejection of some role models or ideals. For Guichard, this first kind of reflexivity leads toward the structuring of the whole self-system from this unique future perspective (often anchored in past experiences).

The second form of reflexivity, which is called triadic reflexivity (as it involves a continuous move from the "I," "you," and "s/he" discursive positions), goes in the opposite direction.

It creates a distance from one's own past and present experiences and specific anticipations by looking at them from other points of view. This ongoing process of interpretation is a sense-making process during which individuals reflect on the multiple possible interpretations of their past and present commitments and those they anticipate. In this ternary reflexivity, with reference to Wiley (1994):

> individuals articulate in their minds their own points of view of "I" with the system of the other "I" that form a human society.... Such a reducing is possible only if the other "I" is considered merely as one of the possible figures in a narration. (Guichard & Pouyaud, 2014).

As described by Peirce (Colapietro, 1989) and Jacques (1991), the dialogical process constitutes the person. It is an intraindividual and interindividual process that involves three dialogical positions: the "I," the "you," and the "he/she." In discourse, when we speak to ourselves within these three positions, we construct new "interpretants," which are ways to construct new knowledge about ourselves. Such dialogical processes are at the core of the life design dialogues described by Guichard (see Chapter 2). The creation of new interpretants through language can also be linked with the previous description of the contextual embedded self-construction, and the creation of be-goals in language must be conceived here in a wide perspective, as both inner language and dialogical interaction are involved in self-construction. "This type of reflexivity enables individuals to engage in an indefinite process of interpretations and re-interpretations of their past and present experiences that lead them to sketch out, and sometimes specify, new potential future prospects" (Guichard & Pouyaud, 2014). What might be important are therefore the individuals' abilities to balance both processes in order to construct themselves in an innovative manner being guided by their projects.

The life path consists in a succession of periods sometimes centered on person, sometimes on personalization. When people need to be engaged in actions, to achieve their objectives, to develop competencies, then dual reflexivity processes might be dominant. When people need to make sense of their lives, then the ability to engage in triadic reflexivity is crucial. A "pathological" focus on the first process will restrain the ability to explore multiple SIFs. This can be related, for example, to the concept of "foreclosed identity status." On the other hand, a never-ending self-analysis based only on triadic reflexivity without any clear identification could lead to vocational indecision.

A Synthetic Perspective of Identity Construction

The vision of narrative identity developed by Ricoeur is a common root that can lead to a useful synthesis for constructivist career counseling theories. Ricoeur considers identity as a narration that links the two poles of idem and ipse, which are conditioned by multiple experiences of alterity. Each of the above-mentioned approaches contains some elements of this definition in relation to career counseling issues. The four previous theoretical approaches can also be seen as life design propositions, as each of them emphasizes a particular dimension of this paradigm:
- The emphasis on the *storytelling process* and the issue of the career plot as support for counseling;
- The emphasis on how *actions take part in the construction of the self*, and how actions and narration are linked through projects and career construction;

- The emphasis on the *conflictual nature of the identity* construction process, and on the strategic relation of the individual with society and institutions. This also questions the role of the counseling relationship as a strategic practice;
- The emphasis on the *processes of reflexivity* involved in the dialogical relation of otherness experiences.

The second part of this article summarizes the relations described between these theoretical approaches in order to propose an integrated view of self-construction that can contribute to the development of interventions and research in the life design perspective.

The Bicycle Metaphor

Identity is both volatile and talkative ("voluble"). This means that it can be seen only through the creative tool of language, in the temporary shape built between the two poles of the signifier and the signified. The "living metaphor" (*métaphore vive*), described by Ricoeur (2004) is the ultimate form of creativity, but it is also a form of truth. It is the "the rhetorical process by which discourse unleashes the power that certain fictions have to redescribe reality" (Ricoeur, 2004, p. 5). According to Clot (1995), the metaphor is also a process "whose use is required during work each time we try to tame a reality that is impossible to grasp directly" (p. 149, author's translation). With this principle, we attempt here to understand identity construction through a metaphor: the metaphor of identity as a bicycle.

The term *bicycle* is to be understood here in a dual sense (bi-cycle): The first is the object, the bicycle, which represents the dialogical nature of identity; the second is the dynamic dimension of identity. The "be-cycle" represents the process by which identity is generated through a temporal and spiral development.

The Bicycle

The first characteristic of identity within the life design perspective is that, as is the case for a bicycle, identity is a tool, a vehicle that allows us to "drive ourselves," to behave in one direction. This bicycle identity is a psychological transformation of the body in a useful vehicle to conduct ourselves in daily activities and on life's paths.

This image does not mean only that identity supports behaviors: It is much more a way to find motives and meanings (in the short and long term) to transform behavior into resources for adapting and moving forward. Identity is thus a way to transform behaviors into commitments. According to our analogy, if one wants to be a good driver, one also needs to be careful of other vehicles. Context and motives are therefore central. One's bicycle must be adapted to the traffic of other vehicles. One certainly will have to face traffic jams, expressways, or furrowed paths (like career transitions). Sometimes one will want to take the shortest, the quickest, or the most usual path, but at other times, one will just want to go for a stroll and take unknown routes. Identity, like the bicycle, is a form of conveyance, a psychological tool that supports the movement of the self.

Just as movement gives the bicycle balance, identity is kept functional as a vehicle by the movement of perpetual reflexivity and the dialogical relation between idem and ipse. Movement is thus the essence of identity. However, to be a mode of conveyance "for the self," identity also needs individual efforts that support the movement and allow directions to be taken. These efforts to provide balance are particularly required during career transitions and traumas. The ability of the identity to move the self depends on a subtle blend between the field's characteristics (context) and the individual's efforts (reflexivity process) to maintain the movement. A combination of these two factors implies the use of identity strategies that allow one both to maintain and surpass oneself.

The Be-Cycle

The notion of identity also implies a temporal perspective that may be seen as a cycle (a circle in motion) or a process of recycling. The dialogical process of identity is not a form of repetition but of rebuilding, a recycling of the self in the narrative activity. In that sense, identity is also a way to transform commitments into behaviors.

This metaphor emphasizes the idea that the bi-cycle is a vehicle pointing toward the future, designed to "go" (goal-oriented). The only way to turn back is to integrate the past into the present. As there is no reverse on a bicycle, you can always take the same path or return to the beginning, but always through a developmental process, a change, a forward movement.

Life design is an adaptation to the pathways we engage in. Identity is built through reciprocal adaptation. This means that changes are constant but not often radical. All bicycles are pretty much the same in principle (two wheels, handlebars, pedals, and a saddle) and still work the same. However, they are built differently depending on the ground encountered and the technical improvements made over time (better tires, brakes, comfort, etc). These developments are the identity resources, the adaptive capacities, the dimensions which are our progressive "personalization" of the self.

Thirteen Theoretical Propositions for "Cycling"

Figure 5.1 in the appendix graphically summarizes the metaphor. The 13 theoretical propositions in the figure legend allow the figure to be understood, and they provide an overview of the main assumptions of the approaches presented (see Figure 5.1 in the appendix). It gives a compatible view of these approaches and takes into account the presuppositions and propositions made by Savickas and colleagues (2009) to describe the life design paradigm: A holistic view of individuals in their ecosystem, the focus on narrative identity strategies which allow individuals to cope with transitions, the necessity to view counseling as a co-construction where clients work on their subjective and multiple realities, and the necessity of developing models of self-construction that allow researchers to evaluate effectiveness of counseling practices. I argue that it can help to understand the dynamic of identity construction and help career counselors to develop life design practices.

Conclusion: Career Counseling Practices in the Life Design Perspective

Within this framework, how can the counselor help and support the construction of the self? For Ricoeur, "the entire issue of personal identity revolves around this search for a relational invariant, giving it the strong meaning of permanence in time" (Ricoeur, 1992, p. 118). For him, the capable person is he or she who "deliberates well" (Ricoeur, 1992, p. 247) in constructing his own life. Counselors should help individuals to develop their power to act, to deliberate, to tell, to recognize oneself, and to be. Career issues may be seen as situations where the mechanisms of self-development are hindered, like an "impossibility for the subjects to transform their experience into means for living another experience" (Clot, 2006, p. 23, author's translation). Therefore, counselors try momentarily to share the burden of their clients' "deficit" in reflexivity. According to Malrieu, this means supporting the activity of personalization, helping the individual to find project strategies and means of self-development. In all previous approaches, counseling practice has been seen as a form of co-construction of a system of subjective identity forms, of scenarios based on narratives, of joint projects.

The integrated model presented here as a metaphorical tool for practitioners shows in addition the importance of the connection between meaning and action in the counseling process. The counselor therefore should focus on the experiences of otherness and help the subject to direct them by a dialogical process of reflexivity. In particular, this consists in finding (re)sources of self-realization from the experiences of otherness, and in helping the subject to express himself or herself by stating self-evidence through the language of inner and overt speech. This constructed consciousness may renew the commitment to a promise of oneself that the subject will try to keep through action. These resources are to be found in the expression of various relationships that constitute the experiential structure of identity – that is, the framework of the bicycle: relationships between feelings arising from daily actions, others, and oneself.

References

Abel, O., & Porée, J. (2009). *Le vocabulaire de Paul Ricoeur* [The vocabulary of Paul Ricoeur]. Paris, France: Ellipses.

Alheit, P., & Dausien, B. (2000). "Biographicity" as a basic resource of lifelong learning. In P. Alheit, J. Beck, E. Kammler, H. Salling Olesen, & R. Taylor (Eds.), *Lifelong learning inside and outside schools* (Vol. 2, pp. 400–422). Roskilde, Denmark: RUC.

Arrien, S.-J. (2007). Ipséité et passivité: le montage narratif du soi [Ipseity and passivity: The narrative edition of self]. *Laval Théologique et Philosophique, 63*, 445–458. http://doi.org/10.7202/018171ar

Briançon, M. (2008). L'altérité au coeur de l'identité: que peut enseigner l'altérité intérieure? [Alterity in the heart of identity: What can teach the inner alterity?]. *Sciences-Croisées, 2*, 1–22.

Butler, J. (2005). *Giving an account of oneself.* New York, NY: Fordham University Press. http://doi.org/10.5422/fso/9780823225033.001.0001

Carver, C. S., & Scheier, M. F. (1998). *On the sel-regulation of behavior.* Cambridge, UK: Cambridge University Press. http://doi.org/10.1017/CBO9781139174794

Clot, Y. (1995). *Le travail sans l'homme?* [The work without man?]. Paris, France: Editions la Découverte.

Clot, Y. (2006). Après le Guillant: quelle clinique du travail? [After le Guillant: What clinical approach of work?] In L. Le Guillant (Ed.), *Le drame humain du travail* (pp. 7–36). Toulouse, France: Erès.

Colapietro, V. M. (1989). *Peirce approach to the self: A semiotic perspective on human subjectivity.* Albany, NY: State University of New York Press.

Collin, A., & Guichard, J. (2011). Constructing self in career theory and counseling interventions. In P. J. Hartung & L. M. Subich (Eds.), *Constructing self in work and career: Concepts, cases and contexts* (pp. 89–106). Washington, DC: American Psychological Association.

Dupuy, R., & Leblanc, A. (2001). Enjeux axiologiques et activités de personalisation dans les transitions professionnelles [Axiological issues and activities of personalization in vocationnal transitions]. *Connexions, 76*, 61–79. http://doi.org/10.3917/cnx.076.0061

Esparbes-Pistre, S., & Tap, P. (2001). Identité projet et adaptation à l'âge adulte [Identity, project, and adaptation in adulthood]. *Carrierologie, 8*, 133–145.

Guichard, J. (2005). Life-long self-construction. *International Journal for Educational and Vocational Guidance, 5*, 111–124. http://doi.org/10.1007/s10775-005-8789-y

Guichard, J. (2009). Self constructing. *Journal of Vocational Behavior, 75*, 251–258. http://doi.org/10.1016/j.jvb.2009.03.004

Guichard, J., & Pouyaud, J. (2014). Processes of identity construction in liquid modernity: Actions, emotions, identifications and interpretations. In R. Young, L. Valach, & J. F. Domene (Eds.), *Counseling and action: Toward life-enhancing work, relationships, and identity*. New York, NY: Springer Science.

Guichard, J., Pouyaud, J., & Dumora, B. (2011). Self-Identity construction and reflexivity. In M. McMahon & M. Watson (Eds.), *Career counseling and constructivism*. New York, NY: Nova Science.

Jacques, F. (1991). *Difference and subjectivity: Dialogue and personal identity*. New Haven, CT: Yale University Press.

Lazarus, S. R., & Folkman, S. (1984). *Stress, appraisal and coping*. New York, NY: Springer.

Malrieu, P. (2003). *La construction du sens dans les dires autobiographiques* [The construction of meaning in the autobiographical narratives]. Toulouse, France: Erès. http://doi.org/10.3917/eres.malri.2003.01

Malrieu, P., Malrieu, S., & Widlocher, D. (1973). La socialisation [The socialization]. In H. Gratiot-Alphandery & R. Zazzo (Eds.), *Traité de Psychologie de l'enfant. 5. La formation de la personnalité*. Paris, France: PUF.

Mongin, O. (1998). *Paul Ricoeur*. Paris, France: Seuil.

Ricoeur, P. (1983). On interpretation. In A. Montefiore (Ed.), *Philosophy in France today* (pp. 175–197). Cambridge, UK: Cambridge University Press.

Ricoeur, P. (1984, 1985, 1988). *Time and narrative* (Vols. 1–3). Chicago, IL: University of Chicago Press.

Ricoeur, P. (1992). *Oneself as another*. Chicago, IL: University of Chicago Press.

Ricoeur, P. (2004). *The rule of metaphor*. London; UK: Taylor & Francis.

Savickas, M. L. (2001). A developmental perspective on vocational behaviour: Career patterns, salience, and themes. *International Journal for Educational and Vocational Guidance, 1*, 49–57. http://doi.org/10.1023/A:1016916713523

Savickas, M. L. (2011). *Career counseling*. Washington DC: American Psychological Association.

Savickas, M. (2013). Career construction theory and practice. In R. W. Lent & S. D. Brown (Eds.), *Career development and counseling: Putting theory and research to work*. (2nd ed., pp. 147–183). Hoboken, NJ: John Wiley & Sons.

Savickas, M. L., Nota, L., Rossier, J., Dauwalder, J.-P., Duarte, M. E., Guichard, J., . . . van Vianen, A. E. M. (2009). Life designing: A paradigm for career construction in the 21st century. *Journal of Vocational Behavior, 75*, 239–250. http://doi.org/10.1016/j.jvb.2009.04.004

Super, D. E. (1990). A life-span, life-space approach to career development. In D. Brown & L. Brooks (Eds.), *Career choice and dévelopment: Applying contemporary theories to practice* (2nd ed., pp. 197–261). San Francisco, CA: Jossey-Bass.

Tap, P., Esparbes-Pistre, S., & Sordes-Ader, F. (1998). Identité et stratégies de personnalisation [Identity and strategies of personalization]. *Bulletin de Psychologie, 428*, 185–196.

Vygotsky, L. S. (1978). *Mind in society*. Cambridge, MA: Harvard University Press.

Wiley, N. (1994). *The semiotic self*. Cambridge, UK: Polity Press.

Young, R. A., Marshall, S., Valach, L., Domene, J., Graham, M., & Zaidman-Zait, A. (2011). *Transition to adulthood*. New York, NY: Springer. http://doi.org/10.1007/978-1-4419-6238-6

Young, R. A., & Valach, L. (2008). Action theory: an integrative paradigm for research and evaluation in career. In J. Athanasou & R. Van Esbroeck (Eds), *International handbook of career guidance* (pp. 643–658). New York, NY: Springer.

Appendix

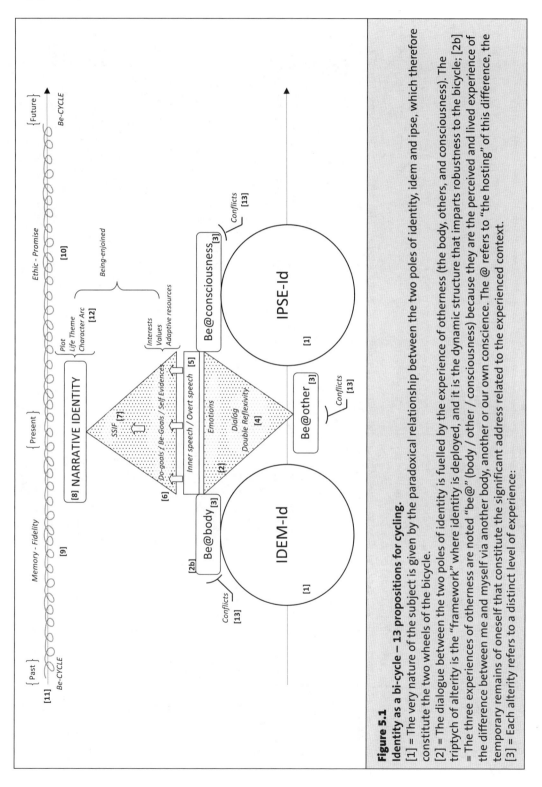

Figure 5.1

Identity as a bi-cycle – 13 propositions for cycling.

[1] = The very nature of the subject is given by the paradoxical relationship between the two poles of identity, idem and ipse, which therefore constitute the two wheels of the bicycle.

[2] = The dialogue between the two poles of identity is fuelled by the experience of otherness (the body, others, and consciousness). The triptych of alterity is the "framework" where identity is deployed, and it is the dynamic structure that imparts robustness to the bicycle; [2b] = The three experiences of otherness are noted "be@" (body / other / consciousness) because they are the perceived and lived experience of the difference between me and myself via another body, another or our own conscience. The @ refers to "the hosting" of this difference, the temporary remains of oneself that constitute the significant address related to the experienced context.

[3] = Each alterity refers to a distinct level of experience:

– Be@body is the pragmatic level of confrontation with reality. Although it does not necessarily come first in time, it serves as the basis, the physical anchoring of identity. It is the saddle of our bicycle.

– Be@consciousness is the disembodied level. It offers its directionality to identity and tries to drive self to a good life. It is the handlebar of the bicycle.

– Be@other is perhaps the most energizing experience of otherness so we situate it in the crank set.

[4] = The three experiences of otherness come together in the processes of reflexivity. In the middle of the triptych, the framework of the bicycle, the two types of reflexivity described by Guichard function alternatively to stabilize or question the self. They support the contradictions of otherness by dialogic activity.

[5] = The process of double reflexivity turns into speech acts by the use of both inner and overt speech. This refers to the role of language described by Vygotsky (1978) as a psychological tool. The two forms of language can be seen as ways to "edit" experiments, just as a film is directed. The edition of experiments is the psychological function of inner and overt speech that gives meaning to experiences. The "recording material" of this "identity movie' is constructed from emotions derived from action.

[6] = On the first level, the process of edition consists in the visible, observable dimensions of individuals: their feelings, attitudes, interests, values, adaptive resources, and skills. This level is widely studied in psychology and is often used to support career counseling. These dimensions can be classified on a continuum that goes from preconscious feelings (linked to action) to more constructed thoughts such as values, beliefs, and commitments. We call these identity dimensions "self-evidences." This involves knowledge about oneself that is gained by the translation of the experiences of otherness through inner and overt speech.

[7] = On the second level, this edition leads to a first form of organization, an identity synthesis that corresponds to a subjective identity form (SIF) map. This is only a primary level, because this map is rooted in the here and now and is like a photograph, without the dynamic function of the system of subjective identity forms (SSIF). It does not exist in itself, as it is only an observed configuration of identity forms in terms of self-evidence. The map actually exists only when it is used by the subject to guide his/her behavior. It then becomes the creative direction of oneself through language. This identity is achieved in the emplotment, by narrative translation into a plot that brings together past events, characters, and the potential future.

[8] = Narrative identity results from self-realization stemming from the dialogical experience transformed into self-evidence. This is a faithful historical reconstruction [9] of experiences of otherness, the search for a commitment of oneself within the promise of ipse [10]. Identity may be seen as the bicycle's center of gravity.

[11] = The path of identity is not like a straight line but is the result of an oscillation, a spiral development involving the relationship "oneself as another" between phases of stabilization and self-questioning.

[12] = What is visible in the identity under development is what is left behind as sediment in the subject's history. It does not translate its entirety but only what has survived. The narrative identity as what has survived is the outcome of the subject's potential. It is what has been allowed by the developmental constraints beyond the conflicts encountered. The narrative identity is therefore still full of the past failures of the developmental process. This is not the best solution – which indeed may forever remain unattained – but only the achieved one. This process of sedimentation, which is dependent on the subject's resources and constraints and on his or her history, which may be found in his or her narratives, is reflected in the life themes, in the character arc, in the plot, and in the "glue" that connects these events in the construction of the sense of self. However, the narrative identity is also underpinned by the promise of self-realization. Finally, the promise of being faithful to oneself as another is the engine that leads to change in the counseling process. This promise can change the course of the plot and the role of characters, provided that it is strong enough to be kept.

[13] = Finally, the bicycle as identity is balance in motion. The paradox of identity is expressed here because balance is related to movement only because it is constantly challenged by it. Movement is thus both an engine for change and for stability. Similarly, identity is stabilized and developed by confrontation with others. As Butler says, "the I is always to some extent dispossessed by the social conditions of its emergence" (Butler, 2005, p. 8). The conflict with others, with the institution, the body, and one's own consciousness leads individuals to keep the promise of the future.

Chapter 6
From Narratives to Action and a Life Design Approach

Mark Watson[1] and Mary McMahon[2]

[1]Department of Psychology, Nelson Mandela Metropolitan University, Port Elizabeth, South Africa
[2]School of Education, The University of Queensland, Brisbane, Australia

Introduction

The subtitle for this handbook, *From Practice to Theory and From Theory to Practice*, reflects a long-standing tension between the more rapid development of career theory and the slower concomitant development of practice models. Indeed, throughout the history of career psychology, there has been a binary relationship between theory and its practical application, counseling. While there have been calls for the field to move from theory to practice, to let career clients' voices determine what model serves them best, the reality remains that theory is more comprehensively described than practice and that theoretical models have invariably been regarded as what Savickas (2010, p. xi) refers to as "recipes." Thus, although our theoretical understanding of career behavior advances and increasingly reflects changes in the global world of work, our ability to translate such theoretical developments into practical tools for career counselors lags behind.

Toward the end of the last century and dominating the present century, several theoretical perspectives emerged in career psychology, resulting in a shift in focus toward a narrative metaphor in career counseling that is embedded in postmodern, constructivist, and social constructionist approaches. Such approaches emphasize a collaborative relationship between the career counselor and the client, in which the focus is on making personal meaning and moving the client toward an action-oriented approach (Patton, 2007). The translation of such approaches into "everyday language conversations between career counsellors and their clients" (Watson & Kuit, 2007, p. 80) is less advanced, however.

The movement of career theory and practice in the present century has been toward an emphasis on the concepts of meaning, identity, and mattering, and away from the 20th century focus on facts and personality (Patton, 2007). This is typified in different forms of narrative career counseling that have subsequently emerged in more recent decades – for example, narrative career counseling (Cochran, 1997); sociodynamic counseling (Peavy, 1998); active engagement (Amundson, 2009); self-construction (Guichard, 2009); life design (Savickas et al., 2009); action theory (Young et al., 2011); chaos theory of careers (Pryor & Bright, 2011); and storytelling (McMahon & Watson, 2012a). Thus narrative career counseling has been described as "one of many identities in the multistoried profession of career counselling" (McMahon, 2007, p. 63). There has been a sustained interest in narrative career counseling approaches, which Del Corso and Rehfuss (2011) believe are "the key to helping individuals adapt in a transitory, ever-changing workplace" (p. 334). Narrative career counseling approaches regard career clients as capable of actively constructing stories that shape their identity by placing emphasis on the constructs of connectedness, meaning making, and agency (McMahon & Watson, 2012a).

Such constructs are indicative of the shift toward more holistic conceptualizations of career theory and the central role of individuals in constructing their careers. Indeed the broad range of career development theories, the consequent need to recognize the significant contributions of all theories, the possibility of convergence between theories or, alternatively, the proposal of a metatheory have been issues in the field for over 2 decades (e.g., Savickas & Lent, 1994). The subsequent proposal of two metatheories, career construction theory (CCT; Savickas, 2002, 2013) and the systems theory framework (STF; McMahon, & Patton, 1995; Patton & McMahon, 1999, 2006) of career development, represents attempts to address such issues. Importantly in the context of this chapter, the developers of these metatheories advocate moving from theory to practice through theory-based narrative approaches to career counseling. CCT is operationalized by its career construction interview approach to career counselling (Savickas, 2013), which incorporates narratability as a goal of intervention. More recently, CCT is one of a number of theories, including self-construction theory (Guichard, 2009), that have informed the life design model for career intervention (Savickas et al., 2009) that is the focus of this book. The STF is operationalized by the systemic storytelling approach to career counseling (McMahon & Watson, 2012a) and by it qualitative career assessment instrument, My System of Career Influences (MSCI), in its adolescent (McMahon, Patton, & Watson, 2005) and adult (McMahon, Watson, & Patton, 2013) versions. With their emphases on story and on clients constructing their careers in context, the STF applications could also be considered in relation to life design. Indeed, Savickas (2012) argues that the qualitative career assessment instruments of the STF are consistent with the life design paradigm for career intervention.

The authors of life design consider one of their next steps to be the development of "ways to use it in life-design counseling" (Savickas et al., 2009, p. 249). However, perhaps reflecting the early stage in the development of life design, Savickas et al. (2009) also describe life design in their seminal article as a "paradigm for career construction" (p. 239), a "model for career intervention" (p. 239), a "framework for counseling" (p. 239), and as a "new paradigm for counseling" (p. 241). Subsequently Savickas (2012) described life design as a "conceptual model for career counseling" (p. 14). Thus the literature on life design is still in the process of conceptual refinement and embryonic practical application at this point in time. For instance, the life design team has described developing counseling methods and materials as "high on the agenda" of their next steps (Savickas et al., 2009, p. 249), and they recognize that existing techniques and tools are suitable for life design counseling.

It is against this background of the emergence of life design that it seems timely in the present chapter to overview the movement from theory to practice of both life design and the STF. The life design approach is described in greater detail elsewhere in this handbook (see Chapters 2 and 4). The motivation for seeking convergence between differing career counseling approaches already exists. For instance, Cochran (2007) has suggested that drawing "from various constructivist theories might enrich practice" (Cochran, 2007, p. 18). Within the perspective of career counseling as a multistoried profession, the present chapter considers potential convergence and divergence between life design and the systemic approaches to career counseling and assessment underpinned by the STF (Patton & McMahon, 2006).

Life Design

Life design is considered the newest model in the movement toward narrative career counseling (Savickas et al., 2009). Its formulation in the present century as a career counseling approach that constructs and deconstructs smaller stories and then reconstructs them into a major narrative that assists career counselors and clients to co-construct a future narrative is consistent with other narrative approaches (e.g., Maree, 2007). Thus, as with other narrative approaches, life design seeks the patterns or themes that provide meaning to individuals' life-career stories (Hartung, 2010).

There are several critical aspects of life design (Savickas et al., 2009) that can be considered in relation to the issue of convergence with other narrative career counseling models. These include life design's basic framework, goals, and five presuppositions, which have been described in detail elsewhere in this book (see Chapter 4 and Chapter 10). However, we briefly reiterate them here for the purpose of considering possible convergence and divergence between life design and the STF and its practical applications. The framework for life design emanates from its theoretical underpinning in career construction and self-construction theories. This framework thus suggests a life-long, holistic, contextual, and preventive perspective on life design interventions. Consistent with this framework, the goals of life design interventions are to increase clients' adaptability, narratability, activity, and intentionality (Savickas et al., 2009).

Stemming from this theoretical framework and the goals of life design are five presuppositions that underpin life design interventions. An important point of convergence with other narrative approaches, including STF applications, is the life design presupposition that career counseling needs to move "from scientific facts to narrative realities" (Savickas et al., 2009, p. 243). Indeed, Savickas (2013) argues that narrative is critical both as a process and as an outcome in life design interventions, that "stories carry the career" (Savickas, 2013, p. 148).

Essentially, life design's presuppositions relate to individuals and their work lives in the context of a changing economy and society. Reflecting concerns about the adequacy of traditional trait-based career counseling to meet the needs of career clients in the 21st century, two further presuppositions concern the need to take greater account of context and to move "from prescription to process" (Savickas et al., 2009, p. 242) – that is, to take greater account of how clients have constructed their lives. This broader perspective requires a move "from linear causality to non-linear dynamics" (Savickas et al., 2009, p. 243). The final presupposition of life design considers the need to move evaluation in career counseling away from standardized approaches. Having briefly outlined the life design framework, goals and presuppositions, the following subsection considers how the life design paradigm may be applied in practice.

Life Design: From Theory to Practice

In general, constructivist and social constructionist career literature is more conceptual than practical, leaving career counselors with few practice models within these more esoteric theoretical frameworks (McMahon, Watson, Chetty, & Hoelson, 2012b; Reid, 2006). While the absence of a "story of application" from most constructivist and social constructionist career counseling approaches may well reflect the constructivist philosophy of not prescribing models and techniques to practitioners, in reality there remains a need to move such theory toward practice. This Savickas et al. (2009) have attempted to do with their life design approach.

Central to CCT and the life design approach to career counseling is the concept of career adaptability (Savickas, 2013; Savickas et al., 2009). Indeed career adaptability has provided a starting point for the development of instruments to operationalize life design in practice. Specifically, the life design team has worked closely with international researchers to develop the Career Adapt-Abilities Scale (CAAS; Porfeli & Savickas, 2012). This instrument, however, is quantitative in nature because of its foundation in logical positivist philosophy, which sees it operationalized in terms of *scores* rather than as *stories* as life design advocates. Further research needs to consider how the CAAS may be qualitatively used within a life design intervention that is primarily narrative in focus.

In this regard, a starting point has been ventured by McMahon, Watson, and Bimrose (2012), who qualitatively considered career adaptability in the narratives of three older women. These authors demonstrated that individuals' stories and their associated reflexive processes may provide a means for qualitatively understanding career adaptability in clients' lives. Inviting individuals to tell a story of their most significant transition, for instance, was suggested as a useful technique for qualitatively exploring career adaptability. Importantly, in the context of the life design presuppositions, framework, and aims, these authors demonstrated that career adaptability was contextually located and involved a recursive reflexive process in which the women responded to internal and external influences.

Drawing on its theoretical bases in CCT (Savickas, 2013) and self-construction (Guichard, 2009), life design interventions largely rely on a process of encouraging clients to narrate autobiographical stories and to identify the themes that emerge from these stories (Savickas, 2012, 2013). There are three steps to counseling related to this process: the construction and deconstruction of a career story with a client, the reconstruction of the story in terms of an occupational plot and a career theme, and the co-construction with the career counselor of the next episode or chapter in the client's story. Construction encourages clients to tell vocational stories about how they have constructed themselves in terms of their career development. Deconstruction allows clients to explore misconceptions they may have about their career development. Reconstruction describes the counseling process in which clients' career stories are themed into a macronarrative or what Savickas calls "a grand story" (Savickas, 2013, p. 170). Co-construction involves the client and the career counselor considering the client's grand narrative and editing it towards a future story. These three steps are common to most narrative career interventions including the systemic storytelling and qualitative career assessment approaches informed by the STF (Patton & McMahon, 2006) of career development. The STF will now be briefly overviewed, followed by a discussion of its systemic applications.

Systems Theory Framework of Career Development

The STF (McMahon & Patton, 1995; Patton & McMahon, 1999, 2006) of career development, like CCT, has been proposed as a metatheoretical framework. It describes traditional influences identified by career theory, research, and practice as well as nontraditional influences that may impact on individual career development. These influences are regarded as reflecting both content and process components of career development. Consistent with the systems theory origins of this metatheory, individuals are regarded as open systems subject to influence from the broader systems in which they live. Content influences consist of intrapersonal influences (such as personality, gender, age) and contextual influences of the social system (such as family and peers) and the environmental-societal system (such as socioeconomic status and geographic location). Process influences comprise recursiveness (described as the interaction within and between influences), change over time, and chance.

The STF emphasizes the "individual in context" and the inseparability of the two. It considers career development as dynamic in its emphasis on the recursive processes of interaction between influences, change over time, and chance. Core constructs of systems theory and the STF are wholes and parts, patterns and rules, acausality, recursiveness, discontinuous change, open and closed systems, abduction (reasoning based on patterns and relationships), and story (for details, see Patton & McMahon, 1999, 2006). These inform its practical applications.

Practical Applications of the STF

Just as life design is moving beyond core constructs and theoretical understanding, so too has the STF (McMahon & Patton, 1995; Patton & McMahon, 1999, 2006) of career development moved toward its own "story of application" through the development of a systemic narrative career counseling approach, storytelling (McMahon & Watson, 2012b), and qualitative career assessment instruments, such as the MSCI (McMahon et al., 2005, 2013), both of which facilitate a process of systemic reflection and storytelling. Indeed, McMahon and Patton (2006) describe the STF as a conceptual and practical map that can guide career interventions.

The storytelling approach to narrative career counseling is based on the theoretical constructs of the individual, systemic thinking, recursiveness, and story that emanate from its foundation in the STF (McMahon, 2005). At a more practical level, career counselors facilitate the counseling relationship and connectedness through the use of story (McMahon, 2005). Connectedness is a multileveled recursive construct that relates to interaction between clients and counselors, clients and their systemic influences, and career counselors and their own systemic influences. Indeed, storytelling's parent framework, the STF, specifically describes recursiveness as the process of interaction within and between influences which are visually presented in both the STF and the MSCI. As with other narrative approaches, including life design, the storytelling approach regards connectedness, meaning making, and agency as core process constructs that emanate from its systemic foundation (McMahon, 2005). Distinguishing storytelling from other narrative approaches is its explicit inclusion of learning and reflection as core process constructs (McMahon, 2005). Despite Krumboltz's (1996) claim over a decade ago that a goal of career counseling is to facilitate learning that enables clients to "create a satisfying life within a constantly changing work environment" (Krumboltz, 1996, p. 75), learning has not been an explicit feature of most narrative approaches.

The life design team has called for research on how to further career counselors' "narrative competence" (Savickas et al., 2009, p. 249). Similarly, Reid (2006) recommends finding ways of assisting career counselors to "do" narrative career counseling, and Heppner and Heppner (2003) have called for research into the process of career counseling. To this end, preliminary research has been conducted on how the five core process constructs of the storytelling approach are operationalized in the storytelling approach to narrative career counselling (McMahon, Watson, Chetty, & Hoelson, 2012a). An important outcome of this research was that the process constructs, in practice, were found to be recursively related. Thus, although process constructs may be viewed as discrete and could be taught as such in order to enhance "narrative competence," in practice, it is their recursive relationship that facilitates a holistic narrative career counseling process. These authors proposed six tentative suggestions for narrative career counsellors: (1) provide a space for reflection, (2) listen deeply for clues in client stories, (3) use the clues to construct brief responses or invitations to tell further stories, (4) assist clients to identify and make explicit the themes and patterns in their stories, (5) connect previously disconnected stories through the identification of themes and patterns, and (6) incorporate themes and patterns as "ingredients" of future stories. These suggestions position both clients and counselors as learners in a reflective learning space, and thus their roles are conceptualized differently from other narrative approaches. For example, the career construction interview sees career counselors asking a predetermined set of questions and providing considerable reflection to clients on the stories they tell in response to these questions; thus career counselors remain to some extent in an expert role even though clients participate more in this approach than in traditional test and tell approaches. By contrast, as learners, career counselors using the storytelling approach base their questions on what clients say and invite greater reflection from clients. Thus they encourage clients to become agentic in the career counseling process. Both the storytelling approach and life design respect and encourage the client's personal agency in enacting their career plans.

In applying the storytelling approach to narrative career counseling, McMahon and Watson (2012a) suggest that career counselors employ "recursive curiosity" and "recursive deep listening" (McMahon & Watson, 2012a, p. 222). These authors consider the recursive process constructs of the storytelling approach and provide examples of three levels of story-crafting questions related to each of the process constructs that career counselors could consider to assist clients to craft stories. Essentially, Level 1 questions focus on facts and content; Level 2 questions focus on subjective experience, interactive processes, and connectedness; and Level 3 questions focus on themes, patterns, and future stories. It is beyond the scope of the present chapter to explain the levels in detail, and readers are referred to the reference list.

There is a history in career psychology of assessment that has been grounded in theory, a history that has predominantly reflected the quantitative assessment of key theoretical constructs. To a lesser extent, narrative approaches to career counseling have also stimulated the use and development of qualitative assessment interventions. However, concern has been expressed that qualitative career assessment instruments are seldom grounded in theory and that there is little research to support their utility (Stebleton, 2010). The STF application, the MSCI (McMahon et al., 2005, 2013), is an example of a qualitative career assessment process that is theoretically grounded, has been rigorously trialed internationally, and has a developing research base.

The MSCI is a reflection process that applies core constructs of its STF theoretical foundation (i.e., the individual, systemic thinking, recursiveness, and story) in a storytelling approach (McMahon & Watson, 2012a). As such, it responds to more recent career theory developments, in its exploration of individuals' contextual influences that may impact on their career development. With its emphasis on holistic and storied approaches to career counseling, the MSCI in its adolescent and adult versions provides a useful stimulus for narrative career counseling.

The MSCI encourages individuals to story their career development through exploring the systems of career influences in their lives and how such influences recursively interrelate (McMahon et al., 2005, 2013). Both the adolescent and adult versions of the MSCI encourage clients to tell their career stories through a step-by-step process in a booklet that sequentially guides them to contextually map their career development over time, to reflect on their map, and to develop an action plan. As such, the developers of the MSCI regard it as providing an active learning process for clients in which they can explore the recursive interaction of their systems of influence. The versatility of this narrative reflection process has been demonstrated in career education interventions in schools (Watson & McMahon, 2006), in career counseling (Watson & McMahon, 2009) and in the training of career counselors. The adult version of the MSCI encourages career exploration, especially in times of career transitions brought on by work restructuring, retrenchment, or dissatisfaction with present working conditions.

A challenge in narrative career counseling has been how to incorporate career assessment. This has been investigated by McMahon et al. (2012b) in relation to the storytelling approach to career counseling with non-Western clients. In particular, the integration of the MSCI and a career values card sort into the storytelling approach was investigated. Results offered support for the guidelines for incorporating career assessment into career counseling proffered by McMahon and Patton (2002). In addition, the results demonstrated how the five recursive process constructs of the storytelling approach – that is connectedness, reflection, meaning making, learning, and agency – were facilitated through the integration of career assessment and narrative career counseling.

The vexed issue of how traditional quantitative career assessment may be employed is central to the challenge of incorporating assessment in narrative career counseling. To this end, an Integrative Structured Interview (ISI) process has been proposed for incorporating quantitative career assessment such as the Self-Directed Search (SDS; Holland, 1997) and a career values card sort into the storytelling approach to narrative career counseling (McMahon & Watson, 2012b; Watson & McMahon, 2014). The ISI process is a series of 13 story-crafting questions structured in six sections. The story-crafting questions of the ISI process operationalize the elements of the SDS as well as the five recursive process constructs of the storytelling approach (McMahon & Watson, 2012b). A similar ISI process has been proposed to incorporate a career values card sort into the storytelling approach to career counseling (Watson & McMahon, 2014). In essence, the story-crafting questions of the ISI facilitate a qualitative exploration of the results of a quantitative career assessment instrument; specifically, quantitative assessment is incorporated into a narrative process.

As described in the previous section, the STF has stimulated a body of research and conceptualization about "doing" narrative career counseling. In the spirit of international collaboration, we now consider convergence and divergence between STF-informed applications and the life design model of career intervention.

Life Design, the STF, and Their Practical Applications: Considering Convergence and Divergence

Constructivist and narrative approaches in career psychology have arisen mainly out of a need to ensure that career counseling remains relevant in the 21st century (McMahon et al., 2012a). The history of newer movements in career psychology such as life design and the practical applications of the STF illustrate how the field responds quickly with the subsequent development of numerous variations along the same story theme. Thus the field is presently experiencing a proliferation of narrative career counseling approaches. There is far greater scope for convergence in these latest developments, however, than with theoretical developments of the last century, given that narrative career counseling approaches share similar conceptual processes. For instance, common to most narrative approaches is their emphasis on storytelling and their definition of clients as active agents who co-construct with the career counselor a future career story (Patton & McMahon, 2006). Seeking convergence within career narrative approaches – for example, through the life design paradigm – would not only ensure a new identity for the field (Watson & McMahon, 2005) but possibly a shared identity or a grand narrative as well.

Divergence, however, between narrative career counseling approaches highlights the strengths and unique contributions of each discrete approach and allows for the development of local narratives. This is evident in the storytelling approach, where research is being conducted with non-Western populations (McMahon et al., 2012a, 2012b). Indeed, the intentional use of the term *storytelling* as the name of the approach is responsive to oral traditions found in non-Western and Western populations. A further example of divergence between storytelling and life design is storytelling's emphasis on learning and reflection as core process constructs. While reflection is common to all narrative approaches including life design, its specific and explicit inclusion as a core construct in storytelling intentionally signals the integral part it plays in narrative career counseling. Learning, as another point of divergence between storytelling and life design, has been present as a relevant construct in career theory throughout its history, but it has seldom been explicitly included in career counseling. Learning acknowledges the new knowledge created by clients through the meaning-making process of construction, deconstruction, and co-construction, and positions the roles of counselors and clients differently from other narrative approaches including life design.

There is certainly room to explore the convergence of practical applications of the STF and a life design paradigm. Savickas (2013) himself has suggested that CCT, a foundation of life design, should make use of other forms of career assessment including quantitative assessment such as Holland's (1997) SDS, as the present authors have already done with their ISI process (McMahon & Watson, 2012b; Watson & McMahon, 2014). It is in this spirit that the present authors explore the potential utility of using the MSCI within a life design approach. McMahon et al. (2012b) have described the life design paradigm as enabling "individuals' narrative life stories to feature in the construction of contextually embedded career plans" (McMahon et al., 2012b, p. 6).

Both the storytelling approach and life design recognize the designing of a life story within the realities of a client's context. The storytelling approach, stimulated by the MSCI, provides a rich, integrated, and interrelated description of systemic influences that impact on the career construction process. Moreover, the MSCI facilitators' guide (McMahon et al., 2013) provides practical learning activities to develop clients' abilities to engage in systemic thinking, offers a framework and guided process for identifying these influences, and engages clients in visual, auditory, and kinesthetic learning processes. Life design's emphasis on the relational and contextual nature of career counseling and process could be supported by the detailed descriptions and rich stories developed through the MSCI storytelling process. Moreover, the MSCI's accommodation of a range of learning styles represents a divergence from life design, which to date, is primarily a discursive process.

The core constructs underpinning the STF, storytelling, and the MSCI reflection process are closely related to the framework, goals, and aims of the life design paradigm, suggesting potential convergence between the two approaches. Indeed, Savickas suggests that the life design paradigm shares the same goal as the MSCI in prompting "meaningful activities that further self-making, identity shaping and career constructing" (Savickas, 2012, p. 15). In this regard, the MSCI assists clients to identify relational and contextual factors and portray them as a holistic diagram reflecting their past, present, and future influences. This diagram then provides a basis for a storytelling process in which autobiographical stories are constructed, guided by the MSCI map (McMahon & Patton 2006). Indeed, the process of identifying influences and representing them visually on an MSCI diagram represents a process of deconstruction, reconstruction, and co-construction consistent with life design (Savickas, 2012). The MSCI also allows for further deconstruction, reconstruction, and co-construction by providing clients with a second opportunity at a later stage of their career narrative to return to earlier reflections of their career influences and reedit these interrelated influences in relation to where they presently perceive their career narrative to be.

Life design interventions encourage clients to be proactive in their career narratives and, together with the career counselor, develop intentional actions that move them toward their preferred futures. Similarly, the career counseling goal of the MSCI is to provide an applied reflective process that offers concrete steps that encourage clients to implement an intentional plan of action. Using the MSCI in conjunction with life design should allow for an in-depth exploration of the dynamics of systemic influences, and an unpacking and repacking of the recursive nature of systemic influences. The ISI process (McMahon & Watson, 2012b; Watson & McMahon, 2014), stimulated by a desire to qualitatively use quantitative career assessment in the storytelling approach and also to avoid an unnecessary divide between quantitative career assessment and narrative career counseling, represents a further potential convergence with life design interventions.

Nothing however is new. Shakespeare, long before the advent of life design or the STF of career development, concluded that "the web of our life is of a mingled yarn." Life is the weaving together of many contextual influences that impact on it, as well as individuals' responses to such influences. Sometimes, to understand the "mingled" nature of our career narrative we have to unpick and reweave it into a more cohesive yarn. Both the STF and life design share this understanding of self-development in career development. To some extent, they share the perception that "a self is built from the outside in, not from the inside out as personality trait theorists would have it" (Savickas, 2013, p. 155).

Conclusion

The issue of convergence in career psychology is not a new one (see Savickas & Lent, 1994). There is a long-standing debate about finding ways to consolidate seemingly diverse approaches in theoretical conceptualization and practice models in the discipline of career psychology. Common to most narrative approaches to career counseling is their emphasis on a holistic approach that allows for the exploration of the complexities embedded in individuals' career stories. Both life design and the STF and its practical applications share much conceptual background – for instance, story is fundamental to both life design and the STF.

McMahon (2006) suggests that there are as many stories about career counseling as there are career counselors in practice and that career counselors need to "make meaning" of their counseling practice as much as their career clients need to make sense of their individual stories. Making meaning for career counselors may involve adopting a personal approach to narrative career counseling that considers an eclectic mix of narrative interventions suited to their clients. For example, a life design approach which is a more recent development in narrative career counseling could benefit from incorporating the practical applications of the STF which was first proposed almost 2 decades ago.

White (1995) uses the term *landscape of action* (p. 31) to suggest that a story is only as complete as much as it includes all the significant parts. This chapter has described the significant introduction of life design into the narrative career counseling landscape and how the development of the STF, storytelling, and the MSCI may converge with life design so that the fullest possible landscape can be considered. While a metanarrative for the field such as life design has the potential to synthesize core constructs relevant to all narrative approaches, the divergences highlighted in the present chapter emphasize the need for, and continued contribution of, discrete approaches such as those emanating from the STF that can bring unique and specialized foci to the field. The chapter suggests that there is a need for the field to consider both metanarrative and discrete career counseling approaches in order to most fully explore clients' career landscapes.

References

Amundson, N. E. (2009). *Active engagement: Enhancing the career counselling process* (3rd ed.). Richmond, Canada: Ergon Communications.

Cochran, L. (1997). *Career counselling: A narrative approach*. Thousand Oaks, CA: Sage.

Cochran, L. (2007). The promise of narrative career counselling. In K. Maree (Ed.), *Shaping the story* (pp. 7–19). Pretoria, South Africa: Van Schaik.

Del Corso, J., & Rehfuss, M. C. (2011). The role of narrative in career construction theory. *Journal of Vocational Behavior, 79,* 334–339. http://doi.org/10.1016/j.jvb.2011.04.003

Guichard, J. (2009). Self-constructing. *Journal of Vocational Behavior, 75,* 251–258. http://doi.org/10.1016/j.jvb.2009.03.004

Hartung, P. J. (2010). Career assessment: Using scores and stories in life designing. In K. Maree (Ed.), *Career counselling: Methods that work* (pp. 1–10). Cape Town, South Africa: Juta.

Heppner, M. J., & Heppner, P. P. (2003). Identifying process variables in career counseling: A research agenda. *Journal of Vocational Behavior, 62,* 429–452. http://doi.org/10.1016/S0001-8791(02)00053-2

Holland, J. L. (1997). *Making vocational choices: A theory of vocational personalities and work environments* (3rd ed.). Odessa, FL: Psychological Assessment Resources.

Krumboltz, J. D. (1996). A learning theory of career counseling. In M. L. Savickas & W. B. Walsh (Eds.), *Handbook of career counseling theory and practice* (pp. 55–80). Palo Alto, CA: Davies Black.

Maree, K. (2007). (Ed). *Shaping the story*. Pretoria, South Africa: Van Schaik.

McMahon, M. (2005). Career counseling: Applying the Systems Theory Framework of career development. *Journal of Employment Counseling, 42,* 29–38. http://doi.org/10.1002/j.2161-1920.2005.tb00896.x

McMahon, M. (2006). Working with story tellers: A metaphor for career counselling. In M. McMahon & W. Patton (Eds.), *Career counselling: Constructivist approaches* (pp. 16–29). Abingdon, UK: Routledge.

McMahon, M. (2007). Life story counselling: Producing new identities in career counselling. In K. Maree (Ed.), *Shaping the story* (pp. 63–72). Pretoria, South Africa: Van Schaik.

McMahon, M., & Patton, W. (1995). Development of a systems theory of career development. *Australian Journal of Career Development, 4,* 15–20. http://doi.org/10.1177/103841629500400207

McMahon, M., & Patton, W. (2002). Using qualitative assessment in career counselling. *International Journal of Educational and Vocational Guidance, 2,* 51–66. http://doi.org/10.1023/A:1014283407496

McMahon, M., & Patton, W. (2006). The Systems Theory Framework: A conceptual and practical map for career counselling. In M. McMahon & W. Patton (Eds.), *Career counselling: Constructivist approaches* (pp. 94–109). Abingdon, UK: Routledge.

McMahon, M., Patton, W., & Watson, M. (2005). *My System of Career Influences (MSCI): Work booklet*. Melbourne, Australia: Australian Council for Educational Research.

McMahon, M., & Watson, M. (2012a). Story crafting: Strategies for facilitating narrative career counselling. *International Journal for Educational and Vocational Guidance, 12,* 211–224. http://doi.org/10.1007/s10775-012-9228-5

McMahon, M., & Watson, M. (2012b). Telling stories of career assessment. *Journal of Career Assessment, 20*, 440–451. http://doi.org/10.1177/1069072712448999

McMahon, M., Watson, M., & Bimrose, J. (2012). Career adaptability: A qualitative understanding from the stories of older women. *Journal of Vocational Behavior, 80*, 762–768. http://doi.org/10.1016/j.jvb.2012.01.016

McMahon, M., Watson, M., Chetty, C., & Hoelson, C. (2012a). Examining process constructs of narrative career counselling: An exploratory case study. *British Journal of Guidance and Counselling, 40*, 127–141. http://doi.org/10.1080/03069885.2011.646949

McMahon, M., Watson, M., Chetty, C., & Hoelson, C. (2012b). Story telling, career assessment and career counselling. *South African Journal of Higher Education, 26*, 729–741.

McMahon, M., Watson, M. B., & Patton, W. (2013). *My System of Career Influences (MSCI) (Adult Version): Work booklet*. Brisbane, Australia: Australian Academic Press.

Patton, W. (2007). Theoretical underpinnings and practical application of constructivist approaches to career counselling. In K. Maree (Ed.), *Shaping the story* (pp. 121–133). Pretoria, South Africa: Van Schaik.

Patton, W., & McMahon, M. (1999). *Career development and systems theory: A new relationship*. Pacific Grove, CA: Brooks/Cole.

Patton, W., & McMahon, M. (2006). *Career development and systems theory: Connecting theory and practice* (2nd ed.). Rotterdam, The Netherlands: Sense.

Peavy, R. V. (1998). *Sociodynamic counselling: A constructivist perspective*. Victoria, Canada: Trafford.

Porfeli, E., & Savickas, M. L. (2012). Career Adapt-Abilities Scale – USA Form: Psychometric properties and relation to vocational identity. *Journal of Vocational Behavior, 80*, 748–753. http://doi.org/10.1016/j.jvb.2012.01.009

Pryor, R. G. L., & Bright, J. E. H. (2011). *The Chaos Theory of careers: A new perspective on working in the twenty-first century*. New York, NY: Routledge.

Reid, H. L. (2006). Usefulness and truthfulness: Outlining the limitations and upholding the benefits of constructivist approaches for career counselling. In M. McMahon & W. Patton (Eds.), *Career counselling: Constructivist approaches* (pp. 17–29). Abingdon, UK: Routledge.

Savickas, M. L. (2002). Career construction: A developmental theory of vocational behavior. In D. Brown & Associates (Eds.), *Career choice and development* (4th ed., pp. 149–205). San Francisco, CA: Jossey-Bass.

Savickas, M. L. (2010). Foreword: Best practices in career intervention. In K. Maree (Ed.), *Career counselling: Methods that work* (pp. xi–xii). Cape Town, South Africa: Juta.

Savickas, M. L. (2012). Life design: A paradigm for career intervention in the 21st century. *Journal of Counseling and Development, 90*, 13–19. http://doi.org/10.1111/j.1556-6676.2012.00002.x

Savickas, M. L. (2013). Career construction theory and practice. In R. W. Lent & S. D. Brown (Eds.), *Career development and counseling: Putting theory and research to work* (2nd ed., pp. 147–193). Hoboken, NJ: Wiley.

Savickas, M. L., & Lent, R. W. (1994). *Convergence in career development theories: Implications for science and practice*. Palo Alto, CA: CPP Books.

Savickas, M. L., Nota, L., Rossier, J., Dauwalder, J.-P., Duarte, M. E., Guichard, J., . . . van Vianen, A. E. M. (2009). Life designing: A paradigm for career construction in the 21st century. *Journal of Vocational Behavior, 75*, 239–250. http://doi.org/10.1016/j.jvb.2009.04.004

Stebleton, M. J. (2010). Narrative-based career counseling perspectives in times of change: An analysis of strengths and limitations. *Journal of Employment Counseling, 47*, 64–78. http://doi.org/10.1002/j.2161-1920.2010.tb00091.x

Watson, M., & Kuit, W. (2007). Postmodern career counselling and beyond. In K. Maree (Ed.), *Shaping the story* (pp. 73–86). Pretoria, South Africa: Van Schaik.

Watson, M., & McMahon, M. (2005). Postmodern (narrative) career counselling and education [Editorial]. *Perspectives in Education, 23*, vii-ix.

Watson, M., & McMahon, M. (2006). My System of Career Influences: Responding to challenges facing career education. *International Journal for Educational and Vocational Guidance, 6*, 159–166. http://doi.org/10.1007/s10775-006-9105-1

Watson, M., & McMahon, M. (2009). Career counselling in South African higher education: Moving forward systemically and qualitatively. *South African Journal of Higher Education, 23*, 470–481.

Watson, M., & McMahon, M. (2014). Making meaning of quantitative assessment in career counseling through a story-telling approach. In G. Arulmani, A. Bakshi, F. Leong, & T. Watts (Eds.), *Handbook of career development: International perspectives*. New York, NY: Springer.

White, M. (1995). *Re-authoring lives: Interviews and essays*. Adelaide, Australia: Dulwich Centre.

Young, R. A., Marshall, S. K., Valach, L., Domene, J. F., Graham, M. D., & Zaidman-Zait, A. (2011). *Transition to adulthood: Action, projects, and counseling*. New York, NY: Springer. http://doi.org/10.1007/978-1-4419-6238-6

Part III
Life Design Across the Life Span

Chapter 7
Life Design in Childhood: Antecedents and Advancement

Paul J. Hartung

Department of Family and Community Medicine, Northeast Ohio Medical University,
Rootstown, OH, USA

Introduction

Life design – a life-long, holistic, contextual, and preventive process of shaping the self through work and relationships (Savickas et al., 2009) – begins in childhood (Ginzberg, Ginsburg, Axelrad, & Herma, 1951; Gottfredson, 1996; Hartung, Porfeli, & Vondracek, 2005; Savickas, 2011a; Super, 1957; Vondracek, Lerner, & Schulenberg, 1986; Watson & McMahon, 2005). Intended to better account for contemporary conditions affecting life and work in the digital age, life design posits that individuals begin making themselves into the persons they want to become from their earliest years of life through interaction with the social world (Guichard, 2005; Savickas, 2011a). They then, in time, may use work to make their lives more meaningful to themselves and of greater consequence to others. With self-construction at its core (Guichard, 2005; Savickas, 2009), life design represents a third paradigm for career studies and career intervention emergent in the 21st century to take its place alongside the vocational guidance (Holland, 1959, 1997; Parsons, 1909) and career development (Super, 1957, 1990) paradigms that predominated during the 20th century.

Considering life design as a paradigm and practice for constructing careers in the 21st century, as it applies to the childhood years, forms the purpose of the present chapter. Recognizing that life design views self-construction through work and relationships as a life-long endeavor, the chapter begins by describing childhood antecedents of this process. A review of established theory and research indicates that the childhood years typically first arouse and shape curiosities, fantasies, interests, and capacities central to life designing as children playfully construct possible future selves projected in work and other social roles (Hartung et al., 2005; Super, 1990). Building upon this work, the chapter then considers career construction principles and practices (Hartung, 2013b; Savickas, 2011a, 2013) as a way to understand and advance life design during the childhood years. A prime exemplar of using the life design paradigm, career construction theory and counseling comprehends and fosters self-making through work and relationships toward achieving life design's core goals of activity, adaptability, narratability, and intentionality. Concluding comments and future directions for advancing life design in childhood close the chapter.

Childhood Origins of Life Design: Theory and Research Perspectives

Traditionally, career theory and research has emphasized the adolescent and adult age periods, with less attention to childhood (Hartung et al., 2005; McMahon & Watson, 2008; Vondracek, 2001). Nonetheless, both established theoretical statements and empirical research findings support a central role of childhood in the core life design processes of activity, adaptability, narratability, and intentionality. The childhood antecedents of life design trace most directly to developmentally based theories that inform life design processes ranging from those of Super (1957) to Gottfredson (1996, 2002). Likewise, reviews of the empirical literature indicate that factors central to life design, such as vocational exploration, career awareness, occupational aspirations, and expectations, vocational interests, and career adaptability begin during the childhood years (Hartung et al., 2005; Watson & McMahon, 2005). Considering these theoretical and research perspectives in turn indicates childhood antecedents of life design.

Theoretical Perspectives

Precursors of life design as a life-long process most prominently include established developmentally based career theories. Taking a life-span perspective, Super (1957, 1990), Ginzberg, Ginsburg, Axelrad, and Herma (1951), and also Havighurst (1951) conceived of childhood as the launching point of an enduring process of vocational development characterized by stages and associated developmental tasks. Combined, such developmental perspectives on career give support to the enduring nature of life design over the life course. Other examples of theories antecedent to the life design paradigm include Gottfredson's (2002) contextually based approach and select person–environment fit models.

Life-Span, Life-Space Theory

Life-span, life-space theory (Hartung, 2013c; Super, 1990) stands out among established career theories that support childhood as a formative life design period. Within this theory, the life stage of career growth, renamed *orientation* in career construction theory (see Savickas, 2013), spans the childhood years and concentrates on the goal of forming an initial and realistic vocational self-concept, in part by identifying with significant others. The budding vocational self-concept reflects the child's formative answer to the question, who am I? in a mental representation of personal strengths, limitations, interests, values, abilities, talents, and personality traits. This self-concept contains the child's public picture and private purpose about the future role of work in her or his life. Society expects that opportunities and experiences afforded at home, play, and school will arouse the child's curiosities, fantasies, interests, and capacities to begin constructing a viable self to be enacted in roles within work, family, community, leisure, and other life domains.

In Super's original model, early childhood fantasy, involving role-play to explore the meanings and possibilities of work, eventually gives way in later childhood to interests and capacities that guide aspirations, activity selection, and career planning. Growth substages for children deal with acquiring rudimentary career adaptability that comprises having concern about the future, control over decision making, curiosity to explore occupations, and confidence to deal with career barriers (Hartung, Porfeli, & Vondracek, 2008; Savickas, 1997;

Savickas & Super, 1993). Children must learn to imagine, be self-responsible, and problem solve to construct a viable future consistent with cultural imperatives of work, love, play, and friendship (Dawis, 1995; Hartung, 2002; Savickas, 1991) conveyed in family and community contexts. The developmental tasks of career growth, or orientation, compel the child to acquire a future orientation characterized by the ability to planfully look ahead (Savickas, 1997; Super, Savickas, & Super, 1996). A critical element in this process, and central to life design, involves envisioning oneself in work and other roles, and comprehending the relative salience, or importance, of these roles in one's life.

During this age period, too, children begin constructing a narrative identity (Ricoeur, 1986) that includes views on self in work, family, community, and other psychosocial roles (McAdams, 2008; Savickas, 2002). Childhood thus figures prominently in shaping the rich context and narratives that comprise life histories and career patterns (Super, 1954). Indeed, childhood plants the seeds from which emerge the theme of the whole life career that follows (Savickas, 2011a). This basic principle of career construction and the life design paradigm seems most aptly and poignantly conveyed in the words of the British novelist Graham Greene (1940) who wrote: "There is always one moment in childhood when the door opens and lets the future in" (p. 15). Through play and exploration, children begin to envision their futures. In his book *Essays on Work and Culture*, H. W. Mabie (1898) asserted that childhood play contains the essential theme of the whole life that is to follow and promotes self-construction, as we imagine ourselves in work and other social roles. This self-construction process continues well into adulthood, as we approach, deal with, and navigate through career transitions (Gottfredson, 2002; Savickas, 2002).

Other Stage-Based Models

Like Super, other developmental theorists formulated stage theories of occupational choice beginning in childhood. Ginzberg et al. (1951) proposed an initial fantasy period wherein children ages 6 to 11 years explore future work possibilities through play and imagination, and realize that work will form a requisite component of their future lives. Children's initial fictive ideas about the world of work and their place in it, give way by the end of the fantasy period and the beginning of the tentative stage to perspectives on work tempered by realism. This is prompted by both cognitive development and social pressures to develop appropriate work habits and is accompanied by initial efforts designed to formulate suitable occupational alternatives based on their emerging self-perceived interests and capacities.

Likewise, Havighurst (1951) conceptualized child vocational development as comprising two distinct periods within the whole of life-span development. Children from about 5 to 10 years of age experience a stage of identification with a worker, in which they must assume the values and ideals of, typically, a parent and develop various competencies, a cooperative spirit, conscience, and personal independence among other essential qualities. From age 10 to 15 years, children enter the period of acquiring the basic habits of industry. This stage demands that children learn to effectively manage their time, complete tasks, and conduct themselves responsibly through associated home- and school-based activities.

Circumscription, Compromise, and Self-Creation

With the life span as one foundational element, context also forms a cornerstone of the life design paradigm. Contextual factors of gender, social status, and class as learned, experienced, and perceived in childhood, figure prominently in the theory of circumscription, compromise, and self-creation (Gottfredson, 1996, 2002). Informed by sociological and psychological perspectives on career, Gottfredson endeavored to link these two disciplines and explained how prevailing social structures and barriers affect vocational development beginning early in life. She proposed that child vocational development proceeds through three stages, orienting first to size and power differences between the child and adults (ages 3 to 5 years), then to occupational sex role typing (ages 6 to 8 years), and finally to social valuation based on social class and intelligence level differences (ages 9 to 12). Consistent with life design (Savickas et al., 2009), the theory merges these contextually centered developmental stages with person–environment fit vocational psychology (Holland, 1997) to describe how children narrow their occupational aspirations based on their perceptions of the social structure and their personality traits.

According to the theory, work careers take root in childhood occupational aspirations, which may reflect ideally desired occupations and realistic choices assuaged by an awareness of obstacles and opportunities. Early gender-role typing, social class, and prestige levels strongly influence the content and development of occupational aspirations. Children also construct common social maps, rudimentary at first and more sophisticated with increasing cognitive development, that eventually prompt them to "come to perceive the same occupational map of the social order as adults do" (Gottfredson, 1996, p. 184). Aspirations consequently change in childhood and throughout life depending on the occupational map constructed and the compatibility of various occupational alternatives with an individual's self-image. Gender circumscribes occupational alternatives from age 6 years and older, and social background circumscribes occupational alternatives beginning at the age of 9. Compromises between ideal and real choices occur when individuals perceive incompatibilities between their preferred occupational choices and the accessibility of those options due to social barriers. Some research suggests genetic (Moloney, Bouchard, & Segal, 1991) and in utero hormonal factors (Sandberg, Ehrhardt, Ince, & Meyer-Bahlburg, 1991) also affect the development of occupational interests and choices from childhood through adulthood. This research supports Gottfredson's (2002) theoretical position that sex and gender identity play a pivotal role in the valuation of occupations and the subsequent circumscription of occupational interests and aspirations.

Person–Environment Fit Models

Developmental career theories most deliberately and clearly identify childhood antecedents of life design goals. Meanwhile, virtually all career theories antecedent to the life design paradigm recognize childhood as a formative age period affecting career planning, exploration, choice, and work adjustment over the life course. Notably, the theory of vocational personalities and work environments underscores the importance of childhood experiences and that "a person's career or development over the life span can be visualized as the long series of person-environment interactions and their outcomes that all people experience as they grow up and age" (Holland, 1997, p. 55). In a similar fashion, the theory of work adjustment describes career development as "the *unfolding* of capabilities and requirements in the course of a person's interaction with environments of various kinds (home, school, play, work) across the life span" (Dawis, 1996, p. 94). Children repeat and rehearse interests, skills, abilities, and other traits in home-, school-, and play-based activities. These behaviors gain consistency and stability to eventually form what may be called the child's recognizable underlying personality or, from a constructionist and life design viewpoint, the child's emerging socially situated reputation (Savickas, 2013).

Research Perspectives

Research reviews support theory to indicate the formative, vital, and very active role childhood plays in career development and life design (Hartung et al., 2005; Watson & McMahon, 2005). These reviews summarize an impressive body of findings that shed light on children's developing vocational exploration, awareness, aspirations, interests, and maturity/adaptability (Hartung et al., 2005), along with the critical role that learning plays in children's career development (Watson & McMahon, 2005). This body of literature clearly indicates that vocational development begins during childhood. During this age period, children must first engage with the world of work to develop career adaptability. As noted above, this involves developing initial concern about the future, control over one's life, curiosity about how to make career decisions, and confidence to make and implement such decisions (Hartung et al., 2008; Savickas, 2002, 2011a). Children as young as 3 to 5 years acquire rudimentary knowledge about occupations, comprehend the existing occupational status hierarchy, and develop distinct attitudes about the suitability for them of particular occupations, albeit often based on stereotyped perceptions and limited information (Dorr & Lesser, 1980; Hartung et al., 2005). Children of about 8 years of age base their perceptions of adult work on a rather loose integration of fantasies or assumptions as well as actual observations of adults working. This loose integration typically gives way by about age 11 to a more realistic understanding of adult work, including gains in knowledge about job salaries, skills, and training requirements (Hill, 1969; Nelson, 1963). Around age 14, when childhood gives way to adolescence, views of adult work become more emotionally overlaid as youths develop awareness of potential negative aspects of work (e.g., dissatisfaction, schedule demands, and role strain), compare the world of work with their own abilities, and grow increasingly aware that entering the work role and making educational and vocational decisions loom as increasingly proximal developmental tasks for them.

As noted in reviews of the child career development literature (Hartung et al., 2005; Watson & McMahon, 2005) and despite a relatively impressive amount of findings, career theory and research – including that within the life design paradigm – has focused in very limited ways on childhood, giving greater emphasis to the adolescent and adult age periods. This has been attributed to two factors. One factor concerns the fact that the most obvious career decision making occurs during adolescence and early adulthood. Another factor relates to society's need to separate children from the duties and responsibilities of paid work in what has been referred to as a cultural moratorium of childhood (Zinnecker, 1995). In any case, the limited focus on childhood has resulted in a great need to consider and make linkages to this age period within career and life design studies and intervention practices (McMahon & Watson, 2008; Vondracek, 2001). Recognizing childhood as the genesis of life design requires looking no further than school-based programs wherein kindergarten to 12th grade (K-12) school counselors and educators have long conducted comprehensive guidance programs that attend to children's vocational development (Gysbers & Henderson, 2012). Likewise, scholars have begun to shift the focus of career studies and career interventions more earnestly to the childhood years (e.g., McMahon & Watson, 2008).

Theory, Research, and Life Design Goals

Theory and research clearly indicate that childhood launches engagement in cognitive, emotional, motivational, and behavioral processes to achieve life design's four central goals of activity, adaptability, narratability, and intentionality. These goals involve, respectively, developing the abilities to (a) *engage* in diverse activities – to identify preferred vocational interests, abilities, and future possible selves; (b) *adapt* to career development tasks, transitions, and traumas – to envision, explore, decide, and problem solve a future; (c) *tell* one's own life story clearly and coherently – to say who one is and who one is becoming; and (d) *interpret* self and situation – to give meaning and direction to one's experiences and circumstances (Savickas et al., 2009). Children begin to move toward these goals to varying degrees through engagement with the social world and based on a host of individual factors such as aptitude and effort, as well as environmental influences such as opportunity and circumstance (Hartung et al., 2005; Watson & McMahon, 2005). Career construction (Savickas, 2011a), a theory of vocational behavior and intervention scheme, offers a model and methods useful for further understanding antecedents and advancement of the core life design intervention goals.

Child Career Construction and Life Design

Career construction theory and practice (Savickas, 2002, 2011a, 2013) views work as a vehicle to making life more meaningful. It rests on the premise that people construct themselves through story beginning at an early age. In telling their life stories, individuals shape their identities in the form of self-defining autobiographical narratives. These narratives hold them during, and carry them through, times of uncertainty and instability, a characteristic of life in the 21st-century digital and global age. Applied to childhood, career construction may be considered in terms of how it understands and fosters life design core goals of (a) activity to shape interests, capacities, and aspirations; (b) adaptability to cope with changes in self and situation; (c) narratability to tell one's story coherently; and (d) intentionality to assign meaning to activities and experiences. In so doing, it can be seen how career construction incorporates self-construction processes antecedent in childhood by integrating three psychological and career counseling paradigms: individual differences (e.g., Holland, 1959, 1997), life-span development (Super, 1990), and life design (Savickas et al., 2009). This integration permits viewing the construction of self as actor, agent, and author, respectively (McAdams, 2013; Savickas, 2011a; 2013). Using these vantage points, career construction counseling offers ways to foster life design's core goals.

Childhood Emergence of Self as Actor, Agent, and Author

Career construction views the self in three ways (Savickas, 2013). First, emerging during early childhood, the self may be viewed as a *social actor* with characteristic traits and playing social roles that resemble social scripts that fit corresponding future work environments. Second, emerging during mid to late childhood, the self mirrors a *motivational agent* with career aspirations exploring possible future life-career plans and projects and developing readiness to fit work into life. Third, arising during adolescence and emerging adulthood, the self represents an *autobiographical author* with a life narrative telling an integrative personal life story about how to shape oneself through work. Accordingly, childhood involves initial and rudimentary orientation to life-long processes of matching self to adult work roles (actor) in the individual differences paradigm, managing self in work and career over the life span (agent) in the developmental paradigm, and making one's self through constructing a personally meaningful and socially useful life career (author) in the life design paradigm.

Childhood as lived primarily within the family of origin as well as within educational, community, and other social contexts launches the core career construction processes of self-making based in the three predominant career theory and intervention paradigms. In turn, children initially learn about themselves and the occupations that befit their *traits*. Much like socially scripted and situationally cued actors, children prepare to perform roles and play parts on future corresponding work stages (Tracey, 2001; Tracey & Sodano, in press). Children begin to acquire and hone interests, abilities, skills, and talents that eventually can be played out in corresponding work settings. They also first deal with developmental *tasks*, much like self-determined and goal-directed agents making future career plans (Hartung et al., 2008; Phillips, 2011). Through fantasy, curiosity, and aspiration, children play with possibilities for making a future self in work roles. During this age period, too, children begin to tell self-defining stories portraying nascent life *themes*, much like budding authors who initially reflect on and narrate their own clear and enduring life-career autobiographies (McAdams, 2013; Savickas, 2011a; Shweder et al., 1998). It is during childhood that a central life theme comprising one's predominant problem in need of a satisfying solution first emerges. As Savickas noted: "Life themes originate in early childhood as unfinished situations and incompletely formed gestalt" (Savickas, 2011a, p. 32). Each one of these self-making processes – actor, agent, author –in turn relates to a core life design intervention goal and becomes a focus of adapting career construction interventions to career counseling with children. Engagement in and movement through these processes occurs, of course, as a function of the child's particular cultural and social context.

Fostering Life Design Goals With Children

Typically applied to career intervention with adults, career construction counseling entails an interpersonal process of helping people author career stories that connect their self-concepts to work roles, fit work into life, and make meaning through work. Using the narrative paradigm, career construction counseling begins with a Career Construction Interview (CCI) comprising five questions about *self* (childhood role models), *setting* (favorite magazines, TV shows, and websites), *story* (current favorite book or movie), *self-advice* (favorite saying), and *scheme* (early childhood memories). Each CCI question prompts individuals to tell small stories about themselves that convey who they are and who they wish to become. Counselor and client collaboratively shape the themes culled from these microstories into a macronarrative about the person's central preoccupation, motives, goals, adaptive strategies, and self-view. This co-construction process empowers individuals to author life-career stories that enhance their experiences of work as personally meaningful and socially useful. They may then use work to actively master what they passively suffer. Applied to career intervention with children, career construction counseling's core assessment method of the CCI and materials such as the *My Career Story* (MCS) workbook (Savickas & Hartung, 2012) may be adapted for use by counselors to promote children's movement toward the core intervention life design goals of activity, adaptability, narratability, and intentionality.

Activity
Activity involves engaging in experiences to rehearse traits such as interests, abilities, and skills that will become recognized by the child's social network as her or his reputation. By

using various self-constructing strategies such as role-playing, introjecting familial guides, and incorporating role models in fantasy and play activities, children perform as social actors (Savickas, 2013). Referencing well-established theories, Magnuson and Starr (2000) aptly underscored the importance of childhood activity consistent with the career construction and life design process of making the self as an actor:

> Children are naturally curious and seek to understand the world (Piaget), look to others (mentors) for guidance in their quest (Vygotsky), are judging themselves by the responses of others to their self-initiated explorations (Erikson), are observing people at work and drawing conclusions about the nature/desirability of the work (Gottfredson), and are forming ideas about themselves and their aspirations (Super). What happens at one level of development will influence subsequent levels. Our responsibility as adults in the lives of children and young adults is to provide many and varied developmentally appropriate opportunities for career awareness, career exploration, and the development of life-career planning skills. To be personally meaningful to children as individuals, the experiences must be accompanied by opportunities to express individual thoughts and beliefs as they develop. (Magnuson & Starr, 2000, p. 98)

Active occupational engagement through enrichment and exploration processes promotes eventual adaptive career decision making (Krieshok, Black, & McKay, 2009) as well as intentional expression of future selves (Savickas et al., 2009). Adapting the CCI question about favorite magazines, TV shows, and websites, counselors can help children to initially reflect on and explore the self they are making in relation to where they may best like to be themselves with regard to work and career situations. Doing so helps children begin early the process that will become more pressing by late adolescence, of authoring career stories that connect their self-concepts (i.e., who they are and who they are becoming) to their educational plans and future work roles. It also assists them to understand how they can use school and work to design their lives and become more complete. Magazines, shows, and websites offer vicarious environments, or *settings,* in which children may immerse themselves (Savickas, 2011a). In these purposefully selected settings, children nurture interests that fit with their emerging social reputations. These settings can be conceptualized according to realistic, investigative, artistic, social, enterprising, and conventional (RIASEC) types (Holland, 1997). For example, *Kids Discover* and *National Geographic Little Kids* magazines expose children to science stories and may hint about a child's preference for a scientific and analytical, or investigative environment. Similarly, an online TV show such as *Secret Millionaires Club* may indicate a preference for a managerial and political, or enterprising type of environment. Knowing what magazines, shows, or websites a child engages with consistently and what she or he likes about them may offer keen insights into where the child may eventually most like to enact the self that she or he is constructing. Other questions, too, such as asking about a child's extracurricular activities and hobbies can indicate what they are training themselves for and on what stage they prefer to enact the self that they are making.

Adaptability

Adaptability involves coping with changes in self and situation so that the developing child can begin to handle life's responsibilities, passages, and strains. In this way, the child becomes much like an agent who must formulate goals and projects that ultimately shape a career. A sense of agency – first emerging by middle childhood (Savickas, 2013) – equips and emboldens the child, and later the adolescent and adult, to deal with typical developmental tasks (e.g., completing chores and school work), successfully navigate transitions (e.g., from home to school and school to work), and cope with traumatic crises (e.g., death, divorce, or serious illness in self or a family member). Skills of career adaptability initially take shape in childhood (Hartung et al., 2008; Savickas, 2013). Career adaptability must then be cultivated throughout the life course across its four skill sets or dimensions of concern (looking ahead), control (owning the future), curiosity (looking around), and confidence (problem solving).

Career construction counseling applied to childhood may most directly aim to increase the concern dimension of career adaptability (Savickas, 2002, 2013). A viable goal is to help children begin to see their futures, perhaps by considering children's career aspirations and using time-perspective interventions (Taber, in press). Such methods intend to help children orient to the future, feel hopeful about it, and begin to plan for it. Counselors may also begin to cultivate children's other developing career adaptability skills. For example, counselors can encourage children's appropriate self-directed activity to feel in control of their own futures; support exploratory behavior to foster their curiosity about work, occupations, and career paths; and promote role-playing and observational learning to nurture children's confidence for pursuing vocational aspirations.

Narratability

Narratability means being able to tell one's story clearly and coherently. Children are encouraged to tell stories about themselves and often do so from an early age (Ahn, 2011). Central to their stories are developing life themes that emerge from their personal experiences. These early experiences prove formative in that children use them to understand themselves and the world. And these stories contain life-long lessons that children will carry with them on into adolescence and adulthood. The significance of early child events in later life design and career construction is summed up well by Alfred Adler (1932) who wrote:

> If ever I am called on for vocational guidance, I always ask how the individual began and what he [sic] was interested in during his first years. His memories of this period show conclusively what he has trained himself for most continuously: they reveal his prototype and his underlying scheme of apperception. (Adler, 1932, p. 242)

Children tell and retell their own personal experiences through playful and structured interactions with the social world (Ahn, 2011). By narrating their experiences and participating in a host of activities, children initially express their emotions and thoughts, rehearse behaviors, and exert their will. In so doing they progress developmentally toward the goal of forming a realistic and viable vocational self-concept in part by identifying with significant others (Super, 1951) and incorporating role models (Savickas, 2011a). An emerging vocational self-concept in childhood prompts formative answers to questions of identity in children's budding mental representations of their perceived strengths, limitations, vocational interests, work values, abilities, talents, and personality traits. This growing self-concept comprises both a public portrayal and a private goal that portends a future role for work and career in the whole of one's life (Super et al., 1996). This role continually gets questioned, shaped, and refined throughout the life course.

Career construction and other approaches within the life design paradigm have promulgated a host of groundbreaking narrative-based intervention schemes throughout the international careers community (e.g., see Hartung, 2013a; Maree, 2007). These schemes recognize that people make themselves and their worlds through the stories they tell. To best achieve life-career success, children can be encouraged to begin to create a story about themselves that expresses very clearly who they are becoming as a person, where they may most like to be in the work world, and how they may want to use work in a way that best allows them to fully be themselves. To construct such a story, it may help children to think of a life career as an ongoing tale with three main parts: a lead character or self that represents who they are, an educational or work setting where they feel most comfortable, and a script with a plot and a central theme that explains and shows them how to use work to best realize the self they are constructing. Knowing and telling one's own life story, or autobiography, adds meaning to career plans and choices. It can also deepen life-career planning and decision making with a clearer sense of direction and purpose. Using questions from the MCS workbook (Savickas & Hartung, 2012) with children may help them tell, hear, and begin to author their own life stories. Telling, hearing, and co-constructing their own story with valued audiences, such as a counselor, coach, teacher, family member, or friend, empowers the child to begin taking authorship of their own life careers.

Intentionality

"Human beings live in the realm of meanings" (Adler, 1932, p. 3). Intentionality denotes a process of engaging meaningfully and purposefully in activities embedded within psychosocial roles. Children engage in intentional action and in so doing begin to meaningfully perform their own life stories. From an early age, children purposefully select activities in play and school in which they perform and explore roles (Smith, 1997). For example, Vandenberg (cited in Smith, 1997) noted a 4-year-old child who "frequently pretends that she is a cheerleader. She dances, jumps, and twirls in youthful imitation of her older heroines" (Smith, 1997, p. 187). On one level, the child's behavior may be viewed as simply role rehearsal and skill development, much like that of the self as actor. On another level, the child's behavior may reflect more intentional action involving the child's early, perhaps introjected choice of cheerleading from among a host of possible roles because her mother was a cheerleader and had discussed this with her daughter. In that sense, the daughter perhaps evinces embryonic signs of a future self as author as she attempts "to construct a possible future for herself as she plays with the meanings of maturity and adulthood that have been presented to her by her mother" (Vandenberg cited in Smith, 1997, p. 187).

Adapting career construction methods of select CCI questions and MCS workbook components for use in the childhood years, counselors can help children begin to tell their budding life stories that include emergent life themes. Reflecting on the answers to CCI and MCS questions promotes both narratability and intentionality (Savickas, 2011a). Doing so assists in a meaning-making process by helping children begin to shape their emerging identities, construct certainty and confidence within themselves, and move into the future with purpose. Using components of the CCI and MCS in whole or in part may offer a useful scheme for empowering children to coherently tell, hear, and retell with deeper clarity their growing life-career stories and identify ways to enact them in home and school-based activities and settings. Envisioning possible selves and future life careers requires action combined with meaning. Such intentionality can and should be nurtured within the developing child.

Conclusion

Childhood begins the life-long process of life design. Amidst the complexities, instability, and uncertainty of work in 21st-century times, engaging children in movement toward key life design goals of activity, adaptability, narratability, and intentionality becomes especially salient and important. Today, individuals must be diligently self-managing, self-regulating, and self-directing if they wish to experience satisfaction and success in their work and careers (Sullivan, 2011). And helping children to develop these attributes is critical. Rather than relying on stable work and organizational structures, people must be increasingly self-reliant to direct and manage their careers.

Meanwhile, an unstable, uncertain, and unpredictable work world has of necessity moved the field of career studies and intervention to adapt itself by looking beyond its twin foci on fitting people to occupations (Holland, 1997; Parsons, 1909) and readying people for careers (Super, 1990), to also see the critical importance and usefulness of reflectively clarifying individual meanings about work and how it can be used to advance one's life story (Collin & Guichard, 2011; Maree, 2007; Savickas, 2011a). This broadened focus embedded within the life design paradigm allows and advances a view of career as projective self-making that begins during the childhood years. This view does not replace but rather augments 20th-century views on career as objective person–occupation match and subjective cycle of self in work over the life span (Savickas, 2011b).

Regarded as the starting place of life design and career construction, childhood provides fertile soil for planting the seeds of attaining life design's core goals. Adapting career construction methods like the CCI and *My Career Story* workbook in whole or in part could help children begin to tell, hear, and enact their own emerging life-career stories. In this way, they can begin to say who they are becoming, where in the world of work they may like to be, and what they think it will take to connect themselves to occupations they may like. Using such methods may prove especially useful for fostering life-career design with children.

References

Adler, A. (1932). *What life should mean to you.* London, UK: Allen & Unwin.

Ahn, J. (2011). Review of children's identity construction via narratives. *Creative Education, 2,* 415–417. http://doi.org/10.4236/ce.2011.25060

Collin, A., & Guichard, J. (2011). Constructing self in career theory and counseling interventions. In P. J. Hartung & L. M. Subich (Eds.), *Developing self in work and career: Concepts, cases, and contexts* (pp. 89–106). Washington, DC: American Psychological Association Books.

Dawis, R. V. (1995). For the love of working on play: Comment on Tinsley and Eldredge (1995). *Journal of Counseling Psychology, 42,* 136–137. http://doi.org/10.1037/0022-0167.42.2.136

Dawis, R. V . (1996). The theory of work adjustment and person-environment correspondence counseling. In D. Brown & L. Brooks (Eds.), *Career choice and development: Applying contemporary theories to practice* (3rd ed., pp. 75–120). San Francisco, CA: Jossey-Bass.

Dorr, A., & Lesser, G. S. (1980). Career awareness in young children. *Communication Research & Broadcasting, No 3,* 36–75.

Ginzberg, E., Ginsburg, S. Axelrad, S., & Herma, J. (1951). *Occupational choice: An approach to a general theory.* New York, NY: Columbia University Press.

Gottfredson, L. S. (1996). Gottfredson's theory of circumscription and compromise. In D. Brown & L. Brooks (Eds.), *Career choice and development: Applying contemporary theories to practice.* (3rd ed., pp. 179–232). San Francisco, CA: Jossey Bass.

Gottfredson, L. S. (2002). Gottfredson's theory of circumscription, compromise, and self-creation. In D. Brown (Ed.), *Career choice and development* (4th ed., pp. 85–148). New York, NY: Wiley.

Greene, G. (1940). *The power and the glory*. New York, NY: Viking Press.

Guichard, J. (2005). Life-long self-construction. *International Journal for Educational and Vocational Guidance, 5,* 111–124. http://doi.org/10.1007/s10775-005-8789-y

Gysbers, N. C., & Henderson, P. (2012). *Developing and managing your school guidance and counseling program* (5th ed.). Alexandria, VA: American Counseling Association.

Hartung, P. J. (2002). Development through work and play. *Journal of Vocational Behavior, 61,* 424–438. http://doi.org/10.1006/jvbe.2002.1884

Hartung, P. J. (2013a). Career as story: Making the narrative turn. In W. B. Walsh, M. L. Savickas, & P. J. Hartung (Eds.), *Handbook of vocational psychology* (4th ed., pp. 33–52). New York, NY: Routledge.

Hartung, P. J. (2013b). Career construction counseling. In A. Di Fabio & K. Maree (Eds.), *Psychology of career counseling: New challenges for a new era* (pp. 15–28). Hauppauge, NY: Nova Science.

Hartung, P. J. (2013c). The life-span, life-space theory of careers. In S. D. Brown & R. W. Lent (Eds.), *Career development and counseling: Putting theory and research to work* (2nd ed., pp. 83–113). Hoboken, NJ: Wiley.

Hartung, P. J., Porfeli, E. J., & Vondracek, F. W. (2005). Vocational development in childhood: A review and reconsideration. *Journal of Vocational Behavior, 66,* 385–419. http://doi.org/10.1016/j.jvb.2004.05.006

Hartung, P. J., Porfeli, E. J., & Vondracek, F. W. (2008). Career adaptability in childhood. *The Career Development Quarterly, 57,* 63–74. http://doi.org/10.1002/j.2161-0045.2008.tb00166.x

Havighurst, R. J. (1951). *Developmental tasks and education.* New York, NY: Longmans/Green.

Hill, J. M. M. (1969). *The transition from school to work: A study of the child's changing perception of work from the age of seven.* London, UK: Tavistock Institute of Human Relations.

Holland, J. L. (1959). A theory of vocational choice. *Journal of Counseling Psychology, 6,* 35–45. http://doi.org/10.1037/h0040767

Holland, J. L. (1997). *Making vocational choices* (3rd ed.). Odessa, FL: Psychological Assessment Resources.

Krieshok, T. S., Black, M. D., & McKay, R. A. (2009). Career decision making: The limits of rationality and the abundance of non-conscious processes. *Journal of Vocational Behavior, 75,* 275–290. http://doi.org/10.1016/j.jvb.2009.04.006

Mabie, H. W. (1898). *Essays on work and culture.* New York, NY: Dodd, Mead, and Company.

Magnuson, C. S., & Starr, M. F. (2000). How early is too early to begin life career planning? The importance of the elementary school years. *Journal of Career Development, 27,* 89–101. http://doi.org/10.1177/089484530002700203

Maree, J. G. (Ed.). (2007). *Shaping the story: A guide to facilitating narrative counselling.* Pretoria, South Africa: Van Schaik.

McAdams, D. P. (2008). Personal narratives and the life story. In O. P. John, R. W. Robins, & L. A. Pervin (Eds.), *Handbook of personality: Theory and research* (3rd ed., pp. 242–262). New York, NY: Guilford Press.

McAdams, D. P. (2013). The psychological self as actor, agent, and author. *Perspectives of Psychological Science, 8,* 272–295. http://doi.org/10.1177/1745691612464657

McMahon, M., & Watson, M. (2008). Children's career development: Status quo and future directions. *The Career Development Quarterly, 57,* 4–6.

Moloney, D. P., Bouchard, T. J., Jr., & Segal, N. L. (1991). A genetic and environmental analysis of the vocational interests of monozygotic and dizygotic twins reared apart. *Journal of Vocational Behavior, 39,* 76–109. http://doi.org/10.1016/0001-8791(91)90005-7

Nelson, R. C. (1963). Knowledge and interests concerning sixteen occupations among elementary and secondary school students. *Educational and Psychological Measurement, 23,* 741–754. http://doi.org/10.1177/001316446302300409

Parsons, F. (1909). *Choosing a vocation.* Boston, MA: Houghton Mifflin.

Phillips, S. D. (2011). Implementing self-concept: Matching, developing, and deciding. In P. J. Hartung & L. M. Subich (Eds.), *Developing self in work and career: Concepts, cases, and contexts* (pp. 161–173). Washington, DC: American Psychological Association Books.

Ricoeur, P. (1986). Life: A story in search of a narrator. In M. Doeser & J. Kray (Eds.), *Facts and values: Philosophical reflections from western and non-western perspectives* (pp. 34–68). Dordrecht, The Netherlands: Nijhoff.

Sandberg, D. E., Ehrhardt, A. A., Ince, S. E., & Meyer-Bahlburg, H. F. L. (1991). Gender differences in children's and adolescents' career aspirations: A follow-up study. *Journal of Adolescent Research, 6,* 371–386. http://doi.org/10.1177/074355489163007

Savickas, M. L. (1991). The meaning of work and love: Career issues and interventions. *The Career Development Quarterly, 4,* 315–324. http://doi.org/10.1002/j.2161-0045.1991.tb00299.x

Savickas, M. L. (1997). Career adaptability: An integrative construct for life-span, life-space theory. *Career Development Quarterly, 45,* 247–259. http://doi.org/10.1002/j.2161-0045.1997.tb00469.x

Savickas, M. L. (2002). Career construction: A developmental theory of vocational behavior. In D. Brown (Ed.), *Career choice and development* (4th ed., pp. 149–205). San Francisco, CA: Jossey-Bass.

Savickas, M. L. (2009). Career studies as self-making and life designing. *Career Research and Development, 24,* 15–17.

Savickas, M. L. (2011a). *Career counseling.* Washington, DC: American Psychological Association Books.

Savickas, M. L. (2011b). The self in vocational psychology: Object, subject, and project. In P. J. Hartung & L. M. Subich (Eds.), *Developing self in work and career: Concepts, cases, and contexts* (pp. 17–33). Washington, DC: American Psychological Association Books.

Savickas, M. L. (2013). Career construction theory and practice. In S. D. Brown & R. W. Lent (Eds.), *Career development and counseling: Putting theory and research to work* (2nd ed., pp. 147–183). Hoboken, NJ: Wiley.

Savickas, M. L., & Hartung, P. J. (2012). *My career story: An autobiographical workbook for life-career success.* Kent, OH: Vocopher. Retrieved from http://www.vocopher.com

Savickas, M. L., Nota, L., Rossier, J., Dauwalder, J.-P., Duarte, M. E., Guichard, J., . . . van Vianen, A. E. M. (2009). Life designing: A paradigm for career construction in the 21st century. *Journal of Vocational Behavior, 75,* 239–250. http://doi.org/10.1016/j.jvb.2009.04.004

Savickas, M. L., & Super, D. E. (1993). Can life stages and substages be identified in students? *Man and Work: Journal of Labor Studies, 4,* 71–78.

Shweder, R. A., Goodnow, J., Hatano, G., Levine, R. A., Markus, H., & Miller, P. (1998). The cultural psychology of development: One mind, many mentalities. In W. Damon (Ed.-in-Chief) & R. M. Lerner (Volume Ed.), *Handbook of child psychology* (5th ed., pp. 865–937). New York, NY: Wiley.

Smith, B. S. (1997). *The ambiguity of play.* Cambridge, MA: Harvard University Press.

Sullivan, S. E. (2011). Self-direction in the boundaryless career era. In P. J. Hartung & L. M. Subich (Eds.), *Developing self in work and career: Concepts, cases, and contexts* (pp. 123–140). Washington, DC: American Psychological Association Books.

Super, D. E. (1951). Vocational adjustment: Implementing a self-concept. *Occupations, 30,* 88–92.

Super, D. E. (1954). Career patterns as a basis for vocational counseling. *Journal of Counseling Psychology, 1,* 12–20. http://doi.org/10.1037/h0061989

Super, D. E. (1957). *The psychology of careers.* New York, NY: Harper and Row.

Super, D. E. (1990). A life-span, life-space approach to career development. In D. Brown & L. Brooks (Eds.), *Career choice and development: Applying contemporary theories to practice* (2nd ed., pp. 197–261). San Francisco, CA: Jossey-Bass.

Super, D. E., Savickas, M. L., & Super, C. M. (1996). The life-span, life-space approach to careers. In D. Brown & L. Brooks (Eds.), *Career choice and development: Applying contemporary theories to practice* (3rd ed., pp. 121–178). San Francisco, CA: Jossey-Bass.

Taber, B. J. (in press). Enhancing future time perspective and exploring occupational possible selves. In P. J. Hartung, M. L. Savickas, & W. B. Walsh (Eds.), *APA handbook of career intervention* (Vol. 2). Washington, DC: American Psychological Association.

Tracey, T. J. G. (2001). The development of structure of interests in children: Setting the stage. *Journal of Vocational Behavior, 59,* 89–104. http://doi.org/10.1006/jvbe.2000.1787

Tracey, T. J. G., & Sodano, S. M. (in press). Assessing children: Interests and personality. In P. J. Hartung, M. L. Savickas, & W. B. Walsh (Eds.), *APA handbook of career intervention* (Vol. 2). Washington, DC: American Psychological Association.

Vondracek, F. W. (2001). The childhood antecedents of adult careers: Theoretical and empirical considerations. In R. K. Silbereisen & M. Reitzle (Eds.), *Bericht ueberden 42. Kongress der Deutschen Gesellschaft fuer Psychologie in Jena 2000* [Report of the 42nd Congress of the German Society for Psychology in Jena 2000] (pp. 265–276). Lengerich, Germany: Pabst Science.

Vondracek, F. W., Lerner, R. M., & Schulenberg, J. E. (1986). *Career development: A life-span developmental approach.* Hillsdale, NJ: Erlbaum.

Watson, M., & McMahon, M. (2005). Children's career development: A research review from a learning perspective. *Journal of Vocational Behavior, 67,* 119–132. http://doi.org/10.1016/j.jvb.2004.08.011

Zinnecker, J. (1995). The cultural modernisation of childhood. In L. Chisholm, P. Büchner, H. H. Krüger, & M. du Bois-Reymond (Eds.), *Growing up in Europe: Contemporary horizons in childhood and youth studies* (pp. 85–94). New York, NY: Walter de Gruyter.

Chapter 8
Career Counseling and the Uniqueness of the Individual Adolescent

Gudbjörg Vilhjálmsdóttir
School of Social Sciences, University of Iceland, Reykjavík, Iceland

Introduction

We live in a fast-moving global economy (Coutinhio, Dam, & Blustein, 2008). The ongoing economic and social changes are comparable to those of the Industrial Revolution in the 18th and 19th centuries (Giddens, 1991). We also live in an environment where young people face higher unemployment than other age groups; a situation that the UK newspaper *The Guardian* described in July 2013 as a "time bomb" (Podesta, 2013). In the last quarter of 2011, the unemployment rates for young people aged 15 to 24 were 22% in the United Kingdom and 48.9% in Spain (Eurostat, n.d.). Statistics from the United States reveal that young people aged 18 to 26 (born in 1980 to 1984) had changed jobs a mean 6.2 times (U.S. Department of Labour – Bureau of Labor Statistics, 2014). This situation is challenging for young people who face choices about careers (Westergaard, 2012). The challenge is no smaller for researchers and practitioners of career counseling. New paradigms are needed in career theory. Kuhn (1962) defines a paradigm as a set of assumptions and beliefs in a particular scientific community that sets the agenda for research and professional practice. The crisis of youth labor is bound to call for a new approach in career counseling that is more successful in solving the problems that face young people today, more successful than previous theoretical paradigms in career counseling. Clearly, a paradigm such as the person–environment (P-E) fit is limiting, because it rests on the premise of relatively stable occupations and a growing labor market. The life design model is a contextualized model based on the epistemology of social constructionism (Savickas et al., 2009). This constructionist approach is in many ways the opposite of the dominant P-E fit approach, as it does not focus on how people fit into work, but on how they are going to fit work into their lives (Savickas, 2011). Careers are constructed through a process of adaptation of the self-concept to changing environments and new subjective realities. The focus in the life design counseling model is therefore on the uniqueness of the individual (Bulletin, contactpoint.ca, n.d.), whereas previous approaches were more focused on universal facts about careers, or career information and how the individual compares with norms. Authors of the life design approach such as Guichard and Savickas have identified three types of interventions: (1) giving information about self, training, and occupations; (2)

preparing for life, such as in psychopedagogical interventions; and (3) life design counseling that includes storying, self-reflection, and meaning making (see Chapter 2; see also Guichard, 2011; Savickas, 2011).

Young people and adolescents in particular have always been of great interest in the field of career counseling, as they are in the process of leaving school and coming to terms with vocational identity and expectations for increasing self-management, personal responsibility, and social participation (Steinberg, 2011). In contemporary Western societies, life roles and life tasks are being postponed, and decisions about careers are on average taken later in life compared with past generations; a situation that is reflected in the new theoretical construct of "emerging adulthood" (Arnett, 2000). It has been the role of school and career counselors to assist adolescents in exploring and finding educational programs and jobs, either in career education or career counseling. Counselors today need to be aware of the changing context of fewer occupational opportunities and of prolonged education, and hence postponement of career and other life choices. They also need to be aware of the fact that in this context, their assistance can no longer be solely to find an educational program or a suitable occupation. Adolescence is a period of growth and major life changes, but it is less and less characterized by being a transition from parental dependency to independency or as the school-leaving age. At the same time, life-decisive changes can take place at adolescence, such as dropping out of school or abusing drugs. This gives counseling for adolescents a whole new dimension where the adolescent has to deal with developing his or her sense of self in a world of growing uncertainties.

The idea of life design implies that the agent is active in shaping his or her work life, something that is necessary in an ever-changing work environment. In adolescence, people are experimenting with such activities, some constructively and others destructively. Life decisions taken in adolescence have been the focus of career counseling theory from its beginnings, and although the dominant theoretical constructs of the P-E approach have been static and directive, others have been dynamic and flexible. This chapter on the life design model in adolescence focuses on some key theoretical constructs of life design in adolescence in preceding theories, such as identity building or career development tasks. These ideas are presented in the sections on historical and developmental perspectives. In the section "Educational Perspectives," research on adolescence is presented, especially preventive and risk factors in adolescence, something that is important to keep in mind with life design in adolescence with its emphasis on the social context (Savickas et al., 2009). The role of social variables in career construction is explored in the following section. The overview of theoretical constructs that have fed into later approaches, such as the life design approach, concludes with a section on the career construction perspective, the main theoretical groundwork of the life design model. Finally, interventions with adolescents from a life design perspective will be discussed and illustrated in a case study. These emphasize a creative approach involving the creation of stories and highlighting the individual uniqueness of each adolescent.

Historical Perspectives

Adolescents have been associated with career problems from the very outset of the profession of career guidance and counseling in the 20th century. Frank Parsons, the father of the guidance movement in the United States, was preoccupied with poor adolescents in the United States in the turmoil of the waves of immigration. Young people were not living up to their potential, because they did not get the information and guidance they needed (Parsons, 1909; Zytowski, 2001).

A decade or so later, in Vienna, another influential figure in the career counseling profession, Alfred Adler, was teaching educators how important it was for adolescents to have decided upon a career goal by the age of 13. This goal might change, but to set a course into the future was important in creating a unique individual lifestyle. Adler also described how students could be discouraged in schools and in that case would seek the company of delinquents outside the schools, and take up socially inappropriate lifestyles (Adler, 1936).

It was the young Erik Homburger, while working as a psychoanalyst in Viennese schools in the 1920s, who became interested in the development of children and adolescents (Homburger (Erikson), 1985) and later, as Erik H. Erikson, he put forward the theory of psychosocial steps (Erikson, 1950/1977). Here the emphasis was on both psychological and social aspects of adolescent development, something that also interested Parsons and Adler. According to Erikson (1968), a basic task in adolescence is creating a self and vocational identity; failure to achieve a sense of identity results in role confusion. "In general it is the inability to settle on an occupational identity which most disturbs young people" (Erikson, 1968, p. 132).

These were some of the important figures in the history of career counseling who stressed, already early in the last century, the importance of adolescence in life creation and that socially deprived adolescents need special attention. Although these ideas, close to the life design paradigm, were present in these early writings, another paradigm, of differential psychology and the P-E fit, became dominant within the guidance field. The proliferation of psychometric tests that were published throughout the 20th century is one explanation for this course of events.

The life design perspective takes an opposite position from trait-factor theories, as it is not preoccupied with fitting the individual to work by comparing him or her with norms, but emphasizes the subjective experience of careers. Professional identity is shaped in an interaction and adaptation with a manifold context not "as static, abstract, and oversimplified profiles of client's test scores" (Savickas et al., 2009, p. 242). At the same time, the life design approach builds on dynamic perspectives and personal patterns, such as the Adlerian one. This dynamic approach is taken further in the construction, co-construction, and reconstruction of narratives, where careers are approached as individual scripts (Savickas et al., 2009). The life design approach also underlines the importance of the preventive aspect of career interventions, in agreement with Adler's view on the importance of setting career goals in adolescence and even at a younger age. In the life design framework, it is important to intervene early, in childhood and early adolescence, to prepare young people for transitions, increase their opportunities for choice, and give attention to at-risk situations (Savickas et al., 2009).

Developmental Perspectives

Adolescence is defined as the transitional period between childhood and adult age. It is a period of growth in more ways than one. As Erikson (1950/1977) and Havighurst (1972, in Dolgin, 2011) pointed out, it is important that the developmental tasks are worked through – if they are not, the outcomes of this growth can harm the adolescent's well-being. Identity, self-knowledge, relationships with parents and peers, and academic development, are all examples of developmental tasks that can result in either good or poor adaptation to the environment. An example of a poor adaptation to the environment is dropping out of school, something that is very likely a failure in construing differentiated (although not confused) and integrated vocational constructs (Vilhjálmsdóttir, 2010).

Super and Gottfredson are the two theoreticians within career counseling theory who have paid particular attention to career development in adolescence. Concepts of interest in understanding career development in adolescence within Super's theoretical framework are the developmental tasks or coping resources needed at the exploration stage (Savickas, 1999) and the importance of a stable self-concept at the end of adolescence. In Gottfredson's theory, it is the concepts of circumscription and compromise that are of interest.

Super's theory evolved from focusing mainly on development and developmental stages, into a more integrative theory (Savickas, 1997). Careers evolve in different developmental stages – namely, growth (ages 4 to 14 years), exploration (ages 15 to 24), establishment (ages 25 to 45), maintenance (ages 46 to 60), and disengagement. At each stage, one has to successfully manage career development tasks that are given at that age level. The vocational development tasks in the exploration stage are crystallization, specification, and implementation. In crystallization, the adolescent is cognitively processing an understanding of his or her interests, skills, and values, and how to pursue career goals; in specification, choosing occupational areas, even occupations of interest; and in implementation, taking steps to actualize career choices (Leung, 2008). The exploration stage with its substages has been used as the framework for career education, where information seeking and attitudes toward careers are stimulated, such as the French Canadian program *Éducation des choix* (Association Trouver/ Créer, 1994). The importance of the self-concept in Super's theory can be seen in the role it plays in his archway figure depicting his theory. The self-concept is the keystone that glues the whole structure of career determinants together (Super, 1990), the self-concept or the idea people have of themselves, and their competencies and interests are expressed in their career development. At the end of adolescence, a somewhat stable self-concept should be established and guide future development (Leung, 2008).

The development of the self-concept is also an interest of Gottfredson's (1981, 2005), especially in childhood and adolescence. The compromise concept refers to how people weigh their possibilities in reaching certain goals by taking into account constraints such as social status and cognitive development (Gottfredson, 1981). Her circumscription concept describes how occupational preferences are gradually circumscribed depending on the development of the self concept. Both Super's and Gottfredson's theories introduced aspects of career development that are important in life design during adolescence – namely, the importance of the self-concept or subjectivity in careers, the multiple sources of influence, and the importance of social variables in career choices. Both theories assume that the individual's self-concept is more or less in place at the end of adolescence.

The life design approach is in many ways linked to developmental approaches of the past. For example, it explains career development with the idea of adaptability rather than maturation. Career adaptability and readiness are examples of concepts used in Savickas's career construction theory that are close to Super's developmental tasks, although the inherent predictability of Super's stages is not included (Savickas, 2013). Maturation occurs best in a stable context, while adaptation is better suited to a changing context. Career development is essential to the life design approach, as different ages, contexts, new events, or situations call for both adaptability and narratability. "Adaptability addresses change while narratability addresses continuity. Together adaptability and narratability provide individuals with the flexibility and fidelity of selves that enables them to engage in meaningful activities and flourish in knowledge societies" (Savickas et al., 2009, p. 245).

Educational Perspectives

The daily life of adolescents centers on school, and experiences in school are of great importance for the developmental progression of careers (Guichard, 2011). On the one hand, school is a social institution with its hierarchy of educational programs (Berthelot, 1984), and on the other hand, it is a pathway toward the future. For some adolescents, this pathway is well paved, whereas for others it is filled with obstacles. Some adolescents become more committed to their studies, whereas others become disinterested and gradually drop out of school. The former group has the support of parents, has learning abilities, knows how to behave in school, and has no drug problems. The latter group is the opposite of the former group in these matters: little support from parents, learning disabilities, behavior problems, and drug abuse. Some young people belong to either of the two opposite groups at different periods in their lives. Without doubt, schooling has a different meaning to these two extremes of behavior in adolescence. Scientists from a wide range of social sciences have tried to explain why students become demotivated or uncommitted in school and eventually drop out. Is it because they experience their weaknesses in schools and look for strengths outside of schools in delinquency (Adler, 1936), or because schools are adapted to certain social classes (Bernstein, 1975; Bourdieu & Passeron, 1990)? Is it the teaching methods (Newmann, 1992), parenting style (Blöndal & Adalbjarnardottir, 2009), or lack of school engagement (Fredricks, Blumenfeld, & Paris, 2004)? This is a vast area of study, where a number of variables come into play. What we know for sure is that there are protective factors and risk factors, and the important ones are engagement and disengagement. Research has shown that dropping out is preceded with a long process of disengagement (Alexander, Entwisle, & Kabbani, 2001; Finn, 1989; Fredricks et al., 2004; Rumberger, 2011). Numerous research projects have revealed that career education and counseling is one of the protective factors in prevention of dropping out (Aðalbergsdóttir, 2006; Vilhjálmsdóttir, 2010). The role of career education and counseling of adolescents is to enhance engagement in schooling. From the point of view of life design, an emphasis needs to be put on the four dimensions of career adaptability and on the meaning of schooling for the adolescent's future. Schooling in itself is planning for the future, and an important career competency is to be able to plan. We need to enhance career adaptability because it "involves planful attitudes, self and environmental exploration and informed decision making" (Savickas, 1997, p. 254). The counseling activities need to enhance the sense of self in the now and in the future so that adolescents care for themselves and their future. This commitment or engagement is about finding strengths within (sense of self in the now) and making sense of those strengths (sense of self in the future).

Role of Social Variables in Career Construction

The emphasis in the field of career counseling has been on individual factors and development. It is nevertheless known that careers are somewhat predictable from social variables and that circumstances create unpredicted curves and bends on an individual's career path (Amundson, 1998; Berthelot, 1984; Goldthorpe, Llewellyn, & Payne, 1980; Halsey et al., 1980; Nash, 1999). Gottfredson (1981, 2005) theorized that gender and socioeconomic status have a major impact on vocational development. The social variables of gender and socioeconomic status act as filters, boys do not "see" women's occupations, they only look at the men's occupations. Gottfredson views the counselor's role as that of helping youths overcome self-limiting social constraints. Other researchers such as Riverin-Simard (1992) or Blustein (2006) have criticized career theory for not taking constraints of social class into account and for allocating privilege to "middle class phenomena" such as self-actualization. The concept of self-actualization in turn can therefore be expected to lead the way in the counseling intervention, whereas sociocultural resources might be a minor aspect of the intervention. Counselors need to bear in mind that "adolescents from various cultures and socioeconomic backgrounds are immersed in the developmental tasks of exploring themselves and their environments, enhancing their basic skills, experimenting with various work roles, struggling to find employment, and making plans for their futures" (Blustein, 1997, p. 387). It is the counselor's role to help people be aware of the role of their cultural background in the progression of their career.

Researchers in career counseling theory have used different educational and sociological theories to strengthen theoretical thinking on the role of social variables in career construction. Sociological theories, such as those of Bourdieu or Goffman, study how individuals construe themselves in a given society. French, English, and Nordic researchers (Colley, 2003; Guichard, 2005; Guichard & Dumora, 2008; Guichard et al., 1994; Hodkinson & Sparkes, 1997; Vilhjálmsdóttir, 2004; Vilhjálmsdóttir & Arnkelsson, 2013) have used Bourdieu's sociological theory to throw light on the social origin of career decisions and how the relation between social position and a social field can explain that sensible decisions are taken without much thinking. A distinguishing factor in the relation between position and field in adolescence are everyday choices and especially the consumption of music and other leisure items (Vilhjálmsdóttir & Arnkelsson, 2013). The analysis of one's social position, or socioanalysis, as Bourdieu calls it (Bourdieu & Wacquant, 1992), can assist adolescents in recognizing the weight of social influences on career paths.

The construction of an individual in a social context is a subject of study in both sociology and social constructionism and is one of the underlying theories of the life design framework. Reality is constructed through social processes and interpersonal relationships (Savickas, 2013), thus making the social aspect of experience just as important as the individual or psychological one. Two principles underlie social constructionism: First, that knowledge and identity are the products of social interaction; and second, that meaning is co-constructed through discourse (Savickas et al., 2009). When the counselor is given access to a story of career change it is important that he or she is aware of how the change came about in complex social interactions.

Career Construction Perspective

Savickas's theory of career construction is fundamental in the life design approach, providing both a conceptual framework and a model for career counseling and life design. According to this theory, individuals construe themselves through interpretive and interpersonal processes; they set course in their vocational behavior and give meaning to their experience. In adolescence, initial steps are taken in setting a direction and making meaning in a career. The competencies of adaptability and identity play a major role in designing a career and making a meaning of it. Both of these competencies emerge in adolescence and are integral in adapting to the environment (Erikson, 1968; Savickas, 1997).

Adolescents face the task of taking career decisions as the end of compulsory education approaches. At the same time, they have little or no experience in taking big decisions by themselves; new demands call for changes in identity, and with increasing independence, adolescents have to rely on their abilities to adapt to environmental changes. They have to decide by themselves what life means to them (Guichard, 2005). This process is a co-construction of a psychological self and social context (Savickas, 2011). While developing skills and talents remains important, having a well-established sense of self provides individuals with a more enduring way of making their lives work. Eccles and associates (1993) have drawn attention to the fact that school environments are not adapted to adolescents' needs for autonomy and relationships, so in this way, schools are not responding to needs of self-construction in adolescence.

The self has three layers according to career construction theory and is composed of the actor, agent, and author. Each can be related to different life stages and to different career theories. The layers of the self also serve as a basis for different kinds of career intervention. The actor builds a reputation, is capable of setting goals and seeing how they resembles people in their surroundings or not. The agent deals with career transitions and includes the four career adaptability dimensions. The author builds on autobiographical stories and uses them to "reflect on life themes with which to construct their careers" (Savickas, 2011, p. 8). All of the layers of the self take shape or are about to take shape in adolescence. Inexperienced, and often without aid in an unknown territory, adolescents find their role models, set goals in their surroundings, face vocational development tasks, and have to write new chapters in their life story. Independent thinking and a sense of self are needed for goal setting and recognizing meaning in life themes. According to Savickas, it is important for individuals to learn how to prepare for environmental changes and develop the abilities needed to adapt to career changes.

The theoretical construct of career adaptability denotes the readiness and resources for making career choices and negotiating career transitions. The four main dimensions of career adaptability describe the main resources for managing occupational transitions, developmental tasks, and work traumas (Savickas, 2005). These four dimensions are concern, control, curiosity, and confidence, and they describe the attitudes and abilities needed when facing career changes. Planning is the essential competency of career concern, and decision making is a basic competency in the career control dimension. Exploring is the crucial competency in career curiosity and problem solving in career confidence. These dimensions represent the strategies used by individuals when facing changes in their careers; they are strategies of career construction and fundamental in the agency of the self (Savickas, 2013).

Each perspective of the self is of importance when contemplating life design at adolescence and the factors and processes of a person's self-construction. One of the contributions of career construction theory is the career construction interview. A case study of a career construction interview will be given at the end of this chapter.

Interventions

Life design is a new conceptual framework that emerged from the integration of, among others, self-construction theory and career construction theory, integrating social and social constructivist theories, as well as intraindividual dynamic and learning processes, such as career adaptability and career competencies. The focus of this chapter has been on theories that have addressed life design in adolescence and have had an impact on the life design framework. Most of these theories assume that the main career competencies needed in adolescence are abilities and attitudes that strengthen vocational identity or a sense of self and aim for adaptation to inner and outer changes or career adaptability. Occupational activities are at the core of the identity structure (Guichard & Dumora, 2008), and vocational identity is the product of social interaction (Savickas et al., 2009) and is explored as such in the career construction interview. Competencies of career adaptability are psychosocial in nature (Savickas, 2013) and necessary when facing career changes. Enhanced vocational identity and career adaptability are important protective factors in adolescent lives. Career competencies in general are listed as follows: (1) self-determination, (2) self-efficacy beliefs, (3) ability to decide thoroughly and rapidly, (4) ability to spot and size opportunities, and (5) power to integrate career moves in a life story that makes sense (Guichard, 2011). These competencies are not formed in a social vacuum, but in an interaction between the inner and outer world. From the perspective of adolescence, it is important to note that career and life constitution competencies develop. Young people construe themselves by relating special skills they perceive, to activities, and they relate to special experiences that inform them about their interests or qualities. This leads people to identify with special fields and try out roles (Guichard, 2011), and the aim of career counseling is the co-construction of meaning in life and careers.

Guichard and Savickas both present career interventions as focusing on (1) information activities, (2) psychopedagogical guidance, and (3) counseling interaction (see Chapter 2; see also Guichard 2011; Savickas, 2011). Vocational guidance concentrates on giving information and looks at the client as actor. Career education focuses on teaching methods in completing career development tasks and looks at the client as agent. The co-construction of stories in a dialogue is in focus in career counseling and the client as author. In vocational guidance and career education planning, resemblance to others and readiness in engaging developmental tasks are at the fore, whereas career construction counseling and the life design model underline the reflexivity on life themes in an emerging story (Savickas, 2011). A life design intervention aims for the ability of entrepreneurship in one's own life, but at the same time to be able to reflect on that experience. Thus a life design intervention has a more encompassing perspective than just choice.

The paradigm of life design centers on individuals as (1) holders of an array of competencies that apply to their social settings and (2) designers and directors of their lives (see Chapter 2). The vantage point of life design is caring for the self and career management. From the point of view of the life design approach, preparing adolescents for the future would be to inform them of the fact that careers are constructed rather than chosen, and that they themselves are actors, agents, and authors of their lives, taking into account the impact of social forces. Preparing them for the future also means informing them about the processes of lifelong self-construction (Guichard, 2005) and that competencies are constructed.

Adolescence is a rather limited period in life, but characterized with an important identity change or change in the person's life story. The life design framework stresses the importance of preventing at-risk situations and beginning early to prepare children and adolescents for life changes in the process of growing up to become an adult. Workshops that actively engage people to explore and construe careers from a holistic point of view are part of the life design framework (Guichard & Dumora, 2008; Savickas et al., 2009). Savickas's career construction interview is an individual intervention focusing on the co-creation of a narrative centered on five questions. The questions are: (1) Who did you admire when you were growing up? (2) What attracts you to your favorite magazines or television shows? (3) What is your favorite book or movie? Tell me the story; (4) Tell me your favorite saying or motto; and (5) What is your earliest recollection? This method has not been used very much with adolescents, but its use with adolescents is explored in the case study below. Career construction theory and the life design framework will be used in interpreting the story.

Case Study

To demonstrate a life design approach, the author conducted a career construction interview with Elsa, a 17-year-old girl who said she was unsure about her future. Although graduation from upper secondary school was 2 years away, the interview revealed that she was currently struggling with career decisions. Listening to her story and having Elsa listen to her own story helped her in figuring out her next steps.

Elsa has just started her second year in upper secondary school. She has entered an educational program in business, because she wants to become an office clerk. But then she really doesn't know what kind of a job that is. Her dad works in an office with desks in an open space, and she just likes the way people communicate there – it is a nice workplace. She is also thinking of being a flight attendant, but then she is not good at languages. The main reason for coming to see a counselor is that she really is unsure about her future. She thinks the counselor can be useful in helping her straighten things out. Elsa came to see me twice. In the first session, she told me her answers to the five questions in the career interview. I will report them here in the same order as I reported them to her in our second session, starting with the earliest recollections.

Her first recollection was from when she was about 6 years old, with her parents. Her mother was not working outside of the home. This was before her brother was born, when the family lived in England. "I remember being in our garden with my mom. We had a lovely garden with squirrels and butterflies, apple trees and plum trees. I remember that I just had to shake the trees and fruits would fall down." The title for that recollection was "It Is Good to Be Abroad." The second recollection was from when Elsa was about 7 years old. She had always wanted a dog, and her dad was kidding her by saying that the new dog stuff that was up in the attic was a giant spider. "But I could see it was for a dog. We saw the dog every Saturday for two months and then he came to live with us, he was so cute." The title for this recollection was "Now the Dog Life Begins." The third story is about when her brother was born, and she was about 8 years old. She remembers that her dad picked her up at school, and they went together to a shop to buy a teddy bear. She remembers picking up a pink teddy bear, but her dad said that they will have to buy a blue one, because it's a boy. When she was at the hospital, she didn't care about the teddy bear. She had a baby brother. The title for this recollection was "Baby Brother Enters the World".

Elsa's recollections tell me that she is preoccupied with life changes and gender roles, something that is typical for adolescents. All of Elsa's early recollections are about a change occurring, in the first recollection she is in a paradise-like world with fruit trees and animals, the world before her brother was born, and she is alone with her mom. The change that occurs is her own doing when she shakes the trees, and wonderful fruit fall down. The second story of a dog life is really a beginning of a career. For the past 5 years Elsa has been a very successful dog coach at dog shows and won many awards, both national and international. To be able to do that she had to overcome her fears in presenting dogs, even dogs she does not know, and making them perform their best. When I tell her that I interpret the first and second story as her questioning whether to continue the "dog life" she says: "Do you read thoughts?" This was exactly what had been bothering her lately, and a few days ago her father was asking her if she was getting tired of it. The third story is about a big life change, it is about gender identity and choice. It is in fact a good example of how young children divide the world between "pink" and "blue" or spheres of work and study "appropriate" for men and women.

Elsa's role models are her aunt and Beyoncé. The aunt is only 10 years older than she is, and they are close friends. "She is a good listener, she gets me through trouble, and she's fun and well dressed. Beyoncé is cool, she makes good songs, she doesn't do drugs and she has a great family." A theme of the good family, good relationships, and solving problems that come up is also predominant in the settings she describes in her choice of magazines and movies. Elsa's favorite movie is *The Notebook*. Elsa says:

> It is a story of a beautiful relationship, caring for each other, being loyal to each other. The man cares for his wife when she is suffering from Alzheimer's disease. Sometimes she recognizes him and sometimes she doesn't. But he is always kind and caring, even though she can be mean to him due to her disease.

In our discussion, she says that a girl has got to do what a girl has got to do. I tell her that her interests are clearly social, but that her career choice of office clerk points to conventional professions and her experience as a dog coach points to the realistic environment. This would be a code of SCR in John Holland's RIASEC type codes of six different types of work environment: realistic, investigative, artistic, social, enterprising, and conventional. Professions like physiotherapist assistants or office workers in social services are examples of professions with the SCR code. Elsa said she could be interested in working in an office that deals with people; actually a relative of her does that. When I ask Elsa about her motto, she answers: "Life is too short for waiting for something special to happen; you just have to carry on." This is the advice Elsa is giving herself. She knows her life is changing, and that she will have to make career choices in the future, but at the same time she knows that she will have to decide soon what to do with her dog-coaching jobs. It is time consuming, and she knows that she only wants to present her own dog at dog shows. A few days earlier her dad had told her that the family would have a new dog, and she says she is willing to coach her own dog and have all of the family come to the dog shows and get together there. Gathering the family together in this activity is important to Elsa. She knows that she is growing up, she has to carry on, but at the same time, she wants to keep the family together. She also knows that she has not decided on a career in business or office work. She still has 2 more years to reflect until she finishes upper secondary school. She made a few changes to the story I told her, based on her answers to the five questions in the first session. Most of the changes were about dogs and dog shows. Elsa also told me that she was going to a big school dance after our session and was very happy about that. After all, Elsa is a teenager stepping into an exciting world filled with fruit trees, but at the same time leaving a world full of niceties, being an adolescent, she has to move on.

Elsa's grandmother brought her to our two sessions. The three of us had a chat in the beginning about the counseling sessions. Elsa was a bit uncomfortable in the beginning of the first session. She was unsure about her choice of an educational program, and as it turned out, she was also hesitating about her quite extensive work as a coach in dog shows. She gained confidence in our interview when she found out that I was not going to ask her about problems, but about things she admired or was thinking about by herself. Elsa was very comfortable when narrating her recollections, and she was quick in making titles for her recollections and her stories. She was discovering the social aspects of her interests, and seemed to be less interested in the office work in the second session. She could nevertheless see the advantage in combining social and conventional work environments. She found it quite amazing that I was detecting her struggle with her work as a professional dog coach. "Can you read thoughts?" she asked, and I said that this was what I thought she was telling me with her recollections. I could also sense that Elsa found this a pleasurable experience, and she wanted to be able to contact me again. She left for the dance with my business card.

Many concepts from the life design approach and underlying constructionist theories can be used to understand Elsa's story, as this was the story she needed to tell at this point (Del Corso & Rehfuss, 2011). It was a story of paradise lost, of a gendered world, of being able to take decisions, of a social person with unique gifts of controlling dogs and having them perform their best. Very little in her story was about office work, and at the end of the second session, she realized that. Her story is filled with people and dogs. She was certainly concerned about her career, but other dimensions of career adaptability were not really activated. Being young, Elsa does not seem to have a strong sense of self, her father is taking decisions, and her grandmother takes her to the session, but she has a strong sense of family and what good family life looks like. During the sessions, she became more alive and gained strength regarding changing her work in coaching dogs. She feels acknowledged for her talents in this field. In her studies, she is gaining competencies in business subjects, and coaching is a source of confidence for her. She has not yet established a connection between herself and occupations, or between her self schemata and occupational prototypes (Guichard & Dumora, 2008).

The intervention with Elsa can be analyzed from the six-step intervention model for life design (Savickas et al., 2009). In the first step, the problem is clarified, and themes and meaning are extracted from the client's narrative, with a focus on emerging life roles. In the second step, Elsa is exploring her system of subjective identity forms, exploring her current work role in presenting dogs at dog shows, and future work roles. In the third step, opening new perspectives is at the fore, and Elsa looks at the social aspects of her interests in caring for other people. The fourth step is about exploring new perspectives that are opened up, something that happened in this interview, as Elsa's social interests were explored. Elsa's counselor could have explored her story of the pink and blue teddy bear in this step, since it can be interpreted as a construction of gender identity. The fifth step on activities and the six step of follow-up were not pursued in Elsa's case, apart from the fact that she was very active in the two sessions; the adventure-like questions of the career construction interview gave the interview an amusing content.

Westergaard (2012) states that the following themes emerged when counselors and therapists shared what works in practice with young people: (1) importance of providing a safe space, (2) the quality of the counselor and the counseling relationship, (3) the need for flexibility, and (4) the use of creative approaches. It can be argued that most theories vouch for some variations of all of these. The advantage of the career construction interview is to provide a safe space because no questions are asked about background or any special problems (like low grades), and having the client narrate stories is definitely both flexible and creative. A great advantage of the career construction interview is that it opens up space to discuss the meaning of wants and likes for the situation at hand and for possible opportunities in the world of work.

Conclusion

Adolescence is a crucial life period in career development, although the direct contact of adolescents with the world of work has diminished. The increase of uncertainties in the world of work means that adolescents have to be prepared differently for it. They need to be prepared for regular career crises in their future, and at the same time, they need to be able to narrate their own story in the world of work and give it meaning. This knowledge needs to be introduced in the school curriculum. Constructive approaches in career intervention, such as the life design approach, offer counseling methods that are more adapted to this new work environment. Career interventions have to offer a safe space for making sense of self and creating ways to explore self and opportunities in study and work. The three types of career interventions – vocational guidance, career education, and career counseling – that explore the aspects of self as actor, agent, and author, have to be available to adolescents. At the same time, career interventions need to have a critical stance on the interplay between individual and social influences on careers and competencies.

In my counseling session with Elsa she asked me, "Can you read thoughts?" Elsa was giving me power, something she is used to in her relationships with adults. But in fact I was talking about the story she told me. Our adolescents have a lot to tell us and teach us about their world. Are we listening?

References

Aðalbergsdóttir, G. (2006). *An investigation into student dropout rates in Icelandic upper-secondary schools.* (Unpublished MPA thesis). University of Warwick, England.

Adler, A. (1936). *Kursus i individualpsykologi* [Course in individual psychology]. Oslo, Norway: H. Aschehoug.

Alexander, K. L., Entwisle, D. R., & Kabbani, N. S. (2001). The dropout process in life course perspective: Early risk factors at home and school. *Teachers College Record, 103*, 760–822. http://doi.org/10.1111/0161-4681.00134

Amundson, N. (1998). *Active engagement. Enhancing the career counseling process.* Richmond, BC: Ergon Communications.

Arnett, J. J. (2000). *Emerging adulthood: A theory of development from the late teens through the twenties, American Psychologist, 55*, 469–480. http://doi.org/10.1037/0003-066X.55.5.469

Association Trouver/Créer. (1994). *Éducation des choix* [Education of choice]. Sainte-Foy, Canada: Éditions Septembre.

Bernstein, B. B. (1975). *Class, codes and control.* London, UK: Routledge & Kegan Paul. http://doi.org/10.4324/9780203011430

Berthelot, J. M. (1984). Orientation formelle et procès sociétal d'orientation [Formal orientation and the processes of social orientation]. *L'Orientation Scolaire et Professionnelle, 13*, 91–113.

Blöndal, K. S., & Adalbjarnardottir, S. (2009). Parenting practices and school dropout. A longitudinal study. *Adolescence, 44*, 729–749.

Blustein, D. L. (1997). The role of work in adolescent development. *Career Development Quarterly, 45*, 381–389. http://doi.org/10.1002/j.2161-0045.1997.tb00541.x

Blustein, D. L. (2006). *The psychology of working: A new perspective for career development, counseling, and public policy.* Mahwah, NJ: Erlbaum.

Bourdieu, P., & Passeron, J. C. (1990). *Reproduction in education, society and culture.* London, UK: Sage. (Original work published 1970)

Bourdieu, P., & Wacquant, L. (1992). *An invitation to reflexive sociology.* Chicago, IL: University of Chicago Press.

Bulletin, contactpoint.ca (n.d.). *Interview with Dr. Mark Savickas*. Retrieved from http://www.contactpoint.ca/index.php?option=com_content&view=article&id=1152%3Afeature-interview-with-dr-mark-savickas&catid=107%3Awinter-2012&Itemid=37

Colley, H. (2003). Engagement mentoring for socially excluded youth: Problematic and holistic approach to creating employability through the transformation of habitus. *British Journal of Guidance and Counselling, 31*, 77–99. http://doi.org/10.1080/0306988031000086189

Coutinhio, M. T., Dam, U. C., & Blustein, D. L. (2008). The psychology of working and globalisation: a new perspective for a new era. *International Journal for Educational and Vocational Guidance, 8*, 5–18. http://doi.org/10.1007/s10775-007-9132-6

Del Corso, J., & Rehfuss, M. C. (2011). The role of narrative in career construction theory. *Journal of Vocational Behaviour, 79*, 334–339. http://doi.org/10.1016/j.jvb.2011.04.003

Dolgin, K. G. (2011). *The Adolescent: Development, relationships, and culture* (13th ed.). Boston, MA: Allyn & Bacon.

Eccles, J. S., Wigfield, A., Midgley, C., Reuman, D., Mac Iver, D., & Feldlaufer, H. (1993). Negative effects of traditional middle schools on students' motivation. *The Elementary School Journal, 93*, 553–574. http://doi.org/10.1086/461740

Erikson, E. H. (1950/1977). *Childhood and society*. St. Albans, UK: Paladin.

Erikson, E. H. (1968). *Identity, youth and crisis*. London, UK: Faber & Faber.

Eurostat. (n.d.). *Unemployment statistics*. Retrieved from http://epp.eurostat.ec.europa.eu/statistics_explained/index.php/Unemployment_statistics#Youth_unemployment_trends

Finn, J. D. (1989). Withdrawing from school. *Review of Educational Research, 59*, 117–142. http://doi.org/10.3102/00346543059002117

Fredricks, J. A., Blumenfeld, P. C., & Paris, A. H. (2004). School engagement: Potential of the concept, state of the evidence. *Review of Educational Research, 74*, 59–109. http://doi.org/10.3102/00346543074001059

Giddens, A. (1991). *Modernity and self identity*. Cambridge, UK: Polity.

Goldthorpe, J. H., Llewellyn, C., & Payne, C. (1980). *Social mobility and class structure in modern Britain*. Oxford, UK: Clarendon Press.

Gottfredson, L. S. (1981). Circumscription and compromise: A developmental theory of occupational aspirations [Monograph]. *Journal of Counseling Psychology, 28*, 545–579. http://doi.org/10.1037/0022-0167.28.6.545

Gottfredson, L. S. (2005). Using Gottfredson's theory of circumscription and compromise in career guidance and counseling. In S. D. Brown & R. W. Lent (Eds.), *Career development and counseling: Putting theory and research to work* (pp. 71–100). New York, NY: Wiley.

Guichard, J. (2005). Life-long self-construction. *International Journal for Educational and Vocational Guidance, 5*, 11–124. http://doi.org/10.1007/s10775-005-8789-y

Guichard, J. (2011). *What competencies do career practitioners need to help clients design and develop their careers and lives?* Erasmus Academic Network Nice [online]. Retrievedfrom: http://www.nicenetwork.eu/fileadmin/erasmus/inhalte/dokumente/Guichard_What_Competencies_do_Career_Practitioners_need_to_help_Clients_design_and_develop_their_Careers_and_Lives_01.pdf

Guichard, J., Devos, P., Bernard, H., Chevalier, G., Devaux, M., Faure, A., . . . Vanesse, V. (1994). Les activités culturelles et de loisirs des adolescents: une approche de la diversité des habitus sociaux [The cultural activities and free-time of adolescents: An approach to the diversity of social habitus]. *L'Orientation Scolaire et Professionnelle, 23*, 381–407.

Guichard, J., & Dumora, B. (2008). A constructivist approach to ethically grounded vocational development interventions for young people. In J. A. Athanasou & Van Esbroeck (Eds.), *International handbook of career guidance* (pp. 187–208). Dordrecht, The Netherlands: Springer.

Halsey, A. H., Heath, A. F., & Ridge, J. M. (1980). *Origins and destinations family class and education in modern Britain*. Oxford, UK: Clarendon Press.

Hodkinson, P., & Sparkes, A. C. (1997). Careership: A sociological theory of decision making. *British Journal of Sociology of Education, 18*, 29–44. http://doi.org/10.1080/0142569970180102

Homburger (Erikson), E. (1985). L'avenir de l'éducation sexuelle et la psychanalyse [The future of sexual education and psychoanlysis]. In M. Cifali & J. Moll (Eds.), *Pédagogie et psychanalyse* (pp. 81–100). Paris, France: Dunod.

Kuhn, T. S. (1962). *The structure of scientific revolutions*. Chicago, IL: University of Chicago Press.

Leung, A. S. (2008). Big five career theories. In J. A. Athanasou & R. Van Esbroeck (Eds.), *International handbook of career guidance* (pp. 120–121). Dordrecht, The Netherlands: Springer.

Nash, R. (1999). Realism in the sociology of education: "Explaining" social differences in attainment. *British Journal of Sociology of Education, 20*, 107–125. http://doi.org/10.1080/01425699995533

Newmann, F. M. (Ed.). (1992). *Student engagement and achievement in American secondary schools.* New York, NY: Teachers College Press.

Parsons, F. (1909). *Choosing a vocation.* Boston, MA: Houghton Mifflin.

Podesta, J. (2013, July 9). Relentlessly high youth unemployment is a global time bomb. *The Guardian.* Retrieved from http://www.theguardian.com/commentisfree/2013/jul/09/youth-unemployment-long-term-effects

Riverin-Simard, D. (1992). Career paths and socio-economic status. *Canadian Journal of Counselling, 26*, 15–28.

Rumberger, R. W. (2011). *Dropping out: Why students drop out of high school and what can be done about it.* Cambridge, MA: Harvard Educational Press. http://doi.org/10.4159/harvard.9780674063167

Savickas, M. L. (1997). Career adaptability: an integrative construct for life-span, life-space theory. *The Career Development Quarterly, 45*, 247–259. http://doi.org/10.1002/j.2161-0045.1997.tb00469.x

Savickas, M. L. (1999). The transition from school to work: A development perspective. *The Career Development Quarterly, 47*, 326–337. http://doi.org/10.1002/j.2161-0045.1999.tb00741.x

Savickas, M. L. (2005). The theory and practice of career construction. In S.D. Brown & R.W. Lent (Eds.), *Career development and counseling: Putting theory and research to work* (pp. 42–70). Hoboken, NJ: Wiley.

Savickas, M. (2011). *Career counseling.* Washington, DC: American Psychological Association.

Savickas, M. L. (2013). Career construction theory and practice. In S. D. Brown & R. W. Lent (Eds.), *Career development and counseling: Putting theory and research to work* (2nd ed., pp. 147–183). Hoboken, NJ: Wiley.

Savickas, M. L., Nota, L., Rossier, J., Dauwalder, J.-P., Duarte, M. E., Guichard, J., . . . van Vianen, A. E. M. (2009). Life designing: A paradigm for career construction in the 21st century. *Journal of Vocational Behavior, 75*, 239–250. http://doi.org/10.1016/j.jvb.2009.04.004

Steinberg, L. (2011). *Adolescence* (11th ed.). New York, NY: McGraw Hill.

Super, D. E. (1990). A life-span, life-space approach to career development. In D. Brown, L. Brooks, & Associates (Eds.), *Career choice and development* (2nd ed., pp. 197–261). San Francisco, CA: Jossey-Bass.

U.S. Department of Labor – Bureau of Labor Statistics. (2014). *America's Young Adults At 27: Labor Market Activity, Education, and Household Composition: Results From A Longitudinal Survey* (USDL-14-0491) Retrieved from http://www.bls.gov/news.release/pdf/nlsyth.pdf

Vilhjálmsdóttir, G. (2004). *Social group differences in occupational conceptualisations: Its relationship to career decision making and the relevance of careers education* (Unpublished doctoral dissertation). Hatfield, UK: University of Hertfordshire.

Vilhjálmsdóttir, G. (2010). Occupational thinking and its relation to school dropout. *Journal of Career Development, 37*, 677–691. http://doi.org/10.1177/0894845309357052

Vilhjálmsdóttir, G., & Arnkelsson, G. B. (2013). Social aspects of career choice from the perspective of habitus theory. *Journal of Vocational Behavior, 83*, 581–590. http://doi.org/10.1016/j.jvb.2013.08.002

Westergaard, J. (2012). Career guidance and therapeutic counseling: Sharing 'what works' in practice with young people. *British Journal of Guidance and Counselling, 40*, 327–339. http://doi.org/10.1080/03069885.2012.687711

Zytowski, D. G. (2001). Frank Parsons and the Progressive Movement. *Career Development Quarterly, 50*, 57–65. http://doi.org/10.1002/j.2161-0045.2001.tb00890.x

Chapter 9
Life Design, Young Adults, and the School-to-Work Transition

Jonas Masdonati and Geneviève Fournier
Laval University, Québec City, Canada

Introduction

The phase of life that young adults go through is difficult to name and define: Sociologists talk about "youth" (Galland, 2006), while in psychology, they are more often referred to as "emerging adults" (Arnett, 2006). Young adults between 16 and 25 years of age find themselves between two better-defined life phases – that is, adolescence and adulthood. These young adults constitute a population with diverse profiles and paths (Dietrich, Parker, & Salmela-Aro, 2012). From an educational and career counseling perspective, young adults in modern Western societies are, for the most part, in contact with two worlds that shape their path: on the one hand, school and the various forms of post–obligatory training; and, on the other, work and, more particularly, the labor market integration processes (Hamilton & Hamilton, 2006). What keeps young adults busy in terms of career development, and what constitutes the development task that marks their entry into adult life, thus revolves around these two worlds and their various overlapping elements. These overlapping elements are commonly referred to as the transition process between school and work (Masdonati, 2007).

In the following sections, school-to-work transition is understood as a process that occurs over time and involves the subjectivity of individuals. Regarding the temporal viewpoint, Hamilton and Hamilton (2006) state that

> the transition from school to work is not a simple one-time change that occurs when school is finished and employment commences. Rather, enrolment and employment are typically interwoven in a wide array of patterns, sequentially and simultaneously, throughout youth and emerging adulthood. (Hamilton & Hamilton, 2006, p. 259)

The adoption of a longitudinal perspective is all the more relevant given the increasing diversification of the pace and paths of education and job market integration over the last 20 years. Accordingly, it has become difficult to establish exactly when this transition begins and when it finishes (occupational stability may occur quite late in one's life course and perhaps never) (cf. Fournier & Bujold, 2005; Trottier, 2000). From a subjective angle, we are not only interested in "objective" changes that are part of every transition, but also in the way people bring these changes about (Dupuy, 1998). This is thus primarily a matter of the personal meaning and social significance that a person, in interaction with multiple environments, attributes to a transition, as well as of the personalization process and identity adjustment that the transition provokes (Baubion-Broye, Dupuy, & Prêteur, 2013; Masdonati, 2007).

The first aim of this chapter is to stress how the *life design* paradigm (Savickas et al., 2009) can lead to a better understanding of the ins and outs of the school-to-work transition process. Particularly, four key processes that mark school-to-work transitions will be described: The influence of the school and job market contexts, the importance of young people's relational environments, their identity construction during the transition, and their relationship to school and work. In the next four sections, we discuss each of these key processes and illustrate their relevance for the understanding of the school-to-work transition, by turning to recent literature and to the results of our own research. The second aim of the chapter is to point out the implications for guidance and counseling practices, of each one of the four key processes when they are analyzed from a life design perspective. These reflections also refer to one or another of the four goals of counseling based on the life design paradigm, as put forward by Savickas et al. (2009): *adaptability, narratability, activity*, and *intentionality*.

The School and Job Market Contexts

The first key process influencing the transition from school to work stresses the importance of contextual factors. As with any other phenomenon related to counseling and career transitions, various contextual elements affect the passage from school to work (Fouad & Bynner, 2008; Schoon & Silbereisen, 2009; Wolbers, 2007). Among these, two contexts play a central role in the way a school-to-work transition occurs: The organization of schooling and the configuration of the labor market (Blustein, 2006; Guichard, 2012).

In modern Western societies, qualifications and training level generally play an important role in the school-to-work transition process, people with higher qualifications being likely to experience more linear, and less chaotic transitions (Bynner & Parsons, 2002; Hamilton & Hamilton, 2006; OECD, 2010; Scarpetta & Sonnet, 2012; Wray-Lake, Syvertsen, Briddell, Osgood, & Flanagan, 2011). Above and beyond this observation, the educational system that is specific to each country or region shapes the way in which school-to-work transitions unfold (Guichard, 2012; Dietrich et al., 2012; Lannegrand-Willems & Bosma, 2006). For example, in countries where work-linked vocational education and training dominates (e.g., Switzerland, Germany, and Austria), the transition takes place at two institutionally stipulated moments – that is, when looking for an apprentice position in a company and at the end of training. Moreover, school–company alternation embeds the notion of post–obligatory training in the socioeconomic fabric such that this alternation has in itself become an established transition between the worlds of education and work (Masdonati, Lamamra, De Puy, & Gaydes-Combes, 2007). Conversely, in countries such as Canada, where work-linked vocational training is less common and where the majority of young people traditionally work during their studies, the school-to-work transition is less confined to a precise moment in the career path. Rather, it occurs progressively and without any real institutional regulation (Masdonati, Fournier, & Pinault, 2014; OECD, 2008). Furthermore, some educational systems, such as that of the United States, result in an early polarization of young people between students pursuing their education at the postsecondary level and those who go directly into the job market (*college*- vs. *work-bound youth*; cf. Hamilton & Hamilton, 2006; Juntunen & Wettersten, 2005;

Mortimer, Zimmer-Gembeck, Holmes, & Shanahan, 2002; Wray-Lake et al., 2011). Finally, the school-to-work transition is more or less dependent on how educational programs are structured and how a person's options depend on educational success. For example, the educational options of young French students are closely linked to their high school grades (Lannegrand-Willems & Bosma, 2006). However, the Finnish system attenuates the impact of the students' grades with a more flexible, less irreversible curricula organization. This includes more permeability between educational tracks and different types of supports when school difficulties arise (Guichard, 2012; Olympio, 2012).

The work market obviously influences the school-to-work transition process, particularly with regard to young people's labor market integration. Some general observations seem to characterize this integration, at least as far as modern Western societies are concerned. First, the various paths taken to enter the labor market are increasing in number and complexity for young people (Bynner & Parsons, 2002; Fournier, Pelletier, & Beaucher, 2003; Mortimer et al., 2002; OECD, 2010; Wray-Lake et al., 2011). Accordingly, the relation between training and work is becoming more elastic, and diplomas are no longer a guarantee of moving straight into a job in a given timeframe (Fournier, Monette, Pelletier, & Tardif, 2000; Papinot & Vultur, 2010; Trottier, 2000). Second, entry into the job market is now often marked by instability and even precariousness (Bynner & Parsons, 2002; Papinot & Vultur, 2010; Schoon & Silbereisen, 2009). Some groups are at greater risk: immigrants, people with low socioeconomic status, young people without qualifications, and from certain angles (particularly salary and part-time work), women (Bynner & Parsons, 2002; OECD, 2010; Wray-Lake et al., 2011). Finally, as with the educational system, the intensity and nature of job market effects are specific for each country and influence labor market integration (Wolbers, 2007). For example, in countries that are less affected by the recent economic recessions, such as Canada, these effects seem to be less intense (OECD, 2010; Scarpetta & Sonnet, 2012; Vuolo, Staff, & Mortimer, 2012).

Taking contextual variables into account in career counseling with young adults who are in transition between school and the work world implies going beyond interventions that focus exclusively on the person. This means both recognizing that contextual constraints may reduce people's control over their own life construction, and identifying strategies to limit or to cope with these constraints (Fournier, 2002; see also Chapter 2). First, since qualifications seem to be a key factor in successfully bridging school-to-work transitions, career counselors must first try to promote post–obligatory training courses that increase employability and work to keep students from dropping out (Lamamra & Masdonati, 2009). Second, career counselors must keep in mind that each school system establishes the key transition moments, and consequently, they should focus their interventions on these moments (Masdonati, 2007). Third, the nature and intensity of career counseling must respect the individual differences of young people in school-to-work transitions. This would involve, for instance, intervening earlier and more continuously with those who have a higher probability of encountering transition difficulties (Masdonati, 2007). Fourth, the increasing length and complexity of the school-to-work transition process suggest that interventions should accompany young people over time, all through the process (Masdonati, 2007). This would imply that counseling services be independent from educational institutions, thereby providing young people with genuine bridges between institutions or between school and work so as to keep them from falling into "gray zones" when they are no longer students and not yet workers.

The notion of *adaptability* allows us to conceive of career counseling that takes into account contextual variables (Savickas et al., 2009). From a life design perspective, adaptability is a personal resource that helps young people to cope with contextual constraints and unpredictability. In this sense, fostering clients' adaptability means guiding them to the construction of a vocational self-concept that takes into account contextual characteristics (e.g., expected competences and flexible work or school paths, see Chapter 2). Comprising four types of resources (*concern, control, curiosity,* and *confidence*; see Savickas & Porfeli, 2012), this notion encourages career counselors to help young people to "anticipate changes and their own future in changing contexts" (Savickas et al., 2009, p. 245). For example, counselors can help young people in transition to develop their *control* by (1) aiding them to set up strategies to overcome contextual obstacles over which young people have no power (e.g., a high unemployment rate in their region) and (2) identifying those areas which they can influence, where there is room to maneuver (e.g., adjust their approach to job hunting, consider moving, increase their network of contacts). To do so, career counselors can help young people to develop their *curiosity* with regard to different possibilities in labor market integration. This type of counseling is all the more relevant in the current unstable and unpredictable context in which new options unexpectedly emerge (Boutinet, 2007). In the same vein, career counselors should assist young adults in developing their *confidence* so that they will not give up too easily on their projects when they encounter apparently insurmountable situations. Counselors should likewise help young adults to explore the different paths leading to their goals and to keep their aspirations and objectives alive despite the difficulties of labor market integration. Finally, it is essential that young people become *concerned* about their personal projects and invest in these present and future endeavors.

Young People's Relational Environments

Young adults' social environments are the second key process playing a central role in the school-to-work transition (Blustein, 2011; Fournier et al., 2003; Masdonati, Lamamra, & Jordan, 2010; Phillips, Christopher-Sisk, & Gravino, 2001). Influence initially comes from family, peers, school personnel, and eventually work colleagues and policies for integrating new employees. This influence can take the form of social support or the transmission of particular representations of school or work.

In the academic field, teachers' social support is a determining factor in educational success (Knesting & Waldron, 2006). By way of illustration, a study conducted among young people who dropped out of vocational training in Switzerland showed that the quality of the relationship with the person in charge of the apprentice's training in a company was often the determining factor in the decision to continue or stop the training (Masdonati & Lamamra, 2009; Masdonati et al., 2010). In the work world, social support has an impact on several key factors, such as employability (Fournier et al., 2003); work satisfaction (Lent & Brown, 2006); self-efficacy and self-esteem with regard to employment integration (Monette & Fournier, 2000); well-being in, and expectations toward, the first job (Murphy, Blustein, Bohlig, & Platt, 2010); the construction of a professional identity and the work socialization of young people (Cohen-Scali, 2003); career choices (Phillips et al., 2001); and career adaptability (Kenny & Bledsoe, 2005).

When we examine the role of social support in school work transitions, it is useful to identify the types (or sources) of support, its possible functions, and their permanent or temporary nature (Goodman, Schlossberg, & Anderson, 2006; Masdonati, 2007). There are generally four types of support: "intimate relationships, family units, network of friends, and the institutions and/or communities of which the people are a part" (Goodman et al., 2006, p. 75). The literature tends to identify five social support functions: emotions, social integration or networking, protection of self-esteem, information, and tangible help (Palladino Schultheiss, Kress, Manzi, & Jeffrey Glasscock, 2001). Finally, social support can endure and be independent of the different roles played by individuals or, conversely, be limited in time and depend on specific roles – student, newcomer, etc. – that people play at given times in their career path (Goodman et al., 2006).

Above and beyond the source, function, and length of social support, the actual effect of this variable on people's occupational behavior depends on how they perceive and use this support (Blustein, 2011; Vanhalakka-Ruoho, 2010). This observation likewise holds for school-to-work transitions (Monette & Fournier, 2000). People can accept offers for support, refuse them, or actively pursue other offers (Phillips et al., 2001). In other words, not all social support is automatically useful, and in certain cases, it can even represent a barrier to a person's vocational development (Sarason & Sarason, 2009).

The relational environments also have an impact on the school-to-work transition process when they are analyzed from a representational viewpoint: Young people's educational and career choices and, therefore, their school-to-work transition are influenced by representations that are conveyed by their family, friends, and colleagues (Blustein, 2011; Vilhjálmsdóttir & Arnkelsson, 2007). A study underway shows, for example, that young people who were finishing their vocational training in Québec considered that this type of training had a negative social representation in Québec and was not highly thought of (Masdonati, Fournier, & Pinault, 2014). Though they were sensitive to this negative representation, the young people interviewed showed they were able to develop arguments that countered this representation and to continue their training. Part of this motivational support involved convincing their family and friends of the quality of the programs. Furthermore, the fact that these young people succeeded in changing their family's and friends' representations of vocational training made it easier for them to continue.

These observations lead to numerous implications for career counseling. Overall, it seems necessary to help young adults identify and take into consideration the resources and constraints in their relational environments if they wish to maximize their chances of successfully completing their education and entering the labor market. Career counselors can also constitute a source of social support during transitions. Their role is all the more important for young people who do not have any proximal support (e.g., parents, close friends, acquaintances) to help them in this process. Career counselors can indeed provide at least four of the five functions of social support. First, they can provide emotional support in case of difficulties, obstacles, uncertainty, in-between situations, and even precariousness. Second, they are able to aid young people in their occupational integration by helping them to better activate and enlarge their own network. Third, counselors can strengthen young people's self-esteem, especially when they are unsuccessful in their labor market integration. Fourth, career counselors are well-placed to help young people actively and effectively search for information about the work world or possible training opportunities once mandatory education is over (Masdonati, 2007).

Concerning the function of emotional support in particular, it seems essential for career counselors to build a working alliance with young people in transition. A working alliance consists of a good client–counselor relationship and an agreement concerning the goals of the counseling process and the means to achieve them (Castonguay, Constantino, & Grosse Holtforth, 2006). For example, we showed in a recent study on the effects of career counseling that a high level of working alliance helped to reduce decision difficulties and increase the impact of the counseling process (Masdonati, Massoudi, & Rossier, 2009; Masdonati, Perdrix, Massoudi, & Rossier, 2014). Above and beyond the emotional support benefits of a working alliance, these results illustrate the subjective dimension of the role played by social support: If support is to be effective, young people must first of all realize that it can help them to successfully complete their transition and reach their objectives.

Career counseling should ideally take into consideration all the different roles that young adults have or are likely to have. It must also aim to provide ongoing support that continues once young people have left the educational system (Masdonati, 2007). Likewise, it could be useful to have young people think about how the dominant school-to-work representations of people close to them affect their own representations and attitudes (Fournier, 2002; Masdonati, 2007). The possibility of contacting the proximal environment so as to work directly on their representations is likewise an option.

A brief analysis of the importance of the young people's relational environments in their school-to-work transition suggests that career counselors adopting a life design approach should insist on *activity* when working with young people (Savickas et al., 2009). This means concentrating on what people do and how they act in their actual life, since it is through, and in, action that young people interact with their environment. They obtain feedback, help, and different viewpoints that can lead them to discover new representations of themselves, their abilities, and at the same time, of their transition into the work world (Masdonati, 2007). Moreover, when these interactions take the form of a life design dialogue (see Chapter 2), they can engender *narratability*, which is very helpful in the transition phase (Savickas et al., 2009). Narratability is the process through which individuals narrate their own story, giving it coherence and continuity. As will be shown in the following section, accompanying people in their own self-narration may positively influence their identity construction. Self-narration allows them to search for continuity in a transitional situation, to give it meaning, and to formulate clearer intentions that are better rooted in their personal story.

Young People's Identity Construction

The school-to-work transition occurs during an important phase of identity construction (Arnett, 2006), which makes it the third key process. Identity construction is all the more important and arduous given that, in modern Western societies, the school-to-work transition period is becoming longer, is often accompanied by precariousness and, because of the above-mentioned multiplication of paths, is becoming more individualized (Schwartz, Donnellan, Ravert, Luyckx, & Zamboanga, 2012). On the one hand, the lengthening of the school-to-work transition is forcing some young people to pass through in-between, fuzzy situations that make for identity gray zones during which they are no longer students but not yet full-fledged workers (Fournier & Bourassa, 2000; Lamamra & Masdonati, 2009; Masdonati et al., 2007). On the other hand, the individualization of this transition implies that, due to a lack of stable and predictable social benchmarks, people are increasingly responsible for constructing their own identity (Guichard, 2009; see also Chapter 2).

In the literature, the phenomenon of identity construction during school-to-work transition has been approached from several angles. For example, developmental psychologists (e.g., Luyckx, Schwartz, Goossens, & Pollock, 2008), based on work by Erikson and Marcia, have looked at identity statuses, which are determined by the degree to which people explore and commit to their own identity construction, particularly as it relates to work (Vondracek, 2006). Authors who subscribe to a sociological or psychosociological perspective (e.g., Dubar, 1996; Mègemont & Baubion-Broye, 2001) look at the manner in which occupational socialization influences identity construction in newcomers to the labor market. Finally, authors who adhere to the life course approach (cf. Benson, Johnson, & Elder, 2012) often concentrate on the notions of subjective age and psychosocial maturity as factors that influence the educational and career accomplishments of young adults.

In the counseling field, identity construction is a central theme that has been analyzed from several angles (Cohen-Scali & Guichard, 2008; Vondracek, 2006). It is commonly approached in terms of vocational or occupational identity, a concept which, according to Skorikov and Vondracek, designates "the conscious awareness of oneself as a worker" (Skorikov & Vondracek, 2011, p. 693). This takes the form of "one's perception of occupational interests, abilities, goals, and values" but also involves a "complex structure of meanings in which the individual links his or her motivation and competencies with acceptable career roles" (pp. 693–694). During transition, young people are faced with a twofold identification: a work role identification, which involves the construction of a worker identity, and an occupational role identification, which entails the construction of an occupational identity (Ng & Feldman, 2007). This twofold construction takes place through transactions that are both biographical – that is, between past, present, and future selves – and relational – that is, in dialogue with the view of others (Dubar, 1996, 2007).

The construction of a worker identity arises out of the passage from one distinct world to another – in other words, from that of school and training to that of employment and work. Young people move from a student's or apprentice's identity to that of a person who now contributes to the production system (Ng & Feldman, 2007). From a biographical viewpoint, this generally symbolizes an entry into adulthood, which entails an access to a certain material, symbolic, and affective autonomy (Luyckx et al., 2008). Our research has also shown that building a worker identity sometimes allows students whose perception of school was negative to build a more positive self-image (Lamamra & Masdonati, 2009; Masdonati, Fournier, & Pinault, 2014). These studies also indicate that, from a relational viewpoint, taking on a worker status and role allows young people to become part of society and be recognized by others as "productive."

Young people in transition from school to work likewise construct an occupational identity: Not only do they become workers, they also generally do it in a specific sector or occupation. At this level, the biographical transaction initially consists in people projecting into possible future selves, based on past and present selves, and choosing an occupational field accordingly (Markus & Nurius, 1986; Oyserman & James, 2011). Once young people have begun working in a field with which they identify, they then attempt to fulfill themselves and develop their occupational skills (Fournier & Bujold, 1996). From a relational point of view, this implies a progressive process of identifying with occupational roles and of being recognized by their peers, which in turn can lead to a feeling of belonging to a profession or trade that shares codes, standards, and values, as well as a specific language and rituals (Lamamra & Masdonati, 2009; Lave & Wenger, 2002; Masdonati et al., 2007).

Given the above-mentioned importance of the school-to-work transition in identity construction, it is likewise understandable that this important period also involves sizable risks in terms of identity deconstruction or disruption (Zittoun, 2012). People encounter these risks when it is impossible to build a worker or occupational identity (Meeus, Dekovic, & Iedema,

1997). Those at risk include young people who have left the school system without any qualifications (Lamamra & Masdonati, 2009) and graduates for whom the transition period is longer
than foreseen, whose work-life conditions are more precarious, whose work experience has
become fractured and removed from their occupation, and who cannot progress in the above-
mentioned identification process (Fournier, 2002; Fournier et al., 2003).

Career counselors can contribute considerably to this identity-building process (Guichard,
2009). One of the central counseling tasks consists in helping people to find the biographical
meaning, to find a coherent, common thread in their past and present path, in their educational
experiences, as well as in their career projects and representations of the future (Boutinet,
2007). An analysis of this key process encourages us to pay particular attention to the gray,
fuzzy zones, those in-between, transitional moments during which people are more exposed to
questions and uncertainty about their identity. Here as well, counselors can play a key role as
a reliable benchmark in uncertain situations. This points once again to career counseling that
takes place over time and accompanies young people in the transitional process until they have
entered the job market and have been recognized by their coworkers.

Counseling must therefore focus on a twofold identity construction involving one's
worker and occupational identities, as previously mentioned. As concerns the construction of
a worker identity, career counselors must assist young people in preparing for the work world
(Masdonati, 2007). To do so, they need to become more aware of the many changes that are
part of moving from a student's role to a worker's role. One must understand one's new rights
and responsibilities; be ready to work in a company with colleagues, managers, and bosses;
deal with the economic demands of productivity and performance; manage a salary; etc.
Accompanying young people in building their occupational identity also constitutes a central
task in educational and career counseling. More precisely, it entails working on young people's
career projects. Counselors must ensure that projects are not simply reduced to choosing an
occupation and that they remain flexible enough to be adapted to the ups and downs of job
market integration. Moreover, these projects must have enough meaning, for young people not
to be overcome by job market fluctuations (Boutinet, 2007; Fournier, 2002; Young, Valach, &
Colin, 2002). Finally, in both cases, career counselors must pay even greater attention to young
people who have left the school system without a diploma and for whom identity construction
can prove to be even more difficult. In these cases, more intense support must be provided,
not only to make their job market integration satisfying, but also so that they will not question
their identity when they encounter difficulties.

The identity building aspect of a career counselor's endeavors to assist young people in
transition can be summarized by the notion of *intentionality*, as conceived from a life design
perspective. It calls upon people to "articulat[e] intentions and anticipations regarding possible
selves and life in the future" (Savickas et al., 2009, p. 246). From this viewpoint, accompanying young people in transition consists in bringing them, through narration, to draw biographical links with their past experiences (in particular, their educational path), their present
in-between situation, and their future perspectives as workers, as well as with their roles as
adults, citizens, etc. This work must allow people to give meaning to the current changes in
their lives and help them to confront the challenges of entering the work world: "Today, it is
the life story that holds the individual together and provides a biographical bridge with which
to cross from one job to the next job" (Savickas et al., 2009, p. 246).

Young People's Relationship to School and Work

The fourth key process is in line with our definition of the school-to-work transition as a process involving the subjectivity of individuals. In this sense, it is relevant to pay attention to the way young adults subjectively represent school and work, as well as to the perceived meaning and importance of school and work in their life. These different subjective aspects can be summarized as the young people's *relationship* to school and work. In fact, the literature shows that the configuration of the school-to-work transition process partly depends on the young person's relationship to school and work (Fournier et al., 2003; Johnson, 2001; Lannegrand-Willems & Bosma, 2006; Masdonati, Fournier, & Pinault, 2014). This last is then an aspect of identity construction that deserves separate treatment in regard to the pivotal role it plays in the transition towards the job market.

The relationship to school is generally associated with the relationship to knowledge – that is, "the (organized) set of relations that a human subject (*thus* singular *and* social) maintains with everything related to learning and knowledge" (Charlot, 1999, p. 3, translated by authors). This relationship to knowledge seems to depend on young people's educational experience, their specific life context (Prêteur, Constans, & Féchant, 2004), as well as on the type of school they attend (Capdevielle-Mougnibas, Garric, Courtinat-Camps, & Favreau, 2012). From the viewpoint of transition, it is thus essential to understand the personal meaning and social significance that each person assigns to school (de Léonardis, Capdevielle-Mougnibas, & Prêteur, 2006; Rochex, 2004). The meaning attributed to school refers to its perceived usefulness and its relative and absolute importance, and it influences young people's educational motivations. The significance of school depends particularly on the representation of school among one's family and friends, the habitus, and the inherited educational capital. In Québec, a province of Canada, we observed that there are several types of relationships with vocational training among young adults enrolled in this educational path (Masdonati, Fournier, & Pinault, 2014). In particular, a distinction appears between young people who have either a *compromise* or a *strategic* relationship with this type of training. For the former, vocational training represents a sort of compromise between the social requirement to obtain qualifications and the temptation to enter the labor market without a post–obligatory diploma. For the latter, vocational training represents a path guaranteeing good options for labor market integration. Their relationship is, accordingly, less ambivalent.

The relationship to work can also influence the transition from school to work (Harpaz, Honig, & Coetsier, 2002). This relationship is associated with the satisfaction that people draw from work and the meaning they give to work in their lives (Bujold, Fournier, & Lachance, 2013; Fournier & Gaudron, 2006). Sometimes associated with the notions of work attitude and meaning of work, the relationship to work can be operationalized as a synthesis of the importance that people attribute to work and the values they look for when working (Bujold et al., 2013; Harpaz et al., 2002; Mercure & Vultur, 2010).

The importance of work depends on how significant work is in people's lives (Nicole-Drancourt & Roulleau-Berger, 2001). Culturally dependent (Harpaz et al., 2002), this importance is notably determined by the perceived possibility of fulfilling oneself through work (Sverko, Babarovic, & Sverko, 2008). Our research among young people in transition to the labor market confirms that they generally see work as important in their lives (Fournier & Bourassa, 2000; Masdonati, Fournier, & Boisvert, 2014). The underlying reasons for this importance vary with the objectives that work is intended to meet. The importance of work for young adults thus differs according to whether they want to make money, socialize, grow, structure their life, or contribute to society.

Work values stem from "the relative importance individuals place on various aspects of work, including desirable work settings and work-related outcomes" (Jin & Rounds, 2012, p. 327). They reflect the aspects of work life that are significant for people or their expectations towards work (Hartung, 2006; Ros, Schwartz, & Surkiss, 1999). Among the many work value taxonomies proposed in the literature (cf. Rounds & Armstrong, 2005), one of the most often cited is that of Ros et al. (1999). These authors distinguish between four types of work values: intrinsic (e.g., autonomy, interest, growth), extrinsic (e.g., job security, income), social (e.g., relations, contribution to society), and status (e.g., prestige, authority, influence). Work values vary according to gender, social class, ethnic origin, age, occupational experiences, culture, generation, training projects/ambitions, and type/level of training (Duffy & Sedlacek, 2007; Jin & Rounds, 2012; Johnson, 2001; Warr, 2008; Wray-Lake et al., 2011). With regard to this last factor, we have, for example, shown that young people who finish vocational or technical training in Québec do not mention prestige-related values (Masdonati, Fournier, & Boisvert, 2014).

Examining young people's relationships to work in a school-to-work transition is, generally speaking, equivalent to focusing on what subjectively links them to their work life. For example, people's relationship to work influences their expectations concerning their future role in the workplace. In some cases, the reality of the integration process into the labor market does not meet their expectations. Scholars point out that a gap between expectations and reality may have negative impacts on young people's job satisfaction and on their job stability (Fournier et al., 2003; Hansen & Leuty, 2012; Rounds & Armstrong, 2005).

Career counseling with young people should then address each person's relationship to school and work. On the one hand, taking young people's relationships to school into account makes it possible to target eventual training projects that will be compatible with the personal meaning and social significance that these young people attribute to school or that will lead to other ways of representing school. Taking young people's relationships to work into account, on the other hand, allows counselors to ascertain the importance young people attribute to work, the values they are looking for, and the relation between work expectations and the reality of integration. Concretely speaking, this first of all implies that, to guide young people, one must conceive of and propose life counseling in addition to career counseling. The former can help young people to see work in relation to all the other life areas and find a balance with respect to their own hierarchy of values and priorities (see Chapter 2). Second, counselors must place the work value analysis at the heart of counseling (Savickas, 2005). They must be able to understand what young people are really looking for in work, as well as in possible future training experiences, and adjust their counseling to these values. Helping young people in transition become aware of what they want to achieve in their future jobs makes it possible to guide them toward various occupational fields but also toward companies, organizations, and post–obligatory training that better reflect their values. A third central aspect of counseling might consist in preparing young people for the possible divergences between, on the one hand, their expectations of their job and work integration and, on the other, what they will actually experience (Masdonati, 2007). This could be accomplished by informing them of the realities of the job market, but also by helping young people to concretely anticipate these gaps so that they understand and manage them better when they encounter them.

Narratability, which consists in bringing a person to tell his or her own story, seems to be the goal in life design–based interventions that best corresponds to the need in counseling to consider the relationship to work and school of young people in transition. Through narration, career counselors can explore the dynamic system of young people's subjective identities, analyze their interrelations, and identify the centrality of work and training in this system

(Guichard, 2009). From this viewpoint, counseling "aims to help people become fully aware of the ways in which they articulate their salient life roles and domains (including major past ones) in relation to some major future expectations in one or more roles" (Savickas et al., 2009, p. 245). This type of counseling likewise makes it possible to verify what young people's expectations are with regard to work and then to adapt career counseling to these expectations.

Conclusion

The four key processes of the school-to-work transition we have analyzed throughout this chapter generally confirm the importance of exploring each person's subjectivity and adopting a process-based, temporal perspective. For example, the same context can exert different influences on young people depending on how they interpret and integrate it into their own life story. Moreover, the characteristics of a given context impose a specific pace on the school-to-work transition process and determine the key moments. And even though identity construction is socially influenced, it is also a subjective development process that integrates the views of others, the assimilation of one's social position, but also the construction of a coherent understanding of past experiences, the present situation, and possible future selves.

As we have shown, understanding the challenges of the school-to-work transition for young adults by adopting a life design approach has important implications for career counseling. Overall, this type of career counseling goes beyond simple job market information and requires highly trained professionals who are skilled with advanced analytical tools and in guidance relationships and counseling dialogues (see Chapter 2). Ideally, this also implies that counselors respect the extreme complexity of the school-to-work transition process. We must consider the subjectivity of each young person; integrate the temporal dimension of school-to-work transitions; and target processes such as *adaptability, narratability, activity*, and *intentionality*, all of which help young people construct their identities in a changing context. These counseling approaches and goals are at the core of the life design paradigm and require considerable resources. Work remains to be done in many cases if we are to negotiate these counseling conditions and provide career counselors with the necessary resources to suitably accompany young people in transition. This is all the more important for counselors who work with young people who experience greater difficulties in this phase of life, which is both delicate and fundamental in the development of one's career.

The ideas put forward above have some limitations with regard to their generalizability. They apply, for example, to the school-to-work transition process as it occurs in modern Western societies (see Chapter 2). Unfortunately however, the scientific literature has not yet proposed detailed data or observations on the school-to-work transition process in other cultural contexts (Brown, 2000). There is a pressing research need to study the influence of the cultural variable on this process and thereby fill this counseling gap. Furthermore, research and counseling that targets a particular aspect or population of young people in transition – migrants, young nonconformists, pioneers, etc. – must indicate the specific manner in which these key processes act and are expressed in their precise context.

Finally, our vision of young adults is not neutral, but rather refers to a particular view of men and women – in other words, that of people who are active in a given context. From this viewpoint, the challenge is thus to investigate how individual agency can interact with contextual constraints and possibilities. From both theoretical and empirical viewpoints, it is important to understand the individual, the context, and the interface between these two elements of career development (Blustein, 2006). The life design paradigm, as with other contemporary approaches in fields closely related to counseling, like the life course approach (Elder & Giele, 2009; Vondracek & Hartung, 2002) or critical psychology (Stead & Perry, 2012), can bring us closer to attaining this objective. The practical challenge is twofold. First, it is important to further explore how we can better operationalize these theoretical and empirical indications in the form of coherent and effective counseling. Second, we must defend the independence and central role of career counseling in our societies and work to obtain the resources (in time, means, and counselor training) needed to put a life design–based counseling into practice.

References

Arnett, J. J. (2006). Emerging adulthood: Understanding the new way of coming of age. In J. J. Arnett & J. L. Tanner (Eds.), *Emerging adults in America: Coming of age in the 21st century* (pp. 3–19). Washington, DC: American Psychological Association. http://doi.org/10.1037/11381-001

Baubion-Broye, A., Dupuy, R., & Prêteur, Y. (Eds.). (2013). *Penser la socialisation en psychologie: Actualité de l'oeuvre de Philippe Malrieu* [Thinking about socialization in psychology: The work of Philippe Malrieu]. Toulouse, France: Erès.

Benson, J. E., Johnson, M. K., & Elder, G. H., Jr. (2012). The implications of adult identity for educational and work attainment in young adulthood. *Developmental Psychology, 48*, 1752–1758. http://doi.org/10.1037/a0026364

Blustein, D. L. (2006). *The psychology of working: A new perspective for career development, counseling, and public policy*. Mahwah, NJ: Erlbaum.

Blustein, D. L. (2011). A relational theory of working. *Journal of Vocational Behavior, 79*, 1–17. http://doi.org/10.1016/j.jvb.2010.10.004

Boutinet, J.-P. (2007). L'espace contradictoire des conduites à projet: Entre le projet d'orientation du jeune et le parcours atypique de l'adulte [The contradictory space of project conducts: Between the youth's orientation project and the adult's atypical path]. *L'Orientation Scolaire et Professionnelle, 36*, 19–32. http://doi.org/10.4000/osp.1259

Brown, D. (2000). Theory and the school-to-work transition: Are the recommendations suitable for cultural minorities? *The Career Development Quarterly, 48*, 376–384. http://doi.org/10.1002/j.2161-0045.2000.tb00882.x

Bujold, C., Fournier, G., & Lachance, L. (2013). The meaning of work among nonstandard workers: A multifaceted reality. *Canadian Journal of Counselling and Psychotherapy, 47*, 480–499.

Bynner, J., & Parsons, S. (2002). Social exclusion and the transition from school to work: The case of young people not in education, employment, or training (NEET). *Journal of Vocational Behavior, 60*, 289–309. http://doi.org/10.1006/jvbe.2001.1868

Capdevielle-Mougnibas, V., Garric, N., Courtinat-Camps, A., & Favreau, C. (2012). Formes du rapport au savoir chez des apprentis et lycéens professionnels de niveau V: Approche comparative [Forms of relationship to knowledge of level V (technical school certificate) students and apprentices: Comparative approach]. *Neuropsychiatrie de l'Enfance et de l'Adolescence, 60*, 94–100. http://doi.org/10.1016/j.neurenf.2011.09.003

Castonguay, L. G., Constantino, M. J., & Grosse Holtforth, M. (2006). The working alliance: Where are we and where should we go? *Psychotherapy: Theory, Research, Practice, Training, 43*, 271–279. http://doi.org/10.1037/0033-3204.43.3.271

Charlot, B. (1999). *Le rapport au savoir en milieu populaire* [The relationship to knowledge of the working class]. Paris, France: Anthropos.

Cohen-Scali, V. (2003). The influence of family, social, and work socialization on the construct of the professional identity of young adults. *Journal of Career Development, 29*, 237–249. http://doi.org/10.1023/A:1022987428665

Cohen-Scali, V., & Guichard, J. (2008). Introduction: Identités et orientations [Introduction: Identities and life designing]. *L'Orientation Scolaire et Professionnelle, 37*, 315–320. http://doi.org/10.4000/osp.1714

de Léonardis, M., Capdevielle-Mougnibas, V., & Prêteur, Y. (2006). Sens de l'orientation vers l'apprentissage chez les apprentis de niveau V: Entre expérience scolaire et rapport à l'avenir [Meaning of the entering into apprenticeship for apprentices of level V(technical school certificate): Between experience school and relation to the future]. *L'Orientation Scolaire et Professionnelle, 35*, 5–27. http://doi.org/10.4000/osp.867

Dietrich, J., Parker, P., & Salmela-Aro, K. (2012). Phase-adequate engagement at the post-school transition. *Developmental Psychology, 48*, 1575–1593. http://doi.org/10.1037/a0030188

Dubar, C. (1996). *La socialisation: Construction des identités sociales et professionnelles* [Socialization: The construction of social and occupational identities] (2nd ed.). Paris, France: Armand Colin.

Dubar, C. (2007). La crise des identités professionnelles [The crisis of occupational identities]. In C. Dubar (Ed.), *La crise des identités: L'interprétation d'une mutation* (pp. 95–128). Paris, France: Presses Universitaires de France.

Duffy, R. D., & Sedlacek, W. E. (2007). The work values of first-year college students: Exploring group differences. *The Career Development Quarterly, 55*, 359–364. http://doi.org/10.1002/j.2161-0045.2007. tb00090.x

Dupuy, R. (1998). Transitions et transformation des identités professionnelles [Transitions and transformations of occupational identities]. In A. Baubion-Broye (Ed.), *Evénements de vie, transitions et construction de la personne* (pp. 45–71). Saint-Agne, France: Erès.

Elder, G. H., Jr., & Giele, J. Z. (2009). Life course studies: An evolving field. In G. H. Elder Jr. & J. Z. Giele (Eds.), *The craft of life course research* (pp. 1–24). New York, NY: Guilford Press.

Fouad, N. A., & Bynner, J. (2008). Work transitions. *American Psychologist, 63*, 241–251. http://doi.org/10.1037/0003-066X.63.4.241

Fournier, G. (2002). L'insertion professionnelle: Vers une compréhension dynamique de ce qu'en pensent les jeunes [Professional integration: Towards a dynamic understanding of what young people think]. *Carriérologie, 8*, 365–387.

Fournier, G., & Bourassa, B. (2000). Le travail des 18 à 30 ans: Vers une nouvelle norme [Working between 18 and 30 years old: Towards a new norm]. In G. Fournier & B. Bourassa (Eds.), *Les 18 à 30 ans et le marché du travail: Quand la marge devient la norme...* (pp. 3–31). Québec, Canada: Presses de l'Université Laval.

Fournier, G., & Bujold, C. (1996). Accroissement du sens de l'identité personnelle et sociale au cours de la transition études/travail [The increase of the sense of personal and social identity during the school-to-work transition]. *Revue Canadienne de Counseling/ Canadian Journal of Counseling, 30*, 165–178.

Fournier, G., & Bujold, C. (2005). Nonstandard career trajectories and their various forms. *Journal of Career Assessment, 13*, 415–438. http://doi.org/10.1177/1069072705277917

Fournier, G., & Gaudron, J.-P. (2006). Significations du travail et rôles de vie: perspectives dialectiques et stratégiques [Meanings of work and life roles: Strategic and dialectical perspectives]. *Carriéologie, 10*, 377–392.

Fournier, G., Monette, M., Pelletier, R., & Tardif, P. (2000). Les diplômés et l'insertion socioprofessionnelle: Résignation déguisée ou adaptation saine à un marché du travail insensé [The professional integration of graduates: Disguised resignation or healthy adaptation to a senseless labor market]. In G. Fournier & M. Monette (Eds.), *L'insertion socioprofessionnelle: Un jeu de stratégies ou un jeu de hasard?* (pp. 1–35). Ste-Foy, Canada: Presses de l'Université Laval.

Fournier, G., Pelletier, R., & Beaucher, C. (2003). Types et itinéraires d'insertion socioprofessionnelle de jeunes diplômés: Caractéristiques et profils sociodémographiques [Professional integration types and trajectories of young graduates: Characteristics and sociodemographic profiles]. *The Canadian Journal of Higher Education, 32*, 49–83.

Galland, O. (2006). Jeunesse [Youth]. In S. Mesure & P. Savidan (Eds.), *Le dictionnaire des sciences humaines* (pp. 648–651). Paris, France: Presses Universitaires de France.

Goodman, J., Schlossberg, N. K., & Anderson, M. L. (2006). *Counseling adults in transition: Linking practice with theory* (3rd ed.). New York, NY: Springer.

Guichard, J. (2009). Self-constructiong. *Journal of Vocational Behavior, 75*, 251–258. http://doi.org/10.1016/j. jvb.2009.03.004

Guichard, J. (2012). L'organisation de l'école et la structuration des intentions d'avenir des jeunes [The school organization and the structuring of young people's future intentions]. In F. Picard & J. Masdonati (Eds.),

Les parcours d'orientation des jeunes: Dynamiques institutionnelles et identitaires (pp. 15–50). Québec, Canada: Presses de l'Université Laval.

Hansen, J.-I. C., & Leuty, M. E. (2012). Work values across generations. *Journal of Career Assessment, 20,* 34–52. http://doi.org/10.1177/1069072711417163

Hamilton, S. F., & Hamilton, M. A. (2006). School, work, and emerging adulthood. In A. J. Arnett & J. L. Tanner (Eds.), *Emerging adults in America: Coming of age in the 21st century* (pp. 257–277). Washington, DC: American Psychological Association. http://doi.org/10.1037/11381-001

Harpaz, I., Honig, B., & Coetsier, P. (2002). A cross-cultural longitudinal analysis of the meaning of work and the socialization process of career starters. *Journal of World Business, 37,* 230–244. http://doi.org/10.1016/S1090-9516(02)00090-1

Hartung, P. J. (2006). Values. In J. Greenhaus, & G. Callanan (Eds.), *Encyclopedia of career development* (pp. 844–848). Thousand Oaks, CA: Sage. http://doi.org/10.4135/9781412952675.n291

Jin, J., & Rounds, J. (2012). Stability and change in work values: A meta-analysis of longitudinal studies. *Journal of Vocational Behavior, 80,* 326 339. http://doi.org/10.1016/j.jvb.2011.10.007

Johnson, M. K. (2001). Change in job values during the transition to adulthood. *Work and Occupations, 28,* 315–345. http://doi.org/10.1177/0730888401028003004

Juntunen, C. L., & Wettersten, K. B. (2005). Broadening our understanding of work-bound youth: A challenge for career counseling. In S. D. Brown & R. W. Lent (Eds.), *Career development and counseling: Putting theory and research to work* (pp. 573–599). Hoboken, NJ: Wiley.

Kenny, M. E., & Bledsoe, M. (2005). Contributions of the relational context to career adaptability among urban adolescents. *Journal of Vocational Behavior, 66,* 257–272. http://doi.org/10.1016/j.jvb.2004.10.002

Knesting, K., & Waldron, N. (2006). Willing to play the game: How at-risk students persist in school. *Psychology in the Schools, 43,* 599–611. http://doi.org/10.1002/pits.20174

Lamamra, N., & Masdonati, J. (2009). *Arrêter une formation professionnelle: Mots et maux d'apprenti-e-s* [Interrupting a vocational training program: Words and aches of apprentices]. Lausanne, Switzerland: Antipodes.

Lannegrand-Willems, L., & Bosma, H. A. (2006). Identity development-in-context: The school as an important context for identity development. *Identity: An International Journal of Theory and Research, 6,* 85–113. http://doi.org/10.1207/s1532706xid0601_6

Lave, J., & Wenger, E. (2002). *Situated learning: Legitimate peripheral participation* (10th ed.). Cambridge, UK: University Press.

Lent, R. W., & Brown, S. D. (2006). Integrating person and situation perspectives on work satisfaction: A social cognitive view. *Journal of Vocational Behavior, 69,* 236–247. http://doi.org/10.1016/j.jvb.2006.02.006

Luyckx, K., Schwartz, S. J., Goossens, L., & Pollock, S. (2008). Employment, sense of coherence, and identity formation: Contextual and psychological processes on the pathway to sense of adulthood. *Journal of Adolescent Research, 23,* 566–591. http://doi.org/10.1177/0743558408322146

Markus, H., & Nurius, P. (1986). Possible selves. *American Psychologist, 41,* 954–969. http://doi.org/10.1037/0003-066X.41.9.954

Masdonati, J. (2007). *La transition entre école et monde du travail: Préparer les jeunes à l'entrée en formation professionnelle* [The school-to-work transition: Preparing young people for vocational education and training]. Bern, Switzerland: Peter Lang.

Masdonati, J., Fournier, G., & Boisvert, S. (2014). *Le goût du travail: L'évolution du rapport au travail des jeunes adultes en phase de transition école-emploi. Rapport pour les participant·e·s* [The taste of working: The evolution of the relationship to work of young adults in transition from school to employment. Report for participants]. Retrieved from https://www.fse.ulaval.ca/fichiers/site_crievat/documents/Rapports_de_recherche/Rapport-participants_V5_140905-120dpi.pdf.

Masdonati, J., Fournier, G., & Pinault, M. (2014). *La formation professionnelle: Le regard des élèves* [Vocational education and training in Quebec: The students' points of view]. Manuscript submitted for publication.

Masdonati, J., & Lamamra, N. (2009). La relation entre apprenti-e et personne formatrice au cœur de la transmission des savoirs en formation professionnelle [The relationship between apprentice and trainer as a key feature of the knowledge transmission in vocational education and training]. *Revue Suisse des Sciences de l'Éducation, 31,* 335–353.

Masdonati, J., Lamamra, N., De Puy, J., & Gay-des-Combes, B. (2007). Les enjeux identitaires de la forma-tion professionnelle duale en Suisse: Un tableau en demi-teinte [Identity issues of the Swiss dual vocation-al education and training system: A portrait with mixed results]. *Formation Emploi, 100,* 15–29.

Masdonati, J., Lamamra, N., & Jordan, M. (2010). Vocational education and training attrition and the school-to-work transition. *Education + Training, 52,* 404–414. http://doi.org/10.1108/ 00400911011058343

Masdonati, J., Massoudi, K., & Rossier, J. (2009). Effectiveness of career counseling and the impact of the working alliance. *Journal of Career Development, 36,* 183–203. http://doi.org/10.1177/0894845309340798

Masdonati, J., Perdrix, S., Massoudi, K., & Rossier, J. (2014). Working alliance as a moderator and a media-tor of career counseling effectiveness. *Journal of Career Assessment, 22,* 3–17. http://doi.org/ 10.1177/1069072713487489

Meeus, W., Dekovic, M., & Iedema, J. (1997). Unemployment and identity in adolescence: A social compari-son perspective. *The Career Development Quarterly, 45,* 369–380. http://doi.org/10.1002/j.2161-0045.1997. tb00540.x

Mègemont, J.-L., & Baubion-Broye, A. (2001). Dynamiques identitaires et représentations de soi dans une phase de transition professionnelle et personnelle [Identity dynamics and self representations in a profes-sional and personal transition phase]. *Connexions, 76,* 15–28. http://doi.org/10.3917/cnx.076.0015

Mercure, D., & Vultur, M. (2010). *La signification du travail* [The meaning of work]. Québec, Canada: Presses de l'Université Laval.

Monette, M., & Fournier, G. (2000). Soutien social et adaptation à la transition entre les études et le marché du travail [Social support and adaptation to the transition between education and the labor market]. In G. Fournier & M. Monette (Eds.), *L'insertion socioprofessionnelle: Un jeu de stratégie ou un jeu de hasard?* (pp. 57–76). Sainte-Foy, Canada: Presses de l'Université Laval.

Mortimer, J. T., Zimmer-Gembeck, M. J., Holmes, M., & Shanahan, M. J. (2002). The process of occupation-al decision making: Patterns during the transition to adulthood. *Journal of Vocational Behavior, 61,* 439–465. http://doi.org/10.1006/jvbe.2002.1885

Murphy, K. A., Blustein, D. L., Bohlig, A. J., & Platt, M. G. (2010). The college-to-career transition: An ex-ploration of emerging adulthood. *Journal of Counseling & Development, 88,* 174–181. http://doi. org/10.1002/j.1556-6678.2010.tb00006.x

Ng, W. H. T., & Feldman, D. C. (2007). The school-to-work transition: A role identity perspective. *Journal of Vocational Behavior, 71,* 114–134. http://doi.org/10.1016/j.jvb.2007.04.004

Nicole-Drancourt, C., & Roulleau-Berger, L. (2001). *Les jeunes et le travail: 1950–2000* [Young people and work: 1950-2000]. Paris, France: Presses Universitaires de France.

OECD. (2008). *Jobs for youth: Canada.* Paris, France: Author.

OECD. (2010). *Off to a good start? Jobs for youth.* Paris, France: Author. http://doi.org/10.1787/9789264096127-en

Olympio, N. (2012). Les contextes éducatifs européens à l'épreuve de la théorie des « capabilités » d'Amartya Sen [The European educational contexts to the test of Amartya Sen's capabilities theory]. In F. Picard & J. Masdonati (Eds.), *Les parcours d'orientation des jeunes: Dynamiques institutionnelles et identitaires* (pp. 95–124). Québec, Canada: Presses de l'Université Laval.

Oyserman, D., & James, L. (2011). Possible identities. In S. J. Schwartz, K. Luyckx, & V. L. Vignoles (Eds.), *Handbook of identity theory and research* (pp. 117–145). New York, NY: Springer. http://doi.org/10.1007/978-1-4419-7988-9_6

Palladino Schultheiss, D. E., Kress, H. M., Manzi, A. J., & Jeffrey Glasscock, J. M. (2001). Relational influ-ences in career development: A qualitative inquiry. *The Counseling Psychologist, 29,* 216–241. http://doi. org/10.1177/0011000001292003

Papinot, C., & Vultur, M. (Eds.). (2010). *Les jeunesses au travail: Regards croisés France-Québec* [Youth at work: Crossed views from France and Quebec]. Québec, Canada: Presses de l'Université Laval.

Phillips, S. D., Christopher-Sisk, E. K., & Gravino, K. L. (2001). Making career decisions in a relational con-text. *The Counseling Psychologist, 29,* 193–214. http://doi.org/10.1177/0011000001292002

Prêteur, Y., Constans, S., & Féchant, H. (2004). Rapport au savoir et (dé)mobilisation scolaire chez des collégiens de troisième [Relationship to knowledge and school (de)mobilization among third year students]. *Pratiques Psychologiques, 10,* 119–132. http://doi.org/10.1016/j.prps.2004.04.001

Rochex, J.-Y. (2004). La notion de rapport au savoir: Convergences et débats théoriques [The concept of rela-tionship to knowledge: Convergences and theoretical debates]. *Pratiques Psychologiques, 10,* 93–106. http://doi.org/10.1016/j.prps.2004.03.001

Ros, M., Schwartz, S. H., & Surkiss, S. (1999). Basic individual values, work values, and the meaning of work. *Applied Psychology: An International Review, 48*, 49–71. http://doi.org/10.1111/j.1464-0597.1999.tb00048.x

Rounds, J. B., & Armstrong, P. I. (2005). Assessment of needs and values. In S. D. Brown & R. W. Lent (Eds.), *Career development and counseling: Putting theory and research to work* (pp. 305–329). Hoboken, NJ: Wiley.

Sarason, I. G., & Sarason, B. R. (2009). Social support: Mapping the construct. *Journal of Social and Personal Relationships, 26*, 113–120. http://doi.org/10.1177/0265407509105526

Savickas, M. L. (2005). The theory and practice of career construction. In S. D. Brown & R. W. Lent (Eds.), *Career development and counseling: Putting theory and research into work* (pp. 42–70). Hoboken, NJ: Wiley.

Savickas, M. L., Nota, L., Rossier, J., Dauwalder, J.-P., Duarte, M. E., Guichard, J., . . . van Vianen A. E. M. (2009). Life designing: A paradigm for career construction in the 21st century. *Journal of Vocational Behavior, 75*, 239–250. http://doi.org/10.1016/j.jvb.2009.04.004

Savickas, M. L., & Porfeli, E. L. (2012). Career Adapt-Abilities Scale: Construction, reliability, and measurement equivalence across 13 countries. *Journal of Vocational Behavior, 80*, 661–673. http://doi.org/10.1016/j.jvb.2012.01.011

Scarpetta, S., & Sonnet, A. (2012). Challenges facing European labour markets: Is a skill upgrade the appropriate instrument? *Intereconomics, 1*, 4–10. http://doi.org/10.1007/s10272-012-0402-2

Schoon, I., & Silbereisen, R. K. (2009). Conceptualising school-to-work transitions in context. In I. Schoon & R. K. Silbereisen (Eds.), *Transitions from school to work: Globalization, individualization, and patterns of diversity* (pp. 3–29). Cambridge, UK: Cambridge University Press. http://doi.org/10.1017/CBO9780511605369

Schwartz, S. J., Donnellan, M. B., Ravert, R. D., Luyckx, K., & Zamboanga, B. L. (2012). Identity development, personality, and well-being in adolescence and emerging adulthood: Theory, research, and recent advances. In I. B. Weiner (Series Ed.), R. M. Lerner, A. Easterbrooks, & J. Mistry (Vol. Eds.), *Handbook of Psychology: Vol. 6. Developmental psychology* (pp. 339–364). New York, NY: Wiley.

Skorikov, V. B., & Vondracek, F. W. (2011). Occupational identity. In S. J. Schwartz, K. Luyckx, & V. L. Vignoles (Eds.), *Handbook of identity theory and research* (pp. 693–714). New York, NY: Springer. http://doi.org/10.1007/978-1-4419-7988-9_29

Stead, G. B., & Perry, J. C. (2012). Toward critical psychology perspectives of work-based transitions. *Journal of Career Development, 39*, 315–320. http://doi.org/10.1177/0894845311405661

Sverko, B., Babarovic, T., & Sverko, I. (2008). Assessment of values and role salience. In J. A. Athanasou & R. Van Esbroeck (Eds.), *International handbook of career guidance* (pp. 539–563). Dordrecht, The Netherlands: Springer.

Trottier, C. (2000). Questionnement sur l'insertion professionnelle des jeunes [Questioning the professional integration of young people]. *Lien Social et Politiques - RIAC, 43*, 93–101. http://doi.org/10.7202/005242ar

Vanhalakka-Ruoho, M. (2010). Relational aspects in career and life-designing of young people. *International Journal for Educational and Vocational Guidance, 10*, 109–123. http://doi.org/10.1007/s10775-010-9178-8

Vilhjálmsdóttir, G., & Arnkelsson, G. B. (2007). Les différences liées au sexe dans les représentations professionnelles [Gender differences in cognitive mapping of occupations]. *L'Orientation Scolaire et Professionnelle, 36*, 421–434. http://doi.org/10.4000/osp.1493

Vondracek, F. W. (2006). Identity. In J. Greenhaus & G. Callanan (Eds.), *Encyclopedia of career development* (pp. 372–375). Thousand Oaks, CA: Sage. http://doi.org/10.4135/9781412952675.n130

Vondracek, F. W., & Hartung, P. J. (2002). Introduction: Innovating career development using advances in life course and life-span theory. *Journal of Vocational Behavior, 61*, 375–380. http://doi.org/10.1006/jvbe.2002.1879

Vuolo, M., Staff, J., & Mortimer, J. T. (2012). Weathering the great recession: Psychological and behavioral trajectories in the transition from school to work. *Developmental Psychology, 48*, 1759–1773. http://doi.org/10.1037/a0026047

Warr, P. (2008). Work values: Some demographic and cultural correlates. *Journal of Occupational and Organizational Psychology, 81*, 751–775. http://doi.org/10.1348/096317907X263638

Wolbers, M. H. J. W. (2007). Patterns of labour market entry: A comparative perspective on school-to-work transitions in 11 European countries. *Acta Sociologica, 50*, 189–210. http://doi.org/10.1177/0001699307080924

Wray-Lake, L., Syvertsen, A. K., Briddell, L., Osgood, D. W., & Flanagan, C. A (2011). Exploring the changing meaning of work for American high school seniors from 1976 to 2005. *Youth & Society, 43*, 1110–1135. http://doi.org/10.1177/0044118X10381367

Young, R. A., Valach, L., & Colin, A. (2002). A contextual explanation of career. In D. Brown & Associates (Eds.), *Career choice and development* (4th ed., pp. 206–252). San Francisco, CA: Jossey-Bass.

Zittoun, T. (2012). Une psychologie des transitions: Des ruptures aux ressources [A psychology of transitions: From ruptures to resources]. In P. Curchod, P.-A. Doudin, & L. Lafortune (Eds.), *Les transitions à l'école* (pp. 261–279). Québec, Canada: Presses de l'Université du Québec.

Chapter 10
Life Designing With Adults: Developmental Individualization Using Biographical Bricolage

Mark L. Savickas

Family and Community Medicine Department, Northeast Ohio Medical University, Rootstown, OH, USA

Introduction

The technological revolution of the 21st century, similar to the Industrial Revolution before it, has wrought dramatic changes in the occupational landscape and made it progressively more complex for individuals to choose occupations and adapt to work. The life course has become a "biography of choice" (Heinz, 2002) because adults must repeatedly explore, choose, and change roles and even life structures. In the field which was once simply vocational guidance, an additional paradigm emerged during the last decade to address the new sets of problems experienced by the members of society living in increasingly uncertain and complicated times. During the 20th century, vocational guidance practitioners could focus on helping adolescents in high school and emerging adults in college make "the" choice. The digital revolution and global economy have changed the contract between employers and employees so that school-leavers no longer choose a 30-year career. Today, adults repeatedly encounter the need to make new choices during a 40-year working life. Rather than offering permanent jobs and life-time employment, organizations now increasingly offer fixed-term projects and assignments. Before considering the two more recent paradigms for career services, I will consider briefly the foundational paradigm of vocational guidance.

Vocational Guidance

In response to the Industrial Revolution, society rearranged work into occupations. What had been the routine daily *chores* of farming became separated into distinct *jobs*. The first scientific paradigm for career intervention, known as vocational guidance, was devised by Parsons (1909) as a scientific approach to matching people to occupations and finding jobs in those occupations. Typically, counselors guided – that is, directed or advised – the lost by recognizing who they resembled and then encouraging them to explore occupations in which they would interact with similar personality types. Thus, the paradigm for vocational guidance concentrated on the construct of *resemblance*. Counselors observed individuals and identified their standing on some enduring traits that differentiated among occupational groups. This practice relied on the stability of occupations. Its epistemology of *formism* (Pepper, 1942/1970) assumed that reality is stable and that observers can perceive the essential quality of individuals. With its root metaphor of similarity or type, formism attempts to answer the question, what is it like? by classifying objects in the world. Of course, for vocational guidance, the question became, who does the client resemble? The guidance paradigm was developed primarily by educators to assist students choose academic majors, make occupational choices, and transition from school to work. Originally, this activity was viewed as an event that took place late in adolescence, with the individual expecting to spent 30 years or more working in the same occupation, and possibly even for the same employer. The emblematic representation of occupational choice portrays a young person standing at a crossroads and trying to decide in which direction to move forward.

Career Education

During the 1950s the sense of occupational stability was shaken by social changes in the organization of society following World War II. Western societies experienced the growth of a middle class who lived in suburbs from which they commuted to work in hierarchical corporations. An individual who works in a bureaucratic hierarchy is rewarded by a regular salary and prospects of advancement during a life-time career. Thus career as a progressive trajectory through a corporation emerged as both a creation of, and value for, bureaucracies. Its emblematic representation is climbing a ladder. In response to this new social arrangement of work into *organizational careers*, guidance personnel quickly learned that vocational guidance was less effective for career planning with middle-class adults, because it mainly focused on the initial match of person to position, not a series of progressive positions sequenced along a career path. Assisting people to advance along career trajectories and climb hierarchical ladders of success required a second paradigm, which I call career development education or, for short, career education.

Career educators in the schools, and career coaches in organizations, noted that career development was a life-long process, in comparison with occupational choice which was a point-in-time event. Thus career education concentrated on how individuals cope with a series of social expectations or vocational development tasks about how to advance a career in an organization. Researchers identified the attitudes, beliefs, and competencies (the ABCs of career development) that agents may use to manage developmental tasks and shape their careers according to a grand narrative composed of five stages named growth, exploration, establishment, maintenance, and disengagement. Career educators and coaches tried to make it easier to master these tasks by encouraging people to plan their futures and increase their readiness and resources for progressing up the career ladder. Practitioners taught students and coach clients in making decisions, seeking information, managing time, overcoming barriers, and solving problems.

The philosopher Pepper's (1942/1970) description of organismic epistemology supported the career development paradigm because it addressed the question, how does it develop?

Career development theory stresses an individual's inherent drive to grow toward wholeness through increasing complexity (development) and integration (health). In this paradigm, the self as agent is the source of his or her own development. As agents for their own lives, individuals must ready themselves for the next career stage and its vocational development tasks.

Need for a New Paradigm

So the field's first paradigm for career services was vocational guidance with youth entering the work world. Guidance concentrated on helping youths find their place in a stable world. The second paradigm for career services was career development with adults working in hierarchical organizations. Career development education and coaching concentrated on helping individuals climb the career ladder in hierarchical organizations. In the risk society (Beck, 1992) of the 21st century, practitioners no longer preach planfulness for a stable 30-year career but instead promote adaptability and preparedness for possibilities. Beck (1992) explained that in the 20th century, work was the "axis of living" (p. 139). Globalization of the economy and individualization of the life course has decentered work as the axis around which identity-construction rotates. No longer may individuals identify their place in the world with the work that they perform (Bauman, 1998). The occupational landscape of the 21st century has been referred to as VUCA – that is, volatile, uncertain, complex, and ambiguous With the flattening of hierarchical corporations and the "dejobbing" of employment (Bridges, 1995), occupational careers have become fragmented by multiple transitions and numerous positions characterized as temporary, contingent, contract, adjunct, or part-time. The 30-year trajectory of a corporate career has become outmoded. People now change jobs about every 5 years according to the US Bureau of Labor Statistics (Bureau of Labor Statistics, 2004; Mullins, 2009).

These changes present a new script for individuals in Western societies. Every society fosters adaptation by offering individuals "metanarratives" that confer social meaning. In these life-course scripts, a specific culture in a particular place tells the story of its members' typical life stages and role trajectories as well as the normative social time table for transitions (Macmillan, 2005). The family and social institutions serve as socialization agents in teaching young people these scripts. They act together to deliberately shape individuals to produce similarity among people in a society. The scripts for life are structured by the order and timing of multiple, interlocking social roles over the life span. In Western societies, the normative sequence is school, first job, apartment, marriage, and then children.

During the first half of the 20th century, Western societies increased standardization in role sequences and transition timing by expanding state activities and institutionalizing social life. Sociologist have called this standardization the *first demographic transition* (Lesthaeghe, 2010). In most Western societies, by 1960 a large majority of individuals uniformly followed the scripted order and timetable of events in the transition to adulthood. Unwillingness or inability to adhere to norms led to negative social consequences.

Tightening the sequence and increasing pressure to adhere to it brought the life-course timing of males and females closer together, as well as that of different socioeconomic groups. Of course, there remained broader patterns of stratification, inequality, and differentiation by gender, ethnicity, race, and social class. Yet, at midcentury, Erik Erikson (1950) could delineate the life-course script in his famous eight stages of life. In the vocational domain, Donald Super (1957) adapted the life-course stages first articulated by Charlotte Buhler (1933) into his model of five career stages, each with three substages. As noted previously, this developmental paradigm coincided with the emergence of organizational careers and gave them a formal structure that career educators and coaches could use in their interventions.

Within each stage was a patterning of social roles that Super (1984) later portrayed in his life-career rainbow: child, student, leisurite, citizen, worker, homemaker or parent. The core social roles, according to Adler (1931), were work, friends, and love. From this perspective, which has been shared by the majority of citizens in Western societies, the deep meaning of life could be created in work, community, and marriage. Until the early 1970s, society forcefully endorsed these core roles, with normative pressure regarding their sequence and timing. The institutionalized life course had been sustained by industrial jobs and corporate careers that imposed strong discipline on the order and timing of life events. After 7 decades of increasing standardization, there came in the 1980s a deregulation of life paths and increasing pluralization of both occupational and family trajectories. For example, in 1991, IBM broke their loyalty contract by ending their lifetime employment policy (Hoerr, 1993).

During the 1970s and 1980s, new options led many people to reconsider the social script and ease normative pressure around role sequences and timing. Opportunities were narrowing, and the gap between aspirations and possibilities was widening, leaving many people anxious, uncertain, and confused. What had been viewed as new options, they then reinterpreted as disorderly sequences and timing caused by economic changes. This made the transition to adulthood more difficult (Grubb, 2002), especially for individuals who aspired to having an organizational career. The notion during the 20th century was that men had careers, while women had working lives. In the 21st century both men and women have working lives because the organizational career is dead (Hall, 1996).

While the traditional script of the 20th-century life course was loosening, the new rules were not yet clear (Herzenberg, Alic, & Wial, 1998). Today, they seem quite clear. For example, there is widespread agreement that the transition to adulthood has become later, protracted, and complex (Billari & Liefbroer, 2010). The trend toward greater complexity and diversity of life paths caused a shift from standardized, institutionalized life-course patterns to individualized biographies. According to Leccardi (2005), "Today, the biographical narrative seems to have lost its anchorage in this form of institutionalization of the life course, and the dimension of continuity associated with it" (p. 124). This trend has been characterized as individualization replacing institutionalization. Giddens (1991) suggested that this "detraditionalization" replaces tradition by demanding that individuals engage in reflexivity and meaning making, as they deliberate self-consciously on choices and actions. Some observers such as Mills (2007) regard individualization as the core characteristic of posttraditional society. Individualization denotes the societal transformation of social institutions that changes the relationship of individuals to institutions from dependency to self-reliance. Without strong institutional holding environments, individuals must organize their own lives. Rather than standardized life courses, individuals produce their own unique trajectories. Instead of moving through an orderly sequence of career stages in one organization, they must splice together a patchwork of short-term projects and assignments with different employers into a career story with continuity and coherence. It could be said that modernity made individuals by providing identities, whereas postmodernity requires people to construct themselves by shaping their own identities.

This individualization of risk shifts responsibility from social structures to the individual. The eminent sociologist Zygmunt Bauman (2000) refers to this as "life in fragments" in a "liquid society" where individuals must live without a guidebook. People still need to organize their lives, but planning no longer works because they lack clear coordinates for existence. Smith (1999) wrote that in the 20th century, people could chose

> their destinations early and travel toward them in a straight line toward successful career, good reputation, and happy family. Each life has a sense-making story that is part of a world that is orderly, determined, and predictable. Imposed norms are to be obeyed. Today process of self-constitution has no visible end, not even a stable direction. (Smith, 1999, p. 150).

In the 21st century, it has become quite difficult to envision and plan one's life in terms of a path through a fixed landscape. The 20th-century task of finding out where you fit in society has become a task of making yourself. This self-construction requires that young people, with less external guidance, prepare for life based on decisions about purpose and values. They must face the tasks of self-construction by deliberating autonomously on their interests, goals, and responsibilities. Because individuals lack a stable framework within which to deliberate, they may benefit from the collaboration of counselors who make them aware of alternative strategies and techniques for organizing their lives and work. Accordingly, the work of the counselor requires a third paradigm for career services, one that comprehends the occupational landscape of the 21st century and addresses the needs of adults who must make frequent transitions between jobs, occupations, and organizations. A contextualist paradigm that addresses these needs has its roots in the epistemology of social constructionism (Altman, Blank, & Germer, 1986).

Social Constructionism

As globalization progressed, the postmodern philosophy of social constructionism grew in popularity among social scientists, including career counselors, who have increasingly turned to narrative psychology. From the perspective of social constructionism, career no longer resides in the company; it lives within the narrative or story that people tell about their working lives and the social spaces that they occupy. Individuals author a story about themselves as occupational actors and vocational agents. A new approach to narrative career counseling – namely, life design (Savickas et al., 2009) provides a career service that assists clients to concentrate attention on the stories they are living and their wishes for the future. To help clients design a life, counselors focus reflection on identity themes and then extend them into the future. Counselors attend to uniqueness and emotion, not just simply the similarity of guidance and rationality of development. Attention to emotion is central to counseling, and of course career counseling in a risk society.

The epistemology of life design according to Pepper's (1942/1970) description is contextualism. The contextual world view defines reality as an ongoing and dynamic event. The individual is seen as constantly changing – especially through interaction – and action itself is conceptualized as behavior infused with meaning. Contextualist counselors make distinctions, they do not make classifications. Formism such as Holland's realistic, investigative, artistic, social, enterprising, and conventional (RIASEC) abstract types removes the context, whereas contextualism insists on the particulars of context (Super & Harkness, 2003). According to Pepper (1942/1970), contextualism attempts to answer the question, how does it happen? The root metaphor is an act in context. And its truth criterion is a pragmatic "successful working" (Pepper, 1942/1970, p. 232).

Thus the third paradigm is about uniqueness, not resemblance or paths. It is about individuality not individual differences or stages. Vocational guidance rested on measuring individual differences to objectify clients as scores on variables – a very useful process for assessing whom a client resembles. However, guidance counselors rarely attempted to reassemble the extracted variables back together into whole persons. They forfeited attention to the individual participants as unique composites of social and psychological characteristics in favor of an almost exclusive regard for the variables. To advance career intervention for the 21st century, counselors need to understand persons, not differences between people, especially in assisting adults to make work-role transitions. Individual difference variables are differences not persons (Lamiell, 2003).

Distinctiveness of the individual, not differences or development, has become the quest of the third paradigm for career services. As the form of work changes from stability to mobility, to reflect the labor needs of postcorporate societies, so too must the form of career intervention change. The paradigms of guiding and preparing now must be supplemented with a new paradigm that fully addresses the life design needs of workers in information societies that have destandardized the life course (Duarte, 2009; Macmillan, 2005).

The work of guidance was to think in types, to make diagnoses. The work of counseling is to avoid types. Counseling focuses on uniqueness and helps clients to come to grips with how they feel about things as they face them. The "individualization of the life course" (Beck, 2002) calls for a science of intervention that deals with making a self, shaping an identity, constructing a career, and designing a life. With the shift in responsibility for career from institutions to individuals, people must "get a life" (Habermas & Bluck, 2000) and bridge transitions in that life by using biographicity or biographical learning (Alheit, 1995) and identity work (Sveningsson & Alvesson, 2003). Leccardi (2005) concludes that "biographical subjectivitization" (p. 126) means that individuals must assume greater responsibility for making their own choices and working out projects, and these projects are not long-term because fluidity is more common than fixity. The increased responsibility to decide comes at a time when the life-course reference points have dissolved. The uncertainty and temporality of the risk society leaves adults looking inward for reference points because in this liquid societies the only certainty is within self.

To address the needs of adults living in risk societies, career counselors and researchers have moved to the third paradigm (Savickas, 2012). This pattern for practice moves away from quantitative methods to measure individual differences, to embrace qualitative methods with which to study the experience of individuals in cultural context. Study of the "person as a whole" –what Henry Murray (1938) termed "personology" – cannot be done well with reductionist techniques (Valsiner, 2009, p. 13). This explains the growing importance of understanding individual persons, not parts, as they function in particular contexts. Taking an idiographic perspective with its qualitative methods leads to an appreciation for the structure and process of individual self-construction and social co-construction. It even prioritizes the use of individual case studies for generalization to a phenomenon as a whole and for training counseling interns.

Instead of making long-term plans for one's life, Leccardi's (2005) research suggests that now young adults form guidelines that give a compass for action. The guidelines should provide an "existential direction" (p. 130) and orientation for decision making that people may use as they repeatedly select short-term projects. This strategy of guidelines may be referred to as *developmental individualization*, which Schwartz, Côté, and Arnett (2005) defined as pursuing a life course "based on extensive deliberations of the alternatives and opportunities available – given the decline of traditional social markers and of economic barriers involving gender, ethnicity, and social class – in pursuit of stimulating and liberating possibilities" (Schwartz et al., 2005, p. 204). The alternative is a passive approach in which the circumstances and impulses shape the life course. This passive pathway of *default individualization* involves little agentic investment in preparing to make important decisions and pursuing options that lead to self-improvement. Developmental individualization may be fostered by career interventions that concentrate on life-course transitions, viewing them as opportunities for individuals to actively shape their biographies by defining what comes next (Shanahan, 2000) based on their existential direction and guidelines. A new paradigm called life design provides a model and methods for just such a career intervention.

Life Design: A Paradigm for Career Intervention

The intervention of life design helps people to cope with the uncertainty of life-course transitions by constructing a biographical narrative that contains intentions or guidelines with which to make choices. The life design paradigm for career counseling takes a broader perspective than the vocational guidance and career development paradigms. Its purview is the course and content of life structures designed and constructed by individual strategies and choices. During the course of their lives, individuals structure and restructure their pattern of life roles by changing the salience and prominence of certain roles in relation to other roles in the theaters of work, friendship, intimacy, leisure, and citizenship. At its fullest, life design prompts individuals to reflexively consider life-course strategies and structures as they envision and build a life arranged with viable and fulfilling roles that interact to produce well-being. When life design focuses narrowly on the work role, the intervention still may be called life design, because work is a part of life. However, with a narrow purview on career, applications of the life design paradigm have also been called *career style counseling* (Savickas, 1989), *narrative career counseling* (Cochran, 1997), *vocational designing* (European Society for Vocational Designing and Career Counseling, http://www.unil.ch/esvdc/), *self-constructing* (Guichard, 2009), *career designing* (Pukelis, 2012*)*, and *career constructing* (Maree, 2013). For my purposes, *life design* is the appropriate name, having been established after lengthy negotiations among colleagues from seven countries (Savickas et al., 2009).

Simply stated, the paradigm for life design structures interventions to (a) construct career through small stories, (b) deconstruct these stories and reconstruct them into an identity narrative or life portrait, and (c) co-construct intentions that lead to the next action episode in the real world (Savickas, 2013). Let us consider each element in turn, starting with construction of a career story.

Construction

When individuals are dislocated from their current stories, they begin narrative processing of their biographies (Heinz, 2002). Some individuals seek counseling to assist them in this identity work. With these clients, life design interventions begin by having them describe both (a) the incident that dislocates them from the current episode in their story and (b) their goals for a new scenario that they want to co-construct with a counselor. Often, clients' opening statement includes the exact ending at which we will arrive. They will keep going in the existential direction in which they are already headed. Counseling will articulate explicitly the guidelines and intention they know implicitly. To do this, life design enhances narratability – that is, it increases clients' ability to tell their stories. Thus, the process of counseling helps clients to clarify what they already know and thereby enhances their ability to decide and act.

To help clients articulate their existential direction and form new intentions, life design follows the advice given by Wittgenstein (1953) on how to solve biographical problems: namely, rearranging or reconfiguring a client's past stories to meet present needs. The narrative shaping of transitional discontinuities in a career can be viewed as "bricolage," which means constructing something new with whatever is at hand. The process involves the "decomposition of existing identities into their constituent components and their recombination into a new identity" (Carruthers & Uzzi, 2000, p. 486) These source materials from the text of one's own life, or sources of the self (Taylor, 1992), are old stories that are generalizable to the new problem and may be used to resolve it. Through biographical bricolage (Savickas, 2000), clients engage in a dialogue with the sources of their own self as they rearrange them to address the choices to be made. In due course, they impose a new organization on the base materials to form a narrative that both fits and shapes the project of making new choices and taking action. Through this process, bricoleurs integrate their past stories with new psychosocial situations to form a narrative identity that bridges the discontinuity and fits the new situation.

To prompt biographical bricolage, counselors ask clients to narrate micronarratives, or tell small stories about how they have made their self, shaped their identity, and constructed their career. Life design assumes that nothing can be created from nothing. So counselors inquire about the cultural plots and metaphors a client has used to articulate and illuminate her or his most profound concerns and fundamental truths. In general, individuals retrieve and repeat possibilities of action from communal history as sources of the self. To mold themselves and hold themselves, individuals select base materials from the range of meanings made accessible by their culture. But which plots, metaphors, meanings, and action possibilities did they select as sources for self-construction?

The genius of the counselor is in asking questions, not in finding answers. To elicit a client's sources of self, narrative counselors use questions to prompt clients to narrate their fundamental stories. Telling their stories focuses clients' self-awareness, and hearing their stories invites reflection on what matters most. Life design counseling theory (Savickas, 2011) recommends five simple questions to elicit stories about sources of the self. The questions inquire about their role models, magazines or television shows they read or watch, favorite book or movie, a motto, and early recollections. These story-crafting questions represent the scaffolding for self-assembly and reassembly. They prompt concrete examples of abstract claims about life and provide a reference background or meaning making with which to remake meaning to navigate transitions and troubles. The role models reveal self-conceptions and blueprints for self-construction, the magazines and television shows reveal manifest interests, the favorite story from a book or movies suggests a possible script for the next chapter in life, the proverb offers advice to self on making the transition, and early recollections highlight the perspective the client takes on bridging the discontinuity. The perspective may be simply the standpoint from which they view their current problem. However, more often, it will be a view of the present situation that has reactivated an unresolved experience from the past. That past is not just behind us, it also goes ahead of us as a presupposition, preoccupation, or perspective. For most of us, the preoccupation will lead to an occupation.

Deconstruction

Counseling involves clients in a quest for a different perspective on their lives. Often it involves a poignant process of examining and deconstructing defenses and safeguarding mechanisms they erected while growing up. Thus, counselors listen to client source stories to identify dominating expectations or insidious ideas that suppress more life-enhancing alternatives. Counselors must deconstruct or disrupt what clients take for granted by taking apart these self-limiting ideas, confining roles, and cultural barriers. In particular, counselors should be sensitive to axioms of meaning and ideological biases regarding gender, race, and social status. When stories require deconstruction, counselors may discuss with clients what a story assumes, overlooks, omits, forgets, or inadequately addresses. Having listened closely to how a client constructs her or his career story, and maybe deconstructing some of its ideas and incidents, the time comes to reconstruct the small stories into a large story or autobiography.

Reconstruction

Occupational transitions, developmental tasks, and work traumas require clients to revise their understanding – and understanding is the goal of life design, not explanation, which is the goal of vocational guidance. To foster deeper understanding, counselors assist clients to reconstruct a "life portrait" that cumulates the insights garnered from the constructs the clients used to tell stories about sources of the self. Narrative processing gathers the constructs from the microstories and crafts them together into one tapestry to narrate a unified sense of individuality. Integration of small stories about the self in social situations reconstructs a large story or macronarrative – that is, an identity narrative. Career counseling consists of helping clients to gradually rearrange their identity narrative by selectively and creatively reinterpreting the past to suit future aspirations. They reassemble or re-member preexisting elements in new combinations that are more useful. The emerging macronarrative or life portrait imposes order by highlighting strands of continuity and patterns of meaning that lead to renewed purpose in a changed world. The portrait articulates the client's existential direction and provides a guide in forming new intentions. Thematic continuities offer both fidelity and flexibility in pointing a way forward that maintains continuity yet at the same time alters the course. In short, life portraits are portrayals of personhood that are incomplete yet contain larger meanings relevant to questions asked by client. Remember in this reconstruction, or narrative bricolage, the client is the architect whom the counselor serves as carpenter. As Wittgenstein (1953) stated, problems are often solved by rearranging what a client already knows, rather than by giving new information. For many clients, a transition is bridged by a new perspective and truths, not new knowledge and facts.

Co-Construction

Having reconstructed an identity narrative from the client's micronarratives, the counselor then presents to the client a draft of her or his life portrait. A first goal in narrating the life portrait to clients is to have them consider the macronarrative reconstructed by the counselor. In this way, counselors offer themselves to clients as a medium for transforming stories into meaning. The portrait presented by the counselor should not be a surprise, like an interpretation, just the next step in the story of the life. It should provide a framework that organizes a client's energies and promotes formation of intention. This portraiture is more than an art of resemblance like that of vocational guidance, rather it presents an opportunity to explore emotion and inner thought. It should focus autobiographical reasoning on the change and choices being confronted.

Reflecting on the life portrait typically leads to the client editing the identity narrative. However, revising the macronarrative involves more than just giving accurate voice to the client's life story. The revision involves amendments that correct mistakes, adjustments that come to terms with old conflicts and settle accounts, and alterations that enhance self-esteem and support a more optimistic view of life. Clients need to modify the portrait to make it more livable and then extend it into the future. Revision should also help clients to amplify the career theme in order to better direct, regulate, and sustain their actions as they cope with their current concerns, challenges, and choices.

The co-constructed identity narrative should become a portrayal of personhood that relates clearly to the concerns and questions that the client brought to counseling. That is why they came to counseling. Client and counselor join together to candidly craft a move in meaning that produces a unifying message that signals and compels a choice. The co-construction of a revised life portrait seeks to incorporate the current dislocation in a way that clarifies priorities, mobilizes central tendencies, and increases the possibility of transformation and development. This occurs as clients access different meanings and understandings that open new possibilities and restart stalled initiatives. With new language, fresh perspectives, and expanded vistas, clients may reorganize their meaning system and clarify what is at stake in the next episode of their career story. This self-clarity enables clients to make their intentions more apparent to themselves and their counselors. With this new found clarity, clients may envision the next scene, form intentions, and begin to act. A revised identity narrative, with stabilized new meanings, enables individuals to meet the uncertainties of transition with comforts recalled from the past. Then with this new narrative, clients take action to make their lives happen. As clients go further and deeper into the world, their actions answer the questions brought to counseling. The actions produce further self-making, identity shaping, and career constructing. Ideally, the actions, and interactions with audiences for the new story, ease the life-course transition and insure success and satisfaction. A case study in life design may help readers better understand the model and methods used to help clients who have experiences a succession of work projects to shape an individualized life course that is meaningful journey rather that a patchwork career.

Case Study

The client was a 29-year-old White women who was currently employed as a high school teacher of English and French. When the counselor asked how he could be useful, she replied, "Help me sort out all of the things I've got going right now – job possibilities, making decisions, focusing." The client explained that she had just ended a 3-year romantic relationship because her partner did not want to have a child. She believed it was time to reorganize her own life, beginning with revitalizing her career, moving to a new town, and then forming a new intimate relationship. In sum she said, "I have to get out of here." Upon further questioning about renewing her career, the client explained that she had to choose among four options: continuing her teaching contract, applying for a teaching position in Europe, taking a marketing job with a former employer, or beginning a doctoral program in education. She reported that she had begun college for 2 years as an international relations major because she said her high school history teacher had "opened up the world" and inspired her love of traveling and teaching. After observing that her peers who graduated with majors in international relations were not getting jobs, she switched majors to communication and received a degree in public relations, along with a teaching certificate. She quickly secured a job in the advertising department of a local company. Her employer then encouraged her to apply for a scholarship to study multicultural education in Australia. She won a scholarship and after earning a degree she returned to the United States and worked as an advertising copy writer. After 18 months she moved to London to teach American literature. A year later, she returned home to begin her current teaching position in which she also directs the drama program, supervises the speech club, and advises the student yearbook staff. During evenings for the last 3 years she had earned a master's degree in cultural foundations of education, with an emphasis on multicultural education. She wrote her thesis on White racial identity.

When asked to evaluate her four options, she said: "I like school. I like being in the classroom. I like teaching. I like learning. I am thinking about the doctoral program in cultural foundations. They have suggested a teaching fellowship which is very appealing, but I don't want to get into the wrong thing and hate it. For some reason, I am putting the brakes on that. I think that I would enjoy training, diversity training, and communications training. Intercultural communication would be my first choice of a doctoral program. I could easily do marketing. Millions of people have told me to do sales, but I do not see myself doing that. Nevertheless, money is becoming more important to me. I have been to three other career counselors, each of whom failed to help me make a choice. They all told me that I have strong and equal interests in Enterprising, Artistic, and Social occupations. This only confused me more."

To co-construct a life portrait with her, I conducted the standard Career Construction Interview (Savickas, 2011) by asking about role models, magazines, favorite story, motto, and early recollections. These questions aim to prompt reflection about self-construction and the reflexivity needed to form new intentions for the next episode in life. In naming role models while growing up, she began with her much older brother whom she described as extroverted, fun, someone who could talk with anyone, very gregarious, and social. He hitchhiked around the world. Her second role model was the leading character on the television show *Murphy Brown* because she was funny and kicked butt. Her third role model was Princess Diana. The client recalled that she liked dressing up and still follows the Royal Family. Her favorite magazines were *Self* because of the articles about women's issues, the *New Yorker* for book and theater reviews, and a professional magazine named *Teacher*. Her favorite story currently is the book *All Creatures Great and Small* by James Herriot (1972). She recounted the story about "brave people who are capable of coping with hardships, often in unconventional ways. They face life's ups and downs with both humor and courage. I admire the fiercely independent characters and appreciate the comedy and pathos of their lives. They use humor to deal with conflicts. Also, I love the opening poem."

All things bright and beautiful,
All creatures great and small,
All things wise and wonderful,
The Lord God made them all.

Her favorite saying was "A closed mind is a beautiful thing to waste." She explained its meaning by saying that "I get really frustrated with people who cannot open up their minds to see the value of something different than they have always seen. It's hard with high school students."

She reported four early recollections (ERs), and subsequently gave each a headline.

First ER: "I remember when my Dad got our dog Molly. My dad brought her home from the fire station. She could fit in your hand. I remember he sat her on the kitchen floor. I just remember being happy." Headline = "Abandoned Pup Produces Smiles."

Second ER = "I remember my Dad lying in the coffin. I was 5 years old. It is vivid. I don't know if I felt anything. Well, my Dad was an alcoholic and I knew it at pretty young age. I remember being almost angry, I was crying. And I was thinking 'He was drunk.' So I don't know if I felt anything when I looked at him but I remember seeing my Mom and that … I knew she was unhappy. She was sitting in a chair by herself. He had fallen asleep at the wheel. In my mind, I was positive he was drunk. I must have said something like 'Dad was drunk again.' And my brother backhanded me." Headline: "Mouthy Little Brat Calls It As She Sees It."

Third ER: "I was in the play *The King and I* when I was kid. That was very fun. The drama director let everybody in the cast have their little brothers and sisters in the play. She dressed us all up and painted our faces, gave use slanted eyes." Headline = "I Make My Debut."

Fourth ER: "My mom teaching me to read." Headline = "A Golden Moment."

The Career Construction Interview ended with me saying, "The time is right for you to move and move gracefully, not to move randomly. Some of the moves in the past have been more like adventures – sort of like your brother had. Now it is time to integrate those threads into a tapestry. Maybe it will not be one thing. It has to be complex, it has to be dramatic, and it must make you laugh. In leaving, she said "That's for sure."

Life Portrait

Before seeing her for a second session, I reconstructed a life portrait for her consideration. We used the following portrait to begin co-construction of an identity narrative and career intentions.

> Let's start by saying you are still that mouthy little brat who speaks the truth. One of your self-construction models was Murphy Brown, similar to her, you are a spunky lady who tells it like it is. Similar to a second model, you are gregarious, social, and fun. And of course, you like to dress up. From your favorite magazines, we see that your manifest interests are social (e.g., teaching) and artistic (e.g. book and theater review) – as you already know from previous counselors. In the social and artistic theaters of life, you want to enact the script of working with all things great and small. You know that people are capable of coping with hardships bravely. You want to help people become open-minded and develop the courage to face life's ups and downs, and you wish to teach them this using humor. Like the lead character in your favorite story, you are not afraid to be unpopular with those who you seek to help by telling them necessary truths that they may not want to hear. In your advice to yourself, you dedicate yourself to opening closed minds. Your quest is to speak the truth in a way that can open closed minds. You have done it for yourself by traveling the world and learning

about different cultures. Now you want to do it for others by teaching multiculturalism. But maybe not to high school students. Rather your intended audience is college students who you wish to teach about social justice, as well as organizations where you can offer diversity training. You seem to gravitate toward getting a doctorate, maybe so you have the credentials to become a university professor and an organizational consultant. You are too artistic to keep teaching in high school, and you already know that. You can do sales and marketing and advertising. They can readily achieve your financial goals yet they do not allow you to make a social contribution by speaking the truth. You hope your new position will involve, or at least allow for, travel around the world. And you do not want to go alone. You want to share a committed relationship and have children. So here sits a woman who wants to open minds but not where she is right now. Where will she do it next, and how will she do it?

At the end of the second session, I asked her if she had achieved the goals she set for counseling. The client said, "Yes, I have sorted things out and [am] ready to leave my job and begin a doctoral program."

In many ways, the client had tipped her hand that she wanted to pursue a doctorate in multiculturalism. Co-constructing her life portrait as a "Truth Teller" affirmed and validated her implicit intention. She went on to earn a doctorate in multicultural education, take a position as a university professor of multicultural studies, and serve as a consultant to large multinational corporations for whom she travels the world to present diversity training workshops for executives. For now, she is happy and looking forward to her next life-course transitions, which she hopes will involve marriage and children. She remains confident because she knows where she is going and can rely on her existential direction as a guide in making smart choices to continue the journey.

Conclusion

As the form of work changes from stability to mobility to reflect the labor needs of postcorporate societies, so too must the form of career intervention change. The paradigms of guiding and preparing have been supplemented with a new paradigm that fully addresses the life design needs of adults in information societies that have destandardized the life course. To address the needs of adults living in risk societies, career counselors and researchers have embraced qualitative methods with which to study the experience of individuals in cultural context. A new paradigm called life design provides a model and methods for career interventions that foster developmental individualization. Life design concentrates on life-course transitions, viewing them as opportunities for individuals to actively shape their biographies by defining what comes next, based on their existential direction and guidelines. Through biographical bricolage (Savickas, 2000), clients engage in a dialogue with the sources of their own self as they rearrange them to address the choices to be made. In due course, they impose a new organization on the base materials to form a narrative that both fits and shapes the project of making new choices and taking action. They will repeat this process each time that they encounter a life-course discontinuity.

References

Adler, A. (1931). *What life should mean to you*. Boston, MA: Little Brown.

Altman, I., Blank, T., & Germer, C. (1986). *Contextualism and understanding in behavioral science: Implications for research and theory*. Westport, CT: Praeger.

Alheit, P. (1995). Biographical learning: Theoretical outline, challenges, and contradictions of a new approach in adult education. In P. Alheit, A. Bron-Wojciechowska, E. Brugger, & P. Dominicé (Eds.), *The biographical approach in European adult education* (pp. 57–74). Vienna, Austria: Verband Wiener Volksbildung.

Bauman, Z. (1998). *Work, consumerism, and the new poor*. Buckingham, UK: Open University Press.

Bauman, Z. (2000). *Liquid modernity*. Cambridge, UK: Polity.

Beck, U. (1992). *Risk society: Towards a new modernity*. Cambridge, UK: Polity.

Beck, U. (2002). *Individualization: Institutionalized individualism and its social and political consequences*. London, UK: Sage.

Billari, F. C., & Liefbroer, A. C. (2010). Towards a new pattern of transition to adulthood? *Advances in Life Course Research, 15*, 59–75. http://doi.org/10.1016/j.alcr.2010.10.003

Bridges, W. (1995). *Job shift: How to prosper in workplace without jobs*. Reading, MA: Addison-Wesley.

Buhler, C. M. (1933). *Der menschliche Lebenslauf als psychologisches Problem* [The course of human life as a psychological problem]. Leipzig, Germany: Hirzel.

Bureau of Labor Statistics. (2004, August 25). *Number of jobs held, labor market activity, and earnings among younger baby boomers: Recent results from a longitudinal study*. Washington, DC: US Department of Labor, Bureau of Labor Statistics.

Carruthers, B., & Uzzi, B. (2000). Economic sociology in the new millennium. *Contemporary Sociology, 29*, 486–494. http://doi.org/10.2307/2653936

Cochran, L. (1997). *Career counseling: A narrative approach*. Thousand Oaks, CA: Sage.

Duarte, M. E. (2009). The psychology of life construction. *Journal of Vocational Behavior, 75*, 259–266. http://doi.org/10.1016/j.jvb.2009.06.009

Erikson, E. H. (1950). *Childhood and society*. New York, NY: Norton.

Giddens, A. (1991). *Modernity and self-identity: Self and society in the late modern age*. Palo Alto, CA: Stanford University Press.

Grubb, N. W. (2002). *Who am I: The inadequacy of career information in the information age*. Brussels, Belgium: Organization for Economic Cooperation and Development.

Guichard, J. (2009). Self-constructing. *Journal of Vocational Behavior, 75*, 251–258. http://doi.org/10.1016/j.jvb.2009.03.004

Habermas, T., & Bluck, S. (2000). Getting a life: The development of the life story in adolescence. *Psychological Bulletin, 126*, 748–769. http://doi.org/10.1037/0033-2909.126.5.748

Hall, D. T. (1996). *The career is dead—Long live the career: A relational approach to careers*. San Francisco, CA: Jossey-Bass.

Heinz, W. R. (2002). Transition discontinuities and the biographical shaping of early work careers. *Journal of Vocational Behavior, 60*, 220–240. http://doi.org/10.1006/jvbe.2001.1865

Herriot, J. (1972). *All creatures great and small*. New York, NY: Integrated Media.

Herzenberg, S. A., Alic, J. A., & Wial, H. (1998). *New rules for a new economy: Employment and opportunity in post-industrial America*. Ithaca, NY: Cornell University Press.

Hoerr, J. (1993, December). System crash: Broken social contract. *The American Prospect, 5*. Retrieved online http://prospect.org/article/system-crash

Lamiell, J. T., (2003). *Beyond individual and group differences: Human individuality, scientific psychology, and William Stern's critical personalism*. New York, NY: Sage.

Leccardi, C. (2005). Facing uncertainty: Temporality and biographies in the new century. *Young: The Nordic Journal of Youth Research, 13*, 123–146. http://doi.org/10.1177/1103308805051317

Lesthaeghe, R. (2010). The unfolding story of the second demographic revolution. *Population and Development Review, 36*, 21–25. http://doi.org/10.1111/j.1728-4457.2010.00328.x

Macmillan, R. (2005). The structure of the life course: Classic issues and current controversies. *Advances in Life Course Research, 9*, 3–24. http://doi.org/10.1016/S1040-2608(04)09001-X

Maree, J. G. (2013). *Counselling for career construction*. Rotterdam, The Netherlands: Sense. http://doi.org/10.1007/978-94-6209-272-3

Mills, M. (2007). Individualization and the life course: Towards a theoretical model and empirical evidence. In C. Howard (Ed.), *Contested individualization: Debates about contemporary personhood* (pp. 61–79). London, UK: Palgrave MacMillan.

Mullins, J. (2009, Summer). Career planning the second time around. *Occupational Outlook Quarterly,* 12–15. Retrieved from http://www.bls.gov/opub/ooq/2009/summer/art02.pdf

Murray, H. A. (1938). *Explorations in personality*. Oxford, UK: Oxford University Press.

Parsons, F. (1909). *Choosing a vocation*. Boston, MA: Houghton Mifflin.

Pepper, S. C. (1942/1970). *World hypotheses: A study in evidence*. Berkeley, CA: University of California Press.

Pukelis, K. (2012). Career designing: Why and what? *Career Designing: Research and Counselling, 1,* 12–45.

Savickas, M. L. (1989). Career-style assessment and counseling. In T. Sweeney (Ed.), *Adlerian counseling: A practical approach for a new decade* (3rd ed., pp. 289–320). Muncie, IN: Accelerated Development Press.

Savickas, M. L. (2000). *Career choice as biographical bricolage*. Paper presented at the annual meeting of the National Career Development Association, Pittsburgh, PA, June, 2000.

Savickas, M. L. (2011). *Career counseling*. Washington, DC: American Psychological Association.

Savickas, M. L. (2012). Life design: A paradigm for career intervention in the 21st century. *Journal of Counseling and Development, 90,* 13–19. http://doi.org/10.1111/j.1556-6676.2012.00002.x

Savickas, M. L. (2013). Career construction theory and practice. In R. W. Lent & S. D. Brown (Eds.), *Career development and counseling: Putting theory and research to work* (2nd ed., pp. 147–183). Hoboken, NJ: Wiley.

Savickas, M. L., Nota, L., Rossier, J., Dauwalder, J.-P., Duarte, M. E., Guichard, J., . . . van Vianen, A. E. M. (2009). Life designing: A paradigm for career construction in the 21st century. *Journal of Vocational Behavior, 75,* 239–250. http://doi.org/10.1016/j.jvb.2009.04.004

Schwartz, S. J., Côté, J. E., & Arnett, J. J. (2005). Identity and agency in emerging adulthood: Two developmental routes in the individualization process. *Youth & Society, 37,* 201–229. http://doi.org/10.1177/0044118X05275965

Shanahan, M. (2000). Pathways to adulthood in changing societies: Variability and mechanisms in life course perspective. *Annual Review of Sociology, 26,* 667–692. http://doi.org/10.1146/annurev.soc.26.1.667

Smith, D. (1999). *Zygmunt Bauman: Prophet of postmodernity*. Cambridge, UK: Polity Press.

Super, C. M., & Harkness, S. (2003). The metaphors of development. *Human Development, 46,* 3–23. http://doi.org/10.1159/000067782

Super, D. E. (1957). *The psychology of careers: An introduction to vocational development*. New York, NY: Harper.

Super, D. E. (1984). Career and life development. In D. Brown & L. Brooks (Eds.), *Career choice and development* (pp. 192–234). San Francisco, CA: Jossey-Bass.

Sveningsson, S. & Alvesson, M. (2003). Managing managerial identities: Organizational fragmentation, discourse and identity struggle. *Human Relations, 56,* 1163–1193. http://doi.org/10.1177/00187267035610001

Taylor, C. (1992). *Sources of the self: The making of modern identity*. Cambridge, MA: Harvard University Press.

Valsiner, J. (2009). Integrating psychology within the globalizing world: A requiem to the post-modern experiment with wissenschaft. *Integrative Psychological and Behavioral Science, 43,* 1–21. http://doi.org/10.1007/s12124-009-9087-x

Wittgenstein, L. (1953). *Philosophical investigations*. Oxford, UK: Blackwell.

Part IV
Life Design Interventions and Activities

Chapter 11
Career Adaptability and Life Designing

Jérôme Rossier
Institute of Psychology, University of Lausanne, Switzerland

Introduction

The modern world is characterized by fast modification of work environments, and of social and economical structures, with rapid technological evolution, due notably to globalization and migration flows. In this uncertain and changing context that confronts people with unpredictable and novel tasks, constraints, and situations, career adaptability is a crucial competence to face numerous and frequent career transitions (Hartung, Porfeli, & Vondracek, 2008). Adaptation is necessary throughout the entire life span to maximize situational benefits and minimize situational inconvenience, to successfully navigate career transitions, and to succeed in boundaryless careers (Littleton, Arthur, & Rousseau, 2000). "Vocational [and career] development constitutes a lifelong process of adaptation" (Hartung et al., 2008, p. 66), determined among other things by the expression of coping behaviors or career adapt-abilities as defined within the frame of Savickas's (2005) career construction theory.

> Adaptation, meaning to make more suitable (or congruent) by changing, also coincides with the developmental perspectives on careers. It suggests a flexibility in responding to the environment.... Furthermore, adaptation emphasizes the interaction between the individual and the environment. This shift in attention from the individual to the individual-in-situation coincides with contextual and multicultural perspectives on work. (Savickas, 1997, p. 253)

The life design paradigm implements the theories of self-construction (Guichard, 2005) and career construction (Savickas, 2005), taking into account, among other things, the importance of the contextual factors and the intraindividual dynamic processes (Savickas et al., 2009). According to this the life design paradigm, people can no longer select the work context that suits them and where they can express their vocational personality, but rather they have to constantly adapt to new environments. Professional trajectories are complex and depend on a large number of personal, contextual, cultural, and social factors that coevolve, and these trajectories contribute to the ongoing development of the personal identity. Adaptability is thought to help people to "develop their capabilities to anticipate changes and their own future in changing contexts" (Savickas et al., 2009, p. 245). According to the life design paradigm, career interventions need to be available throughout life, adapted to the circumstances and needs of the counselee, holistic, taking into account the different roles and identities a counselee endorses, being very attentive to the contextual factors related with the expressed need of the counselee, and increasing the counselee's "adaptability, narratability, activity, and intentionality" (Savickas et al., 2009, p. 245). These four processes should contribute to the project of self-construction, or life design. For this reason, interventions that aim at increasing career adaptability of counselees contribute to the development of the life design competencies.

Career Adaptability

More than 30 years ago, Super and Knasel (1981) suggested considering career adaptability as an alternative to vocational maturity, especially for adults, for whom a purely developmental perspective focused on maturation is less adequate compared with a perspective that defines the person as being able to anticipate, plan, and behave proactively. Super and Knasel's conceptualization was in line with a functional psychology perspective that considered that adapting to the environment has practical value and promotes growth or functional enlargement and improvement. Career adaptability not only implies being able to adapt to a variety of circumstances but also to have an impact on the environment to modify it to one's own needs and constraints. This is similar to Piaget's conception of adaptation by accommodation or assimilation that underlies sensorimotor and practical intelligence development (Piaget & Inhelder, 1969). Note that Holland (1997) also suggested that "persons with differentiated and consistent personality patterns and clear identity are more apt to remake the environment" (p. 68). Super and Knasel (1981) consider adaptability as "the individual ... [being] a responsible agent acting within a dynamic environmental setting" (p. 199) and characterize it as including resilience, positivity, and flexibility. This conceptual description is in line with Pratzner and Ashley's (1984) definition of career adaptability as "the ability to adapt to job requirements, and to the ability to change jobs so that they are more suited to individual needs" (p. 26). Considering this definition, career adaptability may include, promote, or be associated with other personal resources facilitating professional transitions and career adjustment, such as employability or the development or availability of transferable skills (e.g., technological skills), and is certainly a process to take into account when studying career paths.

In 1997, Savickas proposed that career adaptability might allow integrating the four different perspectives of the life-span, life-space approach – namely, the individual, the developmental, the identity, and the contextual perspective. For him, career "adaptability, whether in adolescents or in adults, involves planful attitudes, self and environmental exploration, and informed decision making" (Savickas, 1997, p. 254). This was inspired by the substages identified previously for the growth phase (from 3 to 13 years) – namely, concern, control, conviction, and competence (Super, Savickas, & Super, 1996). The four career adaptability subdimensions were further defined by Savickas (2005), and conviction and competence were respectively renamed curiosity and confidence.

> Career concern, with the associated attitude of and competence in planning, fosters coping behaviors of awareness and preparation, assisting individuals to respond to the demands of the work environment. Control fosters personal responsibility for one's career and work experiences. A decisive attitude, engaging in decision-making and behaving in an asser-

tive manner may assist individuals to create the desired work experience. Career curiosity facilitates a good fit between the self and the world of work, and through exploration and risk-taking suggests that individuals gain knew knowledge and competences. Confidence has been likened to self-esteem and self-efficacy (Savickas, 2005) with this belief in the self to master challenges and solve problem suggesting a capacity to respond to stressful situation[s]. (Johnston, Luciano, Maggiori, Ruch, & Rossier, 2013, p. 296)

These processes contribute to regulate the continuous dynamic, multifactorial, multidirectional, and nonlinear interactions between people and their environment, allowing them to adjust to their contextual and social environment. Career adaptability increases people's ability to tolerate and face uncertainty and ambiguity by increasing flexibility and autonomy. To situate more precisely career adaptability, different levels, ranging from the latent disposition to the behavioral expression in context, have to be distinguished: The first level is the adaptability readiness, or *adaptivity,* as a disposition of being flexible and open to change; the second level is the *adaptability* as a process, similar to self-efficacy or resilience, for example; the third level concerns the behavioral *adapting* responses, such as exploration behaviors; finally, the last level is the fit observed as a result of the *adaptation* (Savickas & Porfeli, 2012).

To operationalize Savickas's career adaptability definition, the members of the International Career Adaptability Team jointly developed the Career Adapt-Ability Scale (CAAS), using a multicenter approach and collecting data simultaneously in 13 countries with a research form of 44 items. A series of hierarchical confirmatory factor analyses allowed the selection of 24 items (six items per subdimension) that were simultaneously relevant across all countries. The results suggested that the CAAS measures the same construct across all countries, but that the CAAS does not reach scalar invariance, implying that norms have to be developed for each language version or each country. This result is not surprising, considering that career adaptability is a psychosocial construct assumed to be context dependent. The CAAS is presently available in 10 different languages: Chinese (Hou, Leung, Li, Li, & Xu, 2012), Dutch (Dries, Van Esbroeck, van Vianen, De Cooman, & Pepermans, 2012), English (Savickas & Porfeli, 2012), French (Johnston, Broonen, et al., 2013), German (Johnston, Luciano, et al., 2013), Icelandic (Vilhjálmsdóttir, Kjartansdóttir, Smáradóttir, & Einarsdóttir, 2012), Italian (Soresi, Nota, & Ferrari, 2012), Korean (Tak, 2012), Portuguese (Duarte et al., 2012), and Taiwanese (Tien, Wang, Chu, & Huang, 2012), and has been validated in many countries from North and South America, Europe, Asia, and Oceania. Finally, a shorter version of 12 items was recently created (Maggiori, Rossier, & Savickas, in press). Savickas' conceptualization of career adaptability is not the only model, and several alternatives can be found in the literature. In 2000, Pulakos, Arad, Donovan, and Plamondon (2000) developed a taxonomy of adaptive performance considering eight dimensions, based on the analyses of a large number of critical incidents from 21 different jobs, such as handling emergencies or crisis situations, handling work stress, solving problems creatively, or dealing with uncertain and unpredictable work situations. Interestingly the frequency of each adaptive response varies with the type of job. Considering the theory of work adjustment, Griffin and Hesketh (2003) grouped these eight dimensions into three more general domains: proactive, reactive, and tolerant behaviors. More recently, Ployhart and Bliese (2006) proposed positioning different aspects associated with adaptability on a distal–proximal continuum. Dispositions, such as personality or physical abilities, but also values or interests, are considered as distal, whereas work-related performance is considered as proximal. The sequence of the behavioral expression goes from dispositions to individual adaptability through mediating processes, such as coping skills. They also developed a questionnaire for assessing the dimensions of individual adaptability suggested by Pulakos et al. (2000). Hamtiaux, Houssemand, and Vrignaud (2013) observed that individual adaptability and career adapt-abilities were highly correlated – for example, learning correlated with curiosity and confidence, and uncertainty with control, curiosity, and confidence.

Inspired by Super and Knasel (1981), Ebberwein, Krieshok, Ulven, and Prosser (2004) have developed another model of career adaptability using a qualitative approach. The aim of their study was to identify the core components of career adaptability of adults facing a career transition. They identified three general themes. The "adaptative responses" category includes coping behaviors, such as proactively searching for another job. The "contextual challenges" category includes all environmental factors that have an impact on career transitions, such as financial and social resources. Finally the "insights into the transition" theme includes ideas of suddenly realizing something – for example, that the world of work is changing rapidly. This model recommends taking into account the environment and coping behaviors, and acknowledging that transitions usually also induce a redefinition of the way people understand and perceive themselves and their environment. Recently, Van den Heuvel, Demerouti, Bakker, and Schaufeli (2013), proposed also an alternative model for describing how employed people adapt to their professional environment. They suggested that employee adaptability might be described by considering adaptive resources, attitudes, and behaviors, with attitudes mediating the relationship between resources and behaviors. This causal sequence corresponds to the sequence – adaptivity, adaptability, and adapting – mentioned above. In their study, adaptability captures two components, change information and meaning making, which are respectively similar to curiosity and control, as defined by Savickas (2005).

Career adaptability seems similar to other constructs studied in career guidance and counseling, such as flexibility, employability, or resilience. "Personal flexibility can be described as a composite of such ingredients as basic academic skills; adaptive, transfer, mobility and learning skills; entrepreneurial skills; career maturity and career adaptability (resilience, insight, identity); planfulness; self-organizational understanding; communication and problem-solving skills" (Herr, 1993, p. 220). According to Herr, personality flexibility is a combination of cognitive, emotional, and social skills, which should be dynamically expressed in accordance with feedback from the environment. School should play a major role in the development of this personal flexibility, which might be considered rather as an adaptive disposition helping people endure stressful work conditions. Employability is the ability to find a new job in the labor market and includes the skills, resources, and abilities necessary to adapt to new work environments. Resilience is the ability to cope with stressful situations, which might be considered as an adaptive response influenced by adaptability. All of these constructs share some similar aspects or features. However, according to our understanding and in contrast to the other constructs, career adaptability has to be understood as precisely a set of personal abilities allowing career adaptation.

Notably, the number of studies using Savickas's (2005) definition of career adaptability has been increasing since the publication of the life design paradigm, suggesting that career adaptability is particularly important for career construction, self-construction, or life designing. Moreover, the life design paradigm considers it important to distinguish adaptivity, adaptability, adapting, and adaptation. Most alternative models presented above, include in their adaptability model aspects related to dispositions (adaptivity) or to behaviors (adapting). The life design paradigm defines career adaptability strictly as a set of psychological resources, as more precisely presented in the following section.

Career Adaptability Research

A growing number of studies have analyzed the impact of career adaptability on career-related outcomes, such as employability, work stress, or work engagement; its relationship with other vocational psychological constructs, such as vocational indecision or vocational maturity; and its relationship with dispositions such as cognitive abilities or personality. Moreover, several more recent studies have tried to assess more specifically whether career adaptability could indeed be considered as a process variable that mediates the relationship between dispositions and career-related outcomes. This section will review the growing literature about career adaptability in order to be able to conceptualize more precisely career adaptability as a self-regulation process.

Career Adaptability and Career-Related Outcomes

Career adaptability is defined as abilities that contribute positively to individuals' capability to manage their career or to design their life. For this reason, it should predict career-related outcomes and be positively and strongly linked with "employability skills [that] refer to general and nontechnical competencies required for performing all jobs, regardless of types or levels of jobs, which are identified to be the most critical skills in the current job market" (De Guzman & Choi, 2013, p. 199). In a study conducted in Papua New Guinea, De Guzman and Choi (2013) did indeed observe a high correlation between career adaptability and employability.

Career adaptability correlates meaningfully with different vocational psychological dimensions. For example, Nota, Ginevra, and Soresi (2012) studied the relationships between career adaptability, problem-solving style, and career decision-making profile in a population of Italian adolescents. Confidence correlated positively with the speed of making the final decision, problem-solving engagement, and the self-assurance scales, and negatively with the aspiration for an ideal occupation. Concern correlated positively with information gathering, information processing, effort invested, and problem-solving engagement. The correlations observed for the control or the curiosity subscales were smaller. In general, undecided adolescents score lower on career adaptability, suggesting that high career adaptability facilitates vocational choice and vocational planning as proposed by the original definition. Moreover, career adaptability is positively related to vocational identity and in particular to the processes underlying identity development (Porfeli & Savickas, 2012). Career adaptability is also an important resource for younger individuals at school. Pouyaud, Vignoli, Dosnon, and Lallemand (2012) have shown that career adaptability is highly correlated with motivation at school and negatively correlated with fear of failure. Moreover, adolescents scoring high on the career adapt-abilities scales have a broader range of interests and perceive fewer internal and external barriers (Soresi et al., 2012). Finally, career adaptability, as expected, is positively related to self-esteem (van Vianen, Klehe, Koen, & Dries, 2012), vocational development (Rocha, 2012), and job search self-efficacy, which has an impact on the school-to-work transition in terms of future person–organization fit (Guan et al., 2013).

Concerning work-related variables, career adaptability is positively related to job level, income, work rate, turnover intention, job search, and actual turnover, but negatively with job tenure. Career adaptability is also related to work conditions and is positively associated with decision latitude and social or managerial support, but seems relatively independent from job demands. For example, Table 11.1 presents the correlations between career adaptability, job

Table 11.1
Correlations between career adapt-abilities and some work-related variables in a representative Swiss sample

	1	1.1	1.2	1.3	1.4	2	3	4
1. Adaptability								
1.1 Concern	.82***							
1.2 Control	.86***	.58***						
1.3 Curiosity	.85***	.60***	.63***					
1.4 Confidence	.87***	.58***	.72***	.68***				
2. Job demands	.07**	.06*	.05*	.04	.10***			
3. Decisional latitude	.35***	.29***	.34***	.26***	.30***	.09***		
4. Work rate	.09***	.10***	.08***	.03	.08**	.15***	.12***	
5. Household income	.15***	.15***	.17***	.08**	.10***	.10***	.23***	.06**

Note. Correlations equal to or above .30 (medium effect size) in absolute magnitude are in in bold, and correlations smaller than .10 are associated with a negligible effect size (*N* = 1,880).
* $p < .01$, ** $p < .05$, *** $p < .001$.

demands, decisional latitude, work rate, and household income, observed in a large representative sample from Switzerland. The correlation with decision latitude seemed especially high (see Table 11.1). Career adaptability is also negatively related to burnout and job stress and may constitute a protective factor for coping with job strain (Browning, Ryan, Greenberg, & Rolniak, 2006; Johnston, Broonen, et al., 2013; Johnston, Luciano, et al., 2013).

Moreover, and very interestingly, employment status seems to have a consistent impact on adaptability in several cultural contexts. Indeed, unemployment is associated with higher career adaptability, due to the activation of personal resources in adverse career situations. In Portugal, the effect size of this difference was small for control and medium for curiosity and concern (Duarte et al., 2012). Moreover, people with low career adaptability may be more prone to be in precarious job situations, whereas people unemployed for more than 3 months seem to activate their career adaptability resources (Maggiori, Johnston, Krings, Massoudi, & Rossier, 2013). Similarly, in a organizational restructuring and downsizing context, employees who know that their jobs are considered to be redundant, and that their positions could potentially be cut, seem to activate their adaptability resources and engage "in more adaptive career planning and exploration" (Klehe, Zikic, van Vianen, & De Pater, 2011, p. 226). Thus, career adaptability seems to be a very important resource for successfully facing career transitions.

Career Adaptability and Dispositions

Several studies have investigated the relationships between career adapt-abilities and personal dispositions such as general abilities or personality. General cognitive ability, as measured by the Raven matrices, is only negligibly correlated with career adaptability (van Vianen et al., 2012). Concerning the links with personality dimensions, Teixeira, Bardagi, Lassance, Magalhães, and Duarte (2012) observed that career adaptability correlated negatively with neuroticism, and positively with extraversion, openness, agreeableness, and conscientiousness in a large Brazilian sample. In The Netherlands and in Switzerland, results were similar, with an especially important correlation between career adaptability and conscientiousness (Rossier, Zecca, Stauffer, Maggiori, & Dauwalder, 2012; van Vianen et al., 2012). However, correlations vary slightly from one country to the other and depend on the measurement instrument used and on the personality model considered. It is important to note that career adaptability has an incremental validity over personality when predicting work-related outcomes. Moreover, adaptability partially mediates the relationship between personality and work-related outcomes, such as work engagement (Rossier et al., 2012).

Recently, Johnston, Luciano, and colleagues (2013) studied the relationship between orientations to happiness, career adaptability, and work stress. Orientations to happiness includes three positive aspects: (1) engagement that describes the experience of flow and that is linked to the fit between demands and competences, (2) pleasure that describes the tendency of individuals to maximize pleasure and minimize pain, and (3) meaning that describes the identification of individuals with their virtues and the contribution of those virtues to their identity. They observed that all three positive traits were related to career adaptability. Also, career adaptability had an incremental validity over orientations to happiness when predicting job stress, and control and curiosity partially mediated the relation between orientations to happiness and work stress.

In sum, career adaptability seems to be relatively independent from some dispositions, such as general cognitive abilities, but more related to other dispositions, such as personality traits, or traits that are close to personality traits, such as orientations to happiness. When career adaptability is related to dispositions, it partially mediates the relation between these dispositions and work- or career-related outcomes and seems thus to contribute to the regulation of their expression.

Career Adapt-Abilities as Self-Regulation Processes

By definition, career adapt-abilities are thought to facilitate the expression of adaptive behaviors and ultimately adaptation. For this reason, career adapt-abilities should contribute to the regulation of the expression of career-related behaviors. Several authors have studied the relationship between career adapt-abilities and other regulation processes. Van Vianen and colleagues (2012) observed that career adapt-abilities correlate positively with promotion-focused self-regulation strategies, which imply being goal focused, finding alternative solutions, and being proactive, and negatively with prevention-focused self-regulation strategies, which imply being cautious and avoidant. Zecca and Rossier (2011) observed that career adapt-abilities were positively correlated with task-oriented coping, cognitive reappraisal, and negatively with emotion-oriented coping. Career adapt-abilities could thus be considered as a set of regulation processes, or as promoting regulation processes, that are especially important for designing our lives and that are involved in the expression of career-related behaviors.

Several models suggest that the relationship between dispositions, personal characteristics, or predispositions, and career-related outcomes are regulated by processes such as self-

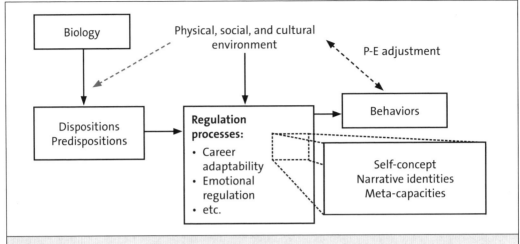

Figure 11.1
Career adapt-abilities as self-regulation processes where career adaptability mediates the relationship between dispositions and behaviors, support the development of the self-concept, and mediate the moderation impact of demographic characteristics and contextual influences. P-E = person–environment.

efficacy beliefs, for the social cognitive career theory (Lent, Brown, & Hackett, 1994); career adapt-abilities, for the career construction theory (Savickas, 2005); the self-concept, for the five-factor model of personality (McCrae & Costa, 1999); and the multiple selves, as delineated in self-construction theory (Guichard, 2005). As expected, career adaptability correlates with variables that are also supposed to mediate the relationship between dispositions and vocational-related outcomes such as self-efficacy or self-esteem (van Vianen et al., 2012). Note that Rossier (2015) has argued that both mediation and moderation effects could be the result of a regulation process. A mediation effect corresponds to a linear regulation of an underlying variable (independently of the level of this underlying variable), whereas moderation might be conceived as a nonlinear regulation, especially effective for some level of this underlying variable. Regulation processes allow adapting the expression of relatively stable dispositions to changing social expectations and evolving environments. These processes are crucial considering that dispositions are evolving slowly and that the environment, and in particular, the contemporary social and economical environment, is evolving rapidly.

The conceptualization of career adapt-abilities as self-regulation processes postulates that dispositions or predispositions are latent variables, not directly expressed and not directly observable, which are strongly biologically rooted. The expression of dispositions in terms of behaviors is regulated by a series of processes, including career adaptability, emotional regulation processes, and coping processes. Regulation processes allow the adapting of this expression of dispositions to the requirement of the environment (see Figure 11.1). Moreover, some dispositions might have an impact on these processes and thus moderate the relation between other dispositions and behaviors (e.g., neuroticism might thus moderate the relationship between general cognitive abilities and job performance). The environment has a direct impact on the regulation processes and as such on the relationship between dispositions and behaviors. This feedback loop (regulation processes-behaviors-environment-regulation processes) can be seen as a rapid mechanism of adaptation that does not affect the latent constitution of the individual. However, this feedback has an impact on the self – which is constantly in self-construction and adapting according to these feedbacks of the environment. Another feedback loop seems to moderate the expression of the biological aspects underlying dispositions (dispositions–regulation processes–behaviors–environment–disposition). This feedback promotes slow but persistent modification of the latent constitution of the individual. Concerning the self-concept or narrative identities, they participate in the regulation process, and have an impact on theses processes by promoting, for example, behavioral continuity and consistency. Importantly, they also contribute to control, to self-direct this regulation, and might thus be conceived as metacapacities (Stauffer, Maggiori, Froidevaux, & Rossier, 2014). Regulation processes are numerous and might be behavior-specific. Self-efficacy or career adapt-abilities are certainly processes particularly involved in the regulation of the expression of career-related behaviors.

The life design paradigm conceives these regulation processes, and in particular, career adaptability and narrative identities, as being key components for career counseling to help individuals to express appropriate career choices and behaviors. These processes represent the dynamic and subjective components of the self, or of the multiple selves, and underlie and promote behavioral flexibility. These resources can be activated and allow the person to adapt to changing conditions. These resources are adaptive only because the feedback loops described above allow them to be context sensitive. According to the life design paradigm, career counseling uses this feedback channel to induce and sustain change.

Career Adaptability and Career Interventions

The main purpose of life design career counseling is to help people to manage their own career by activating and strengthen their resources, to help them to cope with adverse career circumstances or career transitions. "Career construction counseling has a primary aim to increase an individual's level of career adaptability so that they can more effectively produce their own development in changing opportunities and constraints" (Hartung et al., 2008, p. 72). Several studies have confirmed that career adaptability helps people to cope with job insecurity and job strain and might be considered as a resilience factor. Moreover, in adverse situations such as unemployment, people tend to activate their adaptive resources (Maggiori et al., 2013). An increase of career adapt-abilities has a positive influence on job-search strategies, which are more focused and/or deliberate and tend to lead to a higher number of offers. Moreover, this increase also had a direct and positive impact on the quality of reemployment (Koen, Klehe, van Vianen, Zikic, & Nauta, 2010). A recent study conducted by Koen, Klehe, and van Vianen (2012) has shown that a 1-day, group career counseling intervention based on recommendations of Brown et al. (2003) and Hartung et al. (2008) for career counseling interventions had a short- and long-term impact on career adaptability. Moreover, this intervention also had a positive long-term impact on employment quality, job satisfaction, and career success.

Career paths and behaviors are a function of many individual and contextual factors that are not under the control of the individual or cannot be rapidly modified. For this reason, career counseling or life design interventions may focus on increasing personal resources, such as the four career adapt-abilities.

When evaluating individual readiness to adapt, counselors and researchers could assess the processes of adaptability and their developmental course in terms of planful foresight, exploration of the situation, relevant knowledge about self and situation, and decisional skill. The outcome could be assessed in terms of increase or decrease in person-situation congruence and movement toward self-completion. (Savickas, 1997, pp. 254–255)

For example, career exploration can be actively stimulated during life design interventions with "activities, directed toward enhancing knowledge of the self and the external environment, that an individual engages in to foster progress in career development" (Blustein, 1992, p. 175). Such activities should induce an increased exploration and curiosity that contributes to people's adaptability. Such an exploration may also contribute to the redefinition of the self-concept, which may have a positive impact on the control dimension. Moreover, exploration, control, and confidence promotion can be stimulated by modeling and vicarious learning and are related to intrinsic motivational factors and internal rewards (Blustein, 1997). More precisely, career counselors can use orientation exercises to increase career concern, training in decision making to increase career control, information-seeking activities to increase career curiosity, and self-esteem building techniques, such as role play or social modeling, to increase career confidence (Hartung et al., 2008). Moreover, both the overall level of adaptability and the readiness of these resources to being activated might be increased by all these techniques.

Career exploration activities contribute to the definition and development of the self-construct, or the ego identity domain, because they allow people to discover and explore the various aspects and facets of their identity in a variety of settings (Blustein, 1997). For example, Scholl and Cascone (2010) have suggested that the "constructivist résumé" approach, consisting of writing a future-oriented résumé, along with a co-construction of career goals, an action plan, and possibly a redefinition of the counselee's professional identity, may increase not only career adaptability but also professional identity. This suggests that career adaptability may also sustain the identity development or the development of subjective identity forms and might be an important aspect of the development of their structure, as defined by Guichard (2009). According to this conception, career adaptability might be considered as a resource sustaining the self-concept development through the complex interaction between people and their always-changing contexts. In turn, the self-concept may also be conceived as a metacompetency allowing individuals to regulate and allocate personal and process resources (Stauffer et al., 2014). Moreover, the fact of being able to endorse several different subjective identity forms (Guichard, 2009), which can be eventually related to different life roles, is a direct contribution of the self to personal adaptability. Exploring our own career and life history contributes to increased self-awareness as illustrated by the comments of a 32-year-old counselee about the professional and personal lifeline that she was asked to construct for herself at home:

> [this was] what I had to write under personal or extra-professional experiences. As far [as this,] this was easy [showing the part of the lifeline where she had written down her professional history], ... [this] far I waited until the last moment [sic] before to complete [sic] this part [part where she had to write down her personal history]... Every day I was thinking about a new aspect of my life. Yes ... I remember that I have done this ... and I remember that this was pleasant, and that some other history had an impact on me.

And to the question of whether constructing her lifeline allowed her to rediscover her own history, she answered, "Yes, and during all the week I had new part of my own history [sic] that re-emerged in my mind." Life design interventions that propose to deconstruct, reconstruct, and co-construct a career and life project also induce a redefinition of the self.

Moreover, interventions that allow the development of transferrable skills also contribute to the ability to adapt to job requirements and to integration into the world of work, with transferrable skills being important for the development of personal adaptability (Pratzner & Ashley, 1984). Moreover, these skills and resources also permit the changing of one's professional environment, which allows one to occupy the position of active subject, and not only that of the object, in an evolving environment. The idea is that people adjust to their environment and adapt it to their needs and requirements. Establishing a personal portfolio may help people to identify their competences, and their general, specific, and transferrable skills. Increasing people's awareness of their own skills has a positive impact on the development of these same skills. Among these skills, adaptive skills usually include career adaptability and other regulatory resources. Borgen, Amundson, and Reuter (2004) have also suggested that a portfolio workshop might help people to rethink their career histories, to redefine their career goals and plans, and to increase their career resilience and thus their career adaptability.

Finally, several studies have shown that specific psychological interventions may have a positive impact on other types of resources, such as emotional competences, self-efficacy, etc. Nelis, Quoidbach, Mikolajczak, and Hansenne (2009) have shown that a specific intervention focusing on understanding, identifying, expressing, using, and managing emotions induces a very important increase of emotional regulation capabilities, showing that these resources can be activated by a brief psychological intervention (Nelis et al., 2011). Moreover, such an intervention also has an indirect impact on employability, as mediated by emotional intelligence. Notably career adaptability is highly correlated with emotional intelligence (Coetzee & Harry, 2014). However, according to our conception, emotional intelligence does not underlie career adaptability, but rather both of them constitute people's adaptive processes. Moreover, all of the intervention components mentioned by Herr (1993), such as enhancing self-esteem by increasing anxiety management skills, or enhancing job-seeking or work-related skills that "frees [counselees from] the captivity of negative attitudes, irrational beliefs, information deficits, and low self-esteem" (p. 223), certainly also have a positive impact on career adaptability, because flexibility is one aspect of *adaptivity*, a disposition underlying adaptability. The "career insights" Herr mentions can be understood as the result of an identity re-co-construction according to the life design perspective. For such a re-co-construction during a life design intervention, a positive working alliance is important to enable a re-construction together in a secure collaborative atmosphere (Masdonati, Perdrix, Massoudi, & Rossier, 2014).

Life design interventions aim at increasing people's resources, such as career adaptability, and they might be especially useful for adults facing transitions or adverse working conditions. However, it is possible that theses interventions are more effective with already more flexible people or, as suggested by O'Connell, McNeely, and Hall (2008), with more educated people. The "protean career, in which adaptability and identity are key (Hall, 2002), may not be as easily accessible to workers with lower levels of education" (O'Connell et al., 2008, p. 256). This would imply that these interventions could increase social disparities. For this reason, it is crucially important to develop specific interventions for less privileged, vulnerable, or underserved populations, that have an impact on their specific vulnerabilities and help them to maximize their resources. For example, these interventions might be longer, include a systematic follow-up, and accord more importance to identifying, activating, or reactivating the social and contextual resources of the counselees. In this context, prevention is, of course, of prime importance and may help the less privileged or people with fewer psychological resources to be specifically supported. These preventive interventions might help these people to maximize the expression of their resources and help them to overcome their vulnerabilities (see Chapter 13).

Conclusion

Career adaptability is an important set of process resources, the career adapt-abilities, allowing people to face adverse work and professional situations, helping them to master school-to-work and work-to-work transitions. These resources are thus positively related to several positive work-related outcomes such as work engagement, and negatively with negative work-related outcomes such as job stress. Career adaptability also mediates the relationship between personal dispositions and career-related behaviors and promotes adaptation by mediating the moderator impact of the environment. Life design interventions promote career de-co-construction, self-construction, and career resilience by notably stimulating counselees' personal and social resources. Aspects that remain to be studied are whether these interventions are equally effective for all counselees and whether the activation of jeopardized and marginalized subgroups' adaptive resources might be optimized using adapted tools or interventions.

Author Note

The content and examples that illustrate this chapter were partially collected within the framework of the National Competence Center in Research LIVES, Project 7 entitled *Professional trajectories: Impact of individual characteristics and resources, and cultural background* led by Jérôme Rossier. This project is financed by the Swiss National Science Foundation. The author gratefully acknowledges the Swiss National Science Foundation for its financial support and Claire Johnston and Christian Maggiori for feedback, suggestions, and help on earlier drafts of this chapter.

References

Blustein, D. L. (1992). Applying current theory and research in career exploration to practice. *The Career Development Quarterly, 41*, 174–184. http://doi.org/10.1002/j.2161-0045.1992.tb00368.x

Blustein, D. L. (1997). A context-rich perspective of career exploration across the life roles. *The Career Development Quarterly, 45*, 260–274. http://doi.org/10.1002/j.2161-0045.1997.tb00470.x

Borgen, W. A., Amundson, N. E., & Reuter, J. (2004). Using portfolio to enhance career resilience. *Journal of Employment Counseling, 41*, 50–59. http://doi.org/10.1002/j.2161-1920.2004.tb00878.x

Brown, S. D., Ryan Krane, N. E., Brecheisen, J., Castelino, P., Budisin, I., Miller, M., & Edens, L. (2003). Critical ingredients of career choice interventions: More analyses and new hypotheses. *Journal of Vocational Behavior, 62*, 411–428. http://doi.org/10.1016/S0001-8791(02)00052-0

Browning, L., Ryan, C. S., Greenberg, M. S., & Rolniak, S. (2006). Effects of cognitive adaptation on the expectation-burnout relationship among nurses. *Journal of Behavioral Medicine, 29*, 139–150. http://doi.org/10.1007/s10865-005-9028-1

Coetzee, M., & Harry, N. (2014). Emotional intelligence as a predictor of employees' career adaptability. *Journal of Vocational Behavior, 84*, 90–97. http://doi.org/10.1016/j.jvb.2013.09.001

De Guzman, A. B., & Choi, K. O. (2013). The relations of employability skills to career adaptability among technical school students. *Journal of Vocational Behavior, 82*, 199–207. http://doi.org/10.1016/j.jvb.2013.01.009

Dries, N., Van Esbroeck, R., van Vianen, A. E. M., De Cooman, R., & Pepermans, R. (2012). Career Adapt-Abilities Scale–Belgium form: Psychometric characteristics and construct validity. *Journal of Vocational Behavior, 80*, 674–679. http://doi.org/10.1016/j.jvb.2012.01.012

Duarte, M. E., Soares, M. C., Fraga, S., Rafael, M., Lima, M. R., Paredes, I., . . . Djaló, A. (2012). Career Adapt-Abilities Scale–Portugal form: Psychometric properties and relationships to employement status. *Journal of Vocational Behavior, 80*, 725–729. http://doi.org/10.1016/j.jvb.2012.01.019

Ebberwein, C. A., Krieshok, T. S., Ulven, J. C., & Prosser, E. C. (2004). Voices in transition: Lessons on career adaptability. *The Career Development Quarterly, 52*, 292–308. http://doi.org/10.1002/j.2161-0045.2004.tb00947.x

Griffin, B., & Hesketh, B. (2003). Adaptable behaviours for successful work and career adjustment. *Australian Journal of Psychology, 55*, 65–73. http://doi.org/10.1080/00049530412331312914

Guan, Y., Deng, H., Sun, J., Wang, Y., Cai, Z., Ye, L., ... Li, Y. (2013). Career adaptability, job search self-efficacy and outcomes: A three-wave investigation among Chinese university graduates. *Journal of Vocational Behavior, 83*, 561–570. http://doi.org/10.1016/j.jvb.2013.09.003

Guichard, J. (2005). Life-long self-construction. *International Journal for Educational and Vocational Guidance, 5*, 111–124. http://doi.org/10.1007/s10775-005-8789-y

Guichard, J. (2009). Self-constructing. *Journal of Vocational Behavior, 75*, 251–258. http://doi.org/10.1016/j.jvb.2009.03.004

Hall, D. T. (2002). *Careers in and out of organizations*. Thousand Oaks, CA: Sage.

Hamtiaux, A., Houssemand, C., & Vrignaud, P. (2013). Individual and career adaptability: Comparing models and measures. *Journal of Vocational Behavior, 83*, 130–141. http://doi.org/10.1016/j.jvb.2013.03.006

Hartung, P. J., Porfeli, E. J., & Vondracek, F. W. (2008). Career adaptability in childhood. *The Career Development Quarterly, 57*, 63–74. http://doi.org/10.1002/j.2161-0045.2008.tb00166.x

Herr, E. L. (1993). Contexts and influences on the need for personal flexibility for the 21st century: Part II. *Canadian Journal of Counselling, 27*, 219–235.

Holland, J. L. (1997). *Making vocational choices: A theory of vocational personalities and work environment* (3rd ed.). Lutz, FL: PAR.

Hou, Z.-J., Leung, S. A., Li, X., Li, X., & Xu, H. (2012). Career Adapt-Abilities Scale–China form: Construction and initial validation. *Journal of Vocational Behavior, 80*, 686–691. http://doi.org/10.1016/j.jvb.2012.01.006

Johnston, C. S., Broonen, J.-P., Stauffer, S. D., Hamtiaux, A., Pouyaud, J., Zecca, G., . . . Rossier, J. (2013). Validation of an adapted French form of the Career Adapt-Abilities Scale in four Francophone countries. *Journal of Vocational Behavior, 83*, 1–10. http://doi.org/10.1016/j.jvb.2013.02.002

Johnston, C. S., Luciano, E. C., Maggiori, C., Ruch, W., & Rossier, J. (2013). Validation of the German version of the Career Adapt-Abilities Scale and its relation to orientations to happiness and work stress. *Journal of Vocational Behavior, 83*, 295–304. http://doi.org/10.1016/j.jvb.2013.06.002

Klehe, U.-C., Zikic, J., van Vianen, A. E. M., & De Pater, I. E. (2011). Career adaptability, turnover and loyalty during organizational downsizing. *Journal of Vocational Behavior, 79*, 217–229. http://doi.org/10.1016/j.jvb.2011.01.004

Koen, J., Klehe, U.-C., & van Vianen, A. E. M. (2012). Training career adaptability to facilitate a sucessful school-to-work transition. *Journal of Vocational Behavior, 81*, 395–498. http://doi.org/10.1016/j.jvb.2012.10.003

Koen, J., Klehe, U.-C., van Vianen, A. E. M., Zikic, J., & Nauta, A. (2010). Job-search strategies and reemployment quality: The impact of carer adaptability. *Journal of Vocational Behavior, 77*, 126–139. http://doi.org/10.1016/j.jvb.2010.02.004

Lent, R. W., Brown, S. D., & Hackett, G. (1994). Toward a unifying social cognitive theory of career and academic interest, choice, and performance. *Journal of Vocational Behavior, 45*, 79–122. http://doi.org/10.1006/jvbe.1994.1027

Littleton, S. M., Arthur, M. B., & Rousseau, D. M. (2000). The future boundaryless careers. In A. Collin & R. A. Young (Eds.), *The future of career* (pp. 101–114). New York, NY: Cambridge University Press.

Maggiori, C., Johnston, C., Krings, F., Massoudi, K., & Rossier, J. (2013). The role of career adaptability and work conditions on general and professional well-being. *Journal of Vocational Behavior, 83*, 437–449. http://doi.org/10.1016/j.jvb.2013.07.001

Maggiori, C., Rossier, J., & Savickas, M. L. (in press). Career adapt-abilities scale–short form (CAAS-SF): Construction and validation. *Journal of Career Assessment*. http://doi.org/10.1177/1069072714565856

Masdonati, J., Perdrix, S., Massoudi, K., & Rossier, J. (2014). Working alliance as a moderator and a mediator of career counseling effectiveness. *Journal of Career Asssessment, 22*, 3–17. http://doi.org/10.1177/1069072713487489

McCrae, R. R., & Costa, P. T., Jr. (1999). A five-factor theory of personality. In L. A. Pervin & O. P. John (Eds.), *Handbook of personality: Theory and research* (2nd ed., pp. 139–153). New York, NY: Guilford Press.

Nelis, D., Kotsou, I., Quoidbach, J., Hansenne, M., Weytens, F., Dupuis, P., & Mikolajczak, M. (2011). Increasing emotional competence improves prsychological and physical well-being, social relationships, and employ-ability. *Emotions, 11*, 354–366. http://doi.org/10.1037/a0021554

Nelis, D., Quoidbach, J., Mikolajczak, M., & Hansenne, M. (2009). Increasing emotional intelligence: (How) is it possible? *Personality and Individual Differences, 47*, 36–41. http://doi.org/10.1016/j.paid.2009.01.046

Nota, L., Ginevra, M. C., & Soresi, S. (2012). The Career and Work Adaptability Questionnaire (CWAQ): A first contribution to its validation. *Journal of Adolescence, 35*, 1557–1569. http://doi.org/10.1016/j.adoles-cence.2012.06.004

O'Connell, D. J., McNeely, E., & Hall, D. T. (2008). Unpacking personal adaptability at work. *Journal of Leadership & Organizational Studies, 14*, 248–259. http://doi.org/10.1177/1071791907311005

Piaget, J., & Inhelder, B. (1969). *The psychology of child.* London, UK: Routledge & Kegan Paul.

Ployhart, R. E., & Bliese, P. D. (2006). Individual adaptability (I-Adapt) theory: Conceptualizing the anteced-ents, consequences, and measurement of individual differences in adaptability. In S. C. Burke, L. G. Pierce, & E. Salas (Eds.), *Understanding adaptablity: A prerequisite for effective performance within complex en-vironments* (pp. 3–39). Howard House, UK: Emerald.

Porfeli, E. J., & Savickas, M. L. (2012). Career Adapt-Abilities Scale–USA form: Psychometric properties and relation to vocational identity. *Journal of Vocational Behavior, 80*, 748–753. http://doi.org/10.1016/j.jvb.2012.01.009

Pouyaud, J., Vignoli, E., Dosnon, O., & Lallemand, N. (2012). Career Adapt-Abilities Scale–France form: Psychometric properties and relationships to anxiety and motivation. *Journal of Vocational Behavior, 80*, 692–697. http://doi.org/10.1016/j.jvb.2012.01.021

Pratzner, F. C., & Ashley, W. L. (1984). Occupational adaptability and transferable skills: Preparing today's adults for tomorrow's careers. In C. H. Shulman (Ed.), *Adults and the changing workplace: 1985 yearbook of the American vocational association* (pp. 13–22). Arlington, VA: American Vocational Association.

Pulakos, E. D., Arad, S., Donovan, M. A., & Plamondon, K. E. (2000). Adaptability in the workplace: Development of a taxonomy of adpative performance. *Journal of Applied Psychology, 85*, 612–624. http://doi.org/10.1037/0021-9010.85.4.612

Rocha, M. (2012). Transferable skills representations in a Portuguese college sample: Gender, age, adaptabil-ity and vocational development. *European Journal of Psychology of Education, 27*, 77–90. http://doi.org/10.1007/s10212-011-0067-4

Rossier, J. (2015). Personality and career interventions. In P. J. Hartung, M. L. Savickas, & W. B. Walsh (Eds.), *APA handbook of career intervention: Foundations* (Vol. 1, pp. 327–350). Washington, DC: American Psy-chological Association. http://doi.org/10.1037/14438-018

Rossier, J., Zecca, G., Stauffer, S. D., Maggiori, C., & Dauwalder, J.-P. (2012). Career Adapt-Abilities Scale in a French-speaking Swiss sample: Psychometric properties and relationships to personality and work en-gagement. *Journal of Vocational Behavior, 80*, 734–743. http://doi.org/10.1016/j.jvb.2012.01.004

Savickas, M. L. (1997). Adaptability: An integrative construct for life-span, life-space theory. *Career Development Quarterly, 45*, 247–259. http://doi.org/10.1002/j.2161-0045.1997.tb00467.x

Savickas, M. L. (2005). The theory and practice of career construction. In S. D. Brown, & R. W. Lent (Eds.), *Career development and counseling: Putting theory and research to work* (pp. 42–70). Hoboken, NJ: Wiley.

Savickas, M. L., Nota, L., Rossier, J., Dauwalder, J.-P., Duarte, M. E., Guichard, J., . . . van Vianen, A. E. M. (2009). Life designing: A paradigm for career construction in the 21st century. *Journal of Vocational Behavior, 75*, 239–250. http://doi.org/10.1016/j.jvb.2009.04.004

Savickas, M. L., & Porfeli, E. J. (2012). Career Adapt-Abilities Scale: Construction, reliability, and measure-ment equivalence across 13 countries. *Journal of Vocational Behavior, 80*, 661–673. http://doi.org/10.1016/j.jvb.2012.01.011

Scholl, M. B., & Cascone, J. (2010). The constructivist résumé: Promoting the career adaptability of graduate students in counseling programs. *The Career Development Quarterly, 59*, 180–191. http://doi.org/10.1002/j.2161-0045.2010.tb00061.x

Soresi, S., Nota, L., & Ferrari, L. (2012). Career Adapt-Abilities Scale–Italian form: Psychometric properties and relationships to breadth of interests, quality of life, and perceived barriers. *Journal of Vocational Behavior, 80*, 705–711. http://doi.org/10.1016/j.jvb.2012.01.020

Stauffer, S. D., Maggiori, C., Froidevaux, A., & Rossier, J. (2014). Adaptability in action: Using personality, aptitude, and interest data to help clients increase their emotional, social, and cognitive career meta-capacities. In M. Coetzer (Ed.), *Psycho-social career meta-capacities: Dynamics of contemporary career development* (pp. 54–72). Dordrecht, The Netherlands: Springer.

Super, D. E., & Knasel, E. G. (1981). Career development in adulthood: Some theoretical problems and a possible solution. *British Journal of Guidance & Counselling, 9*, 194–201. http://doi.org/10.1080/03069888100760211

Super, D. E., Savickas, M. L., & Super, C. M. (1996). The life-span, life-space approach to careers. In D. Brown & L. Brooks (Eds.), *Career choice and development: Applying contemporary theories to practice* (3rd ed., pp. 121–178). San Francisco, CA: Jossey-Bass.

Tak, J. (2012). Career Adapt-Abilities Scale–Korean form: Psychometric properties and construct validity. *Journal of Vocational Behavior, 80*, 712–715. http://doi.org/10.1016/j.jvb.2012.01.008

Teixeira, M. A. P., Bardagi, M. P., Lassance, M. C. P, Magalhães, M. D., & Duarte, M. E. (2012). Career Adapt-Abilities Scale–Brazilian form: Psychometric properties and relationships to personality. *Journal of Vocational Behavior, 80*, 680–685. http://doi.org/10.1016/j.jvb.2012.01.007

Tien, H.-L. S., Wang, Y.-C., Chu, H.-C., & Huang, T.-L. (2012). Career Adapt-Abilities Scale–Taiwan form: Psychometric properties and construct validity. *Journal of Vocational Behavior, 80*, 744–747. http://doi.org/10.1016/j.jvb.2012.01.010

Van den Heuvel, M., Demerouti, E., Bakker, A. B., & Schaufeli, W. B. (2013). Adapting to change: The value of change information and meaning-making. *Journal of Vocational Behavior, 83*, 11–21. http://doi.org/10.1016/j.jvb.2013.02.004

van Vianen, A. E. M., Klehe, U.-C., Koen, J., & Dries, N. (2012). Career Adapt-Abilities Scale–Netherlands form: Psychometric properties and relationships to ability, personality, and regulatory focus. *Journal of Vocational Behavior, 80*, 716–724. http://doi.org/10.1016/j.jvb.2012.01.002

Vilhjálmsdóttir, G., Kjartansdóttir, G. B., Smáradóttir, S. B., & Einarsdóttir, S. (2012). Career Adapt-Abilities Scale–Icelandic form: Psychometric properties and construct validity. *Journal of Vocational Behavior, 80*, 698–704. http://doi.org/10.1016/j.jvb.2012.01.013

Zecca, G., & Rossier, J. (2011, September). *Relationships between personality factors, affect regulation and career adaptability capacities.* Paper presented at the International Conference, Vocational Designing and Career Counseling: Challenges and New Horizons, Padova, Italy.

Chapter 12
Coaching: A Career Intervention Model Within Life Design

Raoul Van Esbroeck and Marie-Thérèse Augustijnen
Vrije Universiteit Brussel, Belgium

Introduction

The recognition of a life-long development began sometime in the 1930s (Bühler, 1933; Jung, 1933) and resulted in several adult development theories (e.g., Erikson, 1963; Levinson, 1978). Some of these theories gave special attention to the situation of women (e.g., Bardwick, 1980; Levinson, 1996). Career aspects were a key issue in adult development studies and yielded a number of career development theories that originated in different social sciences fields (e.g., Ginzberg et al., 1951; Miller & Form, 1951; Super, 1953). The career development models were extended by introducing concepts from social and cognitive psychology (e.g., Krumboltz, 1979; Lent, Brown & Hackett, 1994; Peterson, Sampson, & Reardon, 1991) and some even converged toward a metatheoretical framework (Patton & McMahon, 1999).

All of these adult development theories fit in very well with the ideas of 20th-century modern society. Life and career were seen as logical, stable, predictable, and depictable. They made it possible to describe development in clearly defined and stable stadia or stages. Work was part of a complex system of roles as identified by Super (1990) in his life-space, life-span model. The existence of different interconnected life roles remains valid in the present postmodern society. But the development of a career is no longer linear, because information societies have "destandardized the life course" (Duarte, 2009). A career becomes "an unpredictable, lifelong evolution of small steps in reaction to the environment" (Van Esbroeck et al., 2005, p. 6). Savickas (2013, p. 150) distinguishes between an "objective" and a "subjective" career, where the subjective career is seen as the "story that individuals tell about their working lives" as constructed by the individual. The construction of this subjective career can be described as a self-construction process (Guichard, 2009). In this process, the self-concepts and the subjective career are continuously reconstructed as part of an interaction between the individual and the environment. This leads to a temporary subjective reality that is given a meaning by the individual. This new paradigm has been described by Savickas and colleagues (2009) as the life design paradigm.

Translating the life design paradigm into adequate career intervention models and methods requires major changes. In these interventions, the individual becomes the author of his or her life project. The individuals synthesize their experiences, actions, and goals into life stories. These stories are built around a number of life themes that have shaped the individuals' past and will model their future developments and choices. The shaping is based on a process of reflection on their stories and life themes. This will allow them to steer the construction of new developments in their lives and determine the choices they make. The entire process becomes a kind of life-long project of successive short or longer periods that fit into the subjective reality as it is constructed by the individual at a given moment. This type of career intervention method fits the description given by Savickas (2011a, 2013) of career counseling and is adapted to the characteristics, demands, and expectations of 21st-century society.

Savickas (2011a) identifies career counseling as a third type of career intervention that "does not replace but rather takes its place among the interventions of vocational guidance and career education" (p. 7). Career guidance and education – though originally developed in the framework of modern society – still play a key role in the present career support scene. McAdams and Olson (2010) identify three perspectives through which life-long development can be observed: The person as "actor" (infants and toddlers), as "agent" (schoolchild and early adolescence) and as "author" (from late adolescence onwards) (Savickas, 2011b). Savickas relates these three types of behavior to the types of career intervention. Career guidance is connected to individuals as actors who discover their identity, career education to individuals as agents who achieve certain goals, and career counseling to individuals as authors who construct a coherent life story and unique identity.

The question, however, is, what is the role of coaching within career interventions? Is this a fourth type of career intervention, or is this – as suggested by Savickas (2013, p. 166) – just a specific alternative to career education? He argues that "career education and coaching meets the needs of individuals climbing the corporate ladder of high modernity" (Savickas, 2013, p. 167) and describes coaching as an intervention to

> (a) assess developmental status, (b) orient to imminent development tasks and occupational transitions, and (c) increase preparedness with relevant coping attitudes, beliefs, and competencies. The outcome for career education and coaching is enhanced adaptability, sometimes called career choice readiness or work adjustment. (Savickas, 2013, p. 167)

Is this interpretation of coaching in line with what is referred to today when speaking about "executive coaching"?

A frequently used definition of executive coaching was formulated by Kilburg (1996), who defined executive coaching as:

> a helping relationship formed between a client who has managerial authority and responsibility in an organization and a consultant who uses a variety of behavioural techniques and methods to assist the client achieve a mutually identified set of goals to improve his or her professional performance and personal satisfaction and consequently to improve the effectiveness of the client's organization within a formally defined coaching agreement. (Kilburg, 1996, p. 142)

This definition is to a large extent in line with Savickas's description of coaching, but adds the aspect of "personal satisfaction." Palmer and Whybrow (2005) underline the importance of coaching in contributing to "well-being and performance in personal life and work domains" (p. 7). The importance of the personal aspects has received attention in recently developed theoretically and experimentally based models in relation to applied methodology, the role of the coach as well as content and goals. These models increasingly rely on counseling and therapy models, such as, for example, rational-emotional behavior therapy (Sherin & Caiger, 2004) and psychotherapy and system therapy in Kilburg's executive coaching model (Kilburg, 2004). The similarities and differences between coaching and other career interventions are still being debated. Attributes and behaviors of coaches are in some ways very similar to those of counselors involved in a counseling and/or therapy relationship (Passmore, 2010). The differences are connected to the fact that coaches have a broader perspective and must consider the organization and their context (Kets de Vries, 2004).

Because of the importance given to personal well-being, however, climbing the corporate ladder – as stressed by Savickas (2013) – is not the only issue in executive coaching. When too much attention is devoted to the ladder-climbing issue, it can become counterproductive for the coaching process. Augustijnen and colleagues (2011) found that environmental variables – in particular, the "organisational attitude towards coaching" (Augustijnen, Schnitzer, & Van Esbroeck, 2011, p. 160) – play a mediating role toward the development and success of the intervention. The coaching process may be rejected or prematurely terminated in situations where the employer and coachee perceive coaching too much as remediation in problem situations and not as an instrument that contributes to personal growth and positive development.

The model of executive coaching as developed by Augustijnen and colleagues (2011) sheds new light on how coaching can be situated in the broader framework of career interventions. In this model, the coaching process is influenced by two mediating variables: organizational attitude toward coaching and location of the coaching sessions. The process itself is run through four phases that concern the role of the coachee: (a) defining formal organization-bound objectives between coach, coachee, and employer, (b) self-reflection, (c) self-awareness, and (d) changes in behavior and personal changes. Finally, it also identifies two central variables: (a) openness to coachee introspection and (b) relationship of trust between coach and coachee. The central variables dynamically steer and guide the development through the stages. This model can be translated into the format that has been proposed by Savickas (2011a) to describe the paradigms in career intervention. Career coaching can accordingly be described as a fourth paradigm that lies somewhere between career education and counseling (see Figure 12.1).

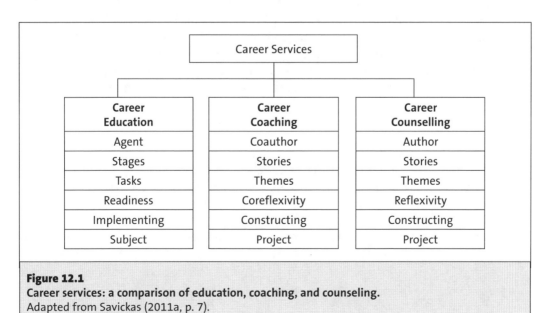

Career Education	Career Coaching	Career Counselling
Agent	Coauthor	Author
Stages	Stories	Stories
Tasks	Themes	Themes
Readiness	Coreflexivity	Reflexivity
Implementing	Constructing	Constructing
Subject	Project	Project

Figure 12.1
Career services: a comparison of education, coaching, and counseling.
Adapted from Savickas (2011a, p. 7).

In executive coaching, the individuals are seen as authors who construct their life and career stories during the coaching process in dialogue with their work organization, by integrating their present and past experiences, activities, and observations. What the stories will be about, however, does not only depend on the individual's personal goals and expectations. On the contrary, the goals will be defined in mutual interaction and agreement between three parties: employer, individual (coachee), and coach.

This agreement will serve as the framework within which the search and construction of life and career themes will evolve. This framework of collaboration may include some constraints, but it will not prevent individuals from developing their broader life stories, which can exceed the career aspects. The coachee remains – as expected within the life design paradigm – the principal author of the story, but it will be written in dialogue with the work organization. In fact it can be considered as a coauthorship of the story. The coaching process includes self-assessment as part of the second (reflexion) stage in the coaching process. This again will be a stage where there is cooperation between the individual and the work environment. It becomes accordingly a kind of coreflexivity between the coachee and the partners of the work environment. The process of construction, deconstruction, reconstruction by the individuals will, as described by Savickas (2013), be part of the self-awareness stage in the coaching process. At the end of the process, the coachee will reach the recognition of changes – changes that can go beyond job- and career-related aspects and may include individual and personal changes. This is the part of the coaching process where the coach and coachee "co-construct the next episode in the story" (Savickas, 2013, p. 167). The content of the next chapter in the life and career story will be steered by the "goals" that have been defined, in mutual agreement between the three actors, at the beginning of the coaching process. This will not prevent the coachee from exceeding these limits as long as they fit the set goals. This can lead to moving toward a life-long holistic story that takes into account social non-work-related contextual aspects which are important to the coachee.

When executive coaching is seen as described above, it fits the life design concept. Indeed, all aspects that are characteristic to life design are present. A coaching intervention supports the coachee in the process of determining which skills and knowledge are needed to deal with current changes and life-long development issues. Coaching aims to increase the clients' adaptability, narratability, and activity. The coaching intervention allows the person to design his or her career development in a broader holistic framework covering a self-construction through all life roles. At the same time, the coaching intervention must play a preventive role that will allow the coachee to effectively identify future developments and how to deal with them.

How these aspects, characteristic of life design, appear in a managerial coaching intervention is illustrated in the case of Catherine. At the same time, the similarities and differences between education, counseling, and coaching intervention are highlighted by comparing the cases of Jef and Catherine. The case of Jef is about a young adult working toward a new major at university, and the case of Catherine is about the coaching process for a woman in the age 30 transition, who is trying to cope with burnout. The similarities and differences between the two cases will illustrate at which point career coaching diverges from, or converges with, counseling and education within a broader life design approach.

Cases

The Case of Jef

Jef was an 18-year-old man and first-year student majoring in Romance languages. He was the youngest of two, with one older sister studying at the same university, and belonged to an upper class family. His father had an engineering degree and was the chief executive officer (CEO) of a large Belgian company, and his mother was a housewife with a degree from an institution of higher education. The family lived in an expensive residential area close to Brussels. Jef went to the local secondary school – a school with a very good reputation for preparing pupils for higher education – and took modern languages as his main subject. He was always a solid average all-round student, who was never held back or failed his grades.

When at school, Jef went through a traditional person–environment (P-E) fit guidance program supported by a career counselor. The program included, as part of self-exploration, a series of tests and a workbook. The self-exploration was rounded off during an individual meeting with the career counselor and with the class mentor (a teacher), who discussed the educational choice made by Jef in the context of his school results and advice formulated by the class council.

The choice of a major in Romance languages at university resulted from this guidance process. Unfortunately, after just 1 week, Jef wanted to explore the possibility of changing his option. He felt uncomfortable in class and doubted that studying Romance languages was really what he wanted. Jef expressed his dissatisfaction with the choice he had made and was clearly uncertain about his interests, values, and skills. This feeling was triggered by the linguistics, etymology, and philology classes. Jef was not expecting to have to spend so much of his time on these subjects. He rather expected to be studying literature and attending writing classes. Jef felt very frustrated.

While reflecting on the guidance process he had gone through in high school, he explained that, originally, when he had made his educational choice at the end of secondary education, he felt very good about his decision. But the problem now was that he doubted if the results of the guidance process had been correct. Jef was unable to fit the information into a broader picture and certainly was unable to express what could be a new option. He was totally undecided and was unable to make a new choice. The idea that he had to choose a new educational option frightened him because he was afraid of making the wrong decision again.

Jef asked if we could help him to clarify his profile and help him find an educational option that would fit his profile, and something he would like to do. The main problem with Jef was his own doubts about his profile. He doubted if the results of the assessments reflected his real self. He was also unable to make a new decision because of his anxiety to get it wrong again. Jef had entered a stage of indecisiveness. The challenge was that he had to rebuild his self-image and identify his life themes.

We opted for a kind of vocational card sort that could stimulate him to identify his life themes and reconstruct his self-image. This choice was supported by Hartung's (1999) observation that card sorts empower "clients to develop their own response categories, construct their own meanings, and reflect on how they personally construe their interests and the career decision-making process." (p. 248). An experimental card set was created on the basis of an outdated set from Maussen and the list of occupational titles used in the Vlaamse Aanpassing Amsterdamse Beroepen Interessen Vragenlijst (Flemish adaptation of the Amsterdam Career Interests Questionnaire; Evers & Van Esbroeck, 1982). The set included 80 occupational titles divided into eight sets of 10 titles. In the case of Jef, the card sort was used in line with the proposals put forward by Tyler (1961 – see Slaney & MacKinnon-Slaney, 1990) – sorting out the occupational titles among "would choose," "would not choose," and "no opinion" – and followed by a structured interview as suggested by Dolliver (1967). Also George Kelly's (1955) personal construct theory was used as a guideline.

Jef was first asked to sort the cards into the three groups. Afterwards, he selected from the "chosen" occupational titles the three most desired or liked ones, followed by the triad of the second most liked, and so on, until all chosen titles were grouped into triads of occupational titles. In the case of Jef, the following triads of occupational titles were constructed, starting with the most liked ones:

> sports coach – tour guide – PR assistant
> social worker – nurse – interior architect
> youth leader – animal carer – medical doctor
> veterinary surgeon – physiotherapist – journalist
> fashion designer – forester – bookshop manager

After the sort, the question-and-answer sequence started. The first question on the most liked triad was, "These are the three occupations you like most. Can you describe what these occupations have in common with you?" After the initial answer, this question was followed by some additional questions asking for further explanation or elaboration on what Jef had said. The second stage in the discussion on the triads started with the question, can you also indicate if there are differences among the three occupations? To explore the answers in depth we also used comparisons in relation to communalities and differences between subsets of two occupations within the original triad. Afterwards, the same procedure was applied to the second and subsequent triads.

Though the goal of this discussion targeted the comparison of what the chosen job titles had in common, it was very often supplemented by little stories and experiences from the past. By way of illustration, when addressing the topic of comparing the jobs of animal carer and medical doctor, Jef indicated that in both roles you were taking care of someone; but at the same time he reflected that "... medical doctor ... how stupid. Obviously, I can't do it. My secondary school option did not prepare me for such an educational track." The same happened while talking about animal carer. He said he liked dogs and sometimes looked after a neighbour's dog; but he also concluded: " ... animal carer ... yeah ... I like animals very much and like to take care of them ... but as a job ... How can you earn a living doing this? It doesn't pay enough." It is clear that while comparing, he talked about important moments and experience from the past and, in so doing, laid the foundation that allowed him to construct the themes.

At the end of the third triad, a wrapping-up sequence started when we asked: "So Jef, we have now finished the analysis of the first three groups of the occupations you liked most. What do you think? How do you feel? Did you find out anything new?" Following these questions, Jef spontaneously started discussing his career constructs and career themes. He said, "It is clear to me ... I do not need to go on anymore ... I am just repeating the same things over and over again while comparing the choices I made. Indeed, I understand now why I chose them."

Jef started to verbalize the themes that had influenced him in the choices he had made to compose and rank the triads. The counselor rephrased what he had said in order to structure and restructure it, and tried to bring his answers to a higher level of generalization. During this discussion, Jef discovered that even some of the more unrealistic choices were meaningful. This interaction between Jef and the counselor resulted in identifying and verbalizing the following themes:

> I want to help someone (people, animals);
> I need recognition, gratitude and respect for what I do;
> I need some freedom;
> The level of my occupation is not so important.

It was a moment of drastic change for Jef. The fact that he himself had discovered the career themes and had been able to express them came as a relief to him. The problem of being undecided and even the feeling of indecisiveness had disappeared. He now knew what he had to look for when choosing a new educational option. Thanks to the self and environmental exploration he had done in secondary school, he was even able to comment on how unrealistic some of his choices had been: "... medical doctor ... how stupid. Obviously, I can't do it. My secondary school option did not prepare me for such an educational track." But also: " ... animal carer ... yeah ... I like animals very much and like to take care of them ... but as a job ... How can you earn a living doing this? It doesn't pay enough."

The counselor and Jef agreed that he would now reflect on the themes he had identified and start exploring possible educational options and make a new appointment when ready. Within a week, Jef made a new appointment. This session started by assessing the extent to which the identified themes were being maintained in his thinking, and whether they reflected his life story and his "me." Jef felt no need to revise the themes; the main topic for him was to present the new education option he had chosen. He opted for a higher education programme in social work at a *Hogeschool* (institution of higher education). He justified his choice by indicating that this program would fit in with his competencies profile and that it was in line with his career themes. Indeed, given that educational prestige was not essential to him, he could easily have chosen a program at a nonacademic institution. Jef was aware that his father, in particular, would be rather disappointed with his choice. More important was the observation that social work would allow him to help people, that he would receive recognition from those who called upon him, and that the job would give him some freedom in how he worked with his clients. Jef was aware that there would be some limitations because most social workers operate within an institutional framework, but he expected to have enough freedom to choose how to work with his clients.

The Case of Catherine

Catherine was a 31-year-old married woman with two children. She worked in a supporting department of an insurance company at middle-management level. She had two younger sisters and one younger brother. Her father held a university degree, and her mother was a nurse. Initially, Catherine started studying commercial engineering, but she switched to applied economic sciences. Her father and Catherine also refer to applied economics as an inferior program. Catherine even considers that she has not been successful in her studies because she does not hold a commercial engineering degree. Catherine has been raised in a family environment that lacked warmth. Her parents paid a lot of attention to academic performance. Her grades were never good enough for her father. Only excellent scores were acceptable, and average scores were considered a failure. After she finished her studies, Catherine worked for 6 years as a junior consultant in finance for a large consultancy agency. She lost this job as a result of a reorganization scheme. Six weeks later she started as a consultant in a service department of an insurance company where she was responsible for loans. She has been working there for 6 years.

Catherine's initial problem when she consulted a coach at her own initiative was burnout. She had been incapable of working for 2 months already and was on sick leave. Her employer was at this stage not aware of this move. She had, however, previously asked her employer that she be given a coach. This request was refused because she was not at the required hierarchical level. The first two coaching sessions could be considered as the first phase (see model, Augustijnen et al., 2011). During this first phase, it emerged that Catherine clearly had a feeling of inferiority with regard to her studies: She was convinced that applied economic sciences was much inferior to commercial engineering, saying, "I am a failure, I don't consider applied economics as university studies." She also had many underlying frustrations with regard to her position at the insurance company. Catherine was very ambitious and thought that she had not been successful in her career, because she did not get the promotions she wanted at the insurance company. The company was working with clear hierarchical levels. Depending on one's education, seniority, and performance evaluations, one could climb the hierarchical ladder. Her colleagues with the same educational level and seniority had already climbed the ladder, and this frustrated her because she was convinced that she did a better job. Catherine was strongly focused on being promoted – saying, "the company should give me a promotion, I am better than my colleagues, they have to do it, I don't understand why I am not getting a promotion" – rather than attaching importance to the content of her actual job. She had very little job satisfaction and displayed this underlying frustration to her line manager. These frustrations were expressed in a rather aggressive and direct manner: "You [line manager] should give me a promotion because of the good work I deliver." During the first phase of the coaching process, it became obvious that Catherine's main objective was to get a promotion within 6 months, when she would be evaluated based on her performance. In this first phase, there was no opening for introspection. She was convinced that she was right and that the company was wrong in not giving her the promotion she felt she deserved.

After the first phase, she entered the second phase of self-reflection, which took three sessions. The dyadic relationship between coach and coachee developed, a mutual trust was developed, and Catherine became mentally ready to continue the process. She demonstrated for the first time openness to introspection: "Maybe, I also have to work on myself…." To have a better idea of what was happening at the company, Catherine allowed the coach to contact her line manager. At this moment, the line manager – to some extent, the work environment – became aware of the ongoing coaching process and that Catherine wanted to work on her problems. The manager had, however, no involvement in the coaching process, nor did he have any influence on the objectives. The employer, however, indirectly influenced what happened in the coaching process and was also going to affect the evaluation of the outcome of the process. To help Catherine in the process of self-evaluation and discover how others assessed her as a person and as a professional, the coach asked her to give a questionnaire to three persons from her private environment and three persons from her work environment. These questionnaires were sent back to the coach. Catherine was described by them as a very hard worker, honest, open, and sociable, but also as a person with a direct communication style. Her line manager even wrote: "Sometimes I have no interest to enter into a discussion with her. In some circumstances, I really don't want to talk with her." Her employer was happy with the quality of her work but could not appreciate her communication attitude. Her colleagues also commented that she gave the feeling of thinking herself superior to her peers, and this could create resistance. Although Catherine functioned well at the level of job content, there was definitely a problem with communication style. She started to recognize this when she said, "Yes indeed, sometimes my colleagues are saying nothing when I am giving a presentation, I think I am overwhelming them." Her direct communication style, however, was based on her extreme urge to be promoted and her sense of inferiority. During the first part of the coaching process, one of the important life topics – that is, her sense of inferiority – had to been addressed. At this stage, Catherine became aware of a new goal: to address her aggressive communication style with regard to her line manager and her peers. The combination of both issues – a sense of inferiority and poor communication style – could be seen as the reasons her career was blocked.

The feedback from her line manager and the results of the questionnaires were also important in helping Catherine in the third stage, that of self-awareness. The third stage took eight sessions in which techniques of mirroring (e.g., "If I understand you correctly, you are convinced that applied economics are not university studies"), listening, confronting (e.g., "Do you really think that someone with an education as a commercial engineer would be more successful in his job … or are there other factors that play a role in being successful?"), giving feedback, and also psychological support were used. As a result, Catherine recognized the role of her feeling of inferiority ("Well yes, maybe it is true being successful depends on other things than education") and her direct communication style.

In the fourth phase, changing behavior and personal change, the challenge for the coach was to rebuild her self-image as well as changing her behavior toward her line manager and colleagues. Approximately eight sessions were spent on this phase. First, her self-image was addressed by employing several techniques, among which were the solution-focused approach. Questions were asked, such as, "give me an example where you were successful, what was the reason you were successful?" This intervention led to the situation where, despite the absence of promotion, she felt successful and handled the assigned projects professionally. While rebuilding her self-image she was able to accept that her feelings of inferiority were not realistic and that they interfered with her behavior and her career. She accepted that her communication style played a part and that it was a major hurdle in further developing her career. Building a new communication style and acquiring the necessary skills became the second focus of attention. In relation to the communication style, a role-playing approach was used. She also included her line manager in this part of the coaching process through continued and regular feedback. After many exercises and a major effort, she adopted another way of communicating. Changing her communication style, but even more importantly, the revision of her self-image, resulted in a renewed interested in her job and even a growing level of job satisfaction. It was no longer the need for promotion, but rather the intrinsic value and content of the job that gave her job satisfaction. The contacts with her colleagues and with her line manager improved. The extent to which she changed was reflected by the midyear and yearly performance reviews. Her scores improved considerably on the level of communication style and teamwork.

At the end of the coaching intervention, she expressed her satisfaction with the result and the important life theme change. Being promoted was no longer crucially important in achieving job satisfaction. Also, communication with colleagues had changed: "Now I am happy when I give a presentation, when people listen to me, and we can have a constructive conversation."

Reflection and Conclusion

The cases of Catherine and Jef differ considerably. As a young adult, Jef approached a career counselor asking for guidance support in the process of revising his educational choice, while Catherine, as an adult woman, requested an intervention – identified by her as coaching support – for a problem of career burnout. Their initial requests, however, led to something much more complex.

Jef and his counselor very soon recognized that traditional career guidance was not going to solve the problem. Jef had received good guidance during his final year in high school, and a new guidance process with new tests and other instruments would not add much to what had already been done. The intervention moved to counseling support where the rebuilding of career themes became the key issue. By using a kind of career card sort, Jef identified his career themes and (re)structured them. The themes were so broad, however, that they could be labeled life themes. Constructing these themes allowed Jef to revise his career choice and bring it in line with what he expected would happen in the new chapter of his life.

Catherine, however, though requesting coaching support, was in fact from the very start asking for counseling. The counselor responded positively to her request for coaching support, but used the first stage of the intervention as a means of helping Catherine to identify the underlying problems that had led to her burnout. Though the coaching process started at the coachee's request, the role of the work organization (line manager and colleagues) became indirectly visible during the process. This led to a situation where Catherine still controlled the process, but it was one in which she actually took into account expectations and goals set by the work environment. While defining the objectives of the coaching, the burnout was related to two problems: redefining the life themes and the need to adapt communication style and acquire new competencies in communication. The request for counseling changed into a coaching process including a combination of reconstructing her self-image – as part of a counseling paradigm – and building new skills – as an aspect of the education paradigm. The integration of both these aspects turned the process into a coaching intervention.

Both cases, though very different in the type of problems presented and the clients' requests, fit the characteristics of life design. The cases illustrate that clients often have specific expectations in relation to what they are looking for, based on previous experiences or knowledge of existing interventions. These expectations concerning the type of intervention considered are not always well founded and do not always make it possible to deal with the problems as presented. As a result, the counselor is faced with the task of using the initial step of the intervention to support a redefinition of the client's request and to help the client become aware of the situation, to rephrase it, and to recognize and accept the goals of the intervention. In both of the cases under scrutiny, it turned out that the counselor could not limit the career intervention to the use of techniques belonging to one paradigm.

Obviously, the specific intervention techniques and methods differed considerably. Jef's case was based on the use of a career card sort technique, a measurement instrument for career guidance, but applied in such a way that it became an instrument for self-reconstruction as part of a broader life design process. In the case of Catherine, a broad range of techniques and instruments was used, from a solution-focused approach as part of the self-reconstruction, to role-playing for adapting the communication style. This wide range of techniques illustrates the fact that life design is not restricted to one single technique. On the contrary, many existing techniques and methods may be used. Whether they fit the life design paradigm depends on how these methods are applied.

The question of the extent to which coaching can be considered as a separate career paradigm is illustrated by Catherine's case. The problems which Catherine presented as a burnout were related to underlying issues of feelings of inferiority and inappropriate communication skills. Though part of the intervention could initially be labeled as counselling, the intervention rapidly became a real career coaching support process where the work environment played a subsidiary, indirect role. To some extent, the indirect role also shaped the construction process and the direction of the self-image reconstruction in which Catherine engaged. The work environment also influenced what happened during the coaching process in relation to the communication style and in assessing the success of this intervention. Catherine's case illustrates the fact that, in a coaching intervention, personal well-being, which will sometimes extend beyond work, is a crucial element. At the same time, Catherine's case illustrates the fact that the aspect of developing new skills or adapting existing ones, needs to operate appropriately in the work environment, which can also be part of the intervention. It is clear that in the case of Catherine, the two aspects could not be dissociated and that working on both was essential to handling her problem.

Given this situation, it can be concluded that in some cases coaching must be considered as a separate paradigm within career support. Indeed the role played by the organization (work environment), the combination of aspects related to skills and attitude development, together with aspects related to personal well-being extending beyond work issues, make the process different from career education and counseling. In any case, executive coaching is often an intervention that includes tightly interwoven aspects of career education and counseling. Given the fact that coaching frequently extends to personal issues that are broader than the narrow work issues, it can be considered a life design intervention.

Analysis of these cases also shows that counselors involved in career interventions cannot limit their activities to one paradigm. They must be prepared to work within the different paradigms in the field of career support, while at the same time focusing on the problems presented by the clients. The need to be able to operate according to different paradigms has many consequences with respect to the competencies needed by counselors who engage in coaching. In the case of Catherine, for instance, the coach needed to have the required competencies as a career guidance practitioner (see, e.g., International Association for Educational and Vocational Guidance, 2008) and a career counselor (see, e.g., National Career Development Association, 1997, 2009), but also meet the required competencies for coaching (see, e.g., International Coach Federation, n.d.). For the coach to recognize the need to work according to different paradigms and with the competencies required for each of these approaches, and to accept that the client is an active author steering the intervention process, is essential for any career intervention that fits within the life design paradigm.

References

Augustijnen, M.-T., Schnitzer, G., & Van Esbroeck, R. (2011). A model of executive coaching: A qualitative study. *International Coaching Psychology Review, 6*, 150–164.

Bardwick, J. (1980). The seasons of a woman's life. In D. McGuigan (Ed.), *Women's lives: New theory, research and policy*. Ann Harbor, MI: University of Michigan.

Bühler, C. (1933). *Der Menschliches Lebenslauf als Psychologisches Problem* [The course of life as a psychological problem]. Leipzig, Germany: Hirzel.

Dolliver, R. H. (1967). An adaptation of the Tyler Vocational Card Sort. *Personnel and Guidance Journal, 45*, 168–174. http://doi.org/10.1002/j.2164-4918.1967.tb04811.x

Duarte, E. (2009). The psychology of life construction. *Journal of Vocational Behavior, 75,* 259–266. http://doi.org/10.1016/j.jvb.2009.06.009

Erikson, E. H. (1963). *Childhood and society* (2nd ed.). New York, NY: Norton.

Evers, A., & Van Esbroeck, R. (1982). *Vlaamse aanpassing van de Amsterdamse Beroepen-Interessen Vragenlijst – Handleiding* [Flemish adaptation of the Amsterdam Career Interests Questionnaire: Manual]. Lisse, The Netherlands: Swets en Zeitlinger.

Ginzberg, E., Ginsburg, S. W., Axelrad, S., & Herma, J. L. (1951). *Occupational choice: An approach to a general theory.* New York, NY: Columbia University Press.

Guichard, J. (2009). Self-construction. *Journal of Vocational Behavior, 75,* 251–258. http://doi.org/10.1016/j.jvb.2009.03.004

Hartung, P. (1999). Interest assessment using card sorts. In M. L. Savickas & A. R. Spokane (Eds.), *Vocational interests* (pp. 235–252). Palo Alto, CA: Davies-Black.

International Association for Educational and Vocational Guidance. (2008). International competences for educational and vocational guidance practitioners. *International Journal for Educational and Vocational Guidance, 8,* 191–195.

International Coach Federation. (n.d.). *Individual credentialing: Core competencies.* Lexington, KY: Author. Retrieved from http://www.coachfederation.org/credential

Jung, C. G. (1933). *Modern man in search of a soul.* New York, NY: Harcourt, Brace, & World.

Kelly, G. A. (1955). *The psychology of personal constructs.* New York, NY: Norton.

Kets de Vries, M. F. (2004). *Coach or couch, anybody? The Zen of creating High-EQ organizations.* Fontainbleau, France: Insead.

Kilburg, R. R. (1996). Toward a conceptual understanding and definition of executive coaching. *Consulting Psychology Journal, 48,* 134–144. http://doi.org/10.1037/1061-4087.48.2.134

Kilburg, R. R. (2004). When shadows fall: Using psychodynamic approaches in executive coaching. *Consulting Psychology Journal: Practice & Research, 56,* 246–268. http://doi.org/10.1037/1065-9293.56.4.246

Krumboltz, J. D. (1979). A social learning theory of career choice. In A. M. Mitchell, G. B. Jones & J. D. Krumboltz (Eds.), *Social learning and career decision making* (pp. 19–49). Cranston, RI: Carroll Press.

Lent, W., Brown, S. D., & Hackett, G. (1994). Toward a unifying sociocognitive theory of career and academic interest, choice, and performance [Monograph]. *Journal of Vocational Behavior, 45,* 79–122. http://doi.org/10.1006/jvbe.1994.1027

Levinson, D. J. (1978). *The seasons of a man's life.* New York, NY: Alfred Knopf.

Levinson, D. J. (1996). *The seasons of a woman's life.* New York, NY: Alfred Knopf.

McAdams, D. P., & Olson, B. D. (2010). Personality development: Continuity and change over the life course. *Annual Review of Psychology, 61,* 517–542. http://doi.org/10.1146/annurev.psych.093008.100507

Miller, D. C., & Form, W. H. (1951). *Industrial sociology.* New York, NY: Harper & Row.

National Career Development Association. (1997). *Career counseling competencies: Revised version.* Broken Arrow, OK: Author. Retrieved from http://www.ncda.org/aws/NCDA/pt/sp/guidelines

National Career Development Association. (2009). *Minimum competencies for multicultural career counselling and development.* Broken Arrow, OK: Author. Retrieved from http://www.ncda.org/aws/NCDA/pt/sp/guidelines

Palmer, S., & Whybrow, A. (2005). The proposal to establish a Special Group in Coaching Psychology. *The Coaching Psychologist, 1,* 5–11.

Passmore, J. (2010). A grounded theory study of the coachee experience: The implications for training and practice in coaching psychology. *International Coaching Psychology Review, 5,* 48–62.

Patton, W., & McMahon, M. (1999). *Career development and systems theory: A new relationship.* Pacific Grove, CA: Brooks/Cole.

Peterson, G. W., Sampson, J. P., & Reardon, R. C. (1991). *Career development and services: A cognitive approach.* Pacific Grove, CA: Brooks/Cole.

Savickas, M. L. (2011a). *Career counselling.* Washington, DC: American Psychological Association.

Savickas, M. L. (2011b). Constructing careers: Actor, agent, and author. *Journal of Employment Counselling, 48,* 179–181. http://doi.org/10.1002/j.2161-1920.2011.tb01109.x

Savickas, M. L. (2013). Career construction theory and practice. In R. W. Lent & S. D. Brown (Eds.), *Career development and counselling* (2nd ed., pp. 147–183) Hoboken, NJ: Wiley.

Savickas, M. L., Nota, L., Rossier, J., Dauwalder, J.-P., Duarte, M. E., Guichard, J., . . . van Vianen, A. (2009).

Life designing: A paradigm for career construction in the 21st century. *Journal of Vocational Behavior, 75*, 239–250. http://doi.org/10.1016/j.jvb.2009.04.004

Sherin, J., & Caiger, L. (2004). Rational emotive behavior therapy: A behavioral change model for coaching. *Consulting Psychology Journal: Practice and Research, 56*, 1065–1083. http://doi.org/10.1037/1065-9293.56.4.225

Slaney, R. B., & MacKinnon-Slaney, F. (1990). The use of vocational card sorts in career counseling. In C. E. Watkins & V. L. Campbell (Eds.), *Testing in counseling practice* (pp. 317–371). Hillsdale, NJ: Erlbaum.

Super, D. E. (1953). A theory of vocational development. *American Psychologist, 8*, 185–190. http://doi.org/10.1037/h0056046

Super, D. (1990). A life-span, life-space approach to career development. In D. Brown & L. Brooks (Eds.), *Career choice theory and development* (2nd ed., pp. 197–261). San Francisco, CA: Jossey-Bass.

Van Esbroeck, R., Tibos, K., & Zaman, M. (2005). A dynamic model of career choice development. *International Journal for Educational and Vocational Guidance, 5*, 5–18. http://doi.org/10.1007/s10775-005-2122-7

Chapter 13
Life Design and Prevention

Laura Nota, Maria Cristina Ginevra, and Sara Santilli
Department of Philosophy, Sociology, Education and Applied Psychology,
University of Padova, Italy

Introduction

As is well known, the challenges posed by the sudden changes that have affected the world of work and of economics have shifted the emphasis from "stability" to flexibility, adaptability, and life-long learning. They have also encouraged the search for methods of *career counseling* that make reference to a dynamic approach, favor creative thinking, and foster the exploration and the planning of possible selves, even in an original fashion. The workers of the 21st century will take on different working roles and positions, sometimes central, sometimes peripheral and marginal. They will have to know how to best invest in their current competencies in order to adapt to and develop new ones to be able to make a contribution to a work market "without clear boundaries." Very likely, they will have to make professional decisions more often than the workers of previous generations, and such decisions will concern above all short-term jobs and activities. They will be more likely to live in a working environment characterized above all by small- and medium-sized businesses. Culkin and Mallick (2011) underline the fact that, despite the crisis, an increase in freelance consultants and microbusinesses – where entrepreneurial abilities and innovation are essential values – has been recorded. Much more than in the past, innovation in its most diverse forms and investment in human capital and in talented individuals are certainly needed. Equally necessary are conditions that can allow people to create new ideas, new technologies, and new products (Moretti, 2012).

The businesses of the near future will very likely be temporary sets of individuals aiming at producing what can satisfy clients' requests, thanks especially to new technologies and the Internet, and will increasingly require teamwork abilities. Hierarchical structures and rigid pyramidal organizations will only be a thing of the past (Ridley, 2010). Moreover, people will have to show their ability to seize and make the most of opportunities, take risks, think strategically, be flexible about work, and show commercial awareness and creativity to favor new forms of business (Culkin & Mallick, 2011). For example, medical doctors will have to acquire social and interactive abilities as they will have to deal with patients increasingly informed about their medical ailments, journalists will have to consider the fact that readers and audiences will increasingly choose and assemble news by themselves, television broadcasters already allow their viewers to choose who will entertain them, and entrepreneurs are enabling clients to choose products à la carte, etc.

Very likely, greater attention will be paid to different needs, stronger specialization will be required in the production of goods and services, and emphasis will be placed on diversified consumption, with technologies and habits that it is not possible to foresee, since innovation and progress have substantially characterized mankind over the centuries. Ridley (2010) maintains that nowadays the world is connected and that ideas are combined in a way as promiscuous as ever; that the rate of innovation will double, and that in the 21st century, financial development will make standards of life skyrocket, helping even the poorest people in the world to fulfill not only their needs but also their desires.

Considering that, the Life Design Group believes that:

> Vocational guidance can no longer confine itself to intervening at transition times and making predictions or proposing suggestions on the basis of present stock taking. It should also include a markedly preventive role. It is necessary to act on settings, looking for early preventive alliances and collaborations. In the framework of life-design counseling this means taking an interest in people's future much earlier than when they have to face the difficulties of transitions, so that their actual choice opportunities can be increased with special attention devoted to at-risk situations. The effectiveness of vocational guidance could be measured by its ability to produce significant changes in the "conclusions" of the life stories of many individuals (Soresi, Nota, Ferrari, & Solberg, 2008) by fostering career adaptability, narratability, activity, and intentionality. (Savickas et al., 2009, p. 245)

We believe that life design counselors are called upon to favor economic progress, innovation, and change in order to reduce inequalities, injustices, exploitation, and poverty, by supporting people and providing them with the necessary psychological and cognitive means to achieve just that. They can act in various ways, with people and the environments they live in, by means of counseling and career education activities, and also through preventive actions. Prevention, in particular, can help us "be prepared" well in advance; have at one's disposal knowledge, attitudes, and behaviors that can favor coping with the difficult times we are going through; but also, and above all, look forward, create, and stimulate progress and greater well-being for everyone.

In this chapter, the issue of prevention will be analyzed, underlining why the bond between life design and prevention is an optimal one, and then some actions that could be implemented with significant figures in this context – that is, parents, but also with their sons and daughters – will be considered.

Prevention, Life Design, and Emphasis on Growth and Development

To analyze the relationship between prevention and life design, the idea of prevention developed in the field of counseling psychology in terms of goals to pursue, characteristics of interventions, and individuals to be helped, will be examined, with the aim of outlining preventive actions for life design counselors.

From the mid-1960s, a number of counseling psychology scholars have addressed the issue of prevention, and focusing on its *definition*, so that the development in the way prevention has been described over the years is understood. Albee and Ryan (1998) asserted that prevention is understood as "doing something now to prevent (or forestall) something unpleasant or undesirable from happening in the future" (p. 441). Romano and Hage (2000) maintained that the definition of prevention should include impeding occurrence, delaying the onset, and reducing the effect of a problem behavior; increasing attitudes, knowledge, and behaviors that enhance physical and emotional well-being; and supporting institutional, community, and government policies which aim to promote physical, emotional, and social well-being. This new notion of prevention shows a shift of focus from problem-centered actions to actions that promote personal well-being. Vera and Polanin (2012) conceptualized prevention as the effort of building a variety of advantages related to avoiding a problem and having a prosperous life during which people can express their own potential.

Specifically for vocational development, Whiston and James (2013) emphasized that prevention should focus on promoting the decision-making process, by identifying career goals and developing skills required to achieve them. All of this is also emphasized by life design, which is structured to be preventive, focused on promoting future career by planning individual, but also small- and large-group prevention programs to be implemented, as mentioned, before a career transition (Nota, Soresi, Ferrari, & Ginevra, 2014). People should not be caught up in thoughts, attitudes, behaviors, and emotional states that do not allow them to "engage in meaningful activities and flourish in knowledge societies" (Savickas et al., 2009, p. 245).

In terms of *aims and goals,* prevention pays special attention to development across the life span and to the personal growth of children, but also of adolescents, adults, and older persons. To examine the *requirements* for *intervention,* an essential prerequisite is cultural competence, which includes not only knowledge of, and respect for, ethnic diversity, but also the institutional culture where prevention counselors can step in (i.e., those who work in school settings must understand the dynamics of school calendars, the roles of the various practitioners, etc.). At the same time, it is necessary to consider scientific progress and the use of new technologies, with the aim of creating large-scale prevention activities and streamline interventions, taking into account the suggestions of the economics of science and cost-benefit analysis. Consideration is given to the importance of focusing on multidisciplinary partnerships for the development of activities more suited to people's needs and to facilitate program implementation and efficacy evaluation (Romano, 2012).

Although the traditional and common tripartite model that considers the three levels of prevention –primary, secondary, and tertiary[1] – is still taken into account, the need for both person- and environment-centered prevention efforts is now emphasized. Person-centered interventions refer to skills building for people who may develop disorders; environment-centered preventions aim to influence the system in which those individuals live (family, community, organizations, peers, school, child care, neighborhood). In either case, interventions should be tailored to individual needs and should stimulate the direct involvement of clients in their career planning (Vera & Polanin, 2012). Life design emphasizes a life-long, holistic, and contextual view, and underscores the need to develop *personalized career counseling activities* that make it possible to approach clients by "giving them a voice," respecting their uniqueness, and creating a relationship based on a working alliance where both client and counselor actively contribute (Nota et al., 2014).

---

[1] Primary prevention aims to prevent new cases of a disorder, is group-oriented, must be realized prior to problem emergence, and focuses on strengthening individual adjustment; secondary prevention refers to early identification and treatment of individuals as being at risk for certain disorders; tertiary prevention includes programs that aim to reduce long-term and negative consequences in people with existing disorders (Vera & Polanin, 2012).

Great prevention efforts should be directed to those possible *clients* who are more vulnerable than others to develop disorders, due to poverty, discrimination, inadequate health care infrastructures, war, or restricted access to services. Particular attention is reserved for parents, who among community members have a significant role in their children's adaptive development, and for teachers and classmates. Life design argues that at-risk individuals in our society include young people, temporary workers, older workers, women, immigrants, and single parents (Nota et al., 2014); it also states that "Life Design counselors must be concerned with disseminating their knowledge and services as part of a knowledge society. This might start in working with parents and teachers" (Savickas et al., 2009, p. 248).

In terms of the *dimensions* to be privileged, the prevention scholars emphasize resilience and emotional, social, cognitive, and behavioral competence. Additionally, they foster critical thinking and decision-making skills, responsibility for one's own actions, self-determination and self-efficacy, moral development, spirituality, and a clear and positive identity (Vera & Polanin, 2012). Also in relation to career development, academic success and investment in education, ability to identify environmental supports, and internal and external resources to pursue own goals are highlighted (Lent & Brown, 2013).

Interventions based on the life design approach should focus on career adaptability, therefore strengthening a set of resources for individuals to handle developmental tasks to prepare for future professional and cope with the difficult times we are going through. These resources have to do with concern, which involves a tendency to consider life within a time perspective anchored in hope and optimism, confidence, control, and curiosity. Life design interventions should also focus on intentionality and action – that is, translating intentions into actions to make sure that what is important to us happens, and on reflexivity, understood as the reflexive project of the self and as taking into account the consequences for close relatives of our own career decisions. Recently, life design has emphasized also the ethical considerations regarding work, work organization, and work for supportable and equitable development (see Chapter 2; also Nota et al., 2014).

Focusing on *methodological issues*, the need for qualitative procedures and narrative approaches in prevention programs has recently been highlighted. Life design counselors have an advantage in this, given that the importance of these procedures has long been emphasized in the life design paradigm. They do not neglect the use of quantitative procedures useful to create a baseline to identify individuals at risk of developing problems or who have already developed them, and to verify efficacy of interventions. However, qualitative procedures can be useful to assign an active role to the client in collecting and interpreting data, emphasize the holistic approach to the individual, and increase intervention personalization (Soresi & Nota, 2010). The use of narratives and storytelling is important in promoting co-construction of clients' lives, reflecting on themselves and on their way of analyzing events experienced, making them take on the role of actors who cobuild their future.

The current economic crisis is clearly revealing that governments are less able or less willing to provide support than they previously were, and the more individualistic social structure in itself also provides less social support (Rubery, 2011). This situation is creating a heavy burden on citizens (Bauman, 2011), a sense of insecurity about the future and a decline in quality of life related to loss of health insurance, lower income, greater pay inequality and instability, and poor labor conditions. Welfare applications have increased for immigrants, young people, temporary workers, older workers, and families having to cope with long periods of their children's school-to-work transitions (Nota et al., 2014).

Life design counselors should therefore urgently adopt a perspective that focuses more on prevention and also fulfills preventive goals. They should aim to (a) involve children and young adolescents, and not only adults who are experiencing difficult career transitions or career problems; (b) focus on those adults who more frequently than in the past have to face the difficulties of transitions (e.g., temporary workers, older people reaching retirement age); (c) take into consideration parents, peers, teachers, other social workers – that is, members sharing the contexts of the individuals that we as counselors are concerned about; (d) privilege those who are experiencing difficult situations or who are more likely to become at-risk individuals; (e) emphasize strengths, resilience, confidence, hope, optimism, career adaptability, career identity, reflexivity; (f) use quantitative and qualitative procedures; (g) promote an optimistic vision of reality and of humankind, and strengthen creativity and innovation; (h) consider different aspects of human life, such as work, family, and leisure, and give emphasis to solidarity within relationships; and (i) guarantee that what life design considers important and essential for individuals (e.g., knowledge, beliefs, etc.) reaches the greatest number of people as quickly as possible.

The attention to prevention advocated by the life design program is in line with what other disciplines (e.g., those in the social and health fields) emphasize. These are engaged in prevention and quality of life and make reference to the need to prevent dissatisfaction, including job dissatisfaction (McCarthy, 2011; Nota et al., 2014). All this emphasizes even more strongly the value of prevention. To address this topic, attention to environment-centered efforts will be paid, focusing on the involvement of parents, and considering some important aspects dear to the life design: work–family balance, optimism, hope, career adaptability, and identity development in the family context.

Life Design Environment-Centered Efforts

Life Design Prevention for the Work-Family Balance

If adults were asked the question: "If you could make three wishes, what would they be?" probably they would mention family, work, and health. These are the most important things in adults' lives. The life design approach emphasizes the need to consider them when reflecting on the future and to give importance to the work–family relationship. As regards the family, the period between 1900 and 1960 witnessed some sort of standardization of people's lives, in line with the requirements of the social system, in which adult age started with work placement and continued with marriage, and which marked the birth of the family (Savickas, 2013).

Recently, a reduction of social ties and a greater presence of nontraditional families are seeing, for example, single-parent families, blended families and stepfamilies, same-sex parents, a single adult who adopts or decides to have a baby without marriage, and aging parents living with their adult children who cannot even start their own family due to economic difficulties or who return to live with their parents because of job loss (Stephens, 2013). Stephens clearly states that these are not "broken," "destroyed," or "inadequate" families, and that it is not possible say whether these changes are negative. Perhaps they represent a sort of personalization of life courses made possible by the well-being and the cultural development that characterize our times, which a life design counselor should make the most of by emphasizing differences.

Adults who devote more time to their family seem to have higher levels of resilience, greater ability to cope with obstacles, and more energy to solve problems. Life design counselors could highlight the strengths and the positive aspects of ties and friendships, of intimate, marital, and parent-child relationships, which, some believe, have a significant role in making one feel loved and valued. They could teach clients to give "time and space" to these relationships, to give more importance to the work–family balance, or, better, to give more importance to the balance between "different times" – that is, time for a job or a job search, time for voluntary activities, time for study and education, time for leisure, and time for the family.

From a preventive perspective, this should take place as soon as possible, both for the adults in the family and for the younger generations that are growing up in it. Reflexivity can be strengthened by stimulating people to think about what they can do for a positive balance, and so for the well-being of the family (Savickas, 2013). Life design counselors can facilitate dialogues in which parent clients narrate events and stories focused on their family and on a positive work–family balance, with phrases such as "I would like very much to stay with you on Saturday afternoons" and "This morning I got up very early to cope with an unexpected task, and this evening I'll probably go to sleep later to finish it, but I would like very much to take a walk with you … we can talk about how you can succeed in doing ..."

Hare and Gray (2013) suggest that – especially with regard to nontraditional families – parents should be helped define the family as a group of people who love and take care of each other. Also they should be helped to encourage their children to think that reciprocal support and assistance give meaning and energy to family life, regardless of who its members are, or, one might add, regardless of work problems that might increase insecurity, fear for the future, and episodes of breakup. Life design counselors can encourage clients to say things like "I enjoyed spending time with you; I had positive feelings …" and "Tomorrow will be a tough and demanding day, but the time we spent together today allowed me to recharge myself...." Hare and Gray (2013) also suggest that parents should be trained to stimulate their children to ask questions about positive and negative situations they are experiencing in the family – for instance, parents' unemployment – and to analyze with them feelings and emotions (e.g., "We're experiencing a difficult situation; my job search may take a long time, and I could be discouraged sometimes"; "This will bring about fewer economic opportunities for …"; "I will need your help …"), and the actions that can be taken.

It can also be helpful to encourage people to appreciate the overall qualities of their families and family members and to underscore family identity. The latter could be achieved through the creation of family trees or maps that link the past to the present and to different potential futures. Moreover, shared rules and commitments, and mutual support and aid are elements on which the concept of solidarity is based. Strengthening a sense of solidarity within the family can also promote solidarity in the community (Komter & Vollebergh, 2002).

This issue requires attention. Opportunities to deal with groups of parents interested in building the future of their children should be created in a variety of contexts – for example, at school, work and in community settings. To stimulate reflexivity, ad hoc materials should be developed with examples and online stories of a positive work–family balance, and seminars on this issue should be held. The family can give out positive energy to spend in other contexts, even in times of financial difficulties. Contributing to family life can help maintain a positive sense of self even in the case of negative work events that can undermine it. Prevention should emphasize all that, and prepare people to take advantage of this psychological capital.

A Push Toward Optimism, Hope, and Career Adaptability as Soon as Possible

The issue of work–family balance is even more significant when parents experience difficult working situations, such as unemployment or underemployment. Conger and Conger (2002) found that economic hardship influences the behavioral and emotional functioning of parents. Financial difficulties are related to parenting quality, reduced parental support and involvement, and, in turn, an increased risk for children to internalize and externalize their anxieties in the form of behavior problems. Johnson, Kalil, and Dunifon (2010) observed an increase of about half of a standard deviation in the level of children's problem behavior, related to job loss in the parents, especially among those with low socioeconomic status. Such conditions can make it less likely for family life to be a source of well-being and energy, and for it to help family members to cope better with the work situations being experienced.

Some resources, such as hope, optimism, emotional stability, and career adaptability, at the family level, may be useful to cope with difficulties. Dispositional optimism is the individual's positive expectation of positive results when dealing with difficult events (Carver & Scheier, 2002). In studying single mothers, Taylor, Larsen-Rife, Conger, Widaman, and Cutrona (2010) found that mothers' optimism moderated the relation between economic stress and children internalizing problems. It negatively predicted maternal internalizing problems and positively predicted child adjustment. Castro-Schilo et al. (2013) observed that parents' dispositional optimism was directly related to quality of parenting, and through the latter, to children's peer competence. Taylor et al. (2012) observed that parents' optimism moderated the relation between economic hardship and internalizing problems, and concluded that parents with high levels of optimism are characterized by greater resilience in the face of economic pressure.

Optimism can be considered a psychological resource that stimulates parents' positive behaviors to overcome difficult events and predicts positive child outcomes. The experience of supportive and optimistic parenting promotes an optimistic view of the world in children, which continues in adulthood. A propensity to optimism in the family fosters higher levels of career exploration, greater career planning, more responsibility about one's future, and career preparedness, because it makes people more aware of the career tasks and occupational transitions they have to overcome and the decisions that they have to make in their future (Savickas & Porfeli, 2012).

Hope is considered as a motivational process based on three components: goals, pathways, and agency goal-directed thinking (Snyder, 2002). Goals can be *approach goals* (e.g., earning a good grade) or *avoidance goals* (e.g., not losing a client). Pathway thinking involves the ability to identify possible paths to achieve a goal. Agency thinking regards the motivation to start and sustain the effort to reach a goal (Snyder, 2002).

In one of his first essays, *The Principle of Hope*, the philosopher Bloch (1959) sees hope as a constant joy, as inspiring energy, as enthusiasm toward the achievement of reachable goals. Hope looks forward, expands the space toward the future, diverts attention from the immediate, and dilates the horizon toward the possible. It has the power to allay our anxieties, make our present bearable, and strengthen our will to fight for what we want. People who have no hope for the future are also those who are less likely to resort to professional assistance, and they allow themselves to sink into desperation and resignation, diminishing their ability to cope with adversities.

Hope has been linked to a variety of mental health and work-related outcomes, such as lower levels of negative affect and depressive symptoms, and better social adjustment, job performance, job management, job satisfaction, work happiness, and organizational commitment (Davidson & Wingate, 2013; Youssef & Luthans, 2007). Faso, Neal-Beevers, and Carlson (2013) involved 71 parents in their study and found that parents' hope negatively correlated with their levels of depression and stress, and positively with life satisfaction. Parents' hope is related also to familial functioning and children's adjustment: In their study involving 252 parents of boys aged between 5 and 12 years, Kashdan et al. (2002) found significant relations between parents' hope and parental and familial functioning (e.g., social adjustment, quality of parent–child relationships, self-esteem). Parents' hope was positively related to positive coping strategies and problem-solving approaches, and negatively associated with maladaptive and passive behaviors (e.g., avoidance and behavioral disengagement). Lastly, parents' hope predicted prosocial parenting behavior (e.g., nurturance, warmth, intimacy) and, in turn, children's social activity, competence, and psychological adjustment. Also in the Italian context, parents' hope is related with their children's levels of hope and optimism: In research involving 100 adolescents and their parents, it was found that parents' hope predicted their children's levels of hope (Father: $\beta = .269$, $p = .043$; Mother: $\beta = .486$, $p = .001$), and that mothers' hope predicted also children's levels of optimism ($\beta = .313$, $p = .007$; Nota, Ginevra, & Santilli, in press).

Career adaptability regards the process through which people dynamically build their professional life. It is a psychosocial construct focused on resources useful to deal with developmental tasks to prepare for future professional roles and to favor well-being (Maggiori, Johnston, Krings, Massoudi, & Rossier, 2013; Nota, Ginevra, Santilli, & Soresi, 2014; Savickas & Porfeli, 2012). Recently, da Conceição and Duarte (2013) examined parental influences on children's career adaptability, in a group of 403 adolescents and their parents. The authors found that children's career adaptability total scores were predicted by mother career adaptability, suggesting the crucial role of mothers on children's career development.

It is then clear that life design counselors should underscore the role of an optimistic, hopeful context rich in career adaptability, informing people regarding these issues, and implementing actions that favor such a context. The parent training activities that Soresi and Nota (2009) have carried out with groups of Italian parents regarding professional planning issues have enabled them to say that parents' way of thinking can indeed be changed. At the end of the interventions, the parents not only showed higher levels of self-efficacy beliefs in managing interactions with their children, but they also focused on planning for the future and on a constructive dialogue between parents and children, which must be properly supported. They gave more importance to the process and to how to get things done, rather than simply proposing their point of view, and took into consideration their children's self-determination and satisfaction (Soresi & Nota, 2009). Starting from these first positive experiences with parents, and in light of what has been expressed in this chapter, at the Laboratory for Research and Intervention in Vocational Designing and Career Counseling (LaRIOS) we (the authors) are reviewing the parents' program and devising sessions on family–work balance and family solidarity, narrability, career adaptability, hope, and optimism.

Based on what has been said above, from a markedly preventive perspective it may be important to work with the parents of preschoolers and elementary school children, but also of kindergarten children, in the pediatric wards, in child and family clinics, and in maternity wards, reaching those that have just become or are about to become parents. Young adults planning their professional life could also be approached and encouraged to think about family life and the roles associated with it. Ad hoc material, with examples and illustrations, can be devised; online materials and videos can be prepared; informational meetings can be held on such issues and also meetings with an educational goal, for example, titled "Nuggets of Optimism and Hope for Parents."

With small groups of parents, or future parents, life design counselors can present the concept of optimism, the consequences of optimistic attitudes, reflect on ways to support and sustain their own and their children's optimism (paying attention to positive things, considering difficulties as challenges, etc.), encourage optimistic relationships in the home by providing examples and reference models (Soresi & Nota, 2009; Soresi et al., 2009). Likewise, it would be interesting to see counselors speak about hope, supplying definitions, research data, and suggestions on how to enhance it, by focusing attention on specific goals, centered on the parents' own work, on the family–work balance, which should be described in a clear, operational way.

Parents can be helped to envisage barriers and obstacles, but especially to think of novel ideas for pursuing their goals (Marques, Lopez, & Pais-Ribeiro, 2011). They can be encouraged to ask first themselves and then their children some questions that support hope – for example, "What do I think makes this life worth living or this job worth doing?" "What would a hopeful person do in such a situation?" "What is the smallest change that could increase hope" "Who has taught you something about hope?" and "Who keeps track of how much you think about hope?" Very likely stories of hope and action could be heard which would favor deeper reflection on these issues, and narrations that could be more hopeful also in the family context (Lopez, 2013). It would also be useful to devote some time to career adaptability and make parents reflect on the idea of career adaptability – on its components and on the importance of attention to the future, of curiosity, of confidence, and of control – and on useful ways to support their career adaptability and that of their children (Soresi & Nota, 2009).

New technologies can be helpful in this. Online sessions and Web-based interventions can be arranged to integrate face-to-face activities, which would have the advantage of containing the costs and times of the interventions and also could reach large numbers of individuals (Whiston & James, 2013). Early interventions with parents on these issues could surely help them reduce the time they devote to "false beliefs" and to not very advantageous ways of spending time with their children and thinking about the future. They would thus increase the time they devote to enjoyable moments, useful in building positive stories of family relationships that can encourage orientation to the future and coping with uncertainty.

Professional Identity in Progress: Enhancing and Strengthening Its Development

Professional identity is surely an important pillar of human growth, and its development is a constant process. It requires a mental activity that, through language and interaction with others, constructs and reconstructs the story of one's own working life in relation to the different roles taken on. Identity us allows to give meaning to certain periods of time, to adaptively integrate new and significant life experiences, and to give meaning to changes, new tasks, and transitions. *Identity* is defined as an ongoing process of self-construction and reconstruction of stories, occurring when individuals feel they are changing but do not yet know what they are becoming, and need to make sense of such changes and experiences. These stories about identity provide self-understanding in the form of an interpretation of self that orients the individual to a social world. Identity is influenced by the social roles and the interactions experienced during the process of constructing stories about the self (Savickas, 2013).

Identity development is one of the major psychosocial events of late adolescence, as a function of maturation of formal operational thinking. It involves the emergence of an autonomous sense of self and, at the same time, the establishment of relationships with significant others (McLean & Mansfield, 2011). According to the narrative approach, identity development is the ability to make meaning of one's past experiences in relation to one's present and future, and thus understanding one's own sense of self through time. Although identity emerges in late adolescence and early adulthood, autobiographical memory consolidates itself in preschool years, and young children begin to elaborate life narratives. Early sharing of personal events during childhood can be considered a precursor of the development of narrative identity (McAdams & McLean, 2013). In all that, and from the early years of life, parents have a crucial role in helping their children organize, interpret, and give meaning to past events, and shape the ideas that they form regarding those events (McLean & Mansfield, 2011). Conversing with their parents about personal events is the foundation on which children learn to give meaning to personal events, and such a meaning-construction process forms the basis for the future development of identity (Fivush, Haden, & Reese, 2006).

A robust area of research focusing on parents' conversational style with their children has highlighted that it influences narrative skills. For example, children of parents who used an elaborate conversational style of past stories, focusing on explanations and causes and emphasizing emotional aspects of personal events, had stronger self-storytelling skills and more elaborate event narratives. Within this perspective, a "repetitive" or "poorly elaborative" style – that is, a tendency to repeat responses until the child answers the question – proves to be little advantageous and provides little additional information about the past event (Fivush et al., 2006). Reese and Newcombe (2007) underline the importance of talking with children about events they have experienced in order to strengthen their elaboration abilities, by asking open questions that encourage children to take part in the conversation (e.g., "What did you do during ...?" "What has so-and-so done...?"); by repeating parts of the answers given to confirm what has been said, at the same time adding details or probing aspects not taken into consideration by the child (e.g., with phrases such as "and so, you ...; I also remember that ..."); by asking further questions, prompted by the answers obtained, so as to keep the interaction going and to enrich it with more details. Also important is the ability to describe one's own personal stories and experiences by supplying details and descriptions.

Narratives useful to strengthen identity should also consider the emotional component. In this respect, Fivush et al. (2006) found that parents who talk about their emotions, using sentences that describe those experienced in past events (e.g., "When I realized .... I felt sad"), mentioning the behavioral components of the emotional sphere ("I cried..."; "...I preferred to move away and be alone..."), reflecting on the causes of emotions ("I think the sadness came from ...."), and stimulating their children to take this component into account at the time they analyze events they have experienced, have children who are more attentive to emotions when reflecting on events, talk more frequently about them with others, and have a more consistent self-concept.

Paying attention to stories and narratives that children spontaneously elaborate is crucial. Talking about past events, even several times, allows life stories to be processed, edited, reinterpreted, and influenced by social and discursive factors, facilitating a more extensive and integrative narrative identity. McAdams and McLean (2013) found that parents are essential in the identity-centered narration process, especially during childhood when they are their children's main audience, but also during adolescence, when peers have an equally important audience function. Indeed because of this, we believe it is important for parents to make the most of the fact that they are reference points. McLean and Mansfield (2011) studied 63 mothers and their adolescents to examine mothers' behaviors during conversations and adolescents' narrative processes of meaning making. Mothers and adolescents were each asked to narrate three events that they considered important, extremely sad, and extremely happy. The authors found that sad events were the occasions when mothers engaged in more confirmations and provided more emotional support. These behaviors were related to greater meaning making in adolescents, and specifically to greater psychological, emotional, or relational insight from the event experienced and its application to broader spheres of their life.

Based on what has been said above, from a preventive perspective, parents can be stimulated to encourage narrations and production of stories centered on aspects and issues concerning school, the school–work relationship, work, and the work–family balance. Parents of very young children can be supported in describing such events, describing those that concern their children, the emotional component involved, the coping methods used, the relationships between those events, the past, and possible futures. Parents can be invited to maintain these activities as their children grow up, so as to favor analysis of situations they experience, meaning making, and analysis of changes taking place. They should be encouraged to focus attention on new events and new tasks (e.g., new disciplines, new school requests, engaging in social activities, etc.), but also on changes and transitions (moving to another class or school, relocations, professional changes, etc.), and on situations of uncertainty and insecurity, such as school or work failure, job loss, financial difficulties, etc., and on supportive actions of solidarity useful to handle difficult times. It is crucial to favor participation, involvement, awareness that these are times that can help the family stay together, think, feeling the solidarity and warmth coming from one's own family members, and also being allowed to have fun with them. Parents must be encouraged to do this; to never give up when facing curt, barely articulate answers, or even nonanswers; to think that such abilities are complex and need time to be strengthened; and to find the right times to devote to this and to their children.

From strengthening optimism, hope, and career adaptability, to developing the skill of telling stories centered on events that help construct and consolidate professional identity, there are many actions that can be carried out with parents in a preventive way to foster positive and advantageous exchanges for identity construction within the family. Positive attitudes and narration are related to each other: McLean and Pratt (2006) have found that the most optimistic parents tell their children stories centered on development and growth, and pay greater attention to meaning making.

Following on from that, we think that life design counselors should believe in the role of prevention and the advantages associated with it. They should move beyond the notion that only individual counseling can produce a sense of fulfillment in individuals suffering discomfort, and embrace the conviction that thanks to conditions that favor well-being, growth, and social justice, the counselor can really make a difference.

Life Design Person-Centered Efforts: From Parents to Their Children

Taking into account the importance of person-centered efforts, sons and daughters will be now considered. From a primary preventive perspective, it can be advantageous to involve developmental age children in vocational guidance projects that consider important issues within life design, such as career adaptability, hope, optimism, and a sympathetic vision of reality (see Chapter 2; also Nota et al., 2014). In this connection, Hartung, Porfeli, and Vondracek (2008) propose a model that sees adult life as strongly influenced by the psychosocial experiences that characterize early childhood, attributing a paramount role to the process of exploration and knowledge of professions, and to learning the characteristics of the world of work. Children are surrounded by a world that talks to them about work all the time: in the family, at school, in interactions with workers they see every day, from the supermarket cashier to the school caretaker, from the pediatrician to the TV journalist. The constant flow of information passing through the mass media cannot be neglected as it can deeply influence the way attitudes toward professions are structured (Schultheiss, 2008).

It may then be important to exploit all that to strengthen career adaptability and its prerequisites (Hartung et al., 2008; Schultheiss, 2008).To that aim it can also be important to act so that children improve their knowledge of the world of work (paying attention to complexity and avoiding coarse judgments and simplistic or stereotyped views), and explore and enhance curiosity, open-mindedness, and supportive attitudes. Children should increase their attention toward the future, develop a strong interest in it, realize that it is full of alternatives and opportunities, get to the conclusion that, with the right amount of commitment and education, it is possible to plan, in a flexible way too, to work hard to achieve one's goals, taking into consideration both work and family life, and act for one's own good and that of others.

Drawing on what Soresi and Nota had done in the 1990s with a program aimed at "training" children to be collaborative, offer help, and act in solidarity with their peers who have difficulties and disabilities; and teaching them to act positively and supportively among themselves before problems could arise (Soresi & Nota, 2001), Nota and Ginevra (in press) devised a 10-unit program for elementary school children called Journey in the World of Professions and Work. In that program, children are encouraged to reflect on what work is and how professions can be explored to learn about them and to analyze their various aspects. They are stimulated to refer to a grid to analyze work, to go deeply into the different professions through specific interviews with working individuals, compare the collected data, and share them with the group. Emphasis is placed on positive, open, and hopeful attitudes to work; concentration is focused on change, on the importance of innovation and creativity; and, to the advantage of integration at the workplace, alternative ideas on gender and cultural barriers – centered on solidarity, hope, and optimism toward their own future ideas – are introduced. The children are invited to share the knowledge they have acquired and then move on to a first project of their own, setting professional and personal goals that encompass all of their many dreams and hopes for the future. The following is a list of the objectives for the didactic units of the Journey in the World of Professions and Work program:

1. *Let's get to know each other to work together.* The first meeting favors reciprocal acquaintance and stimulates children's attention to the issues that will be dealt with and to ways of working. The children are presented with "The Book of the Course: My Future" which will be assembled together over the scheduled meetings.

2. *Let's think about work.* The focus is on the analysis of the idea of work, of the rights and duties that characterize it, the advantages that work brings to people's existence and their quality of life.

3. *Exploring professions beyond their labels.* The children are encouraged to go beyond professional labels and distinguish between professions on the basis of working activities (functions and tasks), of the place where work is done (from the classic ones, indoor or outdoor, to the least considered ones, e.g., places of war or peace), and the instruments used (from the most traditional to the most high-tech, from the most, to the least used, etc.).

4. *Hurrah for school ... for our future.* The children are encouraged to recognize the importance of education and training for their growth, to examine the contribution that each school subject can give to the development of professional activities, and to reflect on the role of keeping up-to-date throughout one's working life. Issues also dealt with

are innovation, creativity, and the importance of getting ready to cope with the new world of work.

5. *Work changes ... let's look for change and think about the future.* Here the focus is on the changes that characterize the work market (in relation to progress, legislation, etc.), on what is needed to sense changes and make good use of them. The children are invited to think of change as a constant, and place emphasis on diverse abilities (social, artistic, etc.) to give their best during their working life.

6. *Let's continue to explore ... probing jobs and workers.* The children are encouraged to keep on going beyond labels given to jobs and grasp differences, by interviewing workers, with the aim also of highlighting the sense that the workers give to their work, the contribution they think they give to society and in their life.

7. *Diversity makes work more meaningful.* The children are encouraged to analyze the differences among human beings, linked to gender, disability, or impairment; the advantages associated with the presence of different individuals at the workplace; and to reflect on how diversity is an added value to working life.

8. *Work, family, community ... hurrah for different relationships.* The children are invited to explore the contexts – work, family, community – in which human life is carried out; the influences between these different areas; and the importance of fostering relationships in all of these contexts to improve one's own and others' quality of life.

9. *Let's project ourselves into the future.* Attention is focused on the profile of the worker of the future – that is, on the characteristics workers will need to have for a better life in a continually evolving world of work, and on ways to set professional goals for one's own future.

10. *Nuggets of optimism and hope.* The children are invited to think of optimism and hope as two fellow travelers, also and above all to form groups of hopeful and optimistic individuals who support one another, show solidarity, and come up with highly creative ideas.

To verify the efficacy of this intervention, Nota and Ginevra (in press) studied 60 children in the last two classes of elementary school, randomly assigned to experimental and control groups. The experimental (participating in the intervention program) and control groups (did not participating in this program) were both assessed in a pretest phase and a posttest phase with the following measures: Pro.Spera (Nota & Soresi, in press) used to asses optimism; My Hopes (Nota & Soresi, in press) used to evaluate hope; the Career Exploration Scale (Tracey, Lent, Brown, Soresi, & Nota, 2006) used to measure the extent to which respondents engaged in career exploratory behaviors; Children's Expected Work Affectivity (Porfeli, Hartung, & Vondracek, 2008) used to measure positive and negative work affectivity; and the Childhood Career Development Scale by Schultheiss and Stead (2004) used to assess awareness of the importance of occupational information, curiosity/exploration, interests, internal locus of control, role models, future time perspective, planning, and awareness of self-knowledge. The experimental and control group students did not differ in pretest levels from the aforementioned variables; but in the posttest situation, students in the experimental group showed higher levels of optimism and hope, greater positive work affectivity, and higher levels of career exploration and curiosity. Moreover, the experimental group presented higher levels of awareness of their career interests, internal locus of control, higher levels of planning and future time perspective, and a greater tendency to use positive role models.

At the LaRIOS institute, specific secondary prevention programs have been devised – that is, career education programs aimed at increasing the strengths of at-risk adolescents in their career choices. Examples of these programs are the following: Difficulties: No Problem! (Nota & Soresi, 2004); Assertive Steps Toward University (Nota & Soresi, 2003); Hope and Expectation Towards the Future: Training to Increase Optimism (Ferrari, Nota, & Soresi, 2012). Also others programs, available only in Italian, were used to enhance attitudes and skills useful to future career planning: Choice for the Future: No Problem! (Nota & Soresi, 1999); First Commandment: I Believe In Myself … Also Because It Is In My Interest (Nota & Soresi, 2000); *Step Toward the Future ... Without Stereotypes!* (Nota, Ginevra, Ferrari, & Soresi, 2010); *I Self-Determine Myself* (Soresi et al., 2009); and *Plans, Itineraries and Possible Steps ... For Your Vocational Projects!* (Soresi et al., 2009).

The various career education programs developed, including the last one for the primary school, have reinforced the idea that prevention can actually help to engage people and to encourage them to think and plan their future in a more advantageous and satisfying way.

Conclusions

Within the life design perspective, prevention activities lead people and those who live with them to engage in actions involving reflection on the future before they have to handle specific transitions, changes at work and at school, or difficult periods at work. The aim of this chapter was to go in depth into some of the actions that can be implemented from a preventive perspective, providing examples of what can be done in the family, with parents, and with those that have to construct their future – our children. Research must continue to do its part, testing fresh interventions and activities that can be made available to life design counselors.

We wish to conclude by emphasizing a number of competencies that life design counselors interested in prevention should have. First of all, it is important to bear in mind that preventive action, besides involving parents, may also require enlisting the help and collaboration of teachers, employers, administrators, health care, and social care providers. It is only through a concerted effort that it is possible to significantly impact the stories of lives at-risk of dissatisfaction and marginalization (Nota et al., 2014). Those who wish to engage in prevention need to be able to create positive relationships with people, both personalized and focused on their needs, but also to implement actions in support of career education, of disseminating knowledge and information using new technologies, and increasing awareness regarding issues dear to them, so as to attract the attention of parents, children, and of those they wish to involve, aiming at reducing the cost of interventions.

At the same time, they must show that they are satisfied with the job they are doing, believe it is important and prestigious, and be able to testify and be a model as regards the characteristics and the abilities they consider crucial, such as career adaptability, career preparedness, optimism, hope, and professional identity (Nota et al., 2014). Life design counselors should aim at innovation, creativity, and support of human capital, to make their contribution to socioeconomic growth. Based on what has been said above, it is clear they are required to become provokers, persuaders, to openly side with people and especially with those who are more likely to have difficulties, by going to look for them in their own settings, before lack of optimism, scarce hope, and low levels of career adaptability can prevail.

References

Albee, G. W., & Ryan, K. (1998). An overview of primary prevention. *Journal of Mental Health, 7*, 441–449. http://doi.org/10.1080/09638239817824

Bauman, Z. (2011). *Collateral damage: Social inequalities in a global age.* Cambridge, UK: Polity.

Bloch, E. (1959). *Das Prinzip Hoffnung* [The principle of hope]. Frankfurt am Main: Suhrkamp.

Carver, C. S., & Scheier, M. F. (2002). Optimism. In C. R. Snyder & S. J. Lopez (Eds.), *Handbook of positive psychology* (pp. 231–243). Oxford, UK: Oxford University Press.

Castro-Schilo, L., Taylor, Z. E., Ferrer, E., Robins, R. W., Conger, R. D., & Widaman, K. F. (2013). Parents' optimism, positive parenting, and child peer competence in Mexican-origin families. *Parenting, 13*, 95–112. http://doi.org/10.1080/15295192.2012.709151

Conger, R. D., & Conger, K. J. (2002). Resilience in Midwestern families: Selected findings from the first decade of a prospective, longitudinal study. *Journal of Marriage and Family, 64*, 361–373. http://doi.org/10.1111/j.1741-3737.2002.00361.x

Culkin, N., & Mallick, S. (2011). Producing work ready graduates: The role of the entrepreneurial university. *International Journal of Market Research, 53*, 347–368. http://doi.org/10.2501/IJMR-53-3-347-368

da Conceição, S. M., & Duarte, M. E. (2013). Parental influence in adolescents' career adaptability. *Proceedings of the International Conference Life Design and Career Counseling: Building Hope and Resilience* (p. 48). Padua, Italy: University of Padova.

Davidson, C. L., & Wingate, L. R. (2013). The glass half-full or a hopeful outlook: Which explains more variance in interpersonal suicide risk in a psychotherapy clinic sample? *The Journal of Positive Psychology: Dedicated to Furthering Research and Promoting Good Practice, 8*, 263–272. http://doi.org/10.1080/17439760.2013.787446

Faso, D. J., Neal-Beevers, A. R., & Carlson, C. L. (2013). Vicarious futurity, hope, and well-being in parents of children with autism spectrum disorder. *Research in Autism Spectrum Disorders, 7*, 288–297. http://doi.org/10.1016/j.rasd.2012.08.014

Ferrari, L., Nota, L., & Soresi, S. (2012). Evaluation of an intervention to foster time perspective and career decidedness in a group of Italian adolescents. *The Career Development Quarterly, 60*, 82–96. http://doi.org/10.1002/j.2161-0045.2012.00007.x

Fivush, R., Haden, C. A., & Reese, E. (2006). Elaborating on elaborations: Role of maternal reminiscing style in cognitive and socioemotional development. *Child development, 77*, 1568–1588. http://doi.org/10.1111/j.1467-8624.2006.00960.x

Hare, J., & Gray, L. A. (2013). *All kinds of families: A guide for parents.* Retrieved from http://www1.cyfernet.org/prog/fam/nontradfam.html

Hartung, P. J., Porfeli, E. J., & Vondracek, F. W. (2008). Career adaptability in childhood. *Career Development Quarterly, 57*, 63–74. http://doi.org/10.1002/j.2161-0045.2008.tb00166.x

Johnson, R. C., Kalil, A., & Dunifon, R. E. (2010). *Mother's work and children's lives: Low-income families after welfare reform.* Kalamazoo, MI: Upjohn Institute for Employment Research.

Kashdan, T. B., Pelham, W. E., Lang, A. R., Hoza, B., Jacob, R. G., Jennings, J. R., ... Gnagy, E. M. (2002). Hope and optimism as human strengths in parents of children with externalizing disorders: Stress is in the eye of the beholder. *Journal of Social and Clinical Psychology, 21*, 441–468. http://doi.org/10.1521/jscp.21.4.441.22597

Komter, A. E., & Vollebergh, A. M. W. (2002). Solidarity in Dutch families family ties under strain? *Journal of Family Issues, 23*, 171–188. http://doi.org/10.1177/0192513X02023002001

Lent, R.W., & Brown, S.D. (2013). Promoting work satisfaction and performance. In S.D. Brown & R.W. Lent (Eds.), *Career development and counseling: Putting theory and research to work* (2nd ed., pp. 621–651). Hoboken, NJ: Wiley.

Lopez, S. J. (2013). *Making hope happen: Create the future you want for yourself and others.* New York, NY: Atria Books.

Maggiori, C., Johnston, C., Krings, F., Massoudi, K., & Rossier, J. (2013). The role of career adaptability and work conditions on general and professional well-being. *Journal of Vocational Behavior, 83*, 437–449. http://doi.org/10.1016/j.jvb.2013.07.001

Marques, S. C., Lopez, S. J., & Pais-Ribeiro, J. L. (2011). "Building hope for the future": A program to foster strengths in middle-school students. *Journal of Happiness Studies, 12*, 139–152. http://doi.org/10.1007/s10902-009-9180-3

McAdams, D. P., & McLean, K. C. (2013). Narrative identity. *Current Directions in Psychological Science, 22*, 233–238. http://doi.org/10.1177/0963721413475622

McCarthy, M. (2011). Health research: Europe's future. *The Lancet, 37*, 1744–1745. http://doi.org/10.1016/S0140-6736(11)60727-7

McLean, K. C., & Mansfield, C. D. (2011). To reason or not to reason: Is autobiographical reasoning always beneficial? *New Directions for Child and Adolescent Development, 131*, 85–97. http://doi.org/10.1002/cd.291 http://doi.org/10.1002/cd.291

McLean, K. C., & Pratt, M. W. (2006). Life's little (and big) lessons: Identity statuses and meaning-making in the turning point narratives of emerging adults. *Developmental Psychology, 42*, 714–722. http://doi.org/10.1037/0012-1649.42.4.714

Moretti, E. (2012). *The new geography of jobs*. Boston, MA: Houghton Mifflin Harcourt.

Nota, L., & Ginevra, M. C. (in press). Il training "Viaggio nel mondo delle professioni e del lavoro" [The "Journey in the World of Professions and Work" program]. *GIPO-Giornale Italiano di Psicologia dell'Orientamento*.

Nota, L., Ginevra, M. C., Ferrari, L., & Soresi, S. (2010). *Un passo dopo l'altro verso il futuro... senza stereotipi* [One step after another toward the future ... without stereotypes]. Firenze, Italy: Giunti.

Nota, L., Ginevra, M. C., & Santilli, S. (in press). Speranza e ottimismo in genitori e figli [Hope and optimism in parents and their children]. *GIPO-Giornale Italiano di psicologia dell'orientamento*.

Nota, L., Ginevra, M. C., Santilli, S., & Soresi, S. (2014). Contemporary career construction: The role of career adaptability. In M. Coetzee (Ed.), *Perspectives on psycho-social career meta-capacities: Dynamics of contemporary career development* (pp. 248–263). New York, NY: Springer.

Nota, L., & Soresi, S. (1999). Il programma "Le scelte per il futuro: no problem!" [The program "Choice for the Future: No Problem!"]. *Supplement to Psicologia e Scuola, 96*, 203–211.

Nota, L., & Soresi, S. (2000). *Autoefficacia nelle scelte* [Self-efficacy and school-career choice]. Firenze, Italy: Giunti.

Nota, L., & Soresi, S. (2003). An assertiveness training program for indecisive students in an Italian university. *The Career Development Quarterly, 51*, 322–334. http://doi.org/10.1002/j.2161-0045.2003.tb00613.x

Nota, L., & Soresi, S. (2004). Improving the problem solving and decision-making skills of a high indecision group of young adolescents: A test of the 'Difficult: No problem!' training. *International Journal for Educational and Vocational Guidance, 4*, 3–21. http://doi.org/10.1023/B:IJVO.0000021054.81492.8d

Nota, L. & Soresi, S. (in press). Gli strumenti Pro.Spera e My Hope [Pro.Spera and My Hope measures]. *GIPO-Giornale Italiano di Psicologia dell'Orientamento*.

Nota, L., Soresi, S., Ferrari, L., & Ginevra, M. C. (2014). Vocational designing and career counseling in Europe: Challenges and new horizons. *European Psychologist*. Advance online publication. http://doi.org/10.1027/1016-9040/9000189

Porfeli, E. J., Hartung, P. J., & Vondracek, F. W. (2008). Children's vocational development: A research rationale. *The Career Development Quarterly, 57*, 25–37. http://doi.org/10.1002/j.2161-0045.2008.tb00163.x

Reese, E., & Newcombe, R. (2007). Training mothers in elaborative reminiscing enhances children's autobiographical memory and narrative. *Child Development, 78*, 1153–1170. http://doi.org/10.1111/j.1467-8624.2007.01058.x

Ridley, M. (2010). *The rational optimist: How prosperity evolves*. London, UK: Fourth Estate.

Romano, J. L. (2012). Prevention in the 21st century. In E. M. Vera (Ed.), *The Oxford handbook of prevention in counseling psychology* (pp. 36–50). Oxford: Oxford University Press.

Romano, J. L., & Hage, S. M. (2000). Prevention and counseling psychology revitalizing commitments for the 21st century. *The Counseling Psychologist, 28*, 733–763. http://doi.org/10.1177/0011000000286001

Rubery, J. (2011). Reconstruction amid deconstruction: Or why we need more of the social in European social models. *Work, Employment and Society, 25*, 658–674. http://doi.org/10.1177/0950017011419718

Savickas, M. L. (2013). Career construction theory and practice. In S. D. Brown & R. W. Lent (Eds.), *Career development and counseling: Putting theory and research to work* (2nd ed.) (pp. 144–180). Hoboken, NJ: Wiley.

Savickas, M. L., Nota, L., Rossier, J., Dauwalder, J.-P., Duarte, M. E., Guichard, J., . . . van Vianen, A. E. M. (2009). Life designing: A paradigm for career construction in the 21st century. *Journal of Vocational Behavior, 75*, 239–250. http://doi.org/10.1016/j.jvb.2009.04.004

Savickas, M. L., & Porfeli, E. J. (2012). Career adapt-Abilities scale: Construction, reliability, and measurement equivalence across 13 countries. *Journal of Vocational Behavior, 80*, 661–673. http://doi.org/10.1016/j.jvb.2012.01.011

Schultheiss, D. E. P. (2008). Current status and future agenda for the theory, research, and practice of childhood career development. *The Career Development Quarterly, 57*, 7–24. http://doi.org/10.1002/j.2161-0045.2008.tb00162.x

Schultheiss, D. E. P., & Stead, G. B. (2004). Childhood career development scale: Scale construction and psychometric properties. *Journal of Career Assessment, 12*, 113–134. http://doi.org/10.1177/1069072703257751

Snyder, C. R. (2002). Hope theory: Rainbows in the mind. *Psychological Inquiry, 13*, 249–275. http://doi.org/10.1207/S15327965PLI1304_01

Soresi, S., & Nota, L. (2001). *La facilitazione dell'integrazione scolastica* [Facilitating school inclusion]. Pordenone, Italy: Erip Editrice.

Soresi, S. & Nota, L. (2009). Career counseling in Italy. In L. Gerstein, P. Heppner, S. Aegisdóttir, A. Leung, & K. Norsworthy (Eds.), *International handbook of cross-cultural counseling: Cultural assumptions and practices worldwide* (pp. 291–300). Thousand Oaks, CA: Sage.

Soresi, S., & Nota, L. (2010). Alcune procedure qualitative per il career counseling [Some qualitative procedures for career counseling]. In L. Nota & S. Soresi (Eds.), *Sfide e nuovi orizzonti per l'orientamento. Metodologie e nuove pratiche* (pp. 100–135). Firenze, Italy: Giunti O.S.

Soresi, S., Nota, L., Ferrari, L., Sgaramella, M. T., Ginevra, M. C., & Carrieri, L. (2009). *Progettazioni itinerari e passi possibili di orientamento* [Planning, pathways and possible steps in career guidance]. Firenze, Italy: Giunti.

Soresi, S., Nota, L., Ferrari, L., & Solberg, V. S. (2008). Career guidance for persons with disabilities. In J. A. Athanasou & R. Van Esbroeck (Eds.), *International handbook of career guidance* (pp. 405–417). Dordrecht, The Netherlands: Springer.

Stephens, M. R. (2013). The non-traditional family: An introduction. *The review of black political economy, 10*, 27–29. http://doi.org/10.1007/s12114-012-9145-3

Taylor, Z. E., Larsen-Rife, D., Conger, R. D., Widaman, K. F., & Cutrona, C. E. (2010). Life stress, maternal optimism, and adolescent competence in single-mother, African-American families. *Journal of Family Psychology, 24,* 468–477. http://doi.org/10.1037/a0019870

Taylor, Z. E., Widaman, K. F., Robins, R. W., Jochem, R., Early, D. R., & Conger, R. D. (2012). Dispositional optimism: A psychological resource for Mexican-origin mothers experiencing economic stress. *Journal of Family Psychology, 26*, 133–139. http://doi.org/10.1037/a0026755

Tracey, T. J. G., Lent, R. W., Brown, S. D., Soresi, S., & Nota, L. (2006). Adherence to RIASEC structure in relation to career exploration and parenting style: Longitudinal and idiothetic considerations. *Journal of Vocational Behavior, 69*, 248–261. http://doi.org/10.1016/j.jvb.2006.02.001

Vera, E. M., & Polanin, M. K. (2012). Prevention and counseling psychology: A simple yet difficult commitment. In E. M. Vera (Ed.), *The Oxford handbook of prevention in counseling psychology* (pp. 3–17). Oxford: Oxford University Press.

Whiston, S. C., & James, B. N. (2013). Interventions to aid job finding and choice implementation. In S. D. Brown & R. W. Lent (Eds.), *Career development and counseling: Putting theory and research to work* (2nd ed., pp. 595–620). Hoboken, NJ: Wiley.

Youssef, C.M., & Luthans, F. (2007). Positive organizational behavior in the workplace: The impact of hope, optimism, and resilience. *Journal of Management, 33*, 774–800. http://doi.org/10.1177/0149206307305562

Chapter 14

Unemployment: Creating and Conserving Resources for Career Self-Regulation

Annelies E. M. van Vianen[1], Jessie Koen[1], and Ute-Christine Klehe[2]

[1]University of Amsterdam, Department of Work and Organizational Psychology, The Netherlands
[2]Justus Liebig University Giessen, Department of Work and Organizational Psychology, Germany

Introduction

Careers have become increasingly unpredictable. Given the technological progress, competitive forces, and turbulent economic climate in the past few years, career transitions occur more frequently in people's lives than ever. By choice or necessity, people are confronted with job changes, periods of unemployment, and uncertain career perspectives (Fugate, Kinicki, & Ashforth, 2004). The current career climate thus requires people to adequately prepare for and respond to these unavoidable career transitions. Based on the life design approach (Savickas et al., 2009) and conservation of resources (COR) theory (Hobfoll, 1989, 2002), we will discuss the resources that may help people to cope with the uncertainties associated with unemployment and their career in the new economy. We believe that these resources can be found in the mental models that people have built of careers and of the self. If, for example, people view career transitions as normal and challenging events that happen in one's life, it may reduce their uncertainty during unemployment. Likewise, if people rely on the self rather than on external factors that influence their careers, it may reduce uncertainty and diminish perceptions of identity threat during unemployment. In other words, these mental models may help people to cope with the unpredictability of their career in the new economy and with the associated periods of unemployment in particular.

Unemployment

Recent European statistics estimate that more than 26 million men and women in the 27 member states of the European Union are unemployed, which is an unemployment rate of 11% (Eurostat, 2013). The unemployment rate in the United States is somewhat lower than in Europe, yet also substantial (7.6%). The European countries with the highest unemployment rates are Greece (27.2%), Spain (26.7%), and Portugal (17.5%). Notably, between 5 and 6 million young people (ages 15 to 24) in the European Union are currently unemployed, which is a youth unemployment rate of 23.5%. The highest youth unemployment rates are in Greece (59.1%), Spain (55.9%), Italy (38.4%), and Portugal (38.3%). These percentages show that the economic crisis has hit young people more than other age groups. Another serious concern is the increasing number of people who are long-term unemployed: About 4.6% of the EU labor force in 2012 had been unemployed for more than 1 year; more than half of these (2.5%) had been unemployed for more than 2 years.

These unemployment statistics are troublesome because unemployment hurts both societies and individuals. At a societal level, unemployment reduces tax revenues and puts pressure on budgets for social benefits. At the individual level, unemployment not only means a loss of income but often also a loss of social contacts, goals, status, time structure, and activity (e.g., Jahoda, 1987). Because of these psychological consequences, unemployment is one of the most stressful, depressing, and literally sickening experiences that people can encounter (Klehe & Van Hooft, in press). Unemployment impairs mental and physical health, leading to unhealthy and self-handicapping behavior such as alcohol consumption, drug abuse, smoking, and risky, even suicidal behaviors (e.g., Paul & Moser, 2009).

In this chapter, we focus on two important components of the distress that accompanies unemployment – namely, uncertainty and identity threats. We specifically address these two components because uncertainty and identity threats are also central features of careers in the new economy (Trevor-Roberts, 2006). Next to the uncertainty that often goes together with the frequent career transitions that are typical for careers in the new economy, these careers also involve regular loss of work-related identities and the need to construct new identities. After all, in careers in the new economy, people's work experiences may not necessarily build on each other, and individuals therefore cannot always lean on prior identities and competencies (Savickas et al., 2009). This idea is also articulated in recent career theories such as the life design approach (Savickas et al., 2009). This theory stresses that careers are unpredictable and encompass more life domains than only the work domain from which people construe their identity. A life design perspective thus views uncertainty and identity construction as natural features of careers.

Uncertainty

The distress that unemployed people encounter during unemployment is largely caused by experiences of uncertainty and associated anxiety (Paul & Moser, 2009). Unemployed people would not suffer that much from their temporary loss of income, or any impact on social contacts, goals, status, time structure, and activity, if they could know for sure when and how this period of unemployment would come to an end (Creed & Klisch, 2004; Fryer, 1995). However, only very few unemployed people are so fortunate as to have a clear notion of what their future will bring. Instead, most of them experience uncertainty about the process and outcomes of this nonwork period in their lives. *Uncertainty* is defined as "an individual's perceived inability to predict something accurately" (Milliken, 1987, p. 136). Indeed, most unemployed people feel unable to predict if and when they will find a suitable job and how their unemployment is going to affect their future: Their career future hinges on an unknown outcome.

Human beings have a fundamental need to feel they are being accurate in their predictions of how the world operates (Heine, Proulx, & Vohs, 2006). This fundamental need stems from an evolutionary past in which inaccurate predictions reduced one's chances of survival. Therefore, individuals inherently dislike uncertain situations. They even prefer to hear bad news about a negative outcome (e.g., the outcome of a medical test) than having to deal with uncertainty (about a possible negative outcome). Several theories such as social identity theory (Hogg, 2000; Tajfel & Turner, 1986), similarity and congruence theories (e.g., Edwards & Cable, 2009), and uncertainty reduction theory of communication (Berger, 2005) view uncertainty reduction as a strong motivational force. People aim to reduce uncertainties as much as they can. This basic human need of uncertainty reduction can already be observed, for example, in the behaviors of young children. In uncertain situations, young children need the company of a caregiver to feel more secure. In addition, they often clamp themselves to a valuable toy to make their situation more predictable. This tendency to stick to familiar persons, objects, or habits also prevails during adulthood. The first response to uncertainty is often trying to regain familiar routines.

Uncertainty is an aversive state that is associated with psychological discomfort, anxiety, and stress (Bordia, Hunt, Paulsen, Tourish, & DiFonzo, 2004). While some people have a dispositional sensitivity for ambiguity and do not tolerate uncertainties at all (Cavanaugh & Sweeny, 2012), a certain intolerance of uncertainty is universal to all human beings. Intolerance of uncertainty comprises cognitive, emotional, and behavioral reactions to uncertainty such as biased information processing, faulty appraisals of threat, anxiety, and reduced coping (e.g., McEvoy & Mahoney, 2012). Uncertainty arouses anxiety especially when people believe that problems are threatening and very difficult to solve (Dugas, Letarte, Rhéaume, Freeston, & Ladouceur, 1995). These beliefs easily emerge because uncertainty makes people more vigilant and sensitive to negative and threatening signals (e.g., Morrison & Robinson, 1997). Moreover, because people are less able to rationalize and normalize uncertain future events, they tend to experience intense emotions with regard to those events (Van Boven & Ashworth, 2007; Wilson, Ceterbar, Kremer, & Gilbert, 2005). The resulting anxiety, in turn, may lead to excessive rumination or, alternatively, to cognitive avoidance. In the latter case, individuals suppress thinking about their problems or imagine that no transitions will be needed because they believe that their prior status quo will reappear. Klehe and colleagues (2011), for example, showed that job insecurity (i.e., uncertainty about possible job loss) "paralyzed" employees rather than activate them to explore other job options.

Uncertainty and anxiety also result from a lack of control (Bordia et al., 2004) – that is, the inability to prepare for, or deal with, a potentially negative unknown. In general, a perceived lack of control reduces people's proneness to initiate action (Anderson & Galinsky, 2006; Lammers, Galinsky, Gordijn, & Otten, 2008). People tend to focus on the regulation of their cognitions and feelings rather than on actions through which they might get more control (such as the seeking of information or the exploration of job alternatives). In times of uncertainty and an experience of lack of control, they get absorbed in their worries and, thus, do not engage in prospective thinking and future planning (Klehe et al., 2011). But also during unemployment, a situation that definitely asks for action, people often involve themselves in inadequate strategies such as procrastination. That is, "they voluntarily delay their intended course of action despite expecting to be worse off for the delay" (Steel, 2007, p. 66). Procrastination and other strategies of cognitive avoidance may initially relieve individuals' problems, but since procrastination also prevents underlying mechanisms from being modified, it may eventually lead to worrisome thoughts after all.

The life design approach (Savickas et al., 2009) recognizes that new-economy careers imply uncertainty, lack of control, and unpredictability. In particular, this approach emphasizes that people's life and work identities will change more frequently during the life span. Indeed, unemployment is often associated with the potential loss of prior identities, which is experienced as threatening.

Identity Threats

Identities are the meanings that people attach to others and the self. These meanings may refer to the social roles that they or others hold (social identity) or to the unique set of attributes they associate with the self or with others (personal identity) (Ashforth & Mael, 1989). Individuals have multiple identities that differ in importance. However, these identities coexist by integrating diverse experiences into a unity that shapes the self (Baumeister, 1998). Identities seem connected to specific life domains such as work, home, and people's social lives. However, identities are also related to each other, such that identity changes in one domain impact on identities that are formed in other domains. The life design approach, therefore, argues that careers (and career counseling) can no longer be addressed from the work domain only, rather that *work* identities should be contextualized because they are the product of interactions between multiple experiences of daily life.

Unemployment may initially evoke threats to, and loss of, former work-related identities. First, employees tend to identify themselves with their organization based on feelings of similarity between their self-concept and the identity they ascribe to their organization. The loss of one's job inherently means the loss of social ties – that is, the loss of an important social identity (Ng & Feldman, 2007). Second, people tend to define themselves in terms of their profession and professional roles and activities (Ibarra, 1999). People's profession and work activities are often critical to their life goals and core sense of self (e.g., Randel & Jaussi, 2003). Hence, the loss of one's job may mean the possible loss of an important part of one's personal identity. Identity theory and research point out that people suffer from identity threats and loss (Ashforth, 2001).

People with a strong work-related identity view paid work as central to their life and are strongly committed to their work (Fugate et al., 2004; McArdle, Waters, Briscoe, & Hall, 2007). This so-called career identity is not tied to a particular job, role, or organization, but derives its meaning from the sequences of work-related experiences (Ashforth & Fugate, 2001; DeFillippi & Arthur, 1994; Fugate et al., 2004; Hall, 2002). People with a strong career identity likely suffer most from being unemployed; they have lost the most valuable part of the self. Although a strong career identity is generally found to be a key driver of (persistence in) job search and contributes to finding stable reemployment (Koen, Klehe, & van Vianen, 2013), many – particularly older – former employees respond to their unemployment with despair and passivity: They need time to mourn over their loss.

At the same time, unemployment not only disrupts existing work-related identities, but also implies threats to projected ones. Young people, for example, lack sequences of work-related experiences but may nevertheless identify themselves with a future work career. Such a *future work self* (cf. Strauss, Griffin, & Parker, 2012) reflects people's hopes and aspirations in relation to their work, and refers to the representation they have of themselves in the future. Like career identity, the future work self provides a cognitive compass for people to navigate through their careers (cf. Fugate et al., 2004). A future work self, however, is explicitly focused on the future, which creates a discrepancy between the future and the present, and thereby motivates proactive career behaviors. The more someone has a clear and salient future work self, the more he or she engages in proactive behaviors such as networking and career planning. Moreover, those with more elaborate future work selves are able to also consider information about potential obstacles and manage threats to their future work self (Strauss et al., 2012).

During unemployment, however, the extent and salience of this future work self are likely to decrease. People may lose their prospective career identity – especially when the time of unemployment is prolonged (e.g., Aaronson, Mazumder, & Schechter, 2010). Additionally, the lack of work-related experiences among unemployed young adults may pose a threat to developing a career identity or elaborating the future work self. Although some young people may have built a career identity during school, others may still need to construct one when making the transition from school to work. Constructing a career identity is essential for having a healthy adult life (e.g., Blustein, 2008) since it helps to find a job and thus to fulfill basic human needs of autonomy (earning an income and thus not being dependent on others), competence (being able to show one's unique capacities), and relatedness (creating social ties with others) (Gagné & Deci, 2005).

Constructing a career identity during secondary school seems, however, far from obvious, because school programs are mostly oriented toward building general knowledge and skills rather than toward building specific professional skills and understanding. Indeed, schools are no longer the direct route to a profession, as has been shown in research that investigated whether young people's initial vocational training matched their first job (Béduwé & Giret, 2011). Strong mismatches were found between the level of students' education and the level of their first job (vertical mismatch) and between the students' field of study and the vocational field in which they found their first job (horizontal mismatch). Students' weak vocational training and their ambiguity about the vocational field they might enter may impede the construction of a career identity. Moreover, the lack of a salient future work self, combined with experiencing difficulties with finding a job, may lead to the total loss of a career identity. These young adults may develop other identities and rather associate themselves with other stigmatized unemployed peers who represent a street culture and a "culture of poverty" (White & Cunneen, 2006).

To summarize, unemployment but also careers in the new economy involve uncertainty and identity threats as a consequence of frequent career transitions. Uncertainty is associated with feelings of anxiety and lack of control. Identity threats concern the possible loss of central parts of the self and the possible demolition of (the building of) hoped-for selves. These features of unemployment and careers raise the question of what resources people should obtain to adequately prepare for and respond to (the often) unwanted but also unavoidable transitions in their lives. In addition, because work and career identities are shaped by multiple experiences in other life domains and thus can no longer be treated as separate constructs, professional identities should be (re)constructed in a holistic, contextual, and – preferably – preventive way (Savickas et al., 2009). In the next paragraph, we will discuss the building of such basic resources by means of the narratives that people may create of their reality, which, in turn, are the vital resources for life design interventions.

Building Resources

COR theory (Hobfoll, 1989, 2002) proposes that individuals attempt to obtain, retain, and protect resources. Resources have been conceptualized as "those things that people value or that serve to help them attain that which they value" (Wells, Hobfoll, & Lavin, 1999, p. 1172). Resources can be contextual or personal. Contextual resources encompass objects (e.g., a property), conditions (e.g., social support, employment), and external means (e.g., time, money). Personal resources concern personal characteristics (e.g., traits) and personal energy (e.g., physical energy). Both types of resources are valued by individuals and help them to attain other valuable resources. Imagine an employee who gets fired. This employee loses an important contextual resource – namely, employment. To find new employment, the employee needs other contextual and personal resources to regulate his or her emotions and (job search) activities. When people's resources fall short, they are less able to cope with the stressors they encounter in their life (Hobfoll, 2002). Hence, inadequate coping mechanisms result when resources get more and more depleted (*loss spiral*).

Resources become less easily depleted when individuals have created a buffer through the generation of additional and more fundamental resources at times when stressors have not yet occurred (Hobfoll, 2002). The resources that individuals have attained may, in turn, lead to a further accumulation of additional recourses, the so-called *gain spiral*. The more resources individuals attain, the better they are able to avoid or to sort out stressors, and the better the surplus of resources can be utilized when specific resources become depleted. Importantly, resources facilitate people's well-being across time and situations, yet some resources are more volatile, whereas others are more structural. Volatile resources cannot be used for different purposes (e.g., physical energy), or they are more temporal (e.g., psychological states such as mood). Structural resources are more permanent because they can be used more often and last for a longer period of time (e.g., continuing social relationships, stable personal characteristics). Obviously, structural resources are especially important for coping with hurdles. Among these structural resources are the so-called *key resources* that facilitate the selection, alteration, and enactment of other resources. Key resources are personal characteristics such as self-esteem, self-efficacy (Kanfer, Wanberg, & Kantowitz, 2001), and optimism (Parker, Bindl, & Strauss, 2001), that all promote effective and active coping.

A basic principle of COR theory is that "people must invest resources in order to protect against resource loss, recover from losses, and gain resources," and "those with greater resources are less vulnerable to resource loss and more capable of orchestrating resource gain" (Hobfoll, 2011, p. 117). Some personal resources such as self-esteem, self-efficacy, and optimism are strongly associated with each other, which indicates that they have been developed together; they form a *resource caravan* (Hobfoll, 2011). Therefore, employees in the new economy need to foster resource caravans that help them to cope with career transitions.

Below, we will discuss some vital resources that may form the resource caravan needed for dealing with uncertainty and identity threats – namely, mental preparation and the mental models that people have built of careers and the self.

Mental Preparation

Arguably, people who accept and expect uncertainties as a normal aspect of their (work) life might be better prepared when actual transitions or changes are nearby (e.g., Lippmann, 2008). However, as people use different coping styles for dealing with strains (i.e., mental versus behavioral coping), they may also use different preparatory styles – that is, some individuals may anticipate an uncertain future primarily by means of preparatory thoughts, whereas others may (also) do so through preparatory behaviors (i.e., problem-focused coping). Preparatory behaviors, such as problem-focused coping, address the threatening issue itself rather than only one's emotional reactions, and they may thus preclude possible threats occurring.

Yet, mental preparation is necessary as it precedes behavioral actions. The question is thus what this mental preparation should include. As argued above, contemplation of future uncertain events may have negative effects because thinking about an uncertain future (with possible spells of unemployment) may evoke intense negative emotions. Consequently, imagining all sorts of career uncertainties may make people worrisome and fearful rather than well prepared. Whether these negative effects indeed occur may to a large extent depend on the meaning that people ascribe to career transitions such as job loss and change.

Human beings are meaning makers. They create mental representations of their reality and identify connections and patterns between elements that may not exist, so as to establish a sense of coherence in their lives. "Meaning is what connects things to other things in expected ways. Meaning connects the people, places, and things around oneself and it connects elements of the self: thoughts, behaviors, desires, attributes, abilities, roles, and autobiographical memories" (Heine, Proulx, & Vohs, 2006, p. 90).

If individuals have a mental representation of specific realities, they experience difficulties with adjusting when this representation is unexpectedly disrupted. This phenomenon was shown in an experiment with playing cards (Bruner & Postman, 1949). Normally there are four suits (spades, hearts, diamonds, and clubs) in two colors (black and red). The researchers changed the red queen of hearts to a black one, and tested how participants in the lab responded. Most participants failed to see the change; apparently, they revised their perception such that the suit and the color matched their mental representation (the black heart was seen as red). Yet, after repeated confrontation with the black heart card most participants gradually became aware of its unusual features and spontaneously revised their playing cards paradigm. A small group of participants were, however, unable to figure out what had happened to the cards; they recognized some unexpected features but were unable to articulate them. These participants felt confused about the original combination of card features and even experienced distress. Because it is unlikely that people are simply aroused by a black queen of hearts, the authors concluded that the distress was probably caused by participants' inability to make meaning of the new situation.

Individuals also ascribe meaning to their career transitions and the loss of their job. It is important that this meaning accords with the new prevailing career realities of unpredictability and change (van Vianen & Klehe, 2013). This means that people should be aware that the sense of coherence in their lives cannot be found in a predictable order of career steps, but through self-narratives (stories that make a point about the narrator) that help them to (re)construct their identities (Ibarra & Barbulescu, 2010). Telling a story helps people create meaning (Gergen, 1994; McAdams, 1996, 1999) and increases the likelihood that their hoped-for identity – or future work self – will be granted (Ashforth, 2001; Van Maanen, 1998). Yet, self-narratives are heavily influenced by the mental models that narrators have of their environment and the self. Below, we will discuss two mental models that are crucial for self-narratives and the construction of identities: mental models of careers and the self.

Mental Models of Careers

Instead of viewing career disruptions as a personal failure (e.g., Feldman, Leana, & Bolino, 2002), people could learn to frame them as normal events that happen in a working life. In a similar vein, instead of experiencing transitions as a loss of or threat to their personal, social, or professional identities, they could conceive of them as chances to make identity shifts (van Vianen & Klehe, 2013) and as an opportunity to reorient themselves and to make new career decisions (e.g., Zikic & Klehe, 2006; Zikic & Richardson, 2007). People may develop a different meaning for their existing identities, or they may, temporarily, shift their focus to other (non-work-related) self-aspects and associated attributes (such as personal characteristics, behaviors, or affect).

If individuals have a more open and positive view toward career transitions, they may, just like their more worrisome counterparts, experience uncertainty, but this uncertainty will be associated with challenge rather than fear. The experience of challenge also comprises uncertainty about one's ability to accomplish a task (finding a job), but this uncertainty is combined with positive arousal (i.e., energy, fascination), which together do not evoke strong feelings of fear (Preenen, 2010). People who associate career transitions with challenge may seek ways to optimize their chances of turning future transitions into a success and engage in preparatory behaviors.

Furthermore, instead of framing careers in terms of objective career outcomes (e.g., income, hierarchical status), careers and career success can be better portrayed in terms of subjective outcomes, such as satisfaction, involvement, health, and need fulfillment (e.g., Hall, 2002). Only a few people are actually able to advance upward. Hence, if they stand by a traditional career conceptualization, they are prone to experience regret and disappointment (Dries, 2011). Careers in the new economy are by definition individual and subjective experiences that will not follow a path that is dictated by societal norms.

Because personal experiences are the core of careers, people should learn to be more self-referent and to primarily rely on their own personal standards and goals rather than comparing themselves with other people or external standards (other-referent). Generally, it is healthier to take the self as the main referent for evaluating one's life (Baumeister, 1998; Thau, Aquino, & Wittek, 2007). Moreover, self-referent satisfaction with one's career tends to advance objective career success. Abele and Spurk (2009) conducted a longitudinal study in which they examined relationships between subjective self-referent, subjective other-referent, and objective career success among a sample of graduate professionals. Although career starters tended to compare themselves with fellow graduates to establish their (subjective) career success, those who were initially satisfied with their career according to their own norms were – in objective terms – more successful in their later career. Hence, initial self-referent satisfaction is beneficial for actual career progress. Most likely, self-referent career evaluations will remain important or become more important in later career stages, when many employees stagnate on their career ladder. Furthermore, the more self-referent people are, the less vulnerable they may be for career uncertainty as caused by external changes and prevailing external norms.

To summarize, key resources for being prepared for (unwanted) career transitions are career mental models that frame transitions as challenges and define career success by means of self-referent norms. The life design approach asserts that narratives are critical in life design interventions. Indeed, narratives uncover people's mental models about their career and the norms and referents they use for establishing their career success. Life design career counselors can help clients to revise their stories into a more adequate and coherent view of their reality. Importantly, volatile economic conditions require that people rely on the self rather than on outside factors that dictate their career. Therefore, career counselors can help clients to attain a vital additional key resource – namely, an adequate mental model of the self.

Mental Models of the Self

People likely derive their self-views from two primary sources. On the one hand, they rely on their beliefs about humans in general – that is, their implicit self-theories. On the other hand, they base their self-views on how they respond to and behave in their daily lives.

People's implicit self-theories have been extensively documented and investigated by Carol Dweck and colleagues. Self-theories are beliefs about either the fixedness or the malleability of personal characteristics (Dweck, 2000). The first type of these beliefs has been referred to as an entity self-theory, whereas the second type of these beliefs reflects an incremental self-theory. Individuals who adhere to an entity theory assume that personal attributes such as capacities and personality are fixed and stable over time and across situations, whereas individuals who hold an incremental theory believe that these attributes are malleable. People's implicit self-theories form the core of their meaning system and direct their attributions and actions. In addition, self-theories orient people to different goals: Incremental theorists place more priority on learning and development than entity theorists (Hong, Chiu, Dweck, Lin, & Wan, 1999). When people believe that their capacities, personality, and skills are fixed, they will be oriented toward retaining the tasks on which they perform well (Dweck & Molden, 2005). In contrast, when people believe that capacities are malleable, they will be willing to learn and invest in their further development.

Since incremental theorists are more open to personal development and do not fear new tasks and situations as much as entity theorists do, they will be better able to cope with the uncertainties associated with unemployment. An incremental mind-set will promote preparatory career behaviors during employment, and it is a key resource for self-efficacy and optimism during career transitions. Hence, an incremental mind-set is essential for new-economy careers.

However, people's self-views originate mostly from their own reflections on their preferences, values, and responses to their environment. For example, they discover that they enjoy specific activities and dislike other activities, experience negative or positive emotions, respond positively or negatively to particular events, and seek out or avoid certain (social) environments. Generally, people prefer activities and environments that match their true or authentic self (van Vianen, 2005).

Aristotle believed that the highest form of excellence people could achieve was through living in accord with one's true self. Like Aristotle, many people are concerned with the question of who they really are, since they assume that their true self is vital for their personal identity. We, therefore, value those aspects of the self that feel authentic, irrespective of whether these true self traits are socially desirable (Schlegel, Hicks, Arndt, & King, 2009). Reflecting on one's true self has positive effects for psychological well-being, such as one's self-esteem, and it promotes active coping (Schlegel, Hicks, King, & Arndt, 2011). Moreover, experienced concordance between the self and the goals people pursue also promotes well-being (e.g., Sheldon & Houser-Marko, 2001). These positive effects of authenticity – the unimpeded functioning of one's true self in daily life – are due to the fact that a true self helps people to create meaning in their life (Schlegel et al., 2011). Career goals and choices become more meaningful if they are consistent with one's true self. Further, the more accessible the true self-concept is or has been made (i.e., by experimental manipulation), the more meaning in life people experience (Schlegel et al., 2009). Therefore, it would be good if the true self were known and easy to imagine: Subjectively experiencing true self-knowledge means experiencing meaning in life.

To summarize, key resources for being prepared for (unwanted) career transitions are mental models of the self that can foster learning and development, and can guide the setting of career goals. People should endorse a personal identity that encompasses both an incremental and a true self-view. Being adaptive and able to learn and change may go well together with adhering to an authentic self.

Above we have argued that people need key preparatory resources for coping with uncertainty and identity threats. Structural key resources that should be obtained, retained, and utilized during transitions are open, positive, and self-referent mental models of careers and incremental and authentic mental models of the self. These mental models of careers likely reduce the anxiety that is often associated with uncertainty, because transitions are no longer viewed as signs of personal failure, but rather as normal and challenging events that happen in one's life. Incremental and authentic mental models of the self may also reduce uncertainty and anxiety, because people believe they can develop and change, and can rely on the (true) self when making choices. In addition, a true self may diminish perceptions of identity threat and may buffer against actual identity loss. Life design career counselors can assist clients to change self-views that are hindering further career exploration, to develop images of possible selves, and finally to construct a self-view that is authentic but not fixed. Below, we further elaborate on how a true self can be constructed.

The Construction of the Self

People engage in forming, repairing, maintaining, strengthening, or revising their identities. This identity work is particularly prevalent during career transitions (Ibarra & Barbulescu, 2010), but given the problems that many people encounter in this period, it is often difficult to accomplish in times of such uncertainty. Identity shifts – an identity restructuring response that encompasses shifts in focus and meaning of the environment and aspects of the self necessary for adequate coping with transitions – are more easily made when individuals appraise transitions as a challenge (rather than threat), have nontraditional conceptions of careers and career success, and already have developed a notion of their true self (see also van Vianen & Klehe, 2013). Identity work is required to sustain feelings of authenticity, despite the changes a person is experiencing (Ibarra, 2003).

Below we will discuss two possible ways in which self-views and identities can be constructed to better cope with uncertainties and identity threats during transitions: abstract self-views and life design dialogues.

Abstract Self-Views

Self-views – how people perceive themselves in relation to their outcomes – vary in content (e.g., "I am cooperative" or "I am competitive"), but they also vary in level of abstractness. Abstract self-views are characterized by broad and abstract descriptions of the self (e.g., "I am a cooperative person"), whereas concrete self-views are detailed descriptions of the self that reflect specific behaviors or events (e.g., "I regularly collaborate with others").

Experimental research has shown that anxiety in situations of uncertainty can be reduced if people use more abstract rather than concrete self-views (Cavanaugh & Sweeny, 2012). Further, self-view abstractness is related to self-esteem and self-esteem stability (Updegraff, Emanuel, Suh, & Gallagher, 2010; Vess, Arndt, & Schlegel, 2011) and well-being (Updegraff

& Suh, 2007). Individuals who use more abstract (and relatively positive) self-descriptions will more quickly recover from blows to their self-esteem, experience smaller fluctuations in self-esteem in response to negative events (Updegraff et al., 2010), and show higher well-being than individuals who use more concrete self-descriptions. In addition, self-view abstractness also predicts the stability of one's self-esteem when controlled for other variables that are known to affect self-esteem, such as positive and negative emotions, self-concept clarity, and neuroticism (Updegraff et al., 2010). These positive effects of abstractness are thought to be due to having "more ways to rationalize and minimize a threat to the self than concrete self-construals" (Updegraff et al., 2010, p. 99). People tend to adopt more flexible, and often more flattering, standards of self-evaluation (Dunning, Leuenberger, & Sherman, 1995), and these self-evaluations are less vulnerable to disconfirmation, such as after personal failure, when defined in abstract rather than concrete terms. Specific events or situations do not easily change abstract (and often positive) self-views (Updegraff et al., 2010; Updegraff & Suh, 2007).

Cavanaugh and Sweeny (2012) showed that self-views are also protective in times of threat posed by uncertainty. In one of their studies, they led participants to believe that a photo of them would be placed on a website and that others would rate their photo. Furthermore, they asked participants to rate a photo of other participants on height (low threat condition) or physical attractiveness (high threat condition), and they were told that others would rate them on a similar criterion (height or attractiveness, respectively). Participants had to wait to the end of the session to receive the evaluations of their photo. Participants who described themselves in more abstract terms experienced less anxiety over uncertainty than people with more concrete self-views. The authors furthermore showed that this result was not due to participants' general positive or negative self-view or their optimism about the evaluation outcome. All in all, during times of uncertainty that are anxiety provoking, abstract self-views seem to function as a buffer and alleviate the anxiety of uncertainty.

Although the level of self-view abstractness differs among individuals, it is also malleable (Updegraff et al., 2010; Updegraff & Suh, 2007). Cavanaugh and Sweeny (2012), for example, also conducted a study in which they manipulated participants' self-views. This study showed similar results to the studies in which participants' spontaneous self-views were measured. Hence, the use of abstract self-views can be enhanced and thereby also their protective function in case of uncertain and negative events. Abstract self-views are particularly protective in situations where uncertainty poses a threat to people's self-worth, which tends to be the case during unemployment. Life design counselors can help unemployed individuals to manage their anxiety by facilitating the construction of abstract self-views so as to detach their self-views from their momentary situation. Constructing these self-views seems relatively simple, even for people who tend toward concrete self-construals (Cavanaugh & Sweeny, 2012).

Although self-views are essential for identity construction, identities also develop through the priorities that people set for themselves. Guichard (see Chapter 2) suggests that counselors can use life design dialogues to assist individuals in developing the reflexivity they need to design their identities.

Life Design Dialogues

A life design perspective views careers as individual and flexible scripts in which work and nonwork activities are interwoven (Savickas et al., 2009). Hence, a life design dialogue should go further than only the domain of employment and should address the norms from which individuals can give meaning to the different domains of their lives. One way to feed this dialogue is to discuss an individual's core values and life priorities. Below, we propose a specific approach to life design dialogues – the good lives model – which counselors can use to help clients to construct their personal identities.

The Good Lives Model

Tony Ward and colleagues (e.g., Ward, 2002; Ward & Brown, 2004) developed the good lives model (GLM) for use in a clinical context – that is, as a positive therapeutic approach to the rehabilitation of clients with a history of offending. However, in our view, this model is highly useful for all kinds of coaching and counseling interventions, such as career interventions.

Ward and colleagues (Ward, 2002; Ward & Brown, 2004) posit that the human basic needs of autonomy, competence, and relatedness (Deci & Ryan, 2000) cause individuals to seek a number of *primary human goods*. Primary goods are "states of mind, personal characteristics, or experiences that are intrinsically beneficial and sought for their own sake. Primary goods create individuals' sense of who they are and what is really worth having in life" (Ward, Yates, & Willis, 2012, p. 95). In their GLM, Ward and colleagues propose 11 classes of primary goods: life (including healthy living and functioning), knowledge, excellence in play, excellence in work (including mastery experiences), excellence in agency (i.e., autonomy and self-directedness), inner peace (i.e., freedom from emotional turmoil and stress), relatedness (including intimate, romantic, and family relationships), community, spirituality (in the broad sense of finding meaning and purpose in life), happiness, and creativity (Ward & Gannon, 2006). These primary goods are not necessarily complete; some of the goods such as relatedness can be divided into more fine-grained goods (friendship, intimacy, support). The priorities that individuals give to specific primary goods reflect their values and life priorities.

GLM-based interventions support clients to focus on their primary goods. For each life domain (e.g., living, work, relationships, leisure activities), clients are asked what they want to pursue in their life (primary goods). Then, they are asked to allocate priority to specific primary goods. The weighting of primary goods reflects a client's personal identity and illuminates the kind of person he or she would like to be. A next step in the intervention is reflection on current goals, obstacles, and context, and the identification of external opportunities and support for gaining primary goods. Finally, counselor and client can then discuss how primary goods can be attained, by identifying a client's resources and strengths, and by determining concrete behaviors that may facilitate securing and attainment of primary goods.

Central to GLM is its emphasis on clients' core values and strengths. It is concerned with the enhancement of clients' capabilities (skills, attitudes, beliefs) to attain primary goods. Furthermore, GLM stresses approach rather than avoidance strategies of goal striving – that is, striving toward the attainment of positive outcomes instead of the avoidance of negative outcomes. There is indeed evidence from diverse reports in the psychological literatures that approach strategies are more effective than avoidance strategies for goal accomplishment and mental health in the longer term and when people potentially have control over their situation (Roth & Cohen, 1986). Also, GLM addresses clients' external conditions (i.e., opportunities and support for gaining primary goods). Finally, GLM focuses on "agency, psychological well-being, and the opportunity to live a different type of life" (Ward & Gannon, 2006, p. 79) (see Table 14.1). Altogether, the model takes into account clients' own primary goods and strengths and relevant life domains and environments, and it addresses what competencies and resources are needed to achieve important primary goods. As such, the model shows an excellent match with the life design approach and provides a tool that is fit for life design counseling. In addition, the intervention steps that are taken in the GLM accord well with those that are recommended in the life design approach (see Savickas et al., 2009).

Table 14.1
Good lives model: intervention steps

1. Identification of primary goods in different life domains
2. Identification of priority of primary goods
2. Identification of current goals, obstacles, and context
3. Identification of external opportunities and support for gaining primary goods
4. Identification of client's resources and strengths (secondary goods) to accomplish or secure primary goods
5. Identification of concrete behaviors that facilitate the attainment of primary goods
6. Planning actions to be taken

Adapted from Ward & Gannon (2006).

Conclusions

In this chapter, we have argued that unemployment and careers in the new economy share some core features: uncertainty and identity threats. People can prepare themselves, both mentally and behaviorally, to cope with these career features by attaining structural key resources. We proposed that pure reflection on future uncertainties may not suffice as an adequate mental preparation for one's career, because these reflections may incite anxiety rather than action. Instead, mental preparation should involve (the construction of) mental models of careers and the self that match (future) reality. Adequate mental models of careers include career disruptions that are considered as normal, challenging, and opportunities to make identity shifts. Furthermore, adequate mental models of careers frame career success in terms of a personal rather than normative endeavor. An adequate mental model of the self comprises self-views that are incremental as well as authentic. Adequate self-views are also easy to recall because they transcend concrete (negative) experiences and thus buffer against daily hassles. Further, adequate self-views are built on the identification and prioritizing of one's primary goods – specific experiences that one wants to pursue – in different life domains.

We derived our propositions from diverse yet relevant research domains. For example, our notion that abstract self-views are helpful in times of uncertainty stems from experimental research in social psychology. Therefore, future research could examine whether abstract self-views are also beneficial during unemployment and in times of career uncertainty: Do abstract self-views indeed promote people's resilience, and how may such processes change over time? Most people, after all, hold generally positive views about themselves, and while positive abstract self-views help people to cope with the adversities of unemployment, the self-views themselves may change as well in response to unemployment. As abstract rather than concrete self-views are more resistant to change, abstract self-views may well prolong the resulting resiliency effects. Yet, we still know little about the resulting self-views once abstract self-views may start to change as well. They may, for example, remain relatively positive on the abstract level while admitting negative components on the more concrete one (e.g., "I am an active person even though I lack meaningful and regular activities in my life right now"). A potential danger, however, may emerge when abstract self-views start to change in valence, rather than in abstractness, as generally we know that unemployment increases the chance of developing depression (Paul & Moser, 2009), a deleterious mood that incorporates generalized negative views about oneself.

In addition, more research is needed on the strategies that people (can) use to mentally prepare themselves for an uncertain future. Are some mental models more useful for career planning than others? Finally, little is yet known about how identity shifts are made, and how salutary identity shifts can be created and supported. We expect that life design dialogues are crucial for the (re)construction of identities, and future research could thus investigate whether and how interventions such as the GLM may facilitate the identity construction process.

Our contention that an adequate mental model of the self encompasses incremental but also true (authentic) self-views may have appeared to be irreconcilable with the fact that true self-views imply a certain degree of fixedness. However, we posit that incremental and true self-views are both essential for healthy career development and are complementary to each other because humans are adaptable (developmental) as well as unique. People have a desire for uniqueness (Brewer, 1991; Hornsey & Jetten, 2004) and a basic need to preserve continuity in their self-views (e.g., Swann, Polzer, Seyle, & Ko, 2004). At the same time, they inherently have to (and seek to) adapt themselves to their environment to have better opportunities to survive (e.g. Baumeister& Muraven, 1996). Incremental self-views allow people to broaden their toolset for dealing with emerging situations and also for giving new meaning to seemingly incompatible situational demands.

Baumeister and Muraven (1996) argued that "individual identity is an adaptation to a social context" (p. 405), to stress that identity and adaptation are related concepts. Further, they noted that "individuals actively choose, alter and modify their identities based on what will enable them to get along best in their context" (p. 405). Hence, to adapt, people should be willing to change but also be aware of their specific qualities and needs – that is, people need an incremental self-theory so that they are willing to adapt, whereas they need a true (authentic) self so that they are able to eventually choose and modify their identity. With Hall (2002), we assert that adaptability and personal identity form the core metacompetencies of a protean career.

Life design counseling with its focus on the development of these metacompetencies seems an adequate approach for producing "significant changes in the conclusions of the life stories of many individuals" (Savickas et al., 2009, p. 7). We recommend that the life design approach embrace knowledge and techniques from other domains in psychology, such as cognitive (e.g., mental models), social (e.g., abstract self-views), and clinical (e.g., GLM) psychology, so that the narratives of people can be employed as an optimized tool for their development and life design.

References

Aaronson, D., Mazumder, B., & Schechter, S. (2010). What is behind the rise in long-term unemployment? *Economic Perspectives, 34*, 28–51.

Abele, A. E., & Spurk, D. (2009). The longitudinal impact of self-efficacy and career goals on objective and subjective career success. *Journal of Vocational Behavior, 74*, 53–62. http://doi.org/10.1016/j.jvb.2008.10.005

Anderson, C., & Galinsky, A. D. (2006). Power, optimism, and the proclivity for risk. *European Journal of Social Psychology, 36*, 511–536. http://doi.org/10.1002/ejsp.324

Ashforth, B. E. (2001). *Role transitions in organizational life: An identity-based perspective*. Mahwah, NJ: Erlbaum.

Ashforth, B. E., & Fugate, M. (2001). Role transitions and the life span. In B. E. Ashforth (Ed.), *Role transitions in organizational life: An identity-based perspective* (pp. 225–257). Mahwah, NJ: Erlbaum.

Ashforth, B. E., & Mael, F. (1989). Social identity theory and the organization. *Academy of Management Review, 14*, 20–39. http://doi.org/10.2307/258189

Baumeister, R. F. (1998). The self. In D. T. Gilbert, S. T. Fiske, & G. Lindzey (Eds.), *Handbook of social psychology* (4th ed., pp. 680–740). New York, NY: McGraw-Hill.

Baumeister, R. F., & Muraven, M. (1996). Identity as adaptation to social, cultural, and historical context. *Journal of Adolescence, 19*, 405–416. http://doi.org/10.1006/jado.1996.0039

Béduwé, C., & Giret, J. (2011). Mismatch of vocational graduates: What penalty on French labour market? *Journal of Vocational Behavior, 78*, 68–79. http://doi.org/10.1016/j.jvb.2010.09.003

Berger, C. R. (2005). Interpersonal communication: Theoretical perspectives, future prospects. *Journal of Communication, 55*, 415–447. http://doi.org/10.1111/j.1460-2466.2005.tb02680.x

Blustein, D. L. (2008). The role of work in psychological health and well-being: A conceptual, historical, and public policy perspective. *American Psychologist, 63*, 228–240. http://doi.org/10.1037/0003-066X.63.4.228

Bordia, P., Hunt, E., Paulsen, N., Tourish, D., & DiFonzo, N. (2004). Uncertainty during organizational change: Is it all about control? *European Journal of Work and Organizational Psychology, 13*, 345–365. http://doi.org/10.1080/13594320444000128

Brewer, M. B. (1991). The social self: On being the same and different at the same time. *Personality and Social Psychology Bulletin, 17*, 475–482. http://doi.org/10.1177/0146167291175001

Bruner, J., & Postman, L. (1949). On the perception of incongruity: A paradigm. *Journal of Personality, 18*, 206–223. http://doi.org/10.1111/j.1467-6494.1949.tb01241.x

Cavanaugh, A. G., & Sweeny, K. M. (2012). Hanging in the balance: The role of self-construal abstractness in navigating self-relevant uncertainty. *Personality and Social Psychology Bulletin, 38*, 520–527. http://doi.org/10.1177/0146167211429806

Creed, P. A., & Klisch, J. (2004). Future outlook and financial strain: Testing the personal agency and latent deprivation models of unemployment and well-being. *International Journal of Psychology, 39*, 382–383.

Deci, E. L., & Ryan, R. M. (2000). The 'what' and 'why' of goal pursuits: human needs and the self-determination of behavior. *Psychological Inquiry, 11*, 227–268. http://doi.org/10.1207/S15327965PLI1104_01

DeFillippi, R. J., & Arthur, M. B. (1994). The boundaryless career: A competency-based perspective. *Journal of Organizational Behavior, 15*, 307–324. http://doi.org/10.1002/job.4030150403

Dries, N. (2011). The meaning of career success: Avoiding reification through a closer inspection of historical, cultural, and ideological contexts. *Career Development International, 16*, 364–384. http://doi.org/10.1108/13620431111158788

Dugas, M. J., Letarte, H., Rhéaume, J., Freeston, M. H., & Ladouceur, R. (1995). Worry and problem solving: Evidence of a specific relationship. *Cognitive Therapy and Research, 19*, 109–120. http://doi.org/10.1007/BF02229679

Dunning, D., Leuenberger, A., & Sherman, D. A. (1995). A new look at motivated inference: Are self-serving theories of success a product of motivational forces? *Journal of Personality and Social Psychology, 69*, 58–68. http://doi.org/10.1037/0022-3514.69.1.58

Dweck, C. S. (2000). *Self-theories: Their role in motivation, personality and development*. Philadelphia, PA: Psychology Press.

Dweck, C., & Molden, D. (2005). Self-theories: Their impact on competence and acquisition. In A. J. Elliot & C. Dweck (Eds.), *The handbook of competence and motivation* (pp. 122–139). New York, NY: Guilford Press.

Edwards, J. R., & Cable, D. M. (2009). The value of value congruence. *Journal of Applied Psychology, 94*, 654–677. http://doi.org/10.1037/a0014891

Eurostat. (2013). *Unemployment statistics*. Retrieved from http://epp.eurostat.ec.europa.eu/statistics

Feldman, D.C., Leana, C. R., & Bolino, M. C. (2002). Underemployment and relative deprivation among re-employed executives. *Journal of Occupational and Organizational Psychology, 75*, 453–471. http://doi.org/10.1348/096317902321119682

Fryer, D. (1995). Labor-market disadvantage, deprivation and mental-health. *Psychologist, 8*, 265–272.

Fugate, M., Kinicki, A. J., & Ashforth, B. E. (2004). Employability: A psycho-social construct, its dimensions, and applications. *Journal of Vocational Behavior, 65,* 14–38. http://doi.org/10.1016/j.jvb.2003.10.005

Gagné, M., & Deci, E. L. (2005). Self-determination theory and work motivation. *Journal of Organizational Behavior, 26,* 331–362. http://doi.org/10.1002/job.322

Gergen, K. J. (1994). *Realities and relationships: Soundings in social constructionism.* Cambridge, MA: Harvard University Press.

Hall, D. T. (2002). *Careers in and out of organizations.* Thousand Oaks, CA: Sage.

Heine, S. J., Proulx, T., & Vohs, K. D. (2006). The meaning maintenance model: On the coherence of social motivations. *Personality and Social Psychological Review, 10,* 88–111. http://doi.org/10.1207/s15327957pspr1002_1

Hobfoll, S. E. (1989). Conservation of resources: A new attempt at conceptualizing stress. *American Psychologist, 44,* 513–524. http://doi.org/10.1037/0003-066X.44.3.513

Hobfoll, S. E. (2002). Social and psychological resources and adaptation. *Review of General Psychology, 6,* 307–324. http://doi.org/10.1037/1089-2680.6.4.307

Hobfoll, S. E. (2011). Conservation of resource caravans and engaged settings. *Journal of Occupational and Organizational Psychology, 84,* 116–122. http://doi.org/10.1111/j.2044-8325.2010.02016.x

Hogg, M. A. (2000). Subjective uncertainty reduction through self-categorization: A motivational theory of social identity processes. *European Review of Social Psychology, 11,* 223–255. http://doi.org/10.1080/14792772043000040

Hong, Y., Chiu, C., Dweck, C. S., Lin, D. M. S., & Wan, W. (1999). Implicit theories, attributions, and coping: A meaning system approach. *Journal of Personality and Social Psychology, 77,* 588–599. http://doi.org/10.1037/0022-3514.77.3.588

Hornsey, M. J., & Jetten, J. (2004). The individual within the group: Balancing the need to belong with the need to be different. *Personality and Social Psychology Review, 8,* 248–264. http://doi.org/10.1207/s15327957pspr0803_2

Ibarra, H. (1999). Provisional selves: Experimenting with image and identity in professional adaptation. *Administrative Science Quarterly, 44,* 764–791. http://doi.org/10.2307/2667055

Ibarra, H. (2003). *Working identity: Unconventional strategies for reinventing your career.* Boston, MA: Harvard Business School Press.

Ibarra, H., & Barbulescu, R. (2010). Identity as narrative: prevalence, effectiveness, and consequences of narrative identity work in macro work role transitions. *Academy of Management Review, 35,* 135–154. http://doi.org/10.5465/AMR.2010.45577925

Jahoda, M. (1987). Unemployed man at work. In D. M. Fryer & P. Ullah (Eds.), *Unemployed people* (pp. 1–73). London, UK: Open University Press.

Kanfer, R. Wanberg, C. R., & Kantowitz, T. M. (2001). Job search and employment: A personality-motivational analysis and meta-analytic review. *Journal of Applied Psychology, 86,* 5, 837–855. http://doi.org/10.1037/0021-9010.86.5.837

Klehe, U.C., & Van Hooft, E.J. (in press). *Handbook of job-loss and job-search.* Oxford: Oxford University Press.

Klehe, U.-C., Zikic, J., van Vianen, A. E. M., & DePater, I. E. (2011). Career adaptability, turnover, and loyalty during organizational downsizing. *Journal of Vocational Behavior, 79,* 217–229. http://doi.org/10.1016/j.jvb.2011.01.004

Koen, J., Klehe, U. C. & van Vianen, A. E. M. (2013). Employability among the long-term unemployed: A futile quest or worth the effort? *Journal of Vocational Behavior, 82,* 37–48. http://doi.org/10.1016/j.jvb.2012.11.001

Lammers, J., Galinsky, A. D., Gordijn, E. H., & Otten, S. (2008). Illegitimacy moderates the effects of power on approach. *Psychological Science, 19,* 558–564. http://doi.org/10.1111/j.1467-9280.2008.02123.x

Lippmann, S. (2008). Rethinking risk in the new economy: Age and cohort effects on unemployment and reemployment. *Human Relations, 61,* 1259–1292. http://doi.org/10.1177/0018726708094912

McAdams, D. P. (1996). Personality, modernity, and the storied self: A contemporary framework for studying persons. *Psychological Inquiry, 7,* 295–321. http://doi.org/10.1207/s15327965pli0704_1

McAdams, D. P. (1999). Personal narratives and the life story. In L. Pervin & O. John (Eds.), *Handbook of personality: Theory and research* (2nd ed., pp. 478–500). New York, NY: Guilford Press.

McArdle, S., Waters, L., Briscoe, J. P., & Hall, D. T. (2007). Employability during unemployment: Adaptability, career identity and human and social capital. *Journal of Vocational Behavior, 71,* 247–264. http://doi.org/10.1016/j.jvb.2007.06.003

McEvoy, M., & Mahoney, A. E. J. (2012). To Be Sure, To be sure: Intolerance of uncertainty mediates symptoms of various anxiety disorders and depression. *Behavior Therapy, 43,* 533–545. http://doi.org/10.1016/j.beth.2011.02.007

Milliken, F. J. (1987). Three types of perceived uncertainty about the environment: State, effect, and response uncertainty. *Academy of Management Review, 12,* 133–143. http://doi.org/10.2307/257999

Morrison, E. W., & Robinson, S. L. (1997). When employees feel betrayed: A model of how psychological contract violation develops. *Academy of Management Review, 22,* 226–256. http://doi.org/10.5465/AMR.1997.9707180265

Ng, T. W. H., & Feldman, D. C. (2007). The school-to-work transition: A role identity perspective. *Journal of Vocational Behavior, 71,* 114–134. http://doi.org/10.1016/j.jvb.2007.04.004

Parker, S. K., Bindl, U. K., & Strauss, K. (2001). Making things happen: A model of proactive motivation. *Journal of Management, 36,* 827–856. http://doi.org/10.1177/0149206310363732

Paul, K. I., & Moser, K. (2009). Unemployment impairs mental health: Meta-analyses. *Journal of Vocational Behavior, 74,* 264–282. http://doi.org/10.1016/j.jvb.2009.01.001

Preenen, P. T. Y. (2010). *Challenge at work: A matter of give and take* (Unpublished doctoral dissertation). Universiteit van Amsterdam, The Netherlands.

Randel, A. E., & Jaussi, K. S. (2003). Functional background identity, diversity, and individual performance in cross-functional teams. *Academy of Management Journal, 46,* 763–774. http://doi.org/10.2307/30040667

Roth, S., & Cohen, L. J. (1986). Approach, avoidance, and coping with stress. *American Psychologist, 41,* 813–819. http://doi.org/10.1037/0003-066X.41.7.813

Savickas, M. L., Nota, L., Rossier, J., Dauwalder, J.-P., Duarte, M. E., Guichard, J., . . . van Vianen, A. E. M. (2009). Life design: A paradigm for career construction in the 21st century. *Journal of Vocational Behavior, 75,* 239–250. http://doi.org/10.1016/j.jvb.2009.04.004

Schlegel, R. J., Hicks, J. A., Arndt, J., & King, L. A. (2009). Thine own self: True self accessibility and meaning in life. *Journal of Personality and Social Psychology, 96,* 473–490. http://doi.org/10.1037/a0014060

Schlegel, R. J., Hicks, J. A., King, L. A., & Arndt, J. (2011). Feeling like you know who you are: Perceived true self-knowledge and meaning in life. *Personality and Social Psychology Bulletin, 37,* 745–756. http://doi.org/10.1177/0146167211400424

Sheldon, K. M., & Houser-Marko, L. (2001). Self-concordance, goal-attainment, and the pursuit of happiness: Can there be an upward spiral? *Journal of Personality and Social Psychology, 80,* 152–165. http://doi.org/10.1037/0022-3514.80.1.152

Steel, P. (2007). The nature of procrastination: A meta-analytic and theoretical review of quintessential self-regulatory failure. *Psychological Bulletin, 133,* 65–94. http://doi.org/10.1037/0033-2909.133.1.65

Strauss, K., Griffin, M. A., & Parker, S. K. (2012). Future work selves: How salient hoped-for identities motivate proactive career behaviors. *Journal of Applied Psychology, 97,* 580–598. http://doi.org/10.1037/a0026423

Swann, W. B., Jr., Polzer, J. T., Seyle, D. C., & Ko, S. J. (2004). Finding value in diversity: Verification of personal and social self-views in diverse groups. *Academy of Management Review, 29,* 9–27. http://doi.org/10.5465/AMR.2004.11851702

Tajfel, H., & Turner, J. C. (1986). The social identity theory of intergroup behavior. In S. Worchel & W. Austin (Eds.), *Psychology of intergroup relations* (pp. 7–24). Chicago, IL: Nelson-Hall.

Thau, S., Aquino, K., & Wittek, R. (2007). An extension of uncertainty management theory to the self: The relationship between justice, social comparison orientation, and antisocial work behaviors. *Journal of Applied Psychology, 92,* 250–258. http://doi.org/10.1037/0021-9010.92.1.250

Trevor-Roberts, E. (2006). 'Are you sure?' The role of uncertainty in career. *Journal of Employment Counseling, 43,* 98–116. http://doi.org/10.1002/j.2161-1920.2006.tb00010.x

Updegraff, J. A., Emanuel, A. S., Suh, E. M., & Gallagher, K. M. (2010). Sheltering the self from the storm: Self-construal abstractness and the stability of self-esteem. *Personality and Social Psychology Bulletin, 36,* 97–108. http://doi.org/10.1177/0146167209353331

Updegraff, J., & Suh, E. (2007). Happiness is a warm abstract thought: Self-construal abstractness and subjective well-being. *Journal of Positive Psychology, 2,* 18–28. http://doi.org/10.1080/17439760601069150

Van Boven, L., & Ashworth, L (2007). Looking forward, looking back: Anticipation is more evocative than retrospection. *Journal of Experimental Psychology–General, 136,* 289–300. http://doi.org/10.1037/0096-3445.136.2.289

Van Maanen, J. (1998). *Identity work: Notes on the personal identity of police officers.* Paper presented at the annual meeting of the Academy of Management, San Diego, CA.

van Vianen, A. E. M. (2005). A review of person-environment fit research: Prospects for personnel selection. In A. Evers, N. Anderson, & O.F. Voskuijl (Eds.), *Handbook of personnel selection* (pp. 419–439). Oxford: Blackwell.

van Vianen, A. E. M., & Klehe, U. C. (2013). New economy careers call for adaptive mental models and resources. In U. C. Klehe & E. J. Van Hooft (Eds.), *Handbook of job-loss and job-search*. Oxford: Oxford University Press.

Vess, M., Arndt, J., & Schlegel, R. J. (2011). Abstract construal levels attenuate state self-esteem reactivity. *Journal of Experimental Social Psychology, 47*, 861–864. http://doi.org/10.1016/j.jesp.2011.02.014

Ward, T. (2002). Good lives and the rehabilitation of sexual offenders: Promises and problems. *Aggression and Violent Behavior, 7*, 513–528. http://doi.org/10.1016/S1359-1789(01)00076-3

Ward, T., & Brown, M. (2004). The good lives model and conceptual issues in offender rehabilitation. *Psychology, Crime, & Law, 10*, 243–257. http://doi.org/10.1080/10683160410001662744

Ward, T., & Gannon, T. A. (2006). Rehabilitation, etiology, and self-regulation: The comprehensive good lives model of treatment for sexual offenders. *Aggression and Violent Behavior, 11*, 77–94. http://doi.org/10.1016/j.avb.2005.06.001

Ward, T., Yates, P. M., & Willis, G. M. (2012). The good lives model and the risk need responsivity model. A critical response to Andrews, Bonta, and Wormith (2011), *Criminal Justice and Behavior, 39*, 94–110. http://doi.org/10.1177/0093854811426085

Wells, J. D., Hobfoll, S. E., & Lavin, J. (1999). When it rains, it pours: The greater impact of resource loss compared to gain on psychological distress. *Personality and Social Psychology Bulletin, 25*, 1172–1182. http://doi.org/10.1177/01461672992512010

White, R., & Cunneen, C. (2006). Social class, youth crime and justice. In B. Goldson & J. Muncie (Eds.), *Youth crime and justice* (pp. 17–29). London, UK: Sage.

Wilson, T. D., Ceterbar, D. B., Kremer, D. A., & Gilbert, D. T. (2005). The pleasures of uncertainty: Prolonging positive moods in ways people do not anticipate. *Journal of Personality and Social Psychology, 88*, 5–21. http://doi.org/10.1037/0022-3514.88.1.5

Zikic, J., & Klehe, U.-C. (2006). Job loss as a blessing in disguise: The role of career exploration and career planning in predicting reemployment quality. *Journal of Vocational Behavior, 69*, 391–409. http://doi.org/10.1016/j.jvb.2006.05.007

Zikic, J., & Richardson, J. (2007). Unlocking the careers of business professionals following job loss: Sensemaking and career exploration of older workers. *Canadian Journal of Administrative Sciences, 24*, 58–73. http://doi.org/10.1002/cjas.5

Chapter 15

Bridging Disability and Work: Contribution and Challenges of Life Design

Lea Ferrari, Teresa Maria Sgaramella, and Salvatore Soresi

Department of Philosophy, Sociology, Education and Applied Psychology,
University of Padova, Italy

Introduction

In the second half of the last century, a number of publications addressed the treatment and inclusion of individuals with different impairments and disabilities. Very few of them were devoted to looking for ways to increase these individuals' likelihood of experiencing satisfactory life conditions and professional realization. On the other hand, even vocational guidance, career education, and career counseling scholars, albeit privileging the analysis of interindividual differences, have actually neglected to apply the results of their research to vulnerable populations. So much so that Blustein (2001) was prompted to say that

> we have developed an elegant science about the work lives of a small proportion of individuals who live in relative affluence in Western countries. Yet, our research has essentially neglected the work lives of the rest of humanity who work primarily to fulfill their basic needs and/or to care for their children and other family members. (Blustein, 2001, p. 171)

Over the last decade, some signs of increased interest by academics and counselors in vulnerable populations and in individuals with disabilities have been recorded. This may also be due to the devastating effects on such groups of people of the current socioeconomic crisis, which is particularly hard for those more at risk for unemployment and in both underground and low-skilled jobs. In this regard, it is relevant to consider the contribution coming from the health and social services, with proposals of actual "work rehabilitation" programs, given that work placement could represent the most certain efficacy index of any rehabilitative model (see Aspinwall & Staudinger, 2003; Keyes & Haidt, 2003; Liberman, 1992; Medley, Powell, Worthington, Chohan, & Jones, 2010). Additionally, in almost all of the models and approaches that today inspire vocational guidance, career education, and career counseling, scholars strongly emphasize the analysis of intraindividual and interindividual differences, such as those associated with gender (Heppner, 2013), impairments (Fabian & Pebdani, 2013), poverty (Juntunen, Ali, & Pierantonio, 2013), and learning difficulties (Morgan, Farkas, & Wu, 2011; Seo, Abbott, & Hawkins, 2008), and those due to language, ethnic, cultural, and religious reasons (Fouad & Kantamneni, 2013). Most career counselors are aware of this complexity and show some thinking, concerns, and ideas regarding the challenges for their profession and for its future (Soresi, Heppner, Nota, & Heppner, 2011). Based on the results of an analysis that aimed to highlight strengths, weaknesses, opportunities, and threats (SWOT) that characterize career counseling (Ferrari & Soresi, 2013), it can be concluded that practitioners are aware that vocational counseling and career counseling can be useful to help people. They understand especially the importance of the need to implement interventions favoring the at-risk groups and those suffering forms of social exclusion, experiencing stereotyping, intolerance, and perpetuating disadvantages due to socioeconomic and gender differences and to disability. In line with what has been said above, and with the emphasis the life design perspective attributes to equal opportunities and prevention, more attention should be paid to people with greater needs, both at the research and practice level.

This chapter: (1) recalls the innovative trends that are currently underlying the cultural-scientific debate on the issues of career design and work inclusion of individuals with impairments and disabilities; (2) underlines the role that can be played by some important and "positive" constructs that are essential to life design; and (3) summarizes competences and attitudes that should characterize life design counselors.

Work and Disability: Stimulating Novel Views

In recent years, the academic debate on the treatment and inclusion procedures for people with disabilities has greatly expanded. This debate has contributed to significant changes in the ways to conceive rehabilitation activity itself and to the definition of the necessary conditions to guarantee these individuals a meaningful existence and quality of life. The "narration" of the changes and the reflections that have been recorded as regards disability and career counseling can be useful in understanding this significant change. There are two "stories" that we wish to base our account on. The first has an international breadth and has been written, on behalf of the World Health Organization (WHO), by a large group of disability experts who have invited all of the countries of the world to review their ways of defining, classifying, and implementing the interventions that can and must be realized in favor of those with disabilities. The second should be the reference platform for all those who deal with work and with disability. It underlines the advantage of resorting to diverse multidisciplinary knowledge to interpret and understand the complexity of the current situations, from the socioeconomic ones to those that specifically characterize the problems of disability.

International Definition of Disability

As regards disability, the main chapters of this development can be found in the *International Classification of Functioning, Disability and Health* (ICF), known also as the biopsychosocial model of disability, promoted at the beginning of this century by WHO (World Health Organization, 2001), and which, in essence, ruled:

a. *The final relinquishment of the traditional views* that focused especially on deficits, impairments, difficulties, and barriers to an autonomous life (see the *International Classification of Diseases* [World Health Organization, 2012] and the *International Classification of Impairments, Disabilities and Handicaps* [World Health Organization, 1980]). Such views could in fact still legitimize special, separate, and institutionalized ways to handle the problems of individuals with disabilities, as well as perpetuate essentially quantitative and normative evaluative and diagnostic procedures (Hughes, 2009; Mitra, 2006). The traditional view located the problem within the individual, gave to the clinician who made the diagnosis the responsibility to provide a cure, and to the individual with a disability the responsibility of overcoming difficulties to reach "normal" levels of functioning (Garden, 2010).

The biopsychosocial view, which is today promoted within the health care world, is decidedly more contextual: It attributes significant roles to relationships, to the stories of those who interact with the world of disability. Such roles can either facilitate or hinder the display of those strengths that, notwithstanding the limitations coming from impairments, do exist and allow the carrying out of activities that are significant for daily living and quality of life. Among these activities the ICF includes work life and the actions necessary to build and plan a life of quality (education, professional training, internships, getting and keeping a decent job, have a paid job, financial self-sufficiency, living within the community, recreation and leisure time, etc.).

b. *The unequivocal recognition of the superiority of the inclusive rehabilitation models* and of those interventions that do not require environmental restrictions. According to the ICF, when choosing treatments, it is essential to privilege analysis and environmental involvement, in its strictly structural, institutional, normative, and relational components. All of this can either favor or hinder people's participation and inclusion on an individual level and, at a community level, can contribute to spread the culture of solidarity and inclusion. It follows that disability or, rather, restrictions in autonomously carrying out necessary daily activities, should be read in light of a complex series of interactions between the health issues that originate impairments and activity limitations, and both the contextual and environmental conditions that may restrict participation. This complex series of interactions ultimately determines an individual's background and his or her levels of activity and autonomy. It also implies that the assessment and treatment of a disability, and therefore career planning itself, cannot be the prerogative of the health care professions, but must involve all those professionals who deal with promoting people's well-being and quality of life. Those who are engaged in career counseling and life design are also included, as they underscore the centrality of the individual from a holistic perspective, thus taking into account what is closely connected with work and other areas of personal and social life.

c. *Relevance attributed to context, family members, and voluntary work.* In dealing with career planning and work inclusion, a new vision of the "context" should be considered. Shogren (2013), for instance, defines it as the set of conditions that account for the high variability of the many aspects of life and for the functioning of every individual. When referring to context, inclusion, and to career planning, the fundamental role of family members (Bedell, Khetani, Cousins, Coster, & Law, 2011; Vargus-Adams & Martin, 2011), schoolmates, teachers, colleagues, and employers cannot be downplayed. Similarly, it is important to acknowledge the role of voluntary workers who, through their involvement in the management of difficult situations, often become effective promoters of inclusion and well-being (Brogan, Lothian, & Smith, 2012). Lastly, it cannot be forgotten that the ICF considers the quality of the natural environment, which must be recognized as a value that can either favor or hinder people's health, well-being, and quality of life. This is much more relevant for people who need specific rehabilitation actions (Day, Theurer, Dykstra, & Doyle, 2012).

Adopting a Multidisciplinary Perspective

The second contribution proceeds directly from a series of socioeconomic reflections that are attracting the attention of those who are engaged in finding solutions, and devising conditions useful to promote a more favorable future. One of the key points concerns the necessity of adopting a multidisciplinary perspective. Especially in the presence of limitations associated with disability or career design, putting the matter in the hands of a single discipline, in only one area of knowledge, is not convenient. This is what is proposed by the so-called philosophy of sharing, whose main representatives include the Hungarian philosopher and humanist Karl Polanyi (Polanyi & Rotstein, 1966) and the economist and academician Raj Patel (2010). Similarities can be also found with the works of Zamagni (2007) and of the Nobel Laureate Amartya Sen (2009). The philosophy of sharing places at its core the obsolescence of *Homo economicus,* engaged in the extreme search for individual profit, in favor of *Homo empathicus.* The latter recognizes his own responsibility toward others and toward the future generations. He thus finds in resource sharing, concern about mankind's well-being, about his family, his nation, or his own self, the key to achieving peace and happiness.

Attention to complexity and "sharing," advocated also by the life design approach, is especially necessary when dealing with those with a disability, which needs to resort to an interdisciplinary perspective – that is, to different languages and paradigms. This means considering those coming from: (a) biomedical sciences, which define impairments; (b) psychosocial sciences, which underscore the importance of the cognitive-emotional components and social behaviors; (c) anthropological, political, and social ones which actually contribute to shape the culture of work and social inclusion (Danermark, 2002).

Disability, Career Planning, and Life Design

Life design (Savickas et al., 2009) is based on a series of important assumptions which could help disability and career counseling practitioners in dealing with challenges, typically occurring in times of crisis such as those we are facing now, and in adopting adequate conceptual instruments, with confidence. The Life Design Group underlines the usefulness of breaking down linear and individualistic perspectives in favor of more "circular" and contextual conceptions. It also emphasizes the use of narrative procedures, which are particularly effective when dealing with *differences* or in giving voice to persons who meet difficulties in openly facing them or when they are inclined to limit themselves. This frequently happens with people with a disability.

According to what we have just mentioned, career counseling activities tailored to these persons frequently use narration and reflexivity to help them in constructing and reconstructing personal stories, finding the most significant aspects and events in their experiences, attributing to them new senses and meanings. Activities conducted by life design counselors stimulate the analysis of diverse life themes and thus facilitate the analysis of an already meaningful person's life, of the barriers and supports, as well as the possible *alliances*. Thanks to their holistic and contextual assumptions, life design counselors may trigger processes of change, emancipation, and participation.

Galvin (2005) asked 92 adults with impairments to describe the way their illness or deficits influenced their own life. In their narratives, the participants referred to significant effects on their independence, their relational and sexual life, and their work. Being unable to work, either because of impairments or discrimination issues, caused them emotional disturbances, and led to consistent threats to their identity. Additionally, when analyzed in a contextual framework, their narratives revealed the importance they ascribed to attitudes and behaviors shown by the others. They referred to the fact that being able to adequately express even their negative experiences and considering their situation with detachment and humor, were useful strategies in managing their low positive representation. Furthermore, persisting in the efforts to see their own rights recognized and to achieve higher levels of inclusion is generally considered a good coping strategy. Finally, participants who mentioned higher levels of independence, higher levels of control over their lives, and characterized themselves as more adapted were also those who referred to easier access to resources and community services.

Moore (2005) came to similar conclusions after interviewing five women with a severe disability. She found that having significant relationships, a paid or nonpaid job, and being anchored to spiritual values were crucial in defining their identity and their perceptions. They referred to the fact that experiencing satisfaction in their relationships helped them in "feeling part of something larger then themselves." This definitively positive thought recurred as a leitmotif in their narratives related to life domains different from work, thus suggesting that these perceptions and these types of supports made them more resilient and able to successfully face difficulties.

Identity and Life Design in Persons With Disability

Disability may influence the way people represent their present, their future, and the goals they consider achievable. Some authors go further and talk about *disability identity* (Dunn & Burcaw, 2013; Foley & Lee, 2012). In regard to this, Dunn and Burcaw (2013) analyzed six stories and found six different ways of describing experiences: sense of belonging, active acceptance of their disability, self-esteem, pride, discrimination, and personal meaning. Sense of belonging refers to the perception of being and becoming active members of groups and associations which are fighting for the recognition of self and other rights. Active acceptance of personal disability refers to recognizing that a disability makes individuals different, but not necessarily inferior to those without any disability. It includes undertaking actions to make their voice and their self-determination heard, and challenging rules and socially shared standards which are not respectful of their identity. Self-esteem refers to self-recognizing strengths and abilities and striving to reach personal goals. Pride refers to being proud of one's personal living condition, of the obstacles already overcome and of results reached, and showing all this rather than being ashamed of oneself. Discrimination refers to the inequality experienced in being treated as a person with a disability in the most diverse situations and to the consequences of this in terms of loss of opportunities, rights, respect, and so on. Finally, personal meaning refers to the searching for a meaning in their life and in their personal condition. During counseling activities, these elements can be used, on the one hand, as a grid in the analysis of stories, detailing the so-called disability identity and, on the other hand, as guidelines in constructing and reconstructing career and life design of persons with impairments.

Additional support to the study of identity in persons with a disability is provided by the analysis of their career stories, which is helpful in capturing the meaning they attribute to different aspects of their own life. Sgaramella (2013), after asking a group of adults who had experienced diverse difficult situations to answer the My System of Career Influences interview constructed by McMahon and Patton (2013), found that most of those living with a neurological disability characterized themselves by mentioning (a) personal characteristics, (b) personal and family values ("I am a husband..."; "I am the father of three daughters"), and (c) work roles they had filled in the past ("I have worked for 7 years as a secretary"; "I was the chief of the factory warehouse"). Rarely did they show any attention to the theme of constructing their future and to goals they pursued in the medium or long term. Persons who showed other types of difficulties (e.g., stories of substance abuse) only recalled their personal characteristics and underlined their weaknesses. They rarely mentioned the roles they had played or made any reference to their diverse identities. This occurred either when they were talking about themselves, anchoring to their past, or when they referred to their present and future life.

Life Design and Future Time Perspective in Disabling Conditions

In times of crisis, the future represents a serious threat for persons who already experience obstacles and barriers in their present life; they represent that future in a markedly negative way. Some studies (Sgaramella, 2011; Soresi, Nota, Ferrari, & Sgaramella, 2013) involving young adults with sensory or motor disabilities have indicated that 21% of those studied were markedly oriented to the present time (the same was shown in 5% of the control group). Work represented a primary goal only for 45% of them (while this was the case for 75% of their nondisabled colleagues). In addition, Carrieri, Sgaramella, and Soresi (2013) asked a group of young adults with an intellectual disability and of adults who showed outcomes from traumatic brain injury, to list their thinking about future goals for different life domains. Only a few of them were able to articulate more than one goal in each of the 10 life domains analyzed, and these goals very seldom showed any explicit elements of a future planning. Although with limited frequencies, the life domains most frequently mentioned were leisure time (12% of persons interviewed) work and romantic relationships (7% and 8% of participants, respectively).

The evidence for different profiles associated with the heterogeneous categories of impairments and disabilities should not, however, stimulate proposals for special approaches, for at least two reasons. Even inside each of these diverse groups, there exists a marked variability, and, besides, the vast majority of elements which arise from these analyses are analogous to those characterizing individuals asking for help in constructing their life. Career counselors and experts in vocational guidance for persons with impairments, using appropriate measures, should take into account the same dimensions and variables which they find relevant in working with people who do not experience a disability. This is also visible in the work of Koenig (2012), who analyzed 12 stories of persons with an intellectual disability: The themes that emerged were very close to those in stories reported by nondisabled persons in previous research. A similar pattern occurred in a series of qualitative studies focusing on the meaning which several groups of persons with different pathologies attributed to work and leisure time activities (Ferrari, Nota, & Soresi, 2008).

A Task for Life Design Professionals

People approaching vocational guidance services or asking for help from life design professionals, irrespective of their undeniable specificity and differences, need help in increasing their well-being, and searching for new meanings and new modalities in managing conflicts and difficult situations. According to life design, for any typology of persons, it is crucial that personal and contextual resources be activated and reorganized with the aim of facilitating choices, life construction, and adaptive changes (Nota, Soresi, Ferrari, & Ginevra, in press).

To reach these goals, as suggested by positive psychology studies involving persons with impairments, it is worth focusing on strengths, and on the personal resources they are able to employ to face everyday challenges and barriers to their life design. This will at the same time avoid reinforcing the generalized inclination to primarily consider inadequacies and deficits (Aspinwall & Staudinger, 2003; Keyes & Haidt, 2003; Seligman & Csikszentmihalyi, 2000; Wehmeyer, 2013). On the other hand, constructs such as hope, optimism, and self-efficacy have been shown to predict positive outcomes for health, adaptive behaviors, and well-being. Consequently, it would be naïve and superficial to leave them out when the goal is helping persons with disabilities in planning and constructing their future (e.g., Rand & Shea, 2013; Seligman & Csikszentmihalyi, 2000).

Career and Life Design Counselors

Professionals who try to help people in designing and building their own future should have adequate training and present very high levels of professionalism, especially if they work with people with disabilities, with activity limitations, and participation restrictions in performing daily living activities. By stimulating the narratives of their clients' stories, these vocational and career counselors should promote the construction of their identity, the development of positive feelings such as hope and optimism toward the future, the perception of adequate efficacy beliefs, and higher levels of career adaptability. Life design professionals should also stimulate reflexivity about searching for meaning to attribute to the interaction between impairments and disabilities, and to different life contexts. This can be done by considering the expectations of others, the conditions of life imposed on them, the presence of obstacles, and also ideological and cultural barriers, or in contrast, the usability of prosthetic and inclusive environments. Consequently, to support the *empathicus,* professional efforts should be devoted to identifying possible supports and aids, searching for possible alliances and resources; sharing cultures, languages, approaches, and forms of collaboration between diverse health and well-being professionals.

Life design counselors, who can instill hope, optimism, and resilience in their clients, offer positive skills that, similar to the more traditional skills, can make a difference in the professional and personal life of those with disabilities. Even if these skills are very difficult to define and measure, they increase the relevance of the services offered and professionalism of those who are in many ways interested in labor issues. As far as this issue is concerned, Larsen, Edey, and LeMay (2007) have stated that if counselors can instill hope in their clients, they are better able to help them in dealing with their problems and uncertainties about the future. Additionally, as Frank (1973) observed, "hopelessness can retard recovery or even hasten death" (p. 136). Furthermore, Talley (1992) affirmed that the best predictor of treatment satisfaction, which explains 68% of the variance, concerns items similar to "the counsellor encouraged me to believe that I could improve my situation." More recently, Lopez and colleagues (2004) have agreed that whatever the type of counseling intervention implemented, beneficial changes can be at least partially attributed to hope. As Edey and Jevne (2003) suggest, hope is "the spark that brings the client for help, the fuel that keeps the counsellor going, the thrust that helps the client try, the outcome of a successful effort. It can be seen as the seed that blossoms into interesting and inspiring counseling interventions" (p. 45). Finally, Larsen and Stege (2012) suggest that a counselor–client alliance stimulates hope when the client feels accepted, heard, understood, and not judged, and when the counselor shows his or her interest and involvement by, for instance, adopting behaviors such as taking notes or smiling.

Besides the ability to sustain clients' resilience, hope, and optimism, life design counselors are more and more asked to be the first to perceive these feelings and to show positive attitudes toward this century's challenges and threats in order to cope with the risk of burnout (Skovholt & Trotter-Mathison, 2011). Bimrose and Hearne (2012) found that almost all career counselors who participated in their qualitative study showed weariness, anxiety, and moderate levels of depression, while only 25% felt themselves to be able to pursue the same job for a long time.

Recently, as previously done with other types of professionals (teachers, psychologists, and educators), Soresi (2013) has studied levels of hope and optimism in Italian professionals who were working in career and job inclusion services for people with a disability. A cluster analysis was run on the 389 responses, on their ability to "instill hope" (e.g., "I can instill hope in people I deal with in my work" and "I can instill trust and hope even in my colleagues"), on their ideas about the future of their careers (e.g., "Surely, in the future, my profession will receive more recognition" and "The working conditions of those engaged in my profession will certainly improve in the future"), and on their perceptions of "work helplessness" (e.g., "In my work it is not possible to program with precision what to do" and "In a job like mine you can't be optimist") (see Table 15.1).

Four groups were identified (see Table 15.1). The largest group included 135 of the participants (34.7%). Although they were sufficiently satisfied with the salary they received, they had only a slightly positive vision of their job. They showed low career self-efficacy beliefs, failed to instill confidence and hope, and did not consider themselves to be capable of coping with difficult situations and occupational stress. Because they adhered to the minimum requirements for their job, without any special strain and at the same time without any particular merit, these counselors were referred to as conventional and neutral. Considering the challenges that vocational counseling and career education counselors have to deal with, this group of professionals seems indifferent, impotent, certainly unable to have an impact on the large number of people who have already had a hard time and to motivate them to design their careers with energy and persistence.

The second group was composed of 106 of the participants (27.3%). These counselors tended to be optimistic, they referred to sufficient career efficacy beliefs, had positive feelings as regards their work and their ability to help people who may have difficulties solving their problems. They know how to be supportive, to encourage and instill hope and confidence, and they appear realistic and moderate. For this reason, these vocational guidance and career counselors were referred to as moderately supportive, optimistic, and realistic.

The third group consisted of 81 counselors (20.8%) and was defined as "very positive, optimistic and resilient" because they basically believed that more positive than negative things

Table 15.1
Ideas and perceptions about their profession in four groups of vocational and career counselors

	Group 1 (n = 135)		Group 2 (n = 81)		Group 3 (n = 106)		Group 4 (n = 67)	
	M	SD	M	SD	M	SD	M	SD
Optimism	13.30	2.23	20.46	1.77	18.38	1.76	15.34	2.09
Hope	24.21	2.15	28.95	1.67	25.08	1.32	20.64	1.70
Work self-efficacy	51.26	6.79	56.67	7.53	53.08	5.98	47.38	7.93
Self-efficacy in establishing positive work relationships with colleagues	27.32	3.41	29.15	2.85	27.82	2.89	26.65	3.51
Self-efficacy in managing clients' difficulties	26.75	3.24	28.83	3.40	27.62	3.04	24.98	3.85
Work realization	30.25	6.39	35.38	4.28	33.42	4.81	30.70	5.48
Able to instill trust and hope	16.56	3.63	19.68	3.24	18.61	2.47	16.02	3.58
Optimism toward the development of the profession	14.51	4.29	18.12	4.42	16.27	3.69	13.20	3.46
Positive representation of one's own work	31.20	6.09	35.99	4.76	34.44	4.67	31.61	6.27
Work satisfaction for collaboration	17.42	4.11	18.42	4.42	18.36	3.88	18.40	3.92
Job satisfaction	19.16	4.29	21.96	3.17	21.01	2.72	18.81	3.37
Satisfaction for career opportunities	7.21	3.26	7.31	3.18	6.76	3.06	6.40	2.83
Salary satisfaction	14.16	5.81	13.46	6.51	13.05	5.16	13.40	4.82
Satisfaction with relationship with managers	26.48	5.98	28.44	5.36	28.78	5.08	27.00	5.75
Resiliency	24.09	3.99	28.73	3.77	26.28	3.48	22.64	3.82

Note. Values are means and standard deviations. N = 389.

can happen, even in times of difficulty and uncertainty. These counselors would then invest energy in pursuing their goals. They considered their work to be valuable, useful, and sufficiently prestigious; they were satisfied with the tasks they perform and consider themselves to be able to establish positive relationships with coworkers and to instill confidence and hope in those who perceive discomfort and difficulties. They appear to be resilient in managing stressful situations. These professionals were exactly those who should take care of people who face the most severe difficulties in choosing and designing their own future. Moreover, they were the colleagues and collaborators all of us would like to have because they are supportive of the leadership and the organizational climate where they work.

The fourth group, fortunately the least numerous, included 67 of the participants (17.2%). These should be considered as decidedly pessimistic about the future and with low career efficacy beliefs. On the professional side they considered themselves to be unfulfilled and unable to cope with difficult and stressful situations. They attributed low prestige and little relevance to the activities they performed. With regard to their chances to be supportive, to be able to instill hope and confidence or to deal with the future of people, there was very little to say: It seemed they were the first who should contact a career counselor!

Besides underlining the fact that different types of counselors can exert diverse impacts on their clients, these clusters suggest the relevance of rethinking the certification of competences and the criteria used to give access to training and the profession, and the need for reviewing the subjects and strategies mastered, when devising training and professional education. These considerations are crucial even from an ethical point of view, especially if counselors are going to work with people with disabilities, who, as it is generally recognized, seem less likely to have decent and satisfying jobs (van Campen & Cardol, 2009).

Conclusion

With this chapter, the authors have tried first of all to give visibility to recent models and principles that are most frequently mentioned in the literature about the difficulties faced by people with disabilities in their daily lives and, specifically, in their careers. The life design approach can easily help unifying the two worlds of disability and career counseling, which have ignored each other and proceeded along parallel trajectories for too long. Not only will research on inclusion of people with disabilities and on career counseling benefit from this "contamination," but more importantly, so too will all of those people who experience difficulties and barriers in designing their future.

The most important merit universally recognized in previously reported models and studies on disability is having placed in the foreground the possibilities and the future of people with disabilities, together with the components of health and strengths. Consequently, the importance of life, education, and work contexts has been emphasized (Soresi, 2007). A significant change in the assessment modalities and, subsequently, in the intervention planning is required next (Soresi et al., 2013).

Although some processes seem to unify diverse situations of impairment or disability, it is worth remembering that even for people showing the same type of injury or disability, aids and supports are markedly heterogeneous and should be found within the same range of assistances that the life design approach may offer to everyone. In doing so, special attention should be devoted to the analysis of positive constructs such as hope, adaptability, and preparedness, equally predictive of the quality of life experience of people with or without a disability (Buchanan & Lopez, 2013; Rand & Shea, 2013). Although research is still needed, these findings are promising both for the way diverse individuals with disabilities may think about their future and for the benefits deriving from approaching life design counselors.

Furthermore, research has shown the relevance for counselors of working on individual characteristics, of undertaking actions involving other life domains beyond work, and taking into account contextual variables (e.g., family, education, family members, and friends, but also relationships at work). These can be either external to the individuals but related to the situations in which both employers and employees live, or environmental, such as facilitators or barriers in their work or in other living environments (Carrieri et al., 2014). For instance, parents and family members should be helped to focus more on their relative's preferences and strengths, to learn more about the services available to them, and to formulate new career plans, thus fostering a positive perspective about their future (Datti, Conyers, & Boomer, 2013; Simonsen & Neubert, 2012). On the other hand, both employers and employees should be helped to develop positive attitudes toward diversity, to reduce irrational beliefs, and promote positive relationships. Research has in fact shown that teams involving "diverse" members are more productive, both in terms of outcomes and problem-solving skills (Bell & Berry, 2007). By encouraging and promoting changes in the context, especially in the work context, life design counselors may then provide concrete and strong foundations for hope and positive outcomes, thus at the same time facilitating work participation and life design.

References

Aspinwall, L. G., & Staudinger, U. M. (2003). *A psychology of human strengths: Fundamental questions and future directions for a positive psychology*. Washington, DC: American Psychological Association.

Bedell, G. M., Khetani, M. A., Cousins, M. A., Coster, W. J., & Law, M. C. (2011). Parent perspectives to inform development of measures of children's participation and environment. *Archives of Physical Medicine and Rehabilitation, 92*, 765–773. http://doi.org/10.1016/j.apmr.2010.12.029

Bell, M. P., & Berry, D. P. (2007). Viewing diversity through different lenses: Avoiding a few blind spots. *The Academy of Management Perspectives, 21*, 21–25. http://doi.org/10.5465/AMP.2007.27895336

Bimrose, J., & Hearne, L. (2012). Resilience and career adaptability: Qualitative studies of adult career counseling. *Journal of Vocational Behavior, 81*, 338–344. http://doi.org/10.1016/j.jvb.2012.08.002

Blustein, D. L. (2001). Extending the reach of vocational psychology: Toward an inclusive and integrative psychology of working. *Journal of Vocational Behavior, 59*, 171–182. http://doi.org/10.1006/jvbe.2001.1823

Brogan, M., Lothian, N. H. S., & Smith, M. (2012). *Telerehabilitation: Exploring the feasibility of using volunteers in the delivery of remote speech and language therapy within community stroke services* [Project evaluation report]. Retrieved from http://www.lothianstrokemcn.scot.nhs.uk/documents/SLTTelerehabilitation-FINAL270412xA.pdf

Buchanan, C. L., & Lopez, S. (2013). Understanding hope in individuals with disabilities. In M. Wehmeyer (Ed.), *The Oxford handbook of positive psychology and disability* (pp. 154–165). Oxford: Oxford University Press.

Carrieri, L., Sgaramella, T. M., & Soresi, S. (2013). Vocational and life design in adults living with intellectual disability: Goals, determinants and profiles. In *Proceedings of the international conference life designing and career counseling: Building hope and resilience* (p. 70). Padua, Italy: University of Padova.

Carrieri, L., Sgaramella, T. M., Bortolon, F., Stenta, G., Fornaro, L., Cracco, A., . . . Soresi, S. (2014). Determinants of on-job-barriers in employed persons with multiple sclerosis: The role of disability severity and cognitive indexes. *Work: A Journal of Prevention, Assessment and Rehabilitation, 47*, 509–520.

Danermark, B. (2002). Interdisciplinary research and critical realism: The example of disability research. *Journal of Critical Realism, 5*, 56–64.

Datti, P. A., Conyers, L. M., & Boomer, K. B. (2013). Factors affecting vocational rehabilitation service use among Latino men with HIV/AIDS: A national perspective. *Journal of Applied Rehabilitation Counseling, 44*, 42–50.

Day, A. M., Theurer, J. A., Dykstra, A. D., & Doyle, P. C. (2012). Nature and the natural environment as health facilitators: The need to reconceptualize the ICF environmental factors. *Disability and Rehabilitation, 34*, 2281–2290. http://doi.org/10.3109/09638288.2012.683478

Dunn, D. S., & Burcaw, S. (2013). Disability identity: Exploring narrative accounts of disability. *Rehabilitation Psychology, 58*, 148–157. http://doi.org/10.1037/a0031691

Edey, W., & Jevne, R. (2003). Hope, illness, and counselling practice: Making hope visible. *Canadian Journal of Counselling, 37*, 44–51.

Fabian, E. S., & Pebdani, R. (2013). The career development of youth and young adults with disabilities. In S. D. Brown & R. W. Lent (Eds.), *Career development and counseling* (*2nd ed*, pp. 357–384). Hoboken, NJ: Wiley.

Ferrari, L., Nota, L., & Soresi, S. (2008). Conceptions of work in Italian adults with intellectual disability. *Journal of Career Development, 34*, 438–464. http://doi.org/10.1177/0894845308316295

Ferrari, L., & Soresi, S. (2013). Crisi economica e orientamento: Il punto di vista degli operatori [Economic crisis and career counseling: Professionals' point of view]. *GIPO Giornale Italiano di Psicologia dell'Orientamento, 13*, 37–47.

Foley, N. M., & Lee, S. (2012). Disability research in counseling psychology journals: A 20-year content analysis. *Journal of Counseling Psychology, 59*, 392–398. http://doi.org/10.1037/a0028743

Fouad, N. A., & Kantamneni, N. (2013). The role of race and ethnicity in career choice, development and adjustment. In S. D. Brown & R. W. Lent (Eds.), *Career development and counseling* (*2nd ed*, pp. 215–243). Hoboken, NJ: Wiley.

Frank, J. D. (1973). *Persuasion and healing: A comparative study of psychotherapy* (Rev. ed.). Baltimore, MD: Johns Hopkins University Press.

Galvin, R. D. (2005). Researching the disabled identity: Contextualising the identity transformations which accompany the onset of impairment. *Sociology of Health & Illness, 27*, 393–413. http://doi.org/10.1111/j.1467-9566.2005.00448.x

Garden, R. (2010). Disability and narrative: New directions for medicine and the medical humanities. *Medical Humanities, 36*, 70–74. http://doi.org/10.1136/jmh.2010.004143

Heppner, M. J. (2013). Women, men, and work: The long road to gender equity. In S. D. Brown & R. W. Lent (Eds.), *Career development and counseling* (2nd ed., pp. 187–214). Hoboken, NJ: Wiley.

Hughes, B. (2009). Disability activisms: Social model stalwarts and biological citizens. *Disability & Society, 24*, 677–688. http://doi.org/10.1080/09687590903160118

Juntunen, C. J., Ali, S. R., & Pierantonio, K. P. (2013). Social class, poverty, and career development. In S. D. Brown & R. W. Lent (Eds.), *Career development and counseling* (*2nd ed*, pp. 245–274). Hoboken, NJ: Wiley.

Keyes, C. L. M., & Haidt, J. (2003). Introduction: Human flourishing: The study of that which makes life worthwhile. In C. L. M. Keyes & J. Haidt (Eds.), *Flourishing: Positive psychology and the life well-lived* (pp. 3–12). Washington, DC: American Psychological Association.

Koenig, O. (2012). Any added value? Co-constructing life stories of and with people with intellectual disabilities. *British Journal of Learning Disabilities, 40*, 213–221. http://doi.org/10.1111/j.1468-3156.2011.00695.x

Larsen, D., Edey, W., & LeMay, L. (2007). Understanding the role of hope in counseling: Exploring intentional uses of hope. *Counseling Psychology Quarterly, 20*, 401–416. http://doi.org/10.1080/09515070701690036

Larsen, D. J., & Stege, R. (2012). Client accounts of hope in early counseling sessions: A qualitative study. *Journal of Counseling & Development, 90*, 45–54. http://doi.org/10.1111/j.1556-6676.2012.00007.x

Liberman, R. (1992). *Handbook of psychiatric rehabilitation*. New York, NY: Macmillan.

Lopez, S. J., Snyder, C. R., Magyar-Moe, J., Edwards, L. M., Pedrotti, J. T., Janowski, K., & Pressgrove, C. (2004). Strategies for accentuating hope. In P. A. Linley & S. Joseph (Eds.), *Positive psychology in practice* (pp. 388–404). Hoboken, NJ: Wiley.

McMahon, M., & Patton, W. (2013). *My System of Career Influences. Adult version*. Camberwell, VIC: ACER.

Medley, A. R., Powell, T., Worthington, A., Chohan, G., & Jones, C. (2010). Brain injury beliefs, self-awareness, and coping: A preliminary cluster analytic study based within the self-regulatory model. *Neuropsychological Rehabilitation, 20*, 899–921. http://doi.org/10.1080/09602011.2010.517688

Mitra, S. (2006). The capability approach and disability. *Journal of Disability Policy Studies, 16*, 236–247. http://doi.org/10.1177/10442073060160040501

Moore, D. L. (2005). Expanding the view: The lives of women with severe work disabilities in context. *Journal of Counseling & Development, 83*, 343–348. http://doi.org/10.1002/j.1556-6678.2005.tb00353.x

Morgan, P. L., Farkas, G., & Wu, Q. (2011). Kindergarten children's growth trajectories in reading and mathematics who falls increasingly behind? *Journal of Learning Disabilities, 44*, 472–488. http://doi.org/10.1177/0022219411414010

Nota, L., Soresi, S., Ferrari, L., & Ginevra, M. C. (in press). Challenges for vocational guidance in the 21st century. *European Psychologist*.

Patel, R. (2010). *The value of nothing: How to reclaim market society and redefine democracy*. New York, NY: Picador.

Polanyi, K. & Rotstein, A. (1966). *Dahomey and the slave trade. An analysis of an archaic economy*. Seattle, WA: University of Washington Press.

Rand, K. L., & Shea, A. M. (2013). Optimism within the context of disability. In M. Wehmeyer (Ed.), *The Oxford handbook of positive psychology and disability* (pp. 48–59). Oxford: Oxford University Press.

Savickas, M. L., Nota, L., Rossier, J., Dauwalder, J.-P., Duarte, M. E., Guichard, J., . . . van Vianen, A. E. M. (2009). Life designing: A paradigm for career construction in the 21st century. *Journal of Vocational Behavior, 75*, 239–250. http://doi.org/10.1016/j.jvb.2009.04.004

Seligman, M. E. P., & Csikszentmihalyi, M. (2000). Positive psychology: An introduction. *American Psychologist, 55*, 5–14. http://doi.org/10.1037/0003-066X.55.1.5

Sen, A. K. (2009). *The idea of justice*. Cambridge, MA: Harvard University Press.

Seo, Y., Abbott, R. D., & Hawkins, J. D. (2008). Outcome status of students with learning disabilities at ages 21 and 24. *Journal of Learning Disabilities, 41*, 300–314. http://doi.org/10.1177/0022219407311308

Sgaramella, T. M. (2011). Time perspective and future goals when university have a disability: Profiles and suggestions for interventions. *Proceedings of Vocational Designing and Career Counseling: Challenges and New Horizons* (p. 73). Padua, Italy: University of Padova.

Sgaramella, T. M. (2013). Qualitative assessment in complex situations: designing the future in case of reduced personal resources and uncertain future time perspective. *Proceedings of the International Conference Life Designing and Career Counseling: Building Hope and Resilience* (p. 78). Padua, Italy: University of Padova.

Shogren, K. A. (2013). Considering context: An integrative concept for promoting outcomes in the intellectual disability field. *Intellectual and Developmental Disabilities, 51*, 132–137. http://doi.org/10.1352/1934-9556-51.2.132

Simonsen, M. L., & Neubert, D. A. (2012). Transitioning youth with intellectual and other developmental disabilities: Predicting community employment outcomes. *Career Development and Transition for Exceptional Individuals, 36,*188–198.

Skovholt, T., & Trotter-Mathison, M. J. (2011). *The resilient practitioner: Burnout prevention and self-care strategies for counselors, therapists, teachers, and health professionals*. New York, NY: Routledge.

Soresi, S. (2007). *Psicologia delle disabilità* [Psychology of disability]. Bologna, Italy: Il Mulino.

Soresi, S. (2013). Helping people build their future. *Proceedings of the International Conference Life Designing and Career Counseling: Building Hope and Resilience* (p. 5). Padua, Italy: University of Padova.

Soresi, S., Heppner, M., Nota, L., & Heppner, P. P. (2011). *Vocational designing and career counseling: Challenges and new horizons thoughts, beliefs, worries and hopes*. Pordenone, Italy: Erip.

Soresi, S., Nota, L., Ferrari, L., & Sgaramella, T. M. (2013). Career development and career thoughts in young and adults with disability. In M. L. Wehmeyer (Ed.), *The Oxford handbook of positive psychology and disability* (pp. 239–264). Oxford: Oxford University Press.

Talley, J. E. (1992). *The predictors of successful very brief psychotherapy: A study of differences by gender, age, and treatment variables*. Springfield, IL: Charles C. Thomas.

van Campen, C., & Cardol, M. (2009). When work and satisfaction with life do not go hand in hand: Health barriers and personal resources in the participation of people with chronic physical disabilities. *Social Science & Medicine, 69*, 56–60. http://doi.org/10.1016/j.socscimed.2009.04.014

Vargus-Adams, J. N., & Martin, L. K. (2011). Domains of importance for parents, medical professionals and youth with cerebral palsy considering treatment outcomes. *Child: Care, Health and Development, 37,*276–281. http://doi.org/10.1111/j.1365-2214.2010.01121.x

Wehmeyer, M. (Ed.). (2013). *The Oxford handbook of positive psychology and disability*. Oxford: Oxford University Press. http://doi.org/10.1093/oxfordhb/9780195398786.001.0001

World Health Organization. (1980). *International classification of impairments, disabilities, and handicaps: A manual of classification relating to the consequences of disease*. Geneva, Switzerland: Author.

World Health Organization. (2001). *International classification of functioning, disability and health (ICF)*. Geneva, Switzerland: Author.

World Health Organization. (2012). *International classification of diseases (ICD)*. Geneva, Switzerland: Author.

Zamagni, S. (2007). *L'economia del bene comune* [The economy of the common good] (Vol. 3). Rome, Italy: Città Nuova.

Chapter 16
Poverty and Life Design

Jacobus G. Maree

Department of Educational Psychology, University of Pretoria, South Africa

Wherever we lift one soul from a life of poverty, we are defending human rights. And, whenever we fail in this mission, we are failing human rights.

Kofi Anan (2000)

Introduction

Much has been written about the value of life design in developed countries, yet little has been said about its applicability in developing countries, particularly in poverty-stricken countries. The author believes that Winslade (2011) is correct in saying that life design today should enable career counselors to answer the following questions on an individual level: How will life design be useful to (a) a young woman from a private school in New York who wishes to study art, (b) a gifted 19-year-old woman in a public school in Zanzibar who wants to become a medical doctor, (c) an inmate in a Mumbai prison who wants to become a lawyer because he wants justice to be seen to be done, and (d) a young man who works as a waiter in Cairo to support his extended family? However, on a collective level, life design should also be useful to (a) a group of citizens living in an affluent suburb in Melbourne, (b) people living in an "average" suburb of London, (c) a group of homeless people occupying a shelter outside Berlin, and (d) the inhabitants of an informal settlement on the outskirts of Johannesburg. What is needed is an approach that will be useful to individuals as well as communities, irrespective of the number of people involved, their ethnic origin, creed, socioeconomic situation, or geographic location. This approach should inform career counseling's individual and collective responses to changes in the world of work. The author thus proposes a shift in the theory and praxis of career counseling toward a present-day, contextualized approach that is built on respect for all human beings and aimed at managing the impact of change and its effects on impoverished people in particular.

Impact of Poverty in Developing Countries

As stated above, the focus in this chapter will be on developing country contexts in general and on impoverished contexts in particular. It is generally agreed that Africa, for instance, finds itself in a particularly invidious position. The many impoverished developing countries on this continent are plagued by, among other things, a severe lack of job opportunities with an ever-shrinking number of available jobs and an ever-growing workforce. Millions of potential employees cannot afford the "luxury" of undergoing career counseling and subsequently constructing careers and designing successful lives. The choice of a career often comes down to accepting any job as long as it brings in the money needed for the survival of the worker and his or her family. This situation is exacerbated by the unavailability of, or limited access to, career counseling; poor health conditions; low literacy levels; extreme poverty; and famine. The following statistics illustrate the seriousness of the situation: "More than 200 million chronically hungry people among the 862 million hungry people globally come from Africa, and 33 million of them are children under the age of five" (Nwonwu, 2009, p. 45).

The above statistics should be seen against the eight goals of the Millennium Declaration (Millennium Development Goals, 2000), which include the eradication of poverty and hunger, the promotion of mental health, and the creation of conditions conducive to the design of successful lives for everyone. Poverty, hunger, and poor economic prospects limit people's chances of choosing careers that will enable them to construct themselves and design successful lives. Conditions of poverty create an environment conducive to the start and continuation of a vicious linear progression: Socioeconomic deprivation leads to inadequate self-construction and life design, which leads to negative impact on the lives of millions of people (young people in particular), and which leads to socioeconomic deprivation. In the case of the youth in particular, the impact of this progression is incalculable.

Wright and Ndong-Jafta (2007) point to the worrying inability of key stakeholders to agree on a unified strategy to combat these challenges. Some education systems even have competing agendas. Whereas the main aim of industrialized and developing countries is to develop an economic workforce and promote national cohesion and identity, the main aim of parents is to prepare their children for "a successful life" (Wright & Ndong-Jafta, 2007, p. 20) and enable them to acquire the skills needed for employment. Children's main aim, on the other hand, is to acquire the competencies needed to "fulfil [their] aspirations" (p. 21). Above all, an education is required that will furnish learners with a means to "escape poverty and participate fully in their communities" (Wright & Ndong-Jafta, 2007, p. 21). The authors agree that the notion of enabling students to choose careers and design successful lives lies at the heart of the Millennium Development Goals (MDGs) (Millennium Development Goals, 2012). In this regard, it is important to note the strong positive association found by Rohlfing, Nota, Ferrari, Soresi, and Tracey (2012) between knowledge of specific occupational types on the one hand and interests and competence perceptions on the other. Given the extremely impoverished context in which the research reported on in this article took place, this finding has special meaning. Very few students in these contexts are ever exposed to more than a handful of stereotypical careers. There is therefore a pressing need to design novel ways to expose learners to the world of careers more adequately and, in doing so, enable them to make sound career choices.

Alston (2005) maintains that the MDGs have not been pursued actively enough by the international human rights community. Some success has been achieved (alleviating poverty in certain regions and ensuring that many children who would otherwise not have done so obtain some form of education), but much remains to be done (Millennium Development Goals Report 2011, 2011) as shown by the spectacular failure of many countries (most of which can be described as developing countries) in international benchmark tests. The apparent belief of the South African state president and the African Union Commission (AUC) chair that Africans can look forward to a well-educated, connected, economically viable, and peaceful continent (Mbeje, 2013) seems to be at odds with the dire situation of millions of people living in abject poverty and unable to find employment. All of the theorizing and speculating about a better future for the impoverished masses have yielded little. What seems to be needed is a change from a "Yes, we can" attitude to a "Yes, we will" and "Yes, we are doing ..." attitude.

The depressing situation described here will continue for many years and, in fact, get worse unless something dramatic is done. What is required is an adaptive response.

Theory of Life Design

The life design framework for career counseling operationalizes and is a natural extension of Guichard's (2005) theory of self-constructing and Savickas's (2005) theory of career construction (both of which describe occupational behavior and its development). Moreover, this framework is structured to be life-long, holistic, and contextual, and to prevent inadequate self-construction (Savickas et al., 2009). It is worthwhile noting Soresi and Nota's (2007) contention in this regard – namely, that preventative guidance should be broadened to include adulthood, as this would enhance our understanding of people and their lived experiences. Furthermore, these ideas build on Van Esbroeck, Tibos, and Zaman's (2005) conceptualization of career choice as a dynamic, flexible, nonhierarchical, and developmental process,

It is also argued that the life design counseling model has liberated the career counseling profession from the shackles imposed on it by an overly positivist approach (Maree, 2013).

The concept of a career as a story or career–life story serves as the basis of career construction theory and life design intervention (Hartung, 2013; Savickas, 2011a). Career counselors regard information presented by clients as meaningful microstories that form part of grand, comprehensive stories (Hartung, 2011), and they attempt to understand the impact of all aspects of people's lives on their lives and careers. People are encouraged to design preferred futures, but, for this to happen, all of the different roles they have to fulfill have to be reconsidered, in addition to the different systems and contexts they are a part of (Campbell & Ungar, 2004a, 2004b).

Interpreting Impoverished Contexts Through a Life Design Lens

Cultural Transition in Impoverished Contexts

Fundamental changes in the global economy over the past few decades, which have prompted dramatic changes in the world of work and careers, have altered the workplace of today and have also brought about changes in the theory and practice of career counseling. Life design can enable counselors to encourage and help people do something about their situation (Savickas, 2010). Savickas (2011b) argues that "these questions arise from the demise of jobs. In response to the recurring transitions that they will face as they move from project to project, individuals cannot maintain their employment, so they must maintain their employability" (Savickas, 2011, p. 256).

Cultural transitions parallel personal transitions, requiring career counselors to think about the past and future of the career counseling profession and to reflect on whether the existing theory and practice of career counseling is still relevant in the 21st century. Duarte (2009) contends that (re)integrating the artificial 20th-century separation of concepts such as "investigation and action, choice and adjustment, guidance and selection, differentialist and developmental perspectives, the study of the individual and of the organization, and the study of education and of industry" (Duarte, 2009, p. 265) constitutes a major challenge in the 21st century. Working from a relational cultural viewpoint (in other words, helping people not only make meaning out of their multiple life experiences but also appreciate how these experiences shape their macrostory or grand life story; Blustein, Schultheiss, & Flum, 2004; Schultheiss, 2011) therefore seems highly advisable in disadvantaged contexts in particular. In doing so, the focus is shifted to providing people with opportunities to use their life experiences to make meaning and to enable them to better understand how the multiple microexperiences shape the grand story or macrostory of their lives.

Vanhalakka-Ruoho (2010) stresses the importance of allowing youths to narrate their stories and elaborate on the relational factors that are peculiar to their decision making by using a variety of classroom-based strategies to draw on personal and group counseling, instead of imposing convenient and inflexible so-called rational decision-making strategies on them. In disadvantaged settings, it is important to adopt a flexible and accommodating approach to enable young people to express themselves truthfully and unreservedly, so as not to curb their self-expression and self-construction but, instead, to "delineate those factors and processes that influence self-construction" (Guichard, 2005, p. 252). The ultimate purpose of this endeavor is to help young people "identize" themselves (Tap, 1980, cited in Guichard, 2009).

Savickas (2008) contends that

> this challenge requires that the profession again address a major cultural transition in a way that best assists individuals adapt to the personal transitions that they face. Thus, the profession of guidance must examine how well its 20th century theories and techniques meet the needs of 21st century clients. My thesis is that each time the social organization of work changes, so do society's methods for helping individuals make vocational choices. (Savickas, 2008, p. 97)

Role Transition

According to Savickas (2008), people are repeatedly called upon to make role transitions to help them gain some perspective on their future lives. All workers today face repeated crossroads in the ever-changing world of work and can best make the necessary role transitions with the help of career counselors who can assist them clarify their goals and make sound decisions.

Collectively and individually, people in impoverished contexts have undergone major role transitions in recent times. Political "freedom" has not always been accompanied by economic liberation. Even though, in theory, many jobs that had previously been reserved for a privileged few are now accessible to all people, the gap between the haves and the have-nots has widened, not only in South Africa. Given the deep-rooted problems in the global economy, the outlook for any improvement in the situation is bleak. Much will have to be done to find ways to help people in the poorest regions in particular escape the cycle and trap of poverty, and overcome the barriers of poor education and the inability to find work.

Society's Response to Changing Contexts and Conditions: One Size Does Not Fit All

Appropriate, accountable career counseling is needed urgently in impoverished contexts where, even in the second decade of the 21st century, the career counseling profession is still characterized by the administration of psychometric assessment tests that were developed in vastly different contexts. Also, the quality of schooling, including the availability of career counseling services, in schools in rural areas, informal settlements, and townships differs widely from that in affluent (mostly private) schools. Career counseling thus remains primarily the preserve of people who can afford this generally expensive service.

The career counseling theory base in these contexts needs updating, and the quality of career counseling, where counseling is available, needs improvement. More importantly, this service needs to be introduced in the numerous impoverished schools where it is not currently offered. Economic growth and political stability are codependent on the availability of career counseling to the millions of people who still have no access to it. Alternative approaches to career counseling and career decision making are also needed.

Eurocentric career counseling theory and intervention in impoverished contexts is widely criticized, resulting in calls for research on approaches more in tune with developing country requirements (Lopez Levers, May, & Vogel, 2011). For career counseling to remain relevant, cultural and educational, gender, and socioeconomic factors have to be taken fully into account (Alika & Egbochuku, 2009; Metz & Guichard, 2009). Questions such as the following should be asked: Can models, strategies, questionnaires, and tests developed in North American and European contexts (which differ widely from Third World contexts) be adapted, restandardized, and successfully implemented in the Third World? Conversely, should research be conducted and models, strategies, questionnaires, and tests developed locally that are better suited for career counseling in impoverished contexts?

All new research should take into account the movement toward a combined qualitative plus quantitative approach in career counseling (Savickas, 2009). The value of qualitative approaches to career counseling in particular has been increasingly recognized with the design, development, and implementation of narrative-based theories and assessment instruments. Career construction counseling (as explained above) entails the belief that incorporation of the objective as well as the subjective meanings people attach to their career and life stories is central to successful career choices and life design. Career counselors who follow this approach are as interested in interpreting the subjective aspects of career counseling (i.e., eliciting clients' career and life stories) as they are in interpreting clients' "objective" test results.

Adopting this approach empowers career counselors to help clients find meaning in their lives; accept authorship of their careers, their life stories, and their actions; and become more adaptable, employable, life-long learners. It also demonstrates how contemporary theories and goals in career counseling can be merged to provide a viable framework for the interpretation, explanation, and directing of career-related behavior and ultimately assist clients choose and construct meaningful careers, design successful lives, and make social contributions through work (Savickas et al., 2009; Sharf, 2010).

Applying the Principle of "Active Mastery of Passive Suffering" in Impoverished Contexts

Mark Savickas (2011a) turned the notion of "active mastery of passive suffering" into a globally recognized basic principle that underlies everything counselors do: helping clients to "actively master what they have passively suffered" (Savickas, 2011a, p. 33). People who have mastered their suffering should also be reminded of their responsibility to use their suffering to help others and, in the process, heal themselves and make social contributions.

The idea of healing oneself by helping others is not new. The author believes it is the task of every counselor to strive toward empowering clients to deal with and transcend their poverty, and the aim of this chapter is to demonstrate how this can be done in practice. The reality of poverty (local and global) and the related suffering should never be ignored. We should also realize that unless poverty is combated and alleviated, local and international stability will be compromised.

Practical Application of Life Design: Putting Practice Into Theory *Intervention Strategy*

The intervention model for life design relies on career–life stories and activities rather than on test scores and profile interpretations. Life design has six general steps, which are informed by the idiosyncratic reality of the unique experience of each individual person and also of communities. First, the problem needs to be defined by the counselor as well as the client.[2] What the client hopes to achieve during the counseling process must also be established. In the next step, the client is encouraged to explore his or her existing system of subjective identity shapes. In the third step, counselor and client focus on broadening the client's perspectives. After the revision of their story, clients place their problem in the revised story (fourth step). In the penultimate step, clients are encouraged to identify activities they can undertake to actualize their new identity. The last (sixth) step comprises short-term and long-term follow-ups (Duarte, 2010; Neimeyer, 2004; Savickas et al., 2009). The project was not initially structured around these six steps. However, upon reflection, 6 years later, the overlap between the six-step structure and the process followed in the actual project is clear. For the purposes of the chapter, and to demonstrate the flexibility of the life design approach, the author has therefore chosen to work deductively, structuring this report around these six steps.

Practical Application of Life Design in an Impoverished Context

It is by examining the actual career–life stories of individuals and communities that we, as researchers, can best learn what works and what does not work in real-life contexts. The remainder of the chapter will therefore report on a longitudinal case study conducted in a deep rural part of South Africa over the past 7 years. It will attempt to show the practical application

---

[2]   In this chapter, the word *client* should be understood in a broad sense as person or community.

of the life design approach discussed thus far in this chapter and explain essential constructs such as adaptability, narratability, biographicity, and identity forms.

Case Study

Background Information

The intervention took place in a predominantly rural region of one of the poorest provinces in South Africa (Limpopo). The intervention was conceptualized in 2006, when the author and coresearchers were conducting research in this province. We were appalled by what we saw. It was not uncommon to see 72, 103, or 136 students crammed into a single classroom. In-depth interviews with the headmasters of the schools we visited revealed deep feelings of demotivation on their part. We saw learners faint from hunger while we were addressing them. They often had to walk 12 km from their homes to schools, and, according to the teachers, children regularly dropped out of school to assume household duties such as looking after siblings. Our research data were often compromised by the desperate socioeconomic conditions in the region, and so we decided to design a project that would entail life story counseling for learners, teachers, and community members.

Project Site

Learners are challenged every day just to get to school, which was founded in 1997 when a prefabricated hall and tents were donated by the community. This area has high levels of unemployment, with most people relying on pensions to survive. Grade 12 school leavers cannot find even short-term employment in the nearby town. The increasing population in the area adds to the problem (Trees for Africa, 2006). Villagers have to travel 32 km to the nearest shopping complex and 128 km to the nearest town.

Project Participants

Twenty-five senior community members participated in the project, including members of the highly motivated school governing body.

Ethics

Informed consent was obtained from all those concerned to record and transcribe all planning sessions, which were held on the school premises. Twelve face-to-face sessions (lasting roughly 2 to 3 hours each) were held in total. Two sessions were conducted in each of the first two stages, one in each of the third and fourth stages, two in the fifth, and four in the sixth stage. Self-reflection was facilitated during each session, and numerous telephone conversations were conducted to ensure the smooth running of the project.

Life Design Intervention

First Stage: Defining the Problem and Identifying What the Client Hopes to Achieve Through the Intervention

Initial Research Project

The author's coresearcher (Dr. Maisha Molepo) and our coworkers initially worked in a number of schools focusing on the students and teachers. Parents, psychologists, and other health professionals involved with the learners were included to develop a joint strategy. Our main aim was to design a blueprint for career counseling in (South) Africa that could help us answer the crucial questions posed in the introductory section of this chapter. More specifically, we hoped to implement the latest developments in career counseling for the benefit of everyone and not just a select few. To this end, we endeavored to help teachers and learners narrate their life stories (narratability) so that they could draw on these stories (biographicity) when life imposed change and related challenges on them.

The Follow-Up Project

In the research project described above (sponsored by the May and Stanley Smith Charitable Trust and the National Research Foundation), we endeavored to exemplify transformation (primary value) in the new democratic South Africa through our research on career counseling in particular. After the initial research project had run its course – having experienced firsthand the extreme poverty levels in the region and especially after discussions with the headmistress – we decided to engage in humanitarian activities to alleviate the poverty and help the school generate employment opportunities for the community at large. In other words, we attempted to instill in the people the courage and skills needed to create holding environments for their communities. To this end, we established a vegetable garden, facilitated the distribution of clothing and technical equipment, and raised funds for clothing and shoe projects (secondary values).

During the first stage of the project (constructing a working alliance), we worked mainly with the headmistress and her staff and then with other project members in an attempt to clarify understanding of the challenge (problem) facing the community. We explained that the community was the architect of its life but that we would collaborate and co-construct a future and codesign a life for its members. In other words, the idea of co-constructing a working alliance was established and "unpacked." Aims agreed upon included dealing with the challenges posed by the community's dire socioeconomic situation, clarifying the different roles of community members, and arriving at a mutual understanding of what it meant to be useful to ("help") the community.

Second Stage: Exploring and Mapping the Current System of Subjective Identity Forms

During the second stage (Guichard, 2005), we asked the project members to reflect on the connection between the community members (distance from mainstream city life, luxuries, and opportunities; poor environment; surviving without support structures; having to adapt to trying circumstances) and their desire to achieve a better quality of life. Community members' experiences, expectations, actions and interactions, relationships with others, and future anticipations were discussed (Savickas et al., 2009). It emerged that community members' expectations were shaped by their background, and a profound disconnect seemed to exist between their identity at the time and their desired identity.

Third Stage: Broadening Perspectives, Discovering and Reauthoring, Reorganizing, Revising and Revitalizing Stories

During the third stage, the community's life story (a story of extreme poverty, and feelings of desperation, suffering, being forgotten and exclusion) was narrated to project members (based on the data obtained during Sessions 1 and 2) and written up. It was crucial at this stage to rekindle hope in the community, and we took pains to ensure that the community did not see itself as a failure, a victim, or backward. We encouraged community members to realize their assets and strengths and to consider their weaknesses as potential strengths. In other words, we attempted to turn what had been implicit into something explicit. By focusing on the rediscovery of hope and reauthoring of the community's story, reorganization, revision, and revitalization of the community's collective life story were achieved.

Fourth Stage: Placing the Problem in the New Story and Putting It Into the New Perspective

During the fourth stage, reinterpretation of the community's situation presented an exciting new perspective and twist in the plot: Reconfirmation of the community's ability to realize its desired identity – namely, to become a beacon of hope and a center of excellence and to serve as an inspiration and a source of food, among other things, for community members.

Various assets and support structures were identified ("discovered") in community life. Overwhelming support was shown by community members for a food gardening project as a feature of our life design project. This project gave the community hope, as community members had been trying to establish something along these lines for years. The headman of the village, who had also been a key player in the construction of the school, gave his full support to the project. Sufficient human capital and capacity as well as the will to initiate poverty alleviation projects were available. Community members could be empowered to (re)construct themselves and restore their sense of self and establish a preferred identity: that of a community working together to redefine and redesign their collective lives and to move from hopelessness to hope.

Fifth Stage: Specifying Activities to Actualize the Established Identity

During the fifth stage, the community members and the counsellors decided on ways of actualizing the envisaged, co-constructed life design strategy. We agreed to work on reinforcing the community's capacity by finding sponsors for a vegetable garden, a shoe and clothing project, and a bread oven project. Our aim was to enable community members to take active charge of their future instead of passively accepting their fate. The initial aims were revisited and overall self-reflection facilitated. In a nutshell: We engaged the community in a number of activities related to the possible self it had narrated. An overarching plan was crafted, and various activities outlined to promote purposeful action (Tiedeman, 1964). The following actions were planned and carried out successfully.

1. Funding was obtained from Nedcor Securities to start and maintain a vegetable garden and to launch a bread oven project. Momentum Lives made funding available for the purchase of shoes, clothing (school uniforms), and toys for all learners. Jopie de Beer and Company funded a soup kitchen.
2. The community supported the projects wholeheartedly and became actively involved. The vegetable garden was developed mainly by unemployed women, young people, and learners. The project gave the community renewed hope, as community members had been trying unsuccessfully to establish something similar for several years. Members of the community, teachers, and learners become involved without expecting anything in return.
3. The headman and councilor of the village – key players in the construction of the school – gave the vegetable garden project their full support and undertook to see this project, and other projects, through to fruition and thereby make a socioeconomic contribution to the community. They would also demonstrate the meaning of resilience to former, current, and future school learners.
4. The headmistress (Ms. Masehela) agreed to oversee all activities including the start-up and long-term management of the garden as well as the involvement of learners, parents and others.
5. Implements such as gardening tools were purchased and used, and a bread oven project was started. Other commodities such as shoes, school clothing, and toys were purchased and given to learners. Permaculture training was provided, and plant materials were purchased. Indigenous trees were planted around the schoolyard and near the school buildings to promote a cool/mild microclimate to mediate the summer heat. Loaves of bread and fresh produce were made available to community members, including learners and their parents, the unemployed, indigent residents and the nearby clinic.

Sixth Stage: Short-, Medium-, and Long-Term Follow-Up and Quality Assurance

As recommended by Savickas et al. (2009), meeting resolutions were studied, and additional advice and help given as and when necessary. Community members were requested to peruse the co-constructed plan of action (drawn up by the research team and themselves) on an ongoing basis and confirm that it was still feasible. Through a collaborative process, all stakeholders helped co-construct chapters in the community's life story through past and present life experiences that encompassed a variety of life roles. We, the researchers, were not seen as experts who could solve all the community's problems. We acted merely as mediators, facilitators, and codesigners of a better life for the community.

In 2009, the school was congratulated by the then minister of education, Ms. Naledi Pandor, for achieving the highest pass rate in the region (Pandor, 2009). The project is still running smoothly today, 8 years after its inception. Clearly, the venture gave the community hope and a vision for the future. Since the project was not experimental by nature, there was no intention to "prove" its success. However, qualitative results confirm its usefulness and effectiveness. Assessment took place in a number of ways:

1. The majority of learners in the sample initially completed the Career Interest Profile (Maree, 2006), the Rothwell-Miller Interest Blank (Hall, Halstead, & Taylor, 1992), life stories, lifelines, genograms, and miscellaneous narrative questionnaires. They also regularly participated in role-play exercises and in in-depth interviews.
2. The majority of teachers in the sample initially completed life stories, lifelines, genograms, and miscellaneous narrative questionnaires.

3. After each session, the teachers and learners answered a number of open-ended questions aimed at assessing their perceptions of the intervention anonymously. In addition, in-depth interviews were conducted with community members on an on-going basis to get their opinions of, and comments on, the project.

It has to be reiterated that traumatized and impoverished research contexts are not conducive to optimal life story counseling. What clearly emerged is that the approach to (career) counseling discussed here yields extremely promising results (an inductive data analysis approach was followed to identify a number of themes and subthemes from participants' responses to the following question: How did you experience the sessions? See Tables 16.1 and 16.2). Judging by this feedback, the project was highly successful and made a positive difference in many people's lives.

Table 16.1
Summary of themes and subthemes that emerged from teachers' and parents' reflective comments about the project (inductive analysis)

Subthemes	Examples of participants' responses:
Theme 1: Experience of presentation	
Positive nature of presentation	It was wonderful to get positive information.
Too little time	It is a pity that we didn't have more time! I could have participated for many more hours.
Practical nature	Appreciated the practical steps to better myself and others.
Theme 2: Personal benefits experienced	
Gained insight	Keep on doing this. It was insightful – an eye opener!
Realized that growth is needed	I now realize how much growth still is necessary in my own life.
Gained self-knowledge	Helped us get to know ourselves better.
Instilled a sense of future orientation	I loved the sessions about ways to handle my uncertainty and stress about the future.
Experienced a sense of being inspired	Very interesting and inspirational.
Added chapters to the own life story	I enjoyed it a lot, learned a lot about myself, and I can now only write a more interesting own life story.
Theme 3: Experience of benefit to the community	
Job creation	Creating jobs in this impoverished part of the world is so important. I hope the project will last forever.
Contributed to rewriting the life story of the community	I am inspired to once again try to help learners but also my community to rewrite their life stories.
Experienced collaboration at all levels	I am amazed to see people work together to reach a common goal. The project has touched the lives of the entire community and not only the school.

Table 16.2
Summary of themes and subthemes that emerged from learners' reflective comments about the project (inductive analysis)

Subthemes	Examples of participants' responses
Theme 1: Personal benefits experienced	
Broadened the learner's horizons	It was an amazing course. The sessions really opened my mind.
Gained self-knowledge	I've learned to get to know myself so much better.
Instilled a sense of future orientation	The sessions were very interesting and an eye opener regarding our careers in the future.
Experienced a sense of being inspired	I am inspired because I have something to work for.
Experienced a sense of self-efficacy	Thanks for helping us understand that we can now guide ourselves.
Received guidance	Thank you for encouraging, counselling and also guiding us through this course.
Received career counseling	It was very enriching. The information on other career choices than the ones we know about was informative. The information about ourselves and careers and what qualifications we need means a lot.
Felt respected	You gave us total respect.
Experienced a holding environment	When stepping in the hall I was scared about what lay ahead, but the security that came from the tone of your voice, calmed me down.
Theme 2: Experiences of benefit to the community	
Contributed to rewriting the life story of the community	I look forward to applying my knowledge and skills in the community.
Experienced a sense of *ubuntu* (connectedness)	I have learnt what makes us human and that others must also benefit from what we do.

Recommendations

First, it should be realized that governments, regardless of where they are in the world and in spite of their often huge investment in social development, will never be able to reach all the citizens in their countries. Second, "ordinary" people should accept the responsibility of helping impoverished communities access services, capital, food, and other basic needs (Jansen, 2006). Third, every attempt should be made to instill hope in the hearts and minds of all people, not just a select few. Fourth, psychologists in general should acquaint themselves with the basic principles of new developments in career counseling (such as life design) and implement these principles whenever possible.

In summary: What is needed is action. Movement forward. All the talking in the world will amount to nothing unless action plans are implemented and properly monitored. Despite predictions that Africa is on its way to redeeming itself and becoming a global power (e.g., references to an African Renaissance and Africa's becoming an economic powerhouse in the next 50 years), there is no good reason to believe that the situation will improve in the years to come unless ordinary people take the lead and actually make the changes themselves. In the words of Mother Teresa: "Do not wait for leaders; do it alone, person to person." The motivation or desire to do something means little as does promising or taking a decision to work (harder) (Krieshok, Black, & McKay, 2009). Intention and action have to be merged (Polkinghorne, 1992). All of us should start contributing to redesigning the lives of billions of people globally – politicians, professionals, nonprofessionals, employers, and employees. Sufficient resources and goodwill exist to secure a better life for all.

Conclusion

What the community achieved with this project is remarkable. Authentic construction occurred when the community reauthored and gave its story a future orientation. A new reality was created through dialogue between community members and ourselves. Deconstruction helped us unpack the stories so that they could be seen from different perspectives. During the project, we were repeatedly confronted with the truth that survival comes first and then education. Our assignment was basically to turn hurt and suffering into hope. We were also reminded that human behavior can be understood only in the context in which it occurs and that individuals define themselves and their environments (Brown & Brooks, 1996). We had to accept the reality of abject poverty and relinquish preconceived ideas of how best to intervene. Instead, we had to draw on the insight of community members themselves into the best way to redesign the life of the community. We moved from gathering information to generating experience through life stories as a team.

Through the life design intervention, we attempted to increase career adaptability by moving from simple advice for decision making to professional co-construction of a more holistic life design. Throughout the project, personal stories were uncovered, and the collective life (re)designed. Our focus was on strategies for survival and the dynamics of coping. The (re)designing of lives entailed the transformation of functionaries from pastor to auditor, beggar to caretaker, unemployed women to chefs, jobless vagrant to baker, headmistress to businessperson (who meticulously submitted timely audited reports), and educator to researcher-practitioner.

To expedite the project and the process of (re)designing the life of the community, we involved many other stakeholders to help us construct a future for the community. Experiencing first hand the extent to which counseling often occurs far from controlled conditions (Savickas et al., 2009), we constantly sought to help the community become more responsive to change and to increase the four dimensions of career adaptability – namely, concern, control, curiosity, and confidence (Savickas et al., 2009). Through the project, job opportunities were created, and emerging entrepreneurs supported. Community members and the research team were offered the opportunity to (re)design the collective lives and life stories of community members from past and present experiences. We experienced the truth of the words "people cannot be separated from their environments" and consequently emphasized personal agency and authoring of the community's story.

The focus in the community has shifted to its ongoing construction and reconstruction of subjective and multiple realities (Savickas et al., 2009). We are therefore striving to forecast emerging stable configurations of variables (Dauwalder, 2003). Research efforts should also be aimed at relieving poverty through advances in science. The overriding aim should be to break the vicious cycle of poor and disadvantaged, inadequate support at school and in society in general, leading to inappropriate and/or inadequate study opportunities, and, ultimately, inadequate realization of personal potential or self-construction (including failure to find suitable employment and to make a meaningful contribution to society at large). A key criterion for evaluating the success of research endeavors is whether it impacts positively on, and improves the living conditions of, poor people. If it does not, the research cannot be considered successful.

This chapter concludes with the sharing of the following remarkable story within a story. In 2007, during the initial stage of the project, the headmistress, Ms. Masehela (who had already obtained a master's degree in education management), indicated her wish to enroll in a doctoral degree program at the University of Pretoria. Regrettably, her initial efforts at enrolling were not supported by "administrative functionaries." The author discussed the issue with the then dean of the Faculty of Education, Prof. Jonathan Jansen, who immediately facilitated her enrollment into a doctoral program. In April 2012, Dr. Masehela received her doctorate from the same university. She had succeeded in adding an inspiring new chapter to her evolving life story. In her own words: "I sincerely thank Prof. Maree who encouraged me to pursue my study. His visit to our school in one of the remotest rural areas of Limpopo and his conscientiousness and timeous follow-ups encouraged me to embark on this study. He remains my role model. I also wish to thank his family, his son Anton in particular, for the care, love, prayers and support during the trying times of my studies" (Masehela, 2011, p. iv).

Acknowledgements

I wish to thank Nedcor Securities, Momentum Lives, and Jopie de Beer and Co. for sponsoring components of this ground-breaking project. Mr. Jean du Plessis (managing director of Nedcor Securities), Ms. Elize Gouws (Momentum Lives) and Dr. Jopie de Beer are especially thanked for their help in securing funding for the project. I also thank all others involved in the project for their cooperation, including Trees for Africa. I hope a blueprint has been provided for similar projects, not only across the country but elsewhere in the world as well. Dr. Masehela, in particular, deserves commendation for her role in bringing hope and meaning to the lives of so many people.

References

Alika, H. I., & Egbochuku, E. O. (2009). Vocational interest, counselling, socio-economic status and age as correlated of re-entry of girls into schools in Edo state. *Edo Journal of Counselling, 2*, 9–16. http://doi.org/10.4314/ejc.v2i1.52649

Alston, P. (2005). Ships passing in the night: The current state of the human rights and development debate seen through the lens of the Millennium Development Goals. *Human Rights Quarterly, 27*, 755–829. http://doi.org/10.1353/hrq.2005.0030

Anan, K. (2000). *Secretary General's address to the General Assembly on the Millennium Development Goals.* New York, NY: United Nations.

Blustein, D. L., Schultheiss, D. E., & Flum, H. (2004). Toward a relational perspective of the psychology of careers and working: A social constructionist analysis. *Journal of Vocational Behavior, 64*, 423–440. http://doi.org/10.1016/j.jvb.2003.12.008

Brown, D., & Brooks, L. (1996). *Career choice and development* (3rd ed.). San Francisco, CA: Jossey-Bass.

Campbell, C., & Ungar, M. (2004a). Constructing a life that works: Part 1: Blending postmodern family therapy and career counseling. *The Career Development Quarterly, 53*, 16–27. http://doi.org/10.1002/ j.2161-0045.2004.tb00652.x

Campbell, C., & Ungar, M. (2004b). Constructing a life that works: Part 2: An approach to practice. *The Career Development Quarterly, 53*, 28–40. http://doi.org/10.1002/j.2161-0045.2004.tb00653.x

Dauwalder, J. P. (2003). Quality in educational and vocational guidance at the beginning of the 21st century: Some introductory statements. In J. P. Dauwalder, R. Kunz, & J. Renz (Eds.), *Quality development in vocational counselling and training* (pp. 22–25). Zürich, Switzerland: SVB.

Duarte, M. E. (2009). The psychology of life construction. *Journal of Vocational behaviour, 75*, 259–266. http://doi.org/10.1016/j.jvb.2009.06.009

Duarte, M. E. (2010, July). *Restructuring career counseling: Objectives and instruments.* Paper presented at the 27th International Congress of Applied Psychology, Melbourne, Australia.

Guichard, J. (2005). Life-long self-construction. *International Journal for Educational and Vocational Guidance, 5*, 111–124. http://doi.org/10.1007/s10775-005-8789-y

Guichard, J. (2009). Self-constructing. *Journal of Vocational Behavior, 75*, 251–258. http://doi.org/10.1016/j.jvb.2009.03.004

Hall, B. A., Halstead, M. E., & Taylor, T. R. (1992). *Manual for the administration of the Rothwell-Miller Interest Blank.* Pretoria, South Africa: HSRC.

Hartung, P. J. (2011). Career construction theory and practice: Structure, strategies, stories, and style. In J. G. Maree (Ed.), *Shaping the story: A guide to facilitating narrative counselling* (pp. 52–62). Rotterdam, The Netherlands: Sense.

Hartung, P. J. (2013). Career construction counselling. In A. Di Fabio & J. G. Maree (Eds.), *Psychology of career counselling: New challenges for a new era* (pp. 15–28). Hauppauge, NY: Nova Science.

Jansen, J. D. (2006). *Press release: At the opening of the Seroka Clinic, Limpopo.*

Krieshok, T. S., Black, M. D., & McKay, R. A. (2009). Career decision making: The limits of rationality and the abundance of non-conscious processes. *Journal of Vocational Behavior, 75*, 75–290. http://doi.org/10.1016/j.jvb.2009.04.006

Lopez Levers, L. L., May, M., & Vogel, G. (2011). Research on counseling in African settings. In E. Mpofu (Ed.), *Counseling people of African ancestry* (pp. 57–74). New York, NY: Cambridge University Press.

Maree, J. G. (2006). *The Career Interest Profile* (Version 1). Randburg, South Africa: Jopie van Rooyen.

Maree, J. G. (2013). *Counselling for career construction: Connecting life themes to construct life portraits: Turning pain into hope.* Rotterdam, The Netherlands: Sense.

Masehela, B. M. M. (2011). *Exploring strategies for the prevention of sexual abuse at schools* (Unpublished doctoral dissertation). University of Pretoria, South Africa.

Mbeje, M. (2013). *Africa should be on equal footing with the world.* Retrieved from http://www.sabc.co.za/news/a/2cfc16804f8f80d5b550f70b5d39e4bb/Africa-should-be-on-equal-footing-with-the-world-20130905

Metz, A. J., & Guichard, J. (2009). Vocational psychology and new challenges. *The Career Development Quarterly, 57*, 310–318. http://doi.org/10.1002/j.2161-0045.2009.tb00116.x

Millennium Development Goals. (2000). Retrieved from http://www.un.org/millennium/declaration/ares552e.pdf

Millennium Development Goals Report 2011. (2011). Retrieved from http://www.un.org/millenniumgoals/

Millennium Development Goals 2015. (2012). Retrieved from http://www.un.org/millenniumgoals/bkgd.shtml

Neimeyer, R. A. (2004). *Constructivist therapy* [DVD]. Washington, DC: American Psychological Association.

Nwonwu, F. (2009). The rise of food prices and the challenge of development in Africa. *Africa Insight, 38*, 44–58.

Pandor, N. (2009, May). *Alleviating poverty thorough science.* Keynote paper presented at NSTF Awards, Johannesburg, South Africa.

Polkinghorne, D. E. (1992). Postmodern epistemology of practice. In S. Kvale (Ed.), *Psychology and postmodernism* (pp. 145–166). Newbury Park, CA: Sage.

Rohlfing, J. E., Nota, L., Ferrari, L., Soresi, S., & Tracey, T .J. G. (2012). Relation of occupational knowledge to career interests and competence perceptions in Italian children. *Journal of Vocational Behaviour, 81*, 330–337. http://doi.org/10.1016/j.jvb.2012.08.001

Savickas, M. L. (2005). The theory and practice of career construction. In S. D. Brown & R.W. Lent (Eds.), *Career development and counseling: Putting theory and research to work* (pp. 42–70). Hoboken, NJ: Wiley.

Savickas, M. L. (2008). Helping people choose jobs: A history of the guidance profession. In J. A. Athanasou & R. Van Esbroeck (Eds.), *International handbook of career guidance* (pp. 97–113). Dordrecht: Springer.

Savickas, M. L. (2009, April). *The essentials of life design counselling*. Invited public lecture, University of Johannesburg, South Africa.

Savickas, M. L. (2010, July). *Life Designing: Framework and introduction*. Paper presented at the 27th International Congress of Applied Psychology, Melbourne, Australia.

Savickas, M. L. (2011a). *Career counseling*. Washington, DC: American Psychological Association.

Savickas, M. L. (2011b). New questions for vocational psychology: Premises, paradigms, and practices. *Journal of Career Assessment, 19*, 251–258. http://doi.org/10.1177/1069072710395532

Savickas, M. L., Nota, L., Rossier, J., Dauwalder, J.-P., Duarte, M. E., Guichard, J., … van Vianen, A. E. M. (2009). Life designing: A paradigm for career construction in the 21st century. *Journal of Vocational Behavior, 75,* 239–250. http://doi.org/10.1016/j.jvb.2009.04.004

Schultheiss, D. E. (2011). Career, migration and the life CV: A relational cultural analysis. *Journal of Vocational Behavior, 78,* 334–341. http://doi.org/10.1016/j.jvb.2011.03.013

Sharf, R.S. (2010). *Applying career development theory to counseling* (5th ed.). Belmont, CA: Brooks/Cole.

Soresi, S., & Nota, L. (2007). L'orientamento come risorsa di prevenzione [Guidance as a preventive resource]. In S. Soresi (Ed.), *Orientamento alle scelte: rassegne, ricerche, strumenti ed applicazioni* (pp. 306–313). Firenze, Italy: Giunti-Organizzazioni Speciali.

Tap, P. (Ed.). (1980). *Identité individuelle et personnalisation* [Individual identity and personalization]. Toulouse, France: Privat.

Tiedeman, D. V. (1964). The cultivation of career in vocational development through guidance-in-education. *Harvard Studies in Career Development*, No. 29.

Trees for Africa. (2006). *Assessment report for Momentum. Rasekgala senior secondary school.* Johannesburg, South Africa: Author.

Van Esbroeck, R., Tibos, K., & Zaman, M. (2005). A dynamic model of career choice development. *International Journal for Educational and Vocational Guidance, 5*, 5–18. http://doi.org/10.1007/s10775-005-2122-7

Vanhalakka-Ruoho, M. (2010). Relational aspects in career and life-designing of young people. *International Journal of Educational and Vocational Guidance, 10*, 109–123. http://doi.org/10.1007/s10775-010-9178-8

Winslade, J. (2011). Constructing a career narrative through the care of the self. In J. G. Maree (Ed.), *Shaping the story: A guide to facilitating narrative counselling* (pp. 52–62). Rotterdam, The Netherlands: Sense.

Wright, C., & Ndong-Jafta, A. T. (2007). *A human rights-based approach to education for all*. New York, NY: United Nations.

Chapter 17
Cultural Perspectives on Life Design

Hsiu-Lan S. Tien
Department of Educational Psychology and Counseling, National Taiwan Normal University, Taipei City, Taiwan

Introduction

Contemporary career counseling is greatly influenced by the reality that diversity and multiculturalism are important factors when we interact with clients. The meaning of career in traditional Eastern society might be different from that in modern Western society. However, there might be similarities when we explore the meaning of career life in the current societies. In this chapter, the meaning of career life from the angles of Western and Easter societies will be reviewed. Traditional versus modern cultural perspectives will also be considered. We also take into account gender issues when we discuss life design competences.

The Meaning of Life Design in Modern Society

In our global, rapidly changing society, we observe significant change in the nature of work and the meaning of career. A century ago, the person–environment match was the main goal of vocational guidance (Parsons, 1909). To achieve this goal, inventories were developed to help individuals understand themselves. Career maturity was assessed by noting which career development tasks had been accomplishment (Super, 1954). Systems for classification of work were also developed for the purpose of person–environment fit (Holland, 1959; Roe, 1959). Decades later, fitting work into life (Richardson, 1996), career as story (Cochran, 1997; Jepsen, 1990), career construction (Savickas, 2005), and life design (Savickas, 2012; Savickas et al., 2009) are the terms used to explicate the meaning of career counseling.

Among these definitions and concepts of career development, Super used the term *life stage* instead of *career stage*. His concepts of life-span and life space even more clearly and broadly defined the meaning of career development. Recently, Savickas et al. (2009) has proposed a new life design approach to describe career self-construction in a changing social and cultural environment and developing career intervention. Collin and Guichard (2011) have also emphasized that the core concern of career development has become the continuous construction of self and life design. *Life design* is therefore a better term to describe career counseling. The main task of vocational guidance is not simply to help individuals find a job. The broadest meaning of *career* is a life-long process of learning and working. *Life design* is more suitable than *career planning* to describe personal-career development in modern society.

Many varieties of counseling activities need to be designed to assist individuals to develop the necessary skills and life attitudes needed to face the many types of transitions which occur at various stages of career development. *Life design competence* is a good phrase to describe the ability to construct a career. In addition, career development cannot be viewed independently from social context and public policy. Savickas et al. (2009) remind us of the important question when we provide services to individuals: "How may individuals best design their own lives in the human society in which they live?" It's obvious that multicultural issues arising from social environments are important when individuals assess opportunities in a multicultural society.

Multicultural Perspective in the Life Design Paradigm

Cultural pluralism has had an important impact on counseling, as has the life design paradigm. Life design is an important approach for an individual to create a meaningful life within the societies in which they live. It is an approach of self-construction (Guichard, 2005). Therefore, it's important for career professionals to keep multicultural perspectives in mind. It is also important for individuals in a global society to be aware of multicultural perspectives in order to competently develop the career and lifestyle they prefer. According to Savickas (2002), the career story and life themes we construct are not individualist constructions. Rather, the meaning given to those constructs are always constructed within the culture in which we interact with others. Career stories and life themes change across time and space as we have new experiences within a social context. Therefore, we should pay attention to the cultural context in which the individual exists.

Since the process and content of life design is tied culture factors related to life design are connected to social structure. As societies have transitioned from traditional to modern, the social structure has evolved from industry-focused to economy-focused and then to the postmodern world. The meaning of career guidance has changed from traditional narrowly focused vocational training to counseling for life design. This approach focuses on the dialogue between a counselor and an individual in certain social contexts. "Liquid modernity" (Guichard, 2012) is a great metaphor to describe the diversity, flexibility, and uncertainty in current societies around the world. The process and content of liquid modernity are changeable but to some degree tied to individual value as are self-construction and life design. In Eastern societies, self-development includes both individual self and collective self. The internal viewpoint is usually neglected in Eastern societies. For the external viewpoint of roles and stages, the role of "student" is the main one that individuals play in their early years in Asian societies. Youths focus attention on examinations for high school, university, and even master's and doctoral programs. It is only in the beginning of university that youths have a chance to think about their career future. While preparing for university entrance examinations, they seek information about the world of work because they have to select a major and department when they register for the exam. The main attention is on "how to get into the top college programs" and not "what kind of career I am actually interested in." Multicultural perspectives of career and life design provide helpful information when we consider the issue of life design globally.

Scope of Culture Issues Discussed in This Chapter

It is quite clear that Eastern societies in countries such as China, Japan, Korea, India, Singapore, and Taiwan focus more on students' learning experiences. The students' main task is to attend a first-rate college or even graduate school. Only when in college, do individuals have the opportunity to focus on the primary career they wish to pursue. For at-risk students, they might need to think about what to do to earn a living but not about eternal life meaning. When youths have an opportunity to explore life meaning, they know that their careers will not only allow them to earn a living but also will add meaning to their lives. Until then they have little chance to reflect on what they would really love to do to shape their personal life meaning.

In Asian societies, it is also possible that a career choice is based on others' expectations, especially for those who attend a medical school or teachers college. Family ties are important, and individuals with excellent levels of performance usually comply with parental expectations. However, they might not actually love to be a doctor or nurse, even if they do have the necessary potential and ability.

In this chapter, the main focus is on discussing multicultural issues in life design. The general traditional Eastern and modernized Western cultures, instead of specific cultures in different countries, will be the main focus for discussion of life design competences. This means that we will focus on global, diverse viewpoints rather than on specific multicultural issues in certain countries or areas.

Traditional Cultures and Ways of Life in Eastern Versus Western Societies

The Process of Life Design From a Multicultural Perspective

Life design is a long-term trajectory process, both personally and professionally. There are a variety of peaks and nadirs in the career development process. Role balance, especially between family, community, and workplace, is always an important issue in this process. From the traditional Eastern viewpoint, people believe that an individual's career choice is ultimately determined by one's destiny. You can make a choice, but the final, long-term results might not be under your control. One cannot control everything. In traditional societies, it is always your fate to be in a certain vocational field. It is, to some degree, similar to Krumboltz's (2009) idea of happenstance. In the modern world, adolescents are educated to be more independent and have their own opinions about future decision making. They are taught to encounter opportunities and take advantage of them. Compared with young adults in Western society, adolescents in Eastern society are more likely to sense the importance of interpersonal harmony and put less emphasis on competition for personal achievement. For coping with future uncertainty, traditional, conservative individuals hope to be well prepared and ready for challenges. Therefore, social contexts influence the individual's trajectories in this long-term process, including personal traits development, information exploration, identity development, decision making, dealing with barriers encountered, coping efficacy, adaptability, and adjustment, etc.

Cultural differences are important and need to be taken into account in the counseling process. For example, when making career decisions, students in Eastern society tend to listen to the opinions of family and parents. Students in Western society tend to be independent and rely on personal preferences. In Eastern society, kids always listen to parents' opinions; while in Western society, parents tend to respect a kid's decision after they discuss the decision with them. Asians, with collectivist cultures, emphasize filial piety and family cohesion (Salili, Chiu, & Lai, 2001). However, Westerners are more individualistic and emphasize the balance between giving and taking. Asians tend to feel responsible to their family and community, while Westerners tend to give more attention to personal desires and needs (Eaton & Dembo, 1997). With regard to self-efficacy beliefs, Eastern adolescents tend to be lower than Western adolescents, but they usually perform better, especially in mathematics. For career decision-making self-efficacy, Eastern adolescents are more collectively oriented and their self-efficacy development may be inhibited; however, Western adolescents are more individually oriented, and the society tends to foster self-efficacy (Mau, 2000). These different cultural perspectives shape different processes of career and life design, especially for females. The process of life design for females always emphasizes the balance between family and work. Males, on the other hand, are traditionally expected to have successful careers. Therefore, during the process of career counseling framed by life design, counselors need to be sensitive to the effects caused by these cultural differences.

Similarities in the Life Design Paradigm Among Different Cultures

Although the differences in the life design process among different cultures are quite obvious, we can still find similarities. For example, people all over the world experience boundarylessness and protean careers. Even those who work from home can still feel the effect of the world. Their lifestyle might be more flexible and active compared with the lifestyle in traditional societies. This is the same for both Westerns and Eastern societies. Hall (2012) mentions that "the picture of stable employment and associated organizational careers is fading" (p. 257). This is also happening in Asian society. Nowadays we experience monumental shifts in the workplace. Employers cannot guarantee any employee's stable place in the globalized world. In addition to professional skills and knowledge, we need to gain the necessary soft skills and relationships to create our own opportunities and shape our personal meaning in life, no matter where we are.

Let's take a specific example: the academic career. Although the patterns of academic careers in Western society are quite different from those in Asia, all academics need to be creative and contribute to the world. Wellman and Spreitzer (2011) have described three crafting strategies to elaborate the meaning of an academic career. These strategies can be applied in both Western and Eastern societies. The three crafting strategies are cognitive crafting, professional crafting, and relational crafting. We need to enlarge our perspective of self-contribution to the world, and benefit society to help it flourish, through professional knowledge, while fostering high-quality connections with colleagues and others. Similarities among different cultures for the life design process are actually obvious: shaping life meaning, making harmonious connections, and facing globalization.

Varieties of the Life Design Pattern Within the Same Culture

However, when counselors interact with others, we have to notice the subtle differences between individuals from the same culture. For example, individuals who would all love to own a tiny coffee shop might have different motivations from each other. Some of them would love to interact with customers through the shop management, some would enjoy decorating the store and making it attractive for artistic customers similar to themselves, and some are curious about types of coffee and would love to investigate those different types. The same occupation, therefore, might mean different things for different individuals. Metaphor can be a technique applied in career counseling, but when we apply it, we have to pay attention to the subtle differences, even among clients who are from the same cultural background.

Actually in the current society, we have found that many young adolescents are Westernized because they have been raised and educated by Westernized parents. In the current Eastern society, fast food is popular, modernized clothing styles are mainstream, city buildings are even higher than those in Western cities, and the lifestyle is similar to that in Western society. Office workers are even busier and more efficient than those in Western society. Overstrained workers are more common in manufacturing, business, scientific research, and medical fields comparing with decades ago. Compared with Western society, the lifestyle in Eastern society is lacking in leisure travel and regular exercise. However, in Eastern society, there are still some different patterns in the lifestyle. Those who emphasize making a contribution to society may spend much more time in community activities. Those who emphasize family and individualized life put more energy into time with family members and personal development. Individual differences can be found within a culture, no matter whether Western or Eastern. In the global world, no matter how similar we are, there are some differences; no matter how different we are, we can still find similarities. Multicultural differences are globalized; modern cultural similarities are also globalized. Similarities and differences actually exist everywhere in the world.

Gender Issues in Career Development and Life Design in Eastern Societies

Characteristics of Female Versus Male Career Issues and Life Design

In Eastern countries, women's participation in the work force has increased during recent decades. However, differences between the career development process for women and men are still quite evident. Variables such as sex-role stereotyping, vocational and educational aspirations, values, work attitudes, and combining career and family remain inherently more complex for women than for men. Because women still assume most of the responsibility for child rearing and homemaking, the career decision-making process for women includes a component that continues to be outside the consideration of men (O'Brien & Fassinger, 1993). These career issues are very salient for women.

In recent years, the percentage of women in traditionally male-dominated professions has increased. However, women still consider a narrower range of career options than men do. The reasons for this are related to career-related barriers, which might or might not be perceived by the individual, especially in Eastern society (Tien, Wang, & Liu, 2009). In a study by Swanson and Tokar (1991), although the main effect for gender was not significant, they still concluded that some gender-related differences in barriers were present. For example, women accounted for almost all of the responses dealing with sacrificing career for children, child concerns, and role conflict. Men, on the other hand, were more likely to indicate financial concerns. The same situation is obvious in Eastern society (Tien, Wang, & Liu, 2009).

Similarly, a summary of the results from two studies (Slaney, 1980; Slaney & Brown, 1983) revealed that approximately 14% of women listed marriage and family pressure as their primary barriers as compared with 1% of men. It seems that social and interpersonal types of career barriers concern women more than men. In Eastern societies, similar concerns are evident (Tien, Lin, & Chen, 2005). Therefore, when we discuss gender differences in life design patterns, the family–work conflict is an important variable. Earning for the family, on the other hand, is a more important concern for men.

Nowadays in Eastern societies, women have begun to move into senior positions such as school principle, business manager, and government department leader. There is still very little empirical research on this. However, we can understand from practical observation that these professional women still encounter more barriers than their male counterparts. For example, it is hard for them to get involved in, and gain support from, informal networks with male peers. This may hinder their performance evaluations and promotion opportunities. The effect of a "chilly climate" for well-performing females may narrow their chances for career advancement.

Women and men follow different routes to get to the upper levels of the career ladder, even when they are in the same profession. Women in a male-dominated profession have to change in some way to fit into the culture in that work environment. They usually have to perform better than their male peers to prove they are excellent.

In addition, gender stereotyping is another obstacle when they have the same qualifications as their male peers related to a more advanced position. For example, a university president will hire a young man as center director instead of a young woman just because of concern about childcare issues if the young woman has young children, even if the young man also has little children. This is still an obvious issue in Asian societies.

Hoobler, Wayne, and Lemmon (2009) proposed a model related to bosses' perceptions of family–work conflicts and women's promotability. The results of a study of that model indicated that women's bosses perceived them as having greater family–work conflicts, although those women did not report more conflict than their male counterparts. These perceptual biases had a significant influence on the women's advancement. Biases like these are the source of the so-called chilly climate which women against the fulfillment of women's potential.

Female Career Development and Life Patterns in Terms of Traditional Versus Modern Societies

In addition to the simple question of gender, culture is an important issue interacting with gender, when we discuss an individual's career development in globalized societies. Traditionally, in Asian societies, women put more emphasis on marriage and family rather than on their professional careers. Child rearing and caring for parents are considered the responsibility of the woman. Women are expected to take care of parents-in-law instead of their own parents.

Nowadays, women have opportunities to ask for external assistance – for example, professional caregivers or community services – to share these tasks. Therefore, the main issues for women's career development in Eastern societies are not simple questions such as, what should I do? or "why should I work? Instead the issues for women are questions such as, what are the factors that affect my career advancement and accomplishment? and/or what is the meaning of my life? How can I create the life pattern I value?

Gender role boundaries are another issue faced by women. Traditionally the collective culture ensured that a women had to adhere closely to what was demanded of her as a woman (Triandis, 1998; Zuo & Bian, 2001). For example, women were to take care of children and their husband. Career advancement was less important than housework in a collective society. Her success on the corporate ladder would be seen as something for her personal achievement rather than for the family. However, a husband might claim his career success as fulfilling the male role and as a big family honor. Nowadays, there is considerable variation in how people respond to individualism and collectivism within cultures. The gender role boundary is ambiguous and flexible. Men and women are perceived as isolated selves. They have equal opportunity to pursue their personal goals, careers, and life patterns.

Traditionally, Super (1957) proposed seven career patterns for women which included stable homemaking, the conventional career pattern, stable working pattern, double-track career pattern, interrupted career pattern, unstable career pattern, and multiple trial pattern. In postmodern society, women have more chances to explore their self and construct their personal and professional identity. Life patterns are even more complicated. It might be hard to categorize different patterns of career lives. Most women work full-time, but some of them live with their husband and parents-in-law; some of them divorce or separate and, as working single mothers, take care of children; some of them work, take care of young children, and meet their husbands only during the weekend, because the husbands work in another city. Lifestyles are varied. In current society, most women prefer to live nearby to their parents-in-law. In such cases, female workers can receive support from the parents-in-law conveniently and also keep their own independent life, although they are married and have kids. Factors entering into decisions related to lifestyle are complicated. Women have to be as comprehensive as possible in the factors they take into consideration in order to create the lifestyle they prefer. Sometimes their preference is not the only consideration. They might put more emphasis on traditional responsibilities as a family caretaker. But career achievement, on the other hand, might be more important when they think about the meaning of life in designing a career.

Formation of Life Pattern and Career Construction for Women in the Postmodern Era

Collectivism and individualism, traditional and modern, feminine and masculine might each be opposite extremes in continua. But they are not necessarily contradictory to each other. A person can be anywhere on these continua at different stages of his or her life. Career process, characterized as individualistic and active, is actually an interactive process between an individual and a social environment, between individuals and others, and also between the individual and himself or herself. In this case, women and men are treated as equals. The formation of a life pattern would be free of concerns about gender discrimination and stereotypes. A narrative approach would be appropriate to help individuals become aware of their life design pattern. To be more specific, Savickas (2012) proposed a new paradigm which contains three important components: (1) constructing career through small stories; (2) deconstructing those stories and reconstructing them into an identity narrative and life portrait; and (3) co-constructing intentions that lead to the next episode in the real world.

Through sharing short stories in different life stages, people become aware of the meaning of those stories either gradually or suddenly. The most important part would be the sudden experience of "Oh! Now I know!" which is a kind of insight expressed by "Ah! Ha!" in Western society. Consistencies and similarities among those stories help individuals comprehend their personality, preferences, interpersonal relationships, values, abilities, etc. These components are important in the process of self-construction and life design.

Since narrative construction helps in a better understanding of life pattern, it's important for us to notice the social context in postmodern society. In the diverse cultures around the world, it is difficult to capture life and career meaning through the description of linear developmental stages. The minicycle (Super, 1957) within the linear life stages related to gender, culture, and the interaction between these two sensitive factors makes the issue of female career design even more complicated and female career design needs further discussion.

Personality is an important factor in determining how women will overcome career barriers. Lambert, Eby, and Reeves (2006) compared gender differences in the network system of white-collar job seekers. They found that a proactive personality was positively related to network intensity, which is an important resource for social support. In addition, awareness of bottlenecks and willingness to break through them is also important. Some women keep going and climb to the top of the ladder; others may choose to maintain the status quo so that they feel more comfortable.

However, women's rate of participation in the work force has increased everywhere in the world, especially in traditionally male-dominated professions. In postmodern society, women are even energized to think about the meaning of life through the balance of work, family, and other life roles. Women significantly underestimate their general learning, verbal, and spatial abilities. This is also supported in Betz's (1994) suggestion that one of the problems in women's career development is the underutilization of their abilities.

Gender issues are always important factors discussed in career development in traditional Eastern societies. Issues discussed include career barriers, self-efficacy, feeling of success, family-related factors, etc. The competence to balance personal and professional life is an important part of a women's life design, especially in Eastern society.

Moderation is an important principle in Chinese culture. Nothing will stay in any extreme forever. *Change* is always the *unchangeable* principle. For keeping balance among all aspects of life, moderation is a good principle. For example, Susan married when she was a doctoral student. As a wife, she needed to learn how to arrange her life schedule to balance her life as a doctoral student and a wife. She always feels disappointed when she needs to stop reading and prepare dinner for her husband. However, a positive approach to thinking about this would be that her role and responsibility as a wife stops her reading only temporarily. Switching from her role as a doctoral student to housework makes her life rich and varied. Too much reading would probably make her life boring. Responsibility for taking care of family might interrupt her research life as a scholar, but it also energizes it. Joyfulness as a mother, wife, and a research worker is then attainable and can be maintained for Susan. The content of life design is constructed through these stories; the meaning of life is deconstructed and reconstructed through components of the meanings involved in different contexts and with awareness and insight. To continue the balance between family and professional development, a woman needs to achieve moderation through the evaluation of her family's needs and the energies required by professional work.

Life Design Competences in Terms of Culture Perspectives

Personal Traits and Competences for Life Design in Terms of Multicultural Issues

In the modernized global society, the work environment has changed. Increased mobility, support from employers, and a dynamic vertical and horizontal interaction in the workplace are important. Kuijpers and Scheerens (2006) have categorized career competences into six areas: career development ability, reflection on capacities, reflection on motives, work exploration, career control, and networking. Tien (2009), regarding Chinese culture, asserted that career-coping behaviors could be categorized into six categories: physical comfort, self-efficacy, life-long learning, interpersonal relationships, family relationships, and spiritual and religious sensitivity. These categories of competences are consistent with the traditional three components of career guidance: self-exploration, world of work exploration, and true reasoning between person and the environment (Parsons, 1909). However, the competences from research studies are more specific. Networking and spirituality are parts that Parsons did not mention.

These competences, to some degree, might relate to an individual's personality traits. In a study by Tien et al. (2013), personality traits measured by the Big Five Personality Test (Goldberg & Somer, 2000) were significantly correlated with career self-efficacy, cognitive complexity, and career adaptability in an adult sample in Taiwan. Career adaptability (Savickas, 1997) includes four important components: concern, control, curiosity, and confidence. This is an important frame for competences and has been verified across different countries around the world. In addition to the four competences, cooperation has been suggested as the fifth component. To be more specific, within the atmosphere of collectivist cultures in Eastern society, people are more likely to stay in their work groups or organization, because networking has been established and makes them feel safe. People in Western individualistic cultures are more likely to change work groups or organizations. They are more likely to recognize opportunities and exhibit job mobility compared with individuals with collectivist orientation.

How to Build Career and Life Design Competences in Multicultural Societies

In Eastern society, people's traits related to career are different from in Western society. For example, extraverted people in Asia might be categorized as introverted in the West. Asians with low math self-efficacy in Eastern cultures may become highly efficacious in a Western context. In this part of the chapter, we focus on how to build life design competences from a multicultural perspective, more particularly for Eastern people in modernized Western societies.

Establish Informal Social Networking

To build career and life design competences, social networking would be important for individuals from a traditional Eastern cultural setting. Many people from Eastern cultures are excellent in professional development, but they are shy and nonassertive in social interaction occasions, especially in situations involving strangers. They probably perform very well in professional development. But when they interact with others, they are modest and do not show what they know. They think that others should already know what they can do if they are really an excellent and acknowledged professional worker. It should be recognized that informal social networks are important for an individual to establish an important support system in a multicultural society. So, attending a social hour whenever the opportunity arises is important. Some colleagues may have a chance to have lunch together. The informal talk during that lunch increases an important support system for when they need help personally or professionally. In the protean society, a boundaryless career emphasizes the importance of network relationships. Social capital relationships with colleagues, friends, and other associates can provide information needed for career opportunities. Many opportunities arise during informal meetings. A happenstance chance might be the turning point in one's career.

Integrate Personality and Soft Skills

Soft skills such as work ethics, communication skills, management ability, problem-solving skills, confidence, leadership ability and cooperative attitude, working under pressure, and learning from criticism are all important soft skills we need to learn in a multicultural world. All of these skills are, to a certain degree, related to personality. The process of personality exploration can be combined with knowledge of soft skills. Being aware of personality and soft skills not only increases one's career competence but also facilitates one's ability to achieve well-being in life. In modern society, soft skills will be needed to be competent in facing planned or accidental transitions.

Modesty is another characteristic of personality traits in Asian culture. However, in Western society, we need to keep records of our contributions and show those accomplishments to others in certain situations. These contributions are all facts and need to be honored. People will not know about your contributions if you do not give them the chance to know about them. Therefore, let people know what you can do appropriately in the proper situation, formally or informally. This is related to communication skills, an important soft skill in Western society. Personality and soft skills are actually interactive with each other. We can try to realize and integrate personal traits and soft skills.

Develop Cognitive Complexity

Cognitive complexity is related to one's intellectual performance. Individuals with higher degrees of thinking complexity can observe interpersonal interactions from multiple perspectives. It also helps an individual think in a deeper and broader way, which leads to the problems being solved. What is true about problem-solving skills as one of the soft skills might relate to this ability as well. In the modern world, we should try to remind ourselves to think in a more complex way, try to think from multiple angles, and think more thoroughly.

Be Aware of Your Career Beliefs

Career beliefs, a concept proposed by Krumboltz (1996) might contain hidden values and ideas that influence an individual's decision-making behavior, not only career decisions but also lifestyle choices. In traditional Chinese society, it is believed that women should stay at home and take care of all of the housework; men, on the other hand, should go out and earn for the whole family. If a woman adheres to this belief, she will probably spend much more time and energy on caring for her children and husband. She will reject opportunities for higher status at work because that would require additional time and energy, though she could also earn a higher salary. If a woman does not think in the traditional way, and instead she believes that men and women have the same obligations and responsibilities for the family, she will probably choose to balance work and family. In this example, we should notice that there is no right or wrong with regard to this belief. It is a personal choice. Different beliefs lead to different actions. Being aware of personal beliefs and possible results caused by the beliefs can help you make better decisions that fit your situation. Some women prefer to stay at home, and others prefer to compete for excellence and achievement. All lifestyles are equal in diversified multicultural societies.

Positive Attitude as Living Habits

Being optimistic is a positive attitude and a necessary habit in the new era. In a multicultural society, varieties of beliefs and styles are respected. To keep a harmonic atmosphere in one's personal and interpersonal life, a positive attitude is important. As we know, it is inevitable that we may encounter barriers during the process of career development. Positive thinking can help us turn the barriers into facilitators. Crisis in Chinese is "危" or "機." It means *dangerous* and *opportunities*. Barriers can be facilitators if we treat the barriers in a positive way. In ancient Chinese culture, it was said, "Crisis is also a kind of turn around." It can be an opportunity to make the crisis situation into something positive. The powers and energies for an individual to make a change are even stronger in a crisis situation.

Management of Physical Health and Leisure Activities

In addition to the above-mentioned competences, physical health is another important aspect we need to pay attention to for designing a quality life. For management of our physical health and leisure activities, we need to be good at time management. Asian people usually emphasize efficiency at work. They prefer to finish lots of work in a short time, and they can usually accomplish that. Is this behavior a good habit? They are so busy that they do not have time to think about the meaning of these behaviors, achievements, or work and lifestyle. We know that Western people usually have regular vacation plans. Many workers have what is called afternoon tea, during their work day. Mogilner (2010) has asserted that people who spend more time with friends are happier. Working hard and interacting less often with friends does not increase happiness. We have heard of many cases of overstretched workers in Taiwan. Most of workers there are willing to work hard. Regular physical exercise and leisure activities are necessary for career and life design.

In summary, these competences are important for career and life design in the postmodern world. However, we should note that varieties of competences are overlapping, and that integrating and applying those competences appropriately is even more important than ever. We call this metacompetence. This could be an issue for further research through the narrative approach.

Strategies for Providing Life Design Competences in Eastern Societies

In the previous session, we described competences and ways to build life design competences in Eastern society. In this section we provide a counseling framework from the counselor's viewpoint to train and then promote individual client's life design competences.

Basic Framework of Life Design Intervention Applied in Eastern Societies

The framework of life design intervention based on construction theory includes the process of construction, deconstruction, reconstruction, co-construction, and action (Savickas, 2012).

In Chinese culture, we have tried three intervention models based on the constructive narrative approach (Tien et al., 2009). The three interventions are (1) life theme construction counseling, (2) strength-centered career counseling, and (3) dream work. The purpose of the three intervention models was to increase people's psychological well-being. The results indicated that there were no significant differences between the three approaches in increasing individual's psychological well-being. All of the participants' posttest scores on psychological well-being increased after the interventions. The framework for each of the three intervention models will be introduced here.

Life Theme Construction Counseling

The life theme approach of career counseling permits a conceptualization of career counseling as a process of articulating a client's life theme (Savickas, 1995). More specifically, the method integrated the psychodynamic life theme model, Alfred Adler's lifestyle analysis model, and Holland's person–environment fit model. Counselors can then use the assessment information from the life theme approach to gain an understanding of life themes and career paths. The framework includes five specific steps: (1) The client tells the story they have brought, (2) the counselor listens carefully and reflects the life themes to the client, (3) the client thinks about the career problems encountered and examines the relationship between the life themes and the career problems, (4) the life themes are extended into the future and an examination is made of the important tasks the client wants or would like to finish, and (5) an attempt is made to create an action plan.

In Chinese culture, clients asking for help usually tell the counselor problems they have encountered and then wait for answers. They do not know that counseling will take time. In the process of counseling, it is important to let them know the structure of the counseling process. If they know that the first step is to state the problem and tell stories related to the problem, they will feel more comfortable about telling the stories. This step is consistent with what Savickas called "construction." In the deconstruction process, the counselor picks different pieces of the stories with the same or similar issue, the so-called life theme. The counselor then reflects the life themes related to the career problems to the client. This is the process of reconstruction. After this, clients with counselors co-construct new ideas, even insights into "who they are" and then create actions about "what they want to do" and "what they can do" next. Storytelling is an easy approach for Chinese people to follow. But they need clear directions and encouragement to tell more to the counselors. Structured facilitation and a warm attitude are important to make Eastern clients more comfortable.

Strength-Centered Career Counseling

The strength-centered approach is a pretty novel approach for Asians. It is not very typical. Asian parents usually scold kids for not doing well. If the kids perform well, they are glad but will not say any word about it. It seems that doing well is a child's obligation. Just like in the Olympic Game, a silver medal winner will feel ashamed of not winning the gold medal. Asian people need to be encouraged to think in a positive way. The strength-centered approach would be something new, and it is worth attempting in the context of Eastern culture. Clients usually feel discouraged at home or even at school because parents and teachers always ask for high scores and will scold the kids for not studying hard and getting higher scores. They need support from friends and counselors.

Strength-centered counseling was developed based on positive psychology of character strengths and virtues and social constructionist therapy (Wong, 2006). According to Peterson and Seligman (2004), character strengths can be distinguished from talents and abilities. Character strengths are usually relatively more malleable, require more effort and will, and fall within the moral domain of life. Gergen (1999) emphasizes the social constructionist view that the therapist and client participate in the co-creation of new meanings concerning clients' subjective experiences. Lopez and Kerr (2006) agree and advocate that in positive psychology we should co-create a new therapy by building on each others' work to help the clients create new meanings for life. The new therapy approach described by Wong (2006) included four phases: explicitizing, envisioning, empowering, and evolving phases. Schutt (2007) developed a strength-based counseling model which was clearly an application of the strength-centered model. The main steps of the counseling approach are: (1) building your strengths, (2) creating an ideal work–life scenario, (3) innovating ways to create the future, and (4) creating an action plan for "will do" goals. In a study by Tien et al. (2009), the specific steps of strength-centered counseling were mainly based on the model developed by Schutt (2007). Chinese people might not be used to this approach. However, many clients did find that they needed encouragement. They did find that the value of being in the world and the increased self-esteem can provide energy for solving problems (Tien et al., 2009).

Narrative Approach of Dream Work

Easterners love to talk about dreams. Sometimes they share dreams in public. But what do they get from talking about them? They also believe that a dream is related to daily life; it is a way for one to retrospect on your lifestyle. Hill and Goates (2004) indicated that dream work has been shown to be effective in helping clients gain insight and increase the depth of counseling sessions. We agree and emphasize that dream work is also a narrative approach of counseling and psychotherapy. In Eastern societies, people are not so comfortable in seeking help from professionals who are strangers. However, they might feel it easier to tell the professional a dream. So the dream could be a good medium for a narrative approach to career counseling.

A study by Tien, Lin, and Chen (2006) suggested that participants receiving a dream session led to a more positive attitude toward dreams. They also found that college students who are not positive toward dream work still perceive gains from the dream work. In a study by Tien et al. (2009), they adapted Hill's (2009) three-part model of dream work: exploration, insight, and action. In the exploration stage, the counselor explains the model and asks the client to tell a dream in the first-person present tense. They then explore the dream through describing, reexperiencing, association, and waking-life triggers (DRAW). In the insight stage, they try to collaborate to construct new meanings for the dream through examination of the experience, waking-life associations, and personality dynamics exploration. They can also gain insight through a spiritual or existential exploration. In the action stage, they work together to see if the dream can be continued or changed in the direction the client wants to go. That change or continuation can then be connected to waking life behaviors. In conclusion, talking about dreams is easy for people in Eastern societies. But the right way to apply dreams in counseling needs to be structured for the client to get any insights for life design.

Professional Competences for Counselors Doing Life Design

When we talked about the career competences, we said that many competences are overlapping. Integrating those competences and applying them appropriately is important. Thinking about how to integrate and apply those competences appropriately is what is referred to as metacompetence. To help clients obtain these competences, the counselor needs to know what competences they themselves need to have to provide services for clients.

The Basic Helping Skills

For career counseling and life design, Savickas (2012) proposed a new paradigm which contains three important components: (1) construct career through stories, (2) deconstruct those stories and reconstruct them into an identity narrative and life portrait, and (3) co-construct intentions that lead to the next episode in the real world. This process is actually consistent with the process of the helping skills model proposed by Hill (2009). In Hill's model, there are three stages in the helping process: exploration, insight, and action. To follow this model, the basic skills include focus, content reflection, reflection of feeling, open-ended questioning, self-disclosure, immediacy, challenge, confrontation, interpretation, direction, and other appropriate cognitive behavior techniques for action and planning. These skills are all required when we provide services for clients with career and/or life problems.

However, cultural issues are also challenging in helping Eastern clients for career and life design. Hill (2009) suggests three specific points in applying her three-stage skills for Asian clients. First, since Asian people usually keep emotions inside, their open expressions vary. In the exploration stage, we need to go slowly and wait for the client's awareness and/or expression. Second, in the insight stage, some skills such as challenges and immediacy might be intrusive and inappropriate. We have to be gentle and tentative when the skills are phrased. However, if the clients are ready for insight, these skills can be very powerful. Third, the action stage might be very comfortable for Asian clients, since they are used to seeking advice. However, they consider the therapist providing advice to be a mentor or teacher who offers guidance. In the process of life design, the three-stage model, which is called the cognitive-experience helping skill model, is appropriate for therapists and clients to use to collaborate and design a career and life future.

Particular Skills for Life Design Counseling

In traditional career counseling, program design, group counseling, assessment and appraisal skills for test interpretation, test development, and program management are all important. However, dialogue between client and counselor is important for life design. How to provide a life meaning is the goal of the dialogue. Since the traditional characteristics of stability and predictability are challenged by the current changing society, we as counseling practitioners need to create programs based on new theoretical approaches integrated with competences of flexibility, adaptability, and life-long learning.

Recently, Savickas (2012) has traced the evolution of career counseling, and he believes that construction and narrative intervention should be the new approach for career design. Storytelling containing lots of dialogue between client and counselor is the main format. Context development in the dialogue depends on the counselor's skills in the process of self/life construction. The stories can first be constructed by the client, with different pieces representing parts of his or her identity. By selectively and creatively reconstructing pieces of the narrative stories with the counselor's help, the client views their career problems from a new perspective and the problem to be solved. The process of collaboration between client and counselor is to co-construct a meaningful identity narrative, which can provide a positive future. Life themes are important components in the process of story co-construction. Clients becomes aware and active in the process. They are energized to shape their own future life and career.

As we mentioned earlier regarding the career competences individuals need to learn, many of the competences are interactive and need to be learned in relationships. We called this metacompetence. Through this process, we shape our own identity. This learning process is the same for counselors. A counselor's self-identity as a professional helper is shaped through the interactive process of metacompetence learning.

Life Design Counseling Competence From a Multicultural Perspective

Cultural-bound values are one of the sources of conflicts and misinterpretation in the counseling process (Sue & Sue, 1999). Cultural values in different social classes in different countries should be part of the counseling training. Because life design is specific to individuals, personal values are important in the process of life design. Cultural competence should be part of the training for professional counselors.

To evaluate the effectiveness of life design counseling in Chinese culture, Tien et al. (2009) conducted a content analysis regarding the participants' perspectives on attending the narrative career program. Each of the 24 participants attended one session, and they listed what they thought was most helpful and least helpful in the counseling session. Through that analysis, we uncovered what competences the counselors should have learned for career counseling. Life theme and strength-centered counseling, and dream work were the three main approaches examined in the study by Tien et al. (2009). The following sections describe their results

Provide Opportunities for Client Self-Reflection in a More Systematic Way
For the life theme approach, 10 out of 24 participants indicated that they did have a chance to achieve a more systematic self-reflection through the life theme approach of career counseling (Tien et al., 2009). For example, some of their experiences might be ignored, but they would still have opportunities to think again in a more systematic way and get insights from those experiences. Five of them indicated that they were provided with chances to clarify their values and beliefs related to their career development. For Chinese people, the power of the life theme is really strong. It energizes an individual's career awareness and development.

Enhance Clients' Confidence and Esteem Through Strength-Centered Counseling
The most helpful event designated by the participants in the strength-centered group was that counseling reminded them of their strengths and increased their self-esteem and self-confidence. Fourteen out of 30 participants indicated that they were more assertive and felt more confident about themselves after the counseling; 10 of them felt it was easier to find energy resources and solve problems they encountered; three of the participants felt they were energized in goal setting, identity achieving, and becoming highly motivated to achieve a goal. More importantly, five of the participants indicated that they were reminded of their peak experiences in the past and become even more assertive about their future.

Dream Work Is Appropriate for Chinese Clients to Increase Awareness and Insight
In the study by Tien et al. (2009), participants in the dream group indicated that dream work helped them understand the association between dream images and daily life. The associations clarified what they were not aware of in the past and increased their self-awareness. In addition, they got more energy and courage to try what they wanted to do. Some of the participants stated that they had opportunities to finish their unfinished business in the dream work. An

example of this was saying specific words to a specific important person in the action stage of the dream work. This was a kind of catharsis or debriefing through which the dreamers felt more comfortable.

Good Advice Needs Enough Information From the Client

Individual clients in Eastern society usually ask for advice. They ask for specific ways to solve problems. However, it is the client who solves the problems, not the counselor. To provide guidance, we need to have enough information. Clients also need to review as much information as possible so that they can clarify and examine their career problems broadly and prudently. For Chinese clients, who tend to be introverted, we have to help clients to talk more. They should be willing to tell us more if we use the right helping skills appropriately.

Fitting Self to Work and Work to Self Is a Dynamic Process

Traditional career counseling matches the relationship between self and the world of work. The step is usually to understand the self and fit it into the work world. Nowadays, contextual factors may influence an individual's values. The structure of the work world is also changing very fast. The relationships between changing self and changing world are interactive. We probably have to fit the self into the world, but changing the world to fit the self would be a more active way to upgrade that self. The interactions between self and work world always continue and progress with regard to both the self and the world.

The assumption of the life design paradigm is to fit the work into your life, instead of fitting your life into the work. However, it depends on the individual's developmental stage. For young adults, especially new workers, fitting the self into the work seems to be unavoidable. They can try to fit the work into their life after they feel comfortable in that work. The fit between self and work is important. The relationship in between is not linear. It's interactive.

Career Responsibility for Self and for the Family

In Western society, we believe that everyone is responsible for his or her own life. In Eastern society, in addition to personal life, people are also considered to be responsible for their family, especially for the parents' life when the parents are getting old. Many aged people also like to depend on, or live with, their children, especially the eldest son, when they are getting old. In ancient times, Chinese people believed that the eldest son had equal power with his uncles. The eldest son, instead of the uncles, would succeed as emperor when the emperor died. Although it is different nowadays, this concept still influences Chinese people inadvertently.

In Eastern society, family is a part of the whole picture for self-construction. We can understand this from the viewpoint of the collective self. People in the Eastern cultures emphasize family and social connections; therefore, role conflicts and family–work balance may be a complex issue to discuss, especially for women. Women, especially those who are daughters-in-law, are under pressure from the husband's family. They need to take care of the young kids, parents-in-law, and husband; sometimes even the husband's other family members. Professional counselors from Western cultures should not be surprised when Asian clients want to take responsibility for a big family.

Conclusion

This chapter has reviewed the concept of career counseling and asserted the importance of its new idea of life design. Since the emergence of constructivism, we believe that individuals are active in planning their career. It is a process of self-construction, which is called life design (Savickas et al., 2009). Life design can be discussed from a variety of angles; multiculturalism is the main perspective taken in this chapter. Although we have emphasized the differences among different cultures, we have also discussed the similarities between different cultures. Practical programs and theoretical concepts should be based on people's needs and indigenous culture.

Since gender is quite a sensitive variable related to cultures in different countries, we also discussed the effects of gender and cultural interactions on individual's process of life design. We finally asserted that moderation is the ultimate truth. Balance between femininity and masculinity is achievable; Eastern orientation and Western approach are not contradictory to each other. Each individual is the subject of his or her own story. Personal life is constructed and designed by self. Gender and race do not matter at all. However, the individuals have to be clear about themselves and the influences from others and the social contexts in different environments.

As far as the life design competences are concerned, we proposed an empirical model, which includes competences at preparation and exploration, establishment and maintenance stages, and transferrable skills. Professional abilities, skills, and positive traits are what we need to prepare to enter the world of work. To establish and maintain your career, it's important to know how to interact and cooperate with others in a friendly way, balance different life roles, and continue your identity as a professional. In addition, transferrable skills and life-long plans are also important components in the life design model. To sum up, individuals in Eastern cultures tend to be work-oriented. They are also collectivistic. Although this is quite different from Western individualization, many characteristics are similar to each other in modernized societies. Research regarding the life design model from a multicultural perspective should be completed and tested in the future.

References

Betz, N. E. (1994). Basic issues and concepts in career counseling for women. In W. B. Wash & S. H. Osipow (Eds.), *Career counselling for women* (pp. 1–41). Hillsdale, NJ: Erlbaum.

Cochran, L. (1997). *Career counseling: A narrative approach*. Thousand Oaks, CA: Sage.

Collin, A., & Guichard, J. (2011). Constructing self in career theory and counseling interventions. In P. J. Hartung & L. M. Subich (Eds.), *Developing self in work and career: Concepts, cases, and contexts* (pp. 89–106). Washington, DC: American Psychological Association.

Eaton, M. J., & Dembo, M. H. (1997). Differences in the motivational beliefs of Asian American and non-Asian students. *Journal of Educational Psychology, 89*, 433–440. http://doi.org/10.1037/0022-0663.89.3.433

Gergen, K. J. (1999). Agency: Social construction and relational action. *Theory & Psychology, 9*, 113–115. http://doi.org/10.1177/0959354399091007

Goldberg, L. R., & Somer, O. (2000). The hierarchical structure of common Turkish person-descriptive adjectives. *European Journal of Personality, 14*, 497–531. http://doi.org/10.1002/1099-0984(200011/12)14:6<497::AID-PER379>3.0.CO;2-R

Guichard, J. (2005). Life-long self-construction. *International Journal for Educational and Vocational Guidance, 5*, 111–124. http://doi.org/10.1007/s10775-005-8789-y

Guichard, J. (2012). How to help emerging adults develop their career and design their lives in an age of uncertainty? *Cypriot Journal of Educational Sciences, 7*, 298–310.

Hall, N. C. (2012). Life in transition: A motivational perspective. *Canadian Psychology/Psychologie Canadienne, 53*, 63–66. http://doi.org/10.1037/a0026044

Hill, C. E. (2009). *Helping skills: Facilitating exploration, insight, and action* (3rd ed.; M. Lin & H. S. Tien, Trans.). Washington, DC: American Psychological Association.

Hill, C. E., & Goates, M. K. (2004). Research on the Hill cognitive-experiential dream model. In C. E. Hill (Ed.), *Dream work in therapy: Facilitating exploration, insight, and action* (pp. 245–288). Washington, DC: American Psychological Association. http://doi.org/10.1037/10624-014

Holland, J. L. (1959). A theory of vocational choice. *Journal of Counseling Psychology, 6*, 35–45. http://doi.org/10.1037/h0040767

Hoobler, J. M., Wayne, S. A., & Lemmon, G. (2009). Bosses' perceptions of family-work conflict and women's promotability: Glass ceiling effects. *Academy of Management Journal, 52*, 939–957. http://doi.org/10.5465/AMJ.2009.44633700

Jepsen, D. A. (1990). Developmental career counseling. In W. B. Walsh & S. H. Osipow (Eds.), *Career counseling: Contemporary topics in vocational psychology* (pp. 117–157). Hillsdale, NJ: Erlbaum.

Krumboltz, J. D. (1996). Competitive grading sabotages good teaching. *Phi Delta Kappan, 78*, 324–326.

Krumboltz, J. D. (2009). The happenstance learning theory. *Journal of Career Assessment, 17*, 135–154. http://doi.org/10.1177/1069072708328861

Kuijpers, M. A. C. T., & Scheerens, J. (2006). Career competencies for the modern career. *Journal of Career Development, 32*, 303–319. http://doi.org/10.1177/0894845305283006

Lambert, T. A., Eby, L. T., & Reeves, M. P. (2006). Predictors of networking intensity and network quality among white-collar job seekers. *Journal of Career Development, 32*, 351–365. http://doi.org/10.1177/0894845305282767

Lopez, S. J., & Kerr, B. A. (2006). An open source approach to creating positive psychological practice: A comment on Wong's strengths-centered therapy. *Psychotherapy: Theory, Research, Practice, Training, 43*, 147–150. http://doi.org/10.1037/0033-3204.43.2.147

Mau, W.-C. (2000). Cultural differences in career decision-making styles and self-efficacy. *Journal of Vocational Behavior, 57*, 365–378. http://doi.org/10.1006/jvbe.1999.1745

Mogilner, C. (2010). The pursuit of happiness: Time, money, and social connection. *Psychological Science, 21*, 1348–1354. http://doi.org/10.1177/0956797610380696

O'Brien, K. M., & Fassinger, R. E. (1993). A causal model of the career orientation and career choice of adolescent women. *Journal of Counseling Psychology, 40*, 456–469. http://doi.org/10.1037/0022-0167.40.4.456

Parsons, F. (1909). *Choosing a vocation*. Boston, MA: Houghton, Mifflin.

Peterson, C., & Seligman, M. E. P. (2004). Previous classifications of character strengths. In C. Peterson & M. E. P. Seligman (Eds.), *Character strengths and virtues: A handbook and classification* (pp. 53–89). Washington, DC: American Psychological Association.

Richardson, M. S. (1996). From career counseling to counseling/psychotherapy and work, jobs, and career. In M. L. Savickas & W. B. Walsh (Eds.), *Handbook of career counseling theory and practice* (pp. 347–360). Palo Alto, CA: Davies-Black.

Roe, A. (1959). Childhood experience with parental attitudes: A test of Roe's hypothesis: Comment. *Journal of Counseling Psychology, 6*, 155–156. http://doi.org/10.1037/h0038871

Salili, F., Chiu, C. Y., & Lai, S. (2001). The influence of culture and context on student's motivational orientation and performance. In F. Salili, C. Chiu, & Y. Hong (Eds.), *Student motivation: The culture and context of learning* (pp. 221–247). New York, NY: Plenum.

Savickas, M. L. (1995). Constructivist counseling for career indecision. *The Career Development Quarterly, 43*, 363–373. http://doi.org/10.1002/j.2161-0045.1995.tb00441.x

Savickas, M. L. (1997). Career adaptability: An integrative construct for life-span, life-space theory. *The Career Development Quarterly, 45*, 247–259. http://doi.org/10.1002/j.2161-0045.1997.tb00469.x

Savickas, M. L. (2002). Reinvigorating the study of careers. *Journal of Vocational Behavior, 61*, 381–385. http://doi.org/10.1006/jvbe.2002.1880

Savickas, M. L. (2005). The theory and practice of career construction. In S. D. Brown & R. W. Lent (Eds.), *Career development and counseling: Putting theory and research to work* (pp. 42–70). Hoboken, NJ: Wiley.

Savickas, M. L. (2012). Life design: A paradigm for career intervention in the 21st century. *Journal of Counseling and Development, 90*, 13–19. http://doi.org/10.1111/j.1556-6676.2012.00002.x

Savickas, M. L., Nota, L., Rossier, J., Dauwalder, J.-P., Duarte, M. E., Guichard, J., . . . van Vianen, A. E. M. (2009). Life designing: A paradigm for career construction in the 21st century. *Journal of Vocational Behavior, 75*, 239–250. http://doi.org/10.1016/j.jvb.2009.04.004

Schutt, D. A. (2007). *A strength-based approach to career development using appreciative inquiry.* Broken Arrow, OK: National Career Development Association.

Slaney, R. B. (1980). Expressed vocational choice and vocational indecision. *Journal of Counseling Psychology, 27*, 122–129. http://doi.org/10.1037/0022-0167.27.2.122

Slaney, R. B., & Brown, M. T. (1983). Effects of race and socioeconomic status on career choice variables among college men. *Journal of Vocational Behavior, 23*, 257–269. http://doi.org/10.1016/0001-8791(83)90040-4

Sue, D. W., & Sue, D. (1999). *Counseling the culturally different: Theory and practice.* New York, NY: Wiley.

Super, D. E. (1954). Career patterns as a basis for vocational counseling. *Journal of Counseling Psychology, 1*, 12–20. http://doi.org/10.1037/h0061989

Super, D. E. (1957). *The psychology of career.* New York, NY: Harper & Row.

Swanson, J. L., & Tokar, D. M. (1991). College students' perceptions of barriers to career development. *Journal of Vocational Behavior, 38*, 92–106. http://doi.org/10.1016/0001-8791(91)90020-M

Tien, H. S. (2009, August). *Effects of narrative counseling on school teachers' psychological wellbeing.* Paper presented at the annual conference of the American Psychological Association, Toronto, Canada.

Tien, H. S., Chu, H., Yang, S., Lin, C., Chen, C., Chi, N., & Lee, S. (2013). *Social cognitive approach of employability: A test of empirical model* (Research report). Taipei, Taiwan: National Taiwan Normal University.

Tien, H. S., Lin, C., & Chen, S. (2005). A grounded analysis of career uncertainty perceived by college students in Taiwan. *Career Development Quarterly, 54*, 162–174. http://doi.org/10.1002/j.2161-0045.2005.tb00148.x

Tien, H.-S., Lin, C., & Chen, S. (2006). Dream interpretation session for college students in Taiwan: Who benefits and what volunteer clients view as most and least helpful. *Dreaming, 16*, 246–257. http://doi.org/10.1037/1053-0797.16.4.246

Tien, H. S., Wang, Y., & Liu, L. (2009). The role of career barriers on high school students' career choice behavior in Taiwan. *Career Development Quarterly, 57*, 274–288. http://doi.org/10.1002/j.2161-0045.2009.tb00112.x

Triandis, H. C. (1998). Vertical and horizontal individualism and collectivism: Theory and research implications for international comparative management. In J. L. C. Cheng & R. B. Peterson (Eds.), *Advances in international comparative management* (*Vol. 12*, pp. 7–35). Stamford, CT: JAI Press.

Wellman, N., & Spreitzer, G. (2011). Crafting scholarly life: Strategies for creating meaning in academic careers. *Journal of Organizational Behavior, 32*, 927–931. http://doi.org/10.1002/job.708

Wong, Y. J. (2006). Strength-centered therapy: A social constructionist, virtues-based psychotherapy. *Psychotherapy: Theory, Research, Practice, Training, 43*, 133–146. http://doi.org/10.1037/0033-3204.43.2.133

Zuo, J., & Bian, Y. (2001). Gendered resources, division of housework, and perceived fairness: A case in urban China. *Journal of Marriage and Family, 63*, 1122–1133. http://doi.org/10.1111/j.1741-3737.2001.01122.x

Chapter 18
A Reflexive Research Approach to Professional Competencies for Life Design

Peter McIlveen
University of Southern Queensland, Toowoomba, QLD, Australia

Introduction

Life design counseling is a "fundamental reordering of career counselling theory that envisions career intervention from a different perspective and elaborates it from new premises about the self and identity" (Savickas, 2012, p. 14). This assertion necessarily calls for research to demonstrate that practitioners require specific training that carefully prepares them for the task of engaging in *life design*. This chapter focuses on the foundations for research into training practitioners for life design counseling. The focus of this chapter is on the counseling processes of one of the two main theoretical foundations of the life design school – namely, career construction theory (Savickas, 2005). There is insufficient space to appropriately address the other major theoretical foundation, life-long self-construction (Guichard, 2005, 2009; Guichard, Pouyaud, de Calan, & Dumora, 2012)

Put succinctly, the Life Design International Research Group stated that:

> Emphasis would be placed on (a) future counselors' active participation during their training, (b) reduction of the gap so often existing between the world of research and that of training and application, (c) ensuring that graduates model what they will advocate, and (d) preparing counselors for collaborative projects. (Savickas et al., 2009, p. 247)

Taken together, rather than as separate agendas, the themes of the training agenda are the reason for this chapter, which is a consideration of the competencies necessary for life design counseling. Indeed, the models of personal knowledge generation in counseling and of practitioner-centered research presented here are a radical departure from the traditions of practitioner training.

Principle and Enhanced Competencies

The professional competencies for life design counseling may be considered against the international backdrop of current competency frameworks for career practitioners that establish parameters of competence for the activity of career counseling (e.g., Career Industry Council of Australia, 2009; International Association for Educational and Vocational Guidance, 2003; National Career Development Association, 1997). Although there are differences in wording among the three frameworks, their respective institutional authors commonly offer descriptors of the knowledge and skills of counseling process and ethics. Typically the frameworks contain statements regarding knowledge of career theories, capacity to establish a working alliance in the counseling relationship, and facility with a variety of counseling processes, including assessment, capacity to support clients with special needs (e.g., a disability), and evaluation of practice. All are relevant to life design and are listed in Table 18.1 as principle competencies.

Table 18.1
Principle and enhanced competencies of life design

Principle competencies	Enhanced competencies
Assessment	Ethic of critical reflexivity
Educational guidance	Dialogical Interpretation
Career development	
Counseling	
Research and evaluation	

Note. Principle competencies are drawn from the International Association for Educational and Vocational Guidance (2003) list of specialized competencies.

Principle Competencies

Given the global membership of the International Association for Educational and Vocational Guidance (IAEVG), its framework of *core competencies* and certain *specialized competencies*, as distinct from competency frameworks of particular nations (e.g., Australia, United States), may be used as the *principle competencies* needed for life design. As shown in Table 18.1, the most relevant IAEVG specialist competencies may serve as life design's principle competencies. Can these principle competencies serve as a foundation for life design counseling? On the whole, yes they can; however, they are insufficiently detailed for establishing a training program for life design counseling. Furthermore, there is a need to include competencies that underpin the complexity of life design counseling.

Enhanced Competencies

Life design counseling that is based upon the career construction theory includes narrative processes such as *construction*, *deconstruction*, *reconstruction*, *co-construction*, and *action*

(Savickas, 2012). These narrative processes demand *enhanced competencies* that are beyond the basic, principle competencies of counseling. There is quite a difference between empathically engaging in client-centered problem solving – a basic counseling process – and reformulating a client's life story. Of course, the so-called *necessary and sufficient conditions of change* (Rogers, 1957) should be present in the counseling encounter for effective implementation of the life design processes. Indeed, research demonstrates the crucial role of a *working alliance* in the effectiveness of career counseling (Masdonati, Massoudi, & Rossier, 2009). This assertion naturally raises the question, what is unique about life design counseling and the competencies required by its practitioners?

Quite crucially, the competency frameworks include statements on practitioners being aware of their limitations. These statements are couched in terms of doing no harm to the client and the profession, which is entirely legitimate. However, such statements open up scope for a broader discussion on practitioner reflexivity, which is addressed in this chapter as a vitally important element of life design counseling. Accordingly, the first enhanced competency is more of a metacompetency; it is the overarching competency that enables the development of professional competence and the production of new knowledge; it is the *ethic of critical reflexivity* that controls practice. The second enhanced competency, *dialogical interpretation,* pertains to working with conversation as the biographical grist of the narrative processes construction, deconstruction, reconstruction, co-construction, and action. What is presented here is a theoretical solution to the problem of modeling those processes in counseling.

The Metacompetency: The Ethic of Critical Reflexivity

Implicit in the Life Design International Research Group's (Savickas et al., 2009) statement on training for the practice of life design counseling is a focus on practitioners' personal attributes. The Group claims that practitioners should "show clear identity and strong adaptability … [and] emerge from training as proactive, self-determined professionals…. [And] they themselves must 'model' narrating their stories and actualizing their identities" (Savickas et al., 2009, p. 247). On the one hand, these statements may apply to any other counseling training program; yet, on the other hand, the practice of the narrative process of life design counseling and its fundamental tenets calls for a different level of critical analysis of the practitioner. I refer to this analytic function as the *ethic of critical reflexivity.*

The ethic of critical reflexivity is informed by the emancipatory communitarian perspective (Blustein, 2006) which holds clients' empowerment and critical consciousness as its goals, and this ethic is an articulation of Blustein's notion of inclusive psychological practice, which emphasizes working alliance, interpretation, exploration of discrepant beliefs and behaviors, and helping clients change (Blustein, 2006, pp. 283–284). Accordingly, I assert that the ethic of critical reflexivity has the following philosophical tenets:

1. It is an ontological position that client and practitioner generate awareness of self and one another through the very process of engaging with one another.
2. It is an epistemological position that the real and imagined (subvocal) dialogue between client and practitioner is a way of generating pragmatic knowledge for living in the world.
3. It is an axiological position that values connectedness and relatedness within counseling and within the many communities in which the client lives.

4. It is a rhetorical form of speaking and listening, whereby empowerment approaches to talk, text, and image are privileged.
5. Finally, the ethic of critical reflexivity is an acceptance of critical research methods that can and should be brought to bear upon the practitioner, as analysis of self by self and through supervision of self by other – thus, to complete the arc of knowledge by returning to the ontology that client and practitioner generate awareness of self and one another.

Thus, the ethic of critical reflexivity demands that practitioners are aware of their own psychological life. This is entirely consistent with the Life Design International Research Group's (Savickas et al., 2009) vision of practitioners who "must 'model' narrating their stories and actualizing their identities through activities that have meaning and mattering" (p. 9).

The term *life design counseling* carries profound implications for theory and reflexive practice. Whether used as a verb or noun, the word *design* implies creation, intent, planning, action, or control, and therefore speaks to power. Implicit in the notion of life design is that a life can be designed. This alludes to a power to create, plan, act, and control one's life. The allusion stands in contrast to the essentialist, developmental view of self as an entity that unfolds over time according to a predefined, psychological ontogeny. Accordingly, in the life design paradigm, self is an "a posteriori story, not an a priori substance defined by a list of properties" (Savickas, 2012, p. 14). As a variant of social constructionism, life design counseling eschews solipsism and asserts that life design is socially contextualized as the acts of social beings – humans do not live disembodied from their minds and the discursive worlds they inhabit. Savickas denotes this social process as thesis, antithesis, and synthesis, whereby the self psychologically confronts the roles afforded in society, to form identity that is socially, discursively mediated. Constitutive of this ontology is that narrative – story and storying – is the psychological fabric of identity; thus, recognizing that story and storying are necessarily social and socialized psychological phenomena.

Within the socially constructed encounter that is counseling, the practitioner is inherently and intimately involved in the narrative processes of life design and must be true to the social constructionist tenets of its practices. In an existential sense, a practitioner is "thrown" into the story of another person's life and, concomitantly, his or her own. Together, the two interlocutors are intimately engaged in the production of an autobiography/biography, with the client as autobiographer and practitioner as biographer, as author and coauthor, editor and coeditor, narrator and conarrator, critic and cocritic. This complexity of cooperative roles implies a marginal, yet radical shift in the boundary of awareness of one and other, and the responsibilities of practitioner to client, whereby the practitioner has no retreat to the relative safety afforded by the notion of clinical objectivity. The taken-for-granted, preestablished boundaries and expectations of the traditional counseling encounter set discursive "lines in the sand" that speak to a clear space, an empty space between the client and practitioner that none shall enter – a psychological no-man's-land with entry prescribed by the conventions of counseling practice. With life design's emphasis on genuinely melding one another's talk together to construct shared understanding, the practitioner must metaphorically take careful steps into that no-man's-land to enter into face-to-face encounter with the client; which is different from the objectivity implied in the expert model of the of practitioner–client dyad, in which the practitioner and client objectively communicate by metaphorically shouting to one another across no-man's-land. To deny this level of intimacy and trust would be to deny the fundamental tenets that underpin the narrative processes of life design counseling.

Thus, in light of the inherent intimacy and requisite trust for life design, the practitioner carries a burden of reflexivity to ensure that not only is the client's story safe and sound, but that the practitioner's is equally so. In terms of the ethic of critical reflexivity, this means two things. First, it demands the scheduling of regular time and space to reflect upon one's practice through the lens of the philosophical tenets of the ethic of reflexivity. Moreover, with respect to the fifth tenet pertaining to research methods, it requires the practitioner to engage in a rigorous analysis via self-analytic procedures or to subject himself/herself to analysis with another through supervision.

Why should the practitioner engage in rigorous analysis? Power. The power of the practitioner to engage in dialogue with a client may leave him or her indelibly changed. This power is no different from that wielded by a psychoanalyst, client-centered counselor, or shaman, who is afforded socially valorized expectations by virtue of their habitus (Foucault, 1973/1994). After all, life design counseling holds to the precept that "storytelling makes the self and crystallizes what clients think of themselves" (Savickas, 2012, p. 15). Storytelling makes the self! Crystallizes what the client thinks! Those words should echo as a clarion that life design counseling openly acknowledges the power relations between practitioner and client, more so than other forms of counseling that posit other constructs and precepts that may surreptitiously afford power to the practitioner (McIlveen & Patton, 2006).

Thus, given the inherent power differential, the accountability of being coauthor, coeditor, conarrator, and cocritic of a life story should be managed within an ethical framework that emphasizes reflexivity in practice and the concomitant generation of personal knowledge. For emphasis, I will repeat some crucial words: "the concomitant generation of personal knowledge." Here I am asserting that the processes of life design are more than processes of counseling; they are ways of knowing for the client and the counselor. For example, if by generating awareness of social circumstances through the emancipatory communitarian lens and its notion of *critical consciousness* (cf. Blustein, 2006), the client and practitioner are effectively taking a particular philosophical stance to make sense of the client's world and to generate actions to better survive in the world – this is generating knowledge together.

There are two facets of the generation of knowledge that must be considered. First and foremost, the processes of life design counseling are, in and of themselves, technologies for the creation of knowledge by the client and counselor in a working alliance, for the benefit of the client. From the social constructivist perspective of Vygotsky, career counseling represents a social process of knowledge generation between two learners within the client's zone of proximal development (Bassot, 2012). Thus, by cooperating with the counselor utilizing life design processes, the client is developing new learning for himself or herself, acting in the world of work in new imagined ways that are germane to his or her sense of self and career, and pragmatically testable in everyday terms to affirm the personal truth of the knowledge. Indeed, Krumboltz (2009) has long described career counseling as a learning process. The social constructionist perspective differs from Krumboltz's theoretical position, however, because the social constructionist approach emphasizes the dialogical, narrative knowing process between client and counselor.

The second facet of the generation of knowledge is focused on the practitioner as a source of knowing. Beyond counseling competencies per se, it is necessary to bring the whole practitioner into focus as a person who engages with the client to effect socially valued changes in the client, that are meaningfully valued by the client. By whole, I mean the entire person, not merely the professional being and his or her visage of professionalism. This is an ethic and burden for all counseling practitioners; however, it is particularly important for life design practitioners because of the power dynamic intrinsic to their work of designing lives. The ethic is more than that of a practitioner abiding by professional ethics in the usual sense of following the rules; it is more than competently practicing the knowledge and skills of effective counseling. Instead, the ethic of critical reflexivity is a way of being, knowing, and doing as a practitioner imbued by the social constructionist paradigm (Noble & McIlveen, 2012). This stance requires the practitioner to deconstruct counseling practices and theory that are unconsciously taken for granted and to confront practices and theory that seem unassailable in their taken-for-grantedness (e.g., that life designing is an effective framework for narrative career counseling). Further, this stance requires the practitioner to theorize and think differently, to constantly find alternative ways of understanding and acting as a life design practitioner. To that end, the qualitative research method autoethnography (Ellis & Bochner, 2000; McIlveen, 2008) may be taken as one disciplined pathway of the ethic of reflexivity. Indeed, autoethnography is rigorous self-analysis writ large.

Within the frame of autoethnography as a research method, the practitioner is situated as a source of knowing; it means that he or she is both the unit of analysis and the analytic lens through which the research is conducted. In this way, practitioners take themselves to be participants in their own research. This is in no way a spiral into solipsism, as autoethnography requires practitioners to theorize themselves beyond the personal limits of themselves. This means extending self into theory and, likewise, drawing theory into oneself. It is important to note that there is a sharp distinction between autobiography and autoethnography. Autobiographical data collection (e.g., personal reflections, notes taken under supervision, audiovisual media) alone is insufficient to fully realize the ethic of reflexivity. These are merely data. A narrative analysis of those data must be conducted – the data must be brought to theory and theory brought to the data to connect practitioner, theory, and practice. The data must be interpreted and realized as knowledge about practice with full regard to self and theory or, more accurately put, self in theory.

Of course, this way of knowing and the resultant knowledge based on a case study have no generalizability, but this is not the purpose of autoethnography. Instead, autoethnography produces an insider's account of such exquisite conceptual depth that its only claim to truth is the extent to which the story resonates with the reader as an empathically felt sharing of perspectives, or moves the reader to a new perspective. Thus, when analyzed through the rigor of autoethnography, a practitioner and his or her counseling practice become another source of knowing. This is akin to the notion of the epistemology of practice (Polkinghorne, 1992) and purports that the insider's view can be as equally informative as the research story told by an outsider looking in through an objective lens.

Autoethnographies may be prepared in a number of genres. Some may be formal journal articles, some may be essays, and others may be poems. The genre chosen depends upon the practitioner and the audience. For example, a life design practitioner may write a study that theorizes his or her psychological transition from a working-class background to that of a middle-class professional. This story of transition may inform or inspire practitioners of similar backgrounds and better enable them to weave their own stories into the counseling of a client who faces similar challenges and dreams of emancipation, empowerment, and autonomy.

Of course, it is preferable, if not desirable with respect to the Life Design International Research Group's requirement for practitioners to model narrative activities, that practitioners publish their autoethnographies because they could be profound stimuli for other scholars' reflections. Indeed, if the life design school is to grow and prosper from its adherents' sharing practices, then autoethnography is an ideal tool because of its capacity to bring new perspectives. However, not all autoethnographies should be shared through publication, because some matters of practice are too private to be feasibly written about without transgressing ethical boundaries of privacy and confidentiality. Nonetheless, within the confines of a formal supervision arrangement, it may be appropriate to present an autoethnography while protecting client confidentiality.

To summarize, life design practitioners are in an extraordinary position of creativity and power. Both demand a profound respect for the client and the procedures of life design. Therefore, it is appropriate that life design practitioners commit themselves to an ethic of reflexivity as its most enhanced competency. While there are many approaches to this ethic of reflexivity, autoethnography offers both a penetrating lens of research and a fertile source of knowledge.

The Process Competency: Dialogical Interpretation

To establish a context for the enhanced competency of dialogical interpretation, it is necessary to conceptually and practically return to the historical roots of counseling theory and practice. These roots include the methods of interpreting a client's past to make meaning of the present, and, moreover, in the case of life design, to remake interpretation as a narrative process of constructing, deconstructing, reconstructing, and co-constructing story with the goal of actively creating a future. Of course, interpretation is part of the canon of counseling practice, harking back to the early work of pioneers such as Freud and Adler. Yet, this is not to say that life design is "old wine in new skins," for its practice also requires a grasp of contemporary concepts and practices that are yet to be fully realized in terms of their potential (e.g., dialogical and emotion-focused methods).

The Adlerian foundations of career construction theory and Savickas's (2011) career counseling methods are evident in his solicitation of early experiences from clients and subsequent interpretations that emphasize overcoming a challenge in early life and reliving this solution in adult life. Therefore, it is apposite to summarize some of the key Adlerian ideas that appear in Savickas's theory and method.

Adler (1932) wrote, "no experience is the cause of success or failure. We do not suffer from the shock – the so-called trauma – but we make out of them just what suits our purposes" (p. 14). Adler did not deny that children experience life challenges that are beyond the norm (e.g., physical disability); however, he argued that the meaning individuals ascribe to their lot in life is the psychological truth of that person. Thus, finding a solution to the human necessity of making a living – of earning to survive – can itself be a solution to the quandary of being human. Adler invoked the notion of *inferiority complex* to explain occupational behavior, both functional and dysfunctional. In the case of functional behavior, some individuals may enter into a profession that represents a solution to a challenge early in life. In the case of dysfunctional behavior:

> there are those people who cannot make up their minds what profession to choose and who keep postponing their decision; others keep changing their profession without ever really accomplishing anything worthwhile in any one field. Some people break down before their examination; others fall ill and avoid a decision by taking refuge in illness. (Adler, 1946, p. 103)

These seemingly commonplace phenomena mentioned by Adler are not at all unfamiliar to career development practitioners. Indeed, it is the grist of their profession's very existence.

As one of the founders of social psychology, Adler knew only too well that humans connect to one another in relationships, and these connections are the sources of meaning. In a prescient statement, he wrote:

> An occupation can sometimes be used to evade and be made into an excuse for evading the problems of society and love. Very often in our social life an exaggeration of activity in business can be chosen as a means to get ride of the problem of love and marriage. A man devotes himself furiously to business and thinks "I have not time to spare for my marriage, and so I am not responsible for its unhappiness." (Adler, 1932, p 250)

In summary, two important points can be drawn from these extracts from Adler's writing: First, career is influenced by meaning making in response to events earlier in life, and that this meaning making persists into adult life; second, career is a psychosocial function that interacts with relationships, which is inherent in the contemporary relational approach to career (cf. Richardson, 2012).

Unlike the traditional practitioner-centered approach to interpretation, the processes of construction, deconstruction, reconstruction, and co-construction, are dependent on interpretation that is collaborative. The main difference appears in the collaborative nature of the process whereby the client and practitioner create knowledge in a dialogical rather than dialectical process. Thus, the technical mechanics of this enhanced competency, dialogical interpretation, draws on a theory of method that reveals how a dialogue is the source of psychological reality within and between the two interlocutors, client and practitioner.

The theory of dialogical self (Hermans & Gieser, 2012; Hermans & Kempen, 1993) can provide a theoretical answer to the question of how career-related life themes are constructed (McIlveen & Patton, 2007). With no allusion to psychotic phenomenology, at any given moment, one may internally hear the chatter, the voices, dominant voices, quiet voices, one's own voice, the voice of others, a monologue, or a conversation. These may be actual conversations that are mentally rehearsed (e.g., trying to remember what my wife told me in the morning), or they may be imagined prospective conversations between oneself and another (e.g., imaging what she will say when she discovers I had forgotten what she asked). This normal cacophony is theorized by Hermans (2006) to be, metaphorically, a theater of voices. Hermans extends the classical I–Me distinction given by James (1890/1952). Instead of a single omnipotent authorial I that observes the many states of Me, Hermans proposes that a person may assume different *I-positions* (e.g., I as a father, as a son, as worker) and that self is a variegation of multiple I-positions. Crucially, each I-position is endowed with its own voice and may engage in dialogue with another I-position. At any given moment, there may be dialogue among the voices, like actors on a theater stage. Also, it is crucial to understand that the self is extended, for a person may generate an I-position that is endowed with the voice and character of another person, thus psychologically removing the internal–external division between the inner and outer worlds.

To be optimally effective in generating a rich career narrative, life design counseling should aim to hear from as many voices as relevant to a person's career. With respect to the process of life design, the dialogical self may assume distinct I-positions of author, narrator, and editor of life themes (McIlveen & Patton, 2007). Both client and practitioner may hold these different I-positions independently of one another; however, the merging of the two sources of

I-positions enlivens the dialogical nexus that is life design counseling. As a confluence of one another in conversation, their I-positions reach toward one another across the internal–external, client–counselor divide – the no-man's-land – to raise the curtain on a psychological theater that creates the story, tells the story, and amends the story of a person's career.

Dialogical interpretation in life design counseling requires the identification of all relevant I-positions. Among others approaches, Hermans (2001) presents the Personal Position Repertoire as a tool for identifying and determining the relationships among I-positions. There is insufficient space in this chapter to describe these methods in detail; therefore, readers should refer to the work of Hermans and others, and also to the works of Guichard and colleagues who address dialogical process from a different theoretical perspective (Bangali & Guichard, 2012; Guichard, 2005, 2009; Guichard et al., 2012). Counseling proceeds on the basis of fostering dialogue among the I-positions to identify signature moments or themes within the emerging narrative. Interpreting those themes in life design counseling is a collaborative process, whereby the client and practitioner with their prominent I-positions of coauthor or coeditor take the lead in the conversations that ensue.

In addition to the current model of dialogical interpretation used for life design that entails the identification of *subjective identity forms* (Bangali & Guichard, 2012; Guichard, 2009; Guichard et al., 2012), there are emergent models of dialogical interpretation that can be used for the processes of construction, deconstruction, reconstruction, and co-construction (McIlveen & du Preez, 2012; Meijers & Lengelle, 2012). As a practitioner-educator, I use semistructured procedures that follow a relatively flexible, yet standard process (viz., Career Systems Interview and My Career Chapter). This serves the pedagogical purpose of demonstrating theory in practice, and it enables practitioners to build their confidence in what is a complex, theoretically informed approach to career counseling. Used together, the Careers Systems Interview, which is an intake interview, and My Career Chapter, which is a written booklet, enable the client to initially talk about and then write a career story. Of conceptual and methodological importance with respect to dialogical self, My Career Chapter facilitates the client taking different I-positions by instructing the client to engage in a conversation with himself or herself as a younger person who speaks from the past into the present to advise the current self on career-related matters. For example, reflect on yourself reading this book right now. What would a younger you – 5 years younger – say about you reading this particular book? Consider your history for a moment. What was your knowledge of, or interest in, life design counseling 5 years ago? Had you heard of it? Imagine; look at yourself through your younger eyes. With your younger voice, say something to the current you in relation to reading this book. Ask a question? Perhaps you might ask, "Why are you reading this book?" And, in response, you – the here-and-now you – answer the younger you. This very simple sample of dialogue demonstrates the to and fro of dialogue across time between two I-positions, both embodied in the same, but different altogether. My Career Chapter also requires clients to read their story aloud. This process enables the client to hear his or her words in his or her own ears, which is phenomenologically different to reading in silence. In addition, at the next session the counselor reads the story aloud. This experience creates a change in consciousness where the client is at once hearing what is familiar, but listening to the story spoken in the first person by a completely different voice emanating from a different position in space, albeit sitting directly in front of him or her. Now, as if with the client's story "over there," the client can engage in constructive dialogue between different I-positions, some spoken by self and others spoken by the counselor.

Dialogical interpretation requires the practitioner to deliberately speak to and listen to the I-positions that he or she may take on (e.g., coauthor, coeditor). This requires a degree of concentration to ensure that "old habits," those over-learned, over-trained, automated responses of being a counselor and doing counseling, are kept in conscious awareness and mediated by an ethic of reflexivity that is fully explicated through autoethnographic analysis. Staying with an I-position of coauthor or coeditor is difficult precisely because it requires that the practitioner to understand his or her own voices emanating from identified I-positions and how to give voice to others, real and imagined. Nonetheless, there is a risk of *slippage* with this collaborative enquiry approach to interpretation. By slippage, I mean those moments when the practitioner speaks from the I-position of expert, when he or she slips back into the role of sage, of clinician, of expert. For example, while I accept the Adlerian notion of inferiority complex and its putative impact upon career decision making, I must ensure that my application of its meaning through the questions I pose in counseling does not become a predominant monologue spoken through an I-position fixed in my own personal and professional antiquity. Therefore I must ensure that my own *countertransference* issues are properly moderated by the ethic of critical reflexivity (see the autoethnography of McIlveen, 2007). This stance ensures that my use of the inferiority complex as a conceptual tool is applied by an appropriate I-position (i.e., a committed coeditor rather than an I-position striving to overcome my own insecurities).

In summary, the enhanced competency of dialogical interpretation is necessary because of the fundamental theories underpinning life design counseling (Guichard, 2005, 2009; Savickas, 2005, 2012, 2013). If life design is to adhere to its narrative metaphor and notions such as life themes, then there must be a theory that describes the psychology of this narrative approach. Dialogical self theory's contribution to life design is that it serves as a theoretical explication of dialogical processes that transpire between client and practitioner, as distinct from leaving these processes unexplored and taken for granted. When left unexplored and taken for granted, counseling processes are liable to bias and slippage, and moreover, there is a need to allow all of the potential voices that a client may speak to be heard. Furthermore, in addition to opening counseling theory and practices to new perspectives on its processes, the theory of dialogical self concomitantly allows for the incorporation of traditional concepts relevant to life design counseling (e.g., Adlerian inferiority complex).

Engaging With Actor and Agent

Before concluding, it is important to make a special comment on one principle competency in particular – namely, assessment, because assessment, in its different forms, is integral to the process of life design counseling and the notions of *actor* and *agent* identified in the career construction theory. Albeit artefacts of postpositivism, the constructs of personality and interest continue to serve practitioners and clients as tools for constructing meaningful patterns of thinking, feeling, and behaving. Despite the current zeitgeist of theory and methods that emphasize the qualitative approaches to research and practice, there remains the professional responsibility to be competent in the selection, application, interpretation, and evaluation of psychometric measures in a manner that is consistent with their epistemological underpinnings – that psychological phenomena can be understood in measurable terms, albeit forced-choice or Likert-scale measurement.

Vocational personality constructs can be quite complex in their conceptualization and measurement, yet very informative with respect to career interventions (Brown & Hirschi, 2013). For example, the broad traits of openness, conscientiousness, extraversion, agreeableness, and neuroticism (McCrae & Costa, 2003) and the hexagonal model of realistic, investigative, artistic, social, enterprising, and conventional occupational interest environments (Holland, 1997) provide useful ways of understanding vocational personality. Therefore practitioners should be able to deploy a range of quantitative and qualitative methods of assessment relevant to the levels of career construction theory: namely, vocational personality – self as actor; adaptability – self as agent; and life themes – self as author. While Savickas's (2011) exemplary model is demonstrably qualitative in the Career Construction Interview, there is every reason to ensure that the life design assessment of vocational personality and adaptability includes psychometric measures. Indeed, there is nothing stopping a practitioner from engaging in qualitative interpretation of psychometric measures, as in an integrated approach (Hartung & Borges, 2005; Hermans, 1988).

Conclusion

This chapter began with the training agenda set by the Life Design International Research Group. In response, I have described two enhanced competencies that are needed for life design counseling, namely the ethic of reflexivity and dialogical interpretation. These two putative enhanced competencies serve as objectives for applied research into the training agenda and the development of pragmatic solutions to practitioners' needs with respect to learning how to personally enact life design and concomitantly evaluate their practices.

An important limitation on the enhanced competencies' implementation in life design counseling and their uptake by practitioners is the international availability of training and continuing professional development for scholars, to enable them to confidently use the research method autoethnography. Furthermore, there is a need for scholarship that demonstrably articulates the theory of dialogical self with the life design paradigm and its constitutive theories (e.g., career construction theory). This is not an insurmountable limitation, however. Platforms for online education and training are now widely available and the Life Design International Research Group has the capacity to commission and lead the design and delivery of a curriculum and online pedagogy for the enhanced competencies.

To conclude, the precepts of life design are suggestive of a new paradigm for career counseling. This does not imply abandonment of all that has come before. Instead, it is suggestive of a new vision that fosters asking new questions of theory, research, and practice. Concomitantly, the field faces the exciting challenge of determining how best to approach professional education and training for this new paradigm. The enhanced competencies presented here are fit for purpose with respect to the training agenda because they engender an active approach to learning, research, and practice, whereby the practitioner must engage reflexively with self, theory, practice, and, moreover, the client.

References

Adler, A. (1932). *What life should mean to you*. London, UK: George Allen & Unwin.
Adler, A. (1946). Individual psychology. In H. Orgler (Ed.), *Alfred Adler: The man and his work. Triumph over the inferiority complex* (pp. 97–120). London, UK: Vision.

Bangali, M., & Guichard, J. (2012). The role of dialogic processes in designing career expectations. *Journal of Vocational Behavior, 81*, 183–190. http://doi.org/10.1016/j.jvb.2012.06.006

Bassot, B. (2012). Career development through participation: Insights from Vygotsky. In P. McIlveen & D. E. Schultheiss (Eds.), *Social constructionism in vocational psychology and career development* (pp. 77–86). Rotterdam, The Netherlands: Sense.

Blustein, D. L. (2006). *The psychology of working: A new perspective for career development, counseling, and public policy*. Mahwah, NJ: Erlbaum.

Brown, S. D., & Hirschi, A. (2013). Personality, career development, and occupational attainment. In S. D. Brown & R. W. Lent (Eds.), *Career development and counseling: Putting theory and research to work* (2nd ed., pp. 299–328). Hoboken, NJ: Wiley.

Career Industry Council of Australia. (2009). *Professional standards for Australian career development practitioners*. Retrieved from http://www.cica.org.au

Ellis, C., & Bochner, A. P. (2000). Autoethnography, personal narrative, reflexivity: Researcher as subject. In N. K. Denzin & Y. S. Lincoln (Eds.), *The handbook of qualitative research* (2nd ed., pp. 733–768). Newbury Park, CA: Sage.

Foucault, M. (1994). *The birth of the clinic* (A. M. S. Smith, Trans., Vintage Books ed.). New York, NY: Random House. (Original work published 1973).

Guichard, J. (2005). Life-long self-construction. *International Journal for Educational and Vocational Guidance, 5*, 111–124. http://doi.org/10.1007/s10775-005-8789-y

Guichard, J. (2009). Self-constructing. *Journal of Vocational Behavior, 75*, 251–258. http://doi.org/10.1016/j.jvb.2009.03.004

Guichard, J., Pouyaud, J., de Calan, C., & Dumora, B. (2012). Identity construction and career development interventions with emerging adults. *Journal of Vocational Behavior, 81*, 52–58. http://doi.org/10.1016/j.jvb.2012.04.004

Hartung, P. J., & Borges, N. J. (2005). Toward integrated career assessment: Using story to appraise career dispositions and adaptability. *Journal of Career Assessment, 13*, 439–451. http://doi.org/10.1177/1069072705277923

Hermans, H. J. M. (1988). On the integration of nomothetic and idiographic research methods in the study of personal meaning. *Journal of Personality, 56*, 785–812. http://doi.org/10.1111/j.1467-6494.1988.tb00477.x

Hermans, H. J. M. (2001). The construction of a personal position repertoire: Method and practice. *Culture & Psychology, 7*, 323–365. http://doi.org/10.1177/1354067X0173005

Hermans, H. J. M. (2006). The self as a theater of voices: Disorganization and reorganization of a position repertoire. *Journal of Constructivist Psychology, 19*, 147–169. http://doi.org/10.1080/10720530500508779

Hermans, H. J. M., & Gieser, T. (Eds.). (2012). *Handbook of dialogical self theory*. Cambridge, UK: Cambridge University Press.

Hermans, H. J. M., & Kempen, H. J. G. (1993). *The dialogical self: Meaning as movement*. San Diego, CA: Academic Press.

Holland, J. L. (1997). *Making vocational choices: A theory of vocational personalities and work environments* (3rd ed.). Odessa, FL: Psychological Assessment Resources.

International Association for Educational and Vocational Guidance. (2003). *International competencies for educational and vocational guidance practitioners*. Retrieved from http://crccanada.org/crc/files/iaevg/Competencies-English.pdf

James, W. (1952). *The principles of psychology*. Chicago, IL: William Benton. (Original work published in 1890).

Krumboltz, J. D. (2009). The happenstance learning theory. *Journal of Career Assessment, 17*, 135–154. http://doi.org/10.1177/1069072708328861

Masdonati, J., Massoudi, K., & Rossier, J. (2009). Effectiveness of career counseling and the impact of the working alliance. *Journal of Career Development, 36*, 183–203. http://doi.org/10.1177/0894845309340798

McCrae, R. R., & Costa, P. T. (2003). *Personality in adulthood: A five-factor theory perspective* (2nd ed.). New York, NY: Guilford Press. http://doi.org/10.4324/9780203428412

McIlveen, P. (2007). The genuine scientist-practitioner in vocational psychology: An autoethnography. *Qualitative Research in Psychology, 4*, 295–311. http://doi.org/10.1080/14780880701522403

McIlveen, P. (2008). Autoethnography as a method for reflexive research and practice in vocational psychology. *Australian Journal of Career Development, 17*, 13–20. http://doi.org/10.1177/103841620801700204

McIlveen, P., & du Preez, J. (2012). A model for the co-authored interpretation of My Career Chapter. *Cypriot Journal of Educational Sciences, 7*, 276–286.

McIlveen, P., & Patton, W. (2006). A critical reflection on career development. *International Journal for Educational and Vocational Guidance, 6*, 15–27. http://doi.org/10.1007/s10775-006-0005-1

McIlveen, P., & Patton, W. (2007). Dialogical self: Author and narrator of career life themes. *International Journal for Educational and Vocational Guidance, 7*, 67–80. http://doi.org/10.1007/s10775-007-9116-6

Meijers, F., & Lengelle, R. (2012). Narratives at work: The development of career identity. *British Journal of Guidance & Counselling, 40*, 157–176. http://doi.org/10.1080/03069885.2012.665159

National Career Development Association. (1997). *Career counseling competencies.* Retrieved from http://associationdatabase.com/aws/NCDA/asset_manager/get_file/3397/counselingcompetencies.pdf

Noble, K., & McIlveen, P. (2012). Being, knowing, and doing: A model for reflexivity in social constructionist practices. In P. McIlveen & D. E. Schultheiss (Eds.), *Social constructionism in vocational psychology and career development.* (pp. 105–113). Rotterdam, The Netherlands: Sense.

Polkinghorne, D. E. (1992). Postmodern epistemology of practice. In S. Kvale (Ed.), *Psychology and postmodernism* (pp. 146–165). London, UK: Sage.

Richardson, M. S. (2012). Counseling for work and relationship. *The Counseling Psychologist, 40*, 190–242. http://doi.org/10.1177/0011000011430097

Rogers, C. R. (1957). The necessary and sufficient conditions of therapeutic personality change. *Journal of Consulting Psychology, 21*, 95. http://doi.org/10.1037/h0045357

Savickas, M. L. (2005). The theory and practice of career construction. In S. D. Brown & R. W. Lent (Eds.), *Career development and counseling: Putting theory and research to work* (pp. 42–70). Hoboken, NJ: Wiley.

Savickas, M. L. (2011). *Career counseling.* Washington, DC: American Psychological Association.

Savickas, M. L. (2012). Life design: A paradigm for career intervention in the 21st century. *Journal of Counseling & Development, 90*, 13. http://doi.org/10.1111/j.1556-6676.2012.00002.x

Savickas, M. L. (2013). Career construction theory and practice. In S. D. Brown & R. W. Lent (Eds.), *Career development and counseling: Putting theory and research to work* (2nd ed., pp. 147–183). Hoboken, NJ: Wiley.

Savickas, M. L., Nota, L., Rossier, J., Dauwalder, J.-P., Duarte, M. E., Guichard, J., . . . van Vianen, A. E. M. (2009). Life designing: A paradigm for career construction in the 21st century. *Journal of Vocational Behavior, 75*, 239–250. http://doi.org/10.1016/j.jvb.2009.04.004

Part V
Conclusion

Chapter 19
Conclusion

Jérôme Rossier[1], Laura Nota[2], Jean-Pierre Dauwalder[1], Maria Eduarda Duarte[3], Jean Guichard[4], Mark L. Savickas[5], Salvatore Soresi[2], Raoul Van Esbroeck[6], and Annelies E. M. van Vianen[7]

[1]Institute of Psychology, University of Lausanne, Switzerland
[2]Department of Philosophy, Sociology, Pedagogy and Applied Psychology, University of Padova, Italy
[3]Faculty of Psychology, Universidade de Lisboa, Alameda da Universidade, Lisbon, Portugal
[4]Institute National du Travail et d'Orientation Professionnelle (INETOP), Conservatoire National des Arts et Métiers (CNAM), Paris, France
[5]Behavioral Sciences Department, Northeastern Ohio Universities College of Medicine (NEOUCOM), Rootstown, OH, USA
[6]Faculty of Psychology and Education, Vrije University Brussel, Belgium
[7]Department of Work and Organizational Psychology, University of Amsterdam, The Netherlands

The *Handbook of Life Design: From Practice to Theory and From Theory to Practice* constitutes a collective effort of more than 25 scholars from four continents to elaborate in more detail the conceptualization presented in the position paper by Savickas and colleagues in 2009. More precisely, this handbook tries to promote a reflexive approach by confronting practice and theory. Indeed, we are convinced that practice should feed theory and the inverse should be true too. The Life Design International Research Group, which includes representatives from seven countries, proposed the life design paradigm. This paradigm will help career practitioners to develop and propose career interventions adapted to the contemporary world characterized by a very rapid evolution of social and economic structures, and help researchers to study and describe this practice and more generally people's career paths across the life span.

People need to develop and manage their lives and careers in an unstable and unpredictable world characterized by rapid social, political, and economic changes and thus have to adapt constantly to changing circumstances. This adaptation implies that people are able to design their own lives to preserve their capacity for being an author, and their capabilities, and not only to react to these changes. Social and economic instability has increased during the last 20 to 30 years, and this evolution has made it necessary to rethink the conceptual framework and practice of vocational guidance and career counseling.

The idea of the Life Design International Research Group was to create a conceptual framework – the life design paradigm – that may be adapted to a large variety of cultural settings, but that also takes into account the specific cultural and social environment of counselees.

This handbook is an attempt to further develop the life design paradigm both conceptually and practically and to provide concrete propositions about how this paradigm can be implemented using life design interventions. Life design interventions aim at allowing counselees to be authors in their own careers by activating, stimulating, and developing their personal resources. This paradigm claims to be rooted in practice and has the ambition to guide practices adapted to the contemporary world.

Being able to act, rather than only to react, is very crucial in current and future careers, but action is not enough. The life design paradigm, as McAdams (2013) noted, considers that people should be agents of their present and future, by having life plans and goals, and by being authors of their life stories or life narratives. The three features of the self (the self as an actor, an agent, and as an author) allow people to design, rather than being shaped by, their lives. As mentioned by Pouyaud (see Chapter 5), the self develops in a particular social and cultural context. The self is context dependent, but it also shapes one's context. One's self-concept, multiple identity forms, and narrative identities are based on self-deliberation activities. Self-deliberation allows subjects to become actors, agents, and authors, and to adapt proactively to changing circumstances. Individual resources, such as career adaptability, self-efficacy beliefs, regulation abilities, optimism, and hope, help people to overcome the barriers that restrain their career development (see Chapter 15).

However, individuals have weaknesses, such as a lack of specific competences, or have to overcome barriers, such as a lack of financial resources, and these difficulties cannot always be modified. An impoverished environment that cannot provide social, material, or financial support to people, constitutes an important barrier that will strongly and negatively impact on people's careers especially when they are lacking personal resources. For this reason, the life design paradigm proposes working on individuals' personal strengths and resources, which can be activated, developed, or constructed, to help them to compensate for or surmount these deficits or difficulties. These resources are especially important in changing conditions, in adverse situations such as poverty (see Chapter 16), to manage career transitions, to avoid risk accumulation, and more generally to manage career paths during the entire life course.

Life design also means that these resources are not only important for career management but also more generally for life management. Work and life cannot be considered separately anymore: The interactions between these two domains are constant, important, and complex. People's resources help them to adapt to their environment but also allow them to change this environment to adjust it to their own needs. A plea for providing people with interventions that increase their resources might be understood as promoting a conception of the world where individuals are responsible for their paths. This is, however, neither our intention nor our vision. In a contemporary economic world, where actors of private and public sectors endorse fewer social responsibilities, it is sometimes a matter of survival for people who lack resources to overcome adverse situations. For this reason, the social justice issue deserves a prominent place in the field of career guidance (Arthur, 2014).

According to the life design approach, career adaptability is an important resource for career path management. Several concrete activities favor the life design de-re-co-construction process and foster adaptability resources (see Chapter 11). In addition to helping clients to build this resource, counselors may function as a social resource, particularly during transitions and when they build high-quality working alliances with their clients (Masdonati, Perdrix, Massoudi, & Rossier, 2014).

Resources are crucial because they promote personal development and adaptation, and allow people to act, plan, and narrate their choices. Resources are dynamic individual features which transform the tension associated with reflexive activities into action and development (see Chapter 3). Reflexive activities support people's need for self-continuity and allow them to cope with disparities emerging in their life stories. To hold and solve internal tensions or conflicts, the (narrative) self must be in a continuous movement of self (re)interpretation and (re)definition. In this way, internal or external tensions can promote personal development and adaptation.

The life design paradigm suggests that the environment always has to be considered when trying to understand any professional path. As mentioned by Duarte and Cardoso (see Chapter 4), personal evolution is the result of an interaction between an individual and his or her proximal and distal environment. This interaction leads to a coevolution. When this coevolution becomes more functional over time, we can speak of adaptation, and when this coevolution becomes less functional, it leads to separation. This view emphasizes that people must be both flexible and able to change their environment so as to adapt it to their own needs. Hence, for describing and understanding career paths, a complex set of factors, which do not always have linear relationships, have to be considered. Indeed as defined by Hartung (see Chapter 7), life design is a life-long holistic and contextual process that underlies self-development through relationships and interactions in various contexts, such as professional life or family. It is especially interesting to observe that during adolescence, people learn to act as social agents and to find a balance between flexibility (complying with social norms of peers or models) and trying to overcome social constrains (or norms of past generations or nonpeers). Adaptability is not only flexibility, since flexibility can be a threat to our identity. Rather, adaptability should sustain self-continuity and narrative identity.

Moreover, the situation of individuals has to be considered in relation to their cultural and social environment. It is very hard to understand the difficulties individuals encounter and the representations they make, if counselors ignore counselees' cultural setting. People's environment is proximal and also distal in that it is constituted by the society in which they live (Fouad & Kantamneni, 2008). The societal environment includes cultural norms and customs that affect the structure of individuals' identity (Guichard's dynamic system of subjective identity forms; see Guichard, 2009). The meanings held by these structures of societal and personal representations may influence each other's *signifié* (de Saussure, 1916). The interaction of different representations may take the form of a negotiation, a dialogue, between the individual and his or her environment, which may, in turn, lead to changes at the level of both the individual and the environment. This negotiation allows societal "metanarratives" to give a meaning to individual choices and paths (Macmillan, 2005). Moreover, the scripts of these metanarratives are continuously becoming more diverse (see Chapter 10).

Life design interventions can be described as dialogues contributing to, for example, the development of counselees' personal identity or identities by inducing reflexive activity, or to the activation or strengthening of personal resources, which might have a preventive impact (see Chapter 11). These interventions are aimed at allowing counselees to be the actors of their own personal development, and to develop professional goals and careers in accordance with their needs, resources, strengths, and weaknesses, taking into account their environment. Several chapters of this book make concrete suggestions concerning life design interventions. Qualitative career assessment instruments might, for example, stimulate narrative processes allowing a de-re-co-construction of the narrative identity. Moreover, interactions between the counselee and counselor might take the form of a life design dialogue that is aimed at increasing and promoting narratability. Thus, as mentioned by Guichard (see Chapter 2), life design interventions should increase the agency liberty and self-directedness of our counselees.

Interventions that induce a reflexive activity encourage, somewhat paradoxically, people to redefine themselves and their position in space and time. Increasing counselees' narratability is thus an important goal of life design interventions.

Being able to tell ourselves our stories helps us to reconstruct our biography and identity, and "bricoleurs integrate their past stories with new psychosocial situations to form a narrative identity that bridges the discontinuity and fits the new situation" (see Chapter 10). This process allows microstories or microcycles to be linked with macro life cycles. Van Esbroeck and Augustijnen (see Chapter 12) speak about a coreflexivity, implying a holistic approach, between the counselee and the career counselor, allowing the emergence of new life projects and career goals and prospects. Life design interventions thus require some specific competences from the counselor, such as the ethic of critical reflexivity or the dialogical interpretation as mentioned by McIlveen (see Chapter 18). This is to note that narrative activities are not sufficient by themselves, because life design interventions must also increase adaptability, activity, and intentionality (Savickas et al., 2009). However, all of these resources are interdependent, and an increasing adaptability, for example, may have a positive impact on people's intentionality, as suggested by the principle of recursivity suggested by Watson and McMahon in their chapter (see Chapter 6).

A life design intervention can take different forms, and its structure and content can be adapted to the counselee and his or her situation. However, the processes that are questioned and activated and the goals always remain the same: to increase adaptability, narratability, activity, and intentionality. Life design is a life-long process that is deployed over space and time, is constituted by a succession of choices (see Chapter 10), and implies life-long learning. This process may allow the structuring of the multiple selves coherently according to the needs, values, expectations, interests, and weaknesses and strengths of the individual. Focusing on people's vulnerabilities may help to understand their social trajectories of exclusion (Spini, Hanappi, Bernardi, Oris, & Bickel, 2014) but the life design paradigm has the ambition to also consider people's strengths and abilities to change themselves and their environment (see Chapter 11). Increasing people's adaptability and intentionality may promote a more positive vision of themselves and their career paths (see Chapter 13). In our societies, work is important for people because it sustains material independence, which is considered as a sign of maturity, but this independence is of course often determined by a social dependence or alienation. In this context, life design interventions may structure the relationship between people's self and their work and social roles, in a storyline, and increase their sense of agency (Savickas, 2013). Self-managing and self-directing abilities allow people to rely less on stable conditions and to experience uncertainty more positively.

The chapters in this book illustrate how the life design paradigm fits the new 21st-century societal developments. They also illustrate that the application of the life design concept requires new attitudes and competences from career counselors. They should help develop the recognition that the clients are leading the intervention process and that they are the authors of the problem they present, their life story, and the meaning they attach to it. Several contributions in this book demonstrate new techniques and methods for a life design approach. Some of these techniques are building upon existing, well-established methods, but are used in another way and within a new framework. The comprehensive analysis of the life design paradigm in this book may give the impression that it tries to replace all other paradigms used in career intervention. This is certainly not the case. The members of the international research group and the authors of this handbook recognize that the life design approach can serve some clients very well. At the same time, however, they recognize that other paradigms may serve the client's needs as well. Which paradigm is to be used depends on the characteristics of the client's profile, their past and present situation, and the problem presented by the client. Certain combinations of these variables justify the use of vocational guidance as the most appropriate approach instead of life design. Though the life design paradigm fits more with present society and is an adequate framework to help individuals who live in liquid modernity coping with the major personal issues they face, it can never be the only paradigm used in career support.

The international research group and the authors are nevertheless aware that the new paradigm, as such, needs to prepare more for some of the major collective issues with which mankind is now confronted. Without being able to produce a comprehensive list of these challenges, two issues which already affect some people's lives – and will affect more and more people in the coming decades, if they are not tackled – should be mentioned. One of them is what the International Labour Office (2001) has called the deficit of decent work in the world. According to the figures published by this organization (International Labour Office, 2006), in 2005 more than 1.4 billion workers were paid less than US $2.00 a day. Such a major problem may need a broad societal and leadership engagement that contributes to the setting up and implementation of an international labor law defining, for example, the minimum standards of a human work activity. The second issue relates to some observations in the 2014 Intergovernmental Panel on Climate Change report (IPCC, 2014). These experts noted that the world population is now 7.1 billion (median age 29.4) and is expected to reach 10 billion before the middle of the 21st century. To meet the needs of this growing population, food production should be increased by 14% each decade. Unfortunately, because of the projected climate changes, a decrease of about 2% each decade is expected.

Obviously many people who design their lives and their working paths are aware of such problems and see them as a key element to consider when they make decisions about their careers and lives. The above-mentioned problems are so acute that the awareness of only some people is not enough to find the urgent treatment they require. Therefore, we believe that one of the major tasks for life and career practitioners and researchers will be to find a way to integrate the life design paradigm and the Jonas (1984) imperative of responsibility: "Act so that the effects of your action are compatible with the permanence of genuine human life" (p. 11). Our experiences and concerns in relation to the broader major collective issues need to be communicated in the most effective way to policy makers and business leaders. We should illustrate that, in addition to effective career support at the individual level, adequate interventions at a broader and societal level are needed to support individual actions.

The life design paradigm was proposed by an international group of career counselors and researchers. This life design group is not only a group of professionals but also a group of friends, a group wherein we can share experiences and ideas. This handbook is an attempt to enlarge our thoughts, our paradigm, with very crucial and important contributions from colleagues from all over the world. Our idea was to invite all of you to join us in contributing to this conceptual co-construction, working on concrete theoretical and practical implications. The aim of this handbook was to further develop the life design paradigm, compare the life design paradigm with other contemporary approaches, to promote reflexivity between practice and theory, and to further develop a conceptual framework and interventions adapted to the contemporary society. After all the work done by all the contributors of this handbook and the multiple discussions we had with many of you, we are convinced that this *Handbook of Life Design: From Practice to Theory and From Theory to Practice* will contribute to the promotion of a reflexive practice.

References

Arthur, N. (2014). Social justice and career guidance in the Age of Talent. *International Journal for Educational and Vocational Guidance, 14*, 47–60. http://doi.org/10.1007/s10775-013-9255-x

de Saussure, F. (1916). *Cours de linguistique générale*. Lausanne, Suisse: Payot.

Fouad, N. A., & Kantamneni, N. (2008). Contextual factors in vocational psychology: Intersections of individual, group, and societal dimensions. In S. D. Brown & R. W. Lent (Eds.), *Handbook of counseling psychology* (4th ed., pp. 408–425). Hoboken, NJ: Wiley.

Guichard, J. (2009). Self-construction. *Journal of Vocational Behavior, 75*, 251–258. http://doi.org/10.1016/j.jvb.2009.03.004

International Labour Office. (2001). *Reducing the decent work deficit: A global challenge. International conference 89th* session 2001 (Report to the Director General). Geneva, Switzerland: Author.

International Labour Office. (2006). The decent work deficit: A new ILO report outlines the latest global employment trends. *World of Work, 56*, 12–15.

IPCC. (2014). *Climate change 2014: Impacts, adaptation, and vulnerability*. Cambridge, UK: Cambridge University Press. Retrieved from http://ipcc-wg2.gov/AR5/report

Jonas, H. (1984). *The imperative of responsibility: In search of an ethics for the technological age*. Chicago, IL: University of Chicago Press.

Macmillan, R. (2005). The structure of the life course: Classic issues and current controversies. *Advances in Life Course Research, 9*, 3–24. http://doi.org/10.1016/S1040-2608(04)09001-X

Masdonati, J., Perdrix, S., Massoudi, K., & Rossier, J. (2014). Working alliance as a moderator and a mediator of career counseling effectiveness. *Journal of Career Assessment, 22*, 3–17. http://doi.org/10.1177/1069072713487489

McAdams, D. P. (2013). The psychological self as actor, agent, and author. *Perspectives on Psychological Science, 8*, 272–295. http://doi.org/10.1177/1745691612464657

Savickas, M. L. (2013). Career construction theory and practice. In S. D. Brown & R. W. Lent (Eds.), *Career development and counseling: Putting theory and research to work* (2nd ed., pp. 147–183). Hoboken, NJ: Wiley.

Savickas, M. L., Nota, L., Rossier, J., Dauwalder, J.-P., Duarte, E., Guichard, J., … van Vianen, A. E. M. (2009). Life designing: A paradigm for career construction in the 21st century. *Journal of Vocational Behavior, 75*, 239–250. http://doi.org/10.1016/j.jvb.2009.04.004

Spini, D., Hanappi, D., Bernardi, L., Oris, M., & Bickel, J.-F. (2014). *Vulnerability across the life course: A theoretical framework and research directions*. Manuscript submitted for publication.

About the Authors

Marie-Therèse Augustijnen holds a master's in business administration and worked for several years in the field of marketing. In 2009, she earned a master's in psychology with a specialization in clinical psychology. Her research on coaching has been published in various books and in the *International Coaching Psychology Review*. After earning her psychology degree, she decided to go through a major career change and founded her own consulting company, Focus on Talent. She specializes in career counseling and coaching for managers and persons working in organizations.

    E-mail: mimi.augustijnen@skynet.be

Paulo Cardoso is an associate professor in the Department of Psychology, University of Évora, Portugal. He teaches vocational psychology and career counseling in the Educational Psychology Master Program. Cardoso's main research interests are career development of special populations and the process of change in career counseling. In addition to his teaching and research, he maintains a limited practice of career counseling at the University of Évora. He is the secretary general of the Portuguese Society of Psychology.

    E-mail: pmscar@gmail.com

Jean-Pierre Dauwalder is an emeritus professor at the University of Lausanne, Switzerland, president of Swiss Federal Authority for Professions in Psychology (PsyKo), and was the president of the European Society for Vocational Designing and Career Counseling (ESVDC). He worked as a clinical psychologist and researcher at the Psychiatric Hospital of the University of Lausanne from 1974 to 1978. He was the head of the Department of Research and Teaching in Social Psychiatry at the University of Bern from 1979 to 1991. He was a full professor for counseling and vocational psychology at the University of Lausanne from 1991 to 2010. He organized international conferences in behavior modification, health psychology, vocational guidance, and self-organization and was a member of many editorial boards. His publication list includes more than 130 articles, books, and chapters. In 2010 he received the Award of the IAAP (Division of Counseling Psychology) in Melbourne. In 2013 he was honored with the first Julius-Suter Medal for applied psychology, in Switzerland.

    E-mail: jean-pierre.dauwalder@unil.ch

Maria Eduarda Duarte is a full professor at the University of Lisbon, Faculty of Psychology, where she directs the master's course Psychology of Human Resources, Work, and Organizations. Her professional interests include career psychology theory and research, with a specific emphasis on issues relevant to adults and the world of work. She is the research director of the Career Guidance and Development of Human Resources Services at the University of Lisbon, Portugal. Her publications and presentations have encompassed topics on adults' career problems, testing and assessment, and counseling processes. Since 2005, she has been the chair of the Portuguese Psychological Society, and director of the Institute of Career Counseling, University of Lisbon; she has also served on editorial boards for several Portuguese, European, and Iberian-American journals.

    E-mail: maria.ec.duarte@gmail.com

Lea Ferrari is an assistant professor in the Department of Philosophy, Sociology, Pedagogy and Applied Psychology, University of Padova, where she teaches diversity management in the workplace and psychology of work inclusion for people with disability. Her research efforts are directed toward the study of variables and processes in life design models, setting up of instruments, planning of interventions programs, and their verification. She is a member of the Italian Society of Vocational Guidance (SIO), of the ESVDC, and of the International Section of Counseling Psychology, Division 17, American Psychological Association (APA). She is a member of the Career Adaptability International Collaborative Group and of the European project University Network for Innovation in Guidance. She is also the coeditor of *The Italian Journal of Vocational Psychology* and the newsletter of the SIO.

E-mail: lea.ferrari@unipd.it

Geneviève Fournier is a full professor of career counseling in the Faculty of Education of Laval University, Quebec City, Canada, and a chief researcher at the Research and Intervention Center on Education and Working Life (CRIEVAT). Her teaching and research activities focus on professional and life transitions, career paths, socioprofessional integration processes, meaning of work, identity construction processes and guidance, and counseling practices.

E-mail: genevieve.fournier@fse.ulaval.ca

Maria Cristina Ginevra, PhD, is a research fellow in the Department of Philosophy, Sociology, Pedagogy and Applied Psychology, University of Padova. She is also an adjunct professor in the Department of Psychology, University of Milan-Bicocca, Italy, where she teaches psychology of disability and school inclusion. She collaborates with the Laboratory for Research and Intervention in Vocational Designing and Career Counseling (LaRIOS) at the University of Padova, Italy. Her research activities concern the field of school-career counseling, and her research efforts are directed toward the analysis of dimensions related to life design approach, setting up of assessment instruments and career education activities aiming at increasing choice abilities. She is a member of the organizing committee of the European Doctoral Programme in Career Guidance and Counseling (funded by the European commission 2013–2015), and a full member of ESVDC, SIO, and the Italian Association of Psychology (AIP).

E-mail: mariacristina.ginevra@unipd.it

Jean Guichard is an emeritus professor of career counseling psychology at The Conservatoire National des Arts et Métiers, Paris, France. He is in charge of the UNESCO chair for Lifelong Guidance and Counseling at Wroclaw University, Poland. His research focuses on the factors and processes of self-construction and on the different modes of relating to occupations and professions. His synthesis of works on the dynamics of subjectivation (lifelong self-construction) provides a general framework for a form of life design dialogues and career education workshops. He has received an honorary doctorate from the universities of East Finland, Lisbon, and Buenos-Aires, and two awards from the APA Society of Counseling Psychology and the ESVDC.

E-mail: jean.guichard@cnam.fr

Paul J. Hartung, PhD, is a professor of family and community medicine at Northeast Ohio Medical University and adjunct professor of counseling at the University of Akron. He has authored over 75 journal articles and book chapters and edited three books dealing with career development theory and practice. Currently, he is the editor of *The Career Development Quarterly* and serves on several editorial boards including those for the *Journal of Vocational Behavior*, the *Journal of Career Assessment*, and the *Journal of Counseling and Development*. He is a fellow of the APA and the National Career Development Association. In 2009, he received the APA Division 17 John L. Holland award for achievement in career and personality research. He is president-elect of Division 16 (Counseling Psychology) of the International Association of Applied Psychology (IAAP).

E-mail: phartung@neomed.edu

Andreas Hirschi, PhD, is a full professor and the chair of the Division of Work and Organizational Psychology at the University of Bern, Switzerland. He obtained his PhD from the University of Zurich and a post–master's degree as a master of advanced studies in psychology of career counseling and human resources management from the universities of Zurich, Berne, and Fribourg, Switzerland. He previously worked at the Pennsylvania State University, United States, the Leuphana University of Lueneburg, Germany, and at the University of Lausanne, Switzerland. His major research interests are career development, career counseling, and subjective well-being at work.

E-mail: andreas.hirschi@psy.unibe.ch

Ute-Christine Klehe, chair of work and organizational psychology at Justus-Liebig-University Giessen (Germany), received her PhD in 2003 from the Rotman School of Management, University of Toronto, Canada. She has since then worked at the universities of Zürich, Switzerland, and Amsterdam, Netherlands. Besides serving on the editorial boards of the *Journal of Applied Psychology*, *Journal of Organizational Behavior*, *Journal of Business and Psychology*, and *Journal of Managerial Psychology*, she is the associate editor of *Applied Psychology: An International Review*. Her research addresses career self-management and career transitions, particularly when faced with economic stressors, as well as personnel selection and performance. She has been published in journals such as the *Journal of Applied Psychology*, *Personnel Psychology*, the *Journal of Vocational Behavior*, and the *Journal of Organizational Behavior,* among others.

E-mail: ute-christine-klehe@psychol.uni-giessen.de

Jessie Koen is an assistant professor in the Department of Work and Organizational Psychology, University of Amsterdam, where she also obtained her PhD (cum laude). Her research focuses on employability and career adaptability during career transitions, as well as work motivation and self-regulation in times of unemployment. Her work has been published in peer-reviewed journals such as the *Journal of Vocational Behavior*. She has presented her work during award-winning symposia at several international conferences, including the annual meetings of the Academy of Management and the Society of Industrial and Organizational Psychology.

E-mail: j.koen@uva.nl

Kobus Maree's (DEd, PhD, DPhil Psychology) research interests include career counseling, giftedness, minority groups, and underprivileged people. He has worked as a registered psychologist in educational institutions and private practices. As the previous editor of the *SA Journal of Psychology* and editor of the *SA Journal of Science and Technology,* he was awarded the Stals Prize of the SA Academy of Science and Arts for exceptional research and contributions to psychology in 2009 and the Stals Prize for Education in 2014. He was awarded the

Chancellor's Medal for Teaching and Learning from the University of Pretoria in 2010 and nominated successfully to be an exceptional academic achiever on four consecutive occasions (2003–2016). As a regular keynote speaker, he was recently invited to be a keynote speaker at the fifth World Conference of Psychology, Counseling and Guidance in Dubrovnik, Croatia (2014) and was one of the State-of-the-Science speakers (Division 16: Counseling Psychology) at the ICAP conference in Paris, France, 2014.

E-mail: kobus.maree@up.ac.za

Jonas Masdonati is an associate professor of career counseling at the Faculty of Education of Laval University, Quebec City, Canada. He is a regular researcher at CRIEVAT. He studied vocational and counseling psychology at the University of Lausanne, Switzerland, and obtained a PhD in education at the University of Fribourg, Switzerland. His teaching and research activities focus on the school-to-work transition, adult career transitions, the meaning of work, identity construction, vocational education and training, vocational psychology theories, group interventions, working alliance, and career counseling processes and outcomes. He is a member of the ESVDC.

E-mail: jonas.masdonati@fse.ulaval.ca

Peter McIlveen, PhD, is an associate professor at the University of Southern Queensland, Australia. He leads a new multidisciplinary research team, the Australian Collaboratory for Career, Employability, and Learning for Living (ACCELL). McIlveen is an international fellow of the National Institute for Career Education and Counseling (UK) and vice president of the Career Development Association of Australia (CDAA). He has served the Career Industry Council of Australia (CICA) as its vice president, and was president of Australia's National Association of Graduate Careers Advisory Services (NAGCAS). He is the editor of the *Australian Journal of Career Development* and serves on the editorial boards of the *Journal of Vocational Behavior* and the *Australian Psychologist*.

E-mail: peter.mcilveen@usq.edu.au

Mary McMahon, PhD, teaches career development and narrative career counseling in the School of Education at The University of Queensland where she works as a senior lecturer. She is interested in the career development of children and adolescents, as well as how young people may be supported by career counseling and career programs. She is the developer, with Dr. Wendy Patton, of the Systems Theory Framework of Career Development. She researches practical applications of her framework including a story-telling approach to career counseling and qualitative assessment instruments. She has published extensively nationally and internationally.

E-mail: marylmcmahon@uq.edu.au

Laura Nota is a professor of career construction and career counseling and psychological counseling for the inclusion of social disadvantage in the Department of Philosophy, Sociology, Education and Applied Psychology, University of Padova. She is the director of LaRIOS, the University Centre for Research and Services on Disability, Rehabilitation and Inclusion, at the University of Padova, and the postgraduate master's course Life Design and Career Counseling. She is president of the SIO, as well as a member of the Executive Board of Division 16 (Counseling Psychology) of the IAAP, and of the Executive Board of the ESVDC. She is a member of the Life Design International Research Group and of the Career Adaptability International

Collaborative Group. She is also part of the Steering Committee of the European project University Network for Innovation in Guidance and the scientific coordinator of the European Doctoral Programme in Career Guidance and Counselling. She is the author of more than 150 scientific articles published in international and national journals as well as more than 10 books.

E-mail: laura.nota@unipd.it

Jacques Pouyaud is a senior lecturer in occupational and vocational psychology at the University of Bordeaux and a member of the laboratory of psychology Health and Quality of Life (EA 4139). He is also an associate member of the laboratory of vocational psychology (EA 4132, Research Center on Work and Development, CNAM). He is member of the governing board of the UNESCO chair Lifelong Guidance and Counseling, and the ESVDC association. He received his PhD in 2008, on the topic of transitions, self-construction, and vocational development. The main themes of his research are the processes of self-construction throughout the life course and psychosocial transitions, as well as the construction of vocational identity through activity. He is also studying counseling processes and developing practical applications for counselors.

E-mail: jacques.pouyaud@u-bordeaux.fr

Jérôme Rossier studied psychology at the University of Lausanne and at the Catholic University of Louvain, Belgium. After work experience at the Academy of Sciences of the Czech Republic, the National Institutes of Health, United States, and the University of Fribourg, Switzerland, he is currently a full professor of vocational and counseling psychology at the Institute of Psychology of the University of Lausanne. He is the editor of the *International Journal for Educational and Vocational Guidance* and a member of several editorial boards of scientific journals such as the *Journal of Vocational Behavior*. His teaching areas and research interests include counseling, personality, psychological assessment, and cross-cultural psychology. He has published more than 100 scientific articles and book chapters mainly about vocational counseling, cross-cultural, and personality issues.

E-mail: jerome.rossier@unil.ch

Sara Santilli is a PhD student in the Doctoral School of Psychological Sciences at the University of Padova, Italy. As a psychologist and holder of a postgraduate degree in career counseling at the University of Padova, she collaborates with LaRIOS, University of Padova, Italy, in the organization of vocational guidance projects and research concerning disability, career guidance, and job placement. Her research interests concern the fields of career counseling and disability. She also collaborates with the University Centre for Research and Services on Disability, Rehabilitation and Inclusion, pertain to the analysis of the factors associated with social and work inclusion, with special attention to career development, career adaptability, employers' attitudes toward people with disabilities as well as parents' and children's attitudes toward students with disabilities.

E-mail: santilli.sara@gmail.com

Mark L. Savickas is professor of family and community medicine at Northeast Ohio Medical University, USA. He served as president of the Division 16, Counseling Psychology, of the IAAP (2011–2014), and as editor of the *Journal of Vocational Psychology* (1999-present), adjunct professor of counselor education at Kent State University, visiting professor in the Institute for Employment Research at The University of Warwick, United Kingdom, and emeritus chair of the Behavioral Sciences Department at Northeast Ohio Medical University. He has received the Leona Tyler Award for Distinguished Contributions to Counseling Psychology from Division 17 of the APA, the Eminent Career Award from the National Career Development Association, and honorary doctorates from the University of Lisbon (Portugal) and the Pretoria University (South Africa).

E-mail: ms@neomed.edu

Teresa M. Sgaramella is an assistant professor at the University of Padova. She teaches models and programs of rehabilitation across the life span, and rehabilitation counseling, and she is a member of the teaching staff in the postgraduate master's course Life Design and Career Counseling. She is a member of LaRIOS and of the University Centre for Research and Services on Disability, Rehabilitation and Inclusion, of the University of Padova. She is also a member of SIO and of the ESVDC. She is one of the Italian representative in the University Network for Innovation in Guidance (NICE) projects, and a member of the organizing committee of the European Doctoral Programme in Career Guidance and Counseling. She is an ad hoc reviewer for several journals: the *Italian Journal of Psychology, Education,* the *International Journal of Brain and Behavioral Sciences,* and the *Journal of Prevention and Treatment.* As a member of the International Hope Research Team (IHRT), she coordinates a research group on hope and time perspective in disability and in psychosocial risk conditions.

E-mail: teresamaria.sgaramella@unipd.it

Salvatore Soresi is a full professor and cofounder of LaRIOS, the University Centre for Research and Services on Disability, Rehabilitation and Inclusion at the University of Padova, and he is a member of SIO and ESVDC. He is also the editor of the *Italian Journal of Vocational Psychology,* a member of the Life Design Group, of the Career Adaptability International Collaborative Group, and of the Steering Committee in the Nice project. He founded IHRT and the Italian University network for counseling (2013). He is the author of about 250 publications, more than 20 books, and a number of important assessment instruments, among which are the portfolios Optimist and Clipper, and the Magellano Project, which received the high patronage of the president of the Italian Republic. In 2008, he received an award from the Society of Counseling Psychology (APA), and in 2013, from the ESVDC for his visionary work in the career field.

E-mail: salvatore.soresi@unipd.it

Hsiu-Lan Shelley Tien, is a professor in the Department of Educational Psychology and Counseling at National Taiwan Normal University (NTNU; 2001 to the present). She also serves as director of the Counseling Center at NTNU. She has been a Fulbright Visiting Scholar in the Department of Psychology at the University of Maryland (2005–2006) and an exchange scholar sponsored by the National Science Council in Taiwan to visit the University of Maryland (2011–2012). She is a licensed psychologist in Taiwan, the editor of the *Journal of Educational Psychology and Counseling,* and also serves on the editorial board and as an advisory editor and/or ad hoc reviewer of the *Career Development Quarterly, Asia Pacific Educational Review*, and *Journal of Career Development.* She was awarded the Distinguished Scholar Award (2004) and Service/Practice Award (2003) from the Taiwan Guidance and Counseling Association.

E-mail: lantien@ntnu.edu.tw

Raoul Van Esbroeck is an emeritus professor in the Faculty of Psychology and Education of the Vrije Universiteit Brussel (Brussels, Belgium) in vocational psychology and career guidance. He has also engaged in research and teaching of career management–related topics such as coaching. He has published a large number of articles, book chapters and books (including the *International Handbook of Career Guidance*) in several languages. He served as editor of the *International Journal for Educational and Vocational Guidance* from 1999 to the end of 2009, and was a member of several editorial boards of international journals. He received several awards for his international contributions, from the Society of Counseling Psychology and the U.S. National Career Development Association.

E-mail: raoul.van.esbroeck@vub.ac.be

Gudbjörg Vilhjálmsdóttir, PhD, is a professor in career guidance and counseling at the University of Iceland. She has been training counselors and been a program director at the university since 1991. Previous to that, she worked as a counselor at the University College of Education. Her research area has been within career development theory with an emphasis on career constructivism and Bourdieu's habitus theory. She has participated in an international research project on career adaptability and developed a measure for career adaptability in Iceland. Her most recent research project is on the use of narrative theory in guidance research. One of her ongoing research interests has been the evaluation of careers education and counseling.

E-mail: gudvil@hi.is

Annelies E. M. van Vianen is a full professor of organizational psychology, and chair of the Department of Work and Organizational Psychology at the University of Amsterdam. She received her PhD from the University of Leiden, Netherlands. Her research interests are career development, person–environment fit, adaptability, aging, leadership, and employee well-being. Her work has been published in journals such as *Personnel Psychology,* the *Academy of Management Journal,* the *Journal of Organizational Behavior,* the *Journal of Vocational Behavior,* the *International Journal of Selection and Assessment, Leadership Quarterly,* and *Psychological Science*. She serves/served on several journal review boards, as guest editor, and as editor of *Behavior & Organization*. She is a member of the ESVDC and the Life design International Research Group, among others.

E-mail: a.e.m.vanvianen@uva.nl

Mark Watson is a distinguished professor in the Psychology Department of the Nelson Mandela Metropolitan University in South Africa. He specializes, researches, and practices in child and adolescent career development, narrative career counseling, and qualitative career assessment. He has published extensively in international journals, has contributed chapters to international career texts, and has coedited several career psychology texts. In addition, he has coedited a book on career psychology in the South African context. He is on the editorial advisory board of several international career journals and is the coeditor of the *International Journal for Educational and Vocational Guidance*. He is an honorary professor at The University of Queensland, Australia, and a research associate at the Institute for Employment Research at the University of Warwick, UK. He is particularly interested in the development of culturally appropriate approaches to career guidance and counseling.

E-mail: mark.watson@nmmu.ac.za